THE FIL.
JEAN SEBERG

# THE FILMS OF JEAN SEBERG

Michael Coates-Smith *and*
Garry McGee

McFarland & Company, Inc., Publishers
*Jefferson, North Carolina, and London*

LIBRARY OF CONGRESS CATALOGUING-IN-PUBLICATION DATA

Coates-Smith, Michael, 1943–
The films of Jean Seberg / Michael Coates-Smith and Garry McGee.
p.    cm.
Includes bibliographical references and index.

ISBN 978-0-7864-6652-8
softcover : acid free paper ∞

1. Seberg, Jean—Criticism and interpretation.
I. McGee, Garry, 1966–   II. Title.
PN2287.S343C63  2012        791.4302' 8092—dc23        2012012654

BRITISH LIBRARY CATALOGUING DATA ARE AVAILABLE

Front cover image: Jean Seberg as St. Joan of Arc in *Saint Joan*, 1957
(Photofest); cover design by David K. Landis (Shake It Loose Graphics)

Manufactured in the United States of America

*McFarland & Company, Inc., Publishers*
*Box 611, Jefferson, North Carolina 28640*
*www.mcfarlandpub.com*

For
Dorothy Arline (Benson) Seberg
[1909–1997]
and
Edward W. Seberg
[1906–1984]

# Table of Contents

# *Preface*

The "Jean Seberg story" is well rehearsed. As a thumbnail sketch, it has been rehashed by journalists a thousand times and more, often colored by personal or political sympathies or sensationalized for the gossip-hungry, and all too often retold with little regard to verified fact. It is, after all, a remarkable story. In spite of this, relatively few people, including those who have written about the actress, appear to be familiar with the full extent and diversity of her career in international cinema. Many people who remember her vividly are unable to name more than a handful of films in which she appeared, and very few indeed have seen all of these. Without such an overview it is difficult to make sense of her personal journey or to form a balanced judgment of her professional career, with all its ups and downs and critical vicissitudes.

This book attempts to present a systematic chronological survey of Seberg's film work in its biographical context, providing essential data and background information in each case and indicating the variety of each film's critical reception. Limitations of space have inevitably brought difficult choices, especially when seeking the right balance between the readable and the purely informative, but some priority has been given to information not readily accessible elsewhere. Bibliographical references are supplied not only to indicate sources used, but also to provide pointers for those wishing to explore further. In Jean Seberg's case, to a notorious degree, what was written about her affected her life and career profoundly. The inclusion of bibliographical references here does not, of course, imply reliability, but the mere fact that this material was published when it was may be significant in itself. The abridged references relate to the full citations in the bibliography at the end of the volume.

Many published accounts of Jean Seberg's life and career have been biased and/or factually inaccurate. For this reason her own comments or those of people who knew her personally have deliberately been given prominence here. The running times of films are approximations, given the variety of different versions in circulation, but generally relate to the original uncut cinematic editions. Jean Seberg's film career included productions in five different languages. The eventual distribution for each one varied, but to help identification alternative and major foreign language titles are indicated where these are known. The authors were guided primarily by their own curiosity. How did this or that film come into being? What is it about? Who was involved? Where and when was it made? We began the project with such questions, and hope that the answers offered will be of wider interest, whether for the films individually or in the broader context of Seberg's little known but extraordinarily diverse career as an actor on screen.

Many individuals have given generous help during the slow development of this book, whether by sharing their memories, lending precious materials, supplying information or,

1

and not least importantly, giving tireless advice and encouragement. We would particularly like to thank Nancy Adams, Jean-Claude Benméziane, John Berry, Manoah Bowman, John Crome, Mylène Demongeot, Fosco Dubini, Donatello Dubini, Nicolas Gessner, Roger Grenier, Maurice and Chantal Guichard, Jean-François Hangouët, Ross Hunter, Irvin Kershner, Eric Monder, François Moreuil, Richard Ness, Betty Nocella, Dan Petrie, Sr., Françoise Prévost, Jude Rawlins, George Schaefer, Marc Simenon, Pauline Smith and Martin, Phillip and Don of the sadly missed "Rare Discs" in London. Many librarians have given unstinting assistance, among them the staff of The British Film Institute in London, La Bibliothèque du Film in Paris, The British Library, The New York Public Library, The Marshall County Historical Society, Il Centro Sperimentale di Cinematografia in Rome, The Margaret Herrick Library in Los Angeles and Det Danske Filminstitut in Copenhagen. The patient moral support of family members and friends too numerous to name has been vital, but here Gerald and Marian McGee and Wendy Coates-Smith deserve exceptional mention.

Jean Seberg, 1969 (courtesy Manoah Bowman, Independent Visions).

The authors have taken pains throughout to present a true factual record, but must accept full responsibility for any shortcomings in the accuracy of transcription or translation, as well as for any other inadvertent errors.

# Technicolor Dreams: A Biography

Jean Seberg was a girl from Marshalltown, Iowa, who dreamed of becoming a movie star. Born November 13, 1938, she was the second of four children. Her childhood was a normal one, with hobbies and activities such as the March of Dimes, an interest in animal rights and work in her father's business, Seberg Pharmacy, which gave her the chance to dip into Hollywood gossip magazines. While attending Marshalltown High School Jean acted in several plays and competed in oratory contests, scoring high marks for what seemed a budding gift. It was Carol Houghton Hollingsworth, the drama and speech coach at the high school, who first noticed in her an unusual talent and drive. While Hollingsworth admitted she would never suggest acting as a career to anyone, she sensed that this girl had something extra.

After graduating from high school in 1956, Seberg appeared in several stock theatre plays on the East Coast. She had planned to study at the University of Iowa, work towards acting on Broadway, and then, with luck, break into film acting. However, the lucky break came earlier than she could have imagined. Carol Hollingsworth had been encouraged to put forward her name for Otto Preminger's highly publicized contest for the film role of *Saint Joan*. Other submissions, including one from the Cape May Playhouse, had already nominated her. Incredibly, before she could join classes at the university, Seberg found herself selected from some 18,000 aspiring young actresses for the opportunity of a lifetime. Preminger was a director with a reputation for audacity. His 1953 film *The Moon Is Blue* had tested the limits of what was permissible simply by using the words "virgin" and "pregnant," while in 1955 he had tackled the theme of heroin addiction in *The Man with the Golden Arm*.

Seberg was just eighteen when she was whisked away to England for the filming of *Saint Joan*. For a beginner who knew little of stagecraft, a leading role alongside such actors as Gielgud, Todd, Widmark and Walbrook was a gamble against long odds. It guaranteed "stardom" of a sort, but made her famous only for failure, since the film flopped both critically and commercially. Inevitably, the newcomer became the scapegoat. When her second picture with Preminger, *Bonjour Tristesse*, fared little better at the hands of the critics the director concluded she was not an asset and sold his contract with her. Perhaps he had been wrong at the outset—yet there were a significant few who thought not, and there were many more who were later to revise an initially negative verdict.

"Preminger was attacked for his presumption," Seberg said, "for trying to make an actress out of a country bumpkin like myself, and I was told [by the critics] to get back to the farm. It was amazing, the cruelty of some of the reviews. I thought when I read them that he would not want me [for *Bonjour Tristesse*]. But because he is a fighter and a stubborn man, he was determined to impose me—to prove these people wrong. He was persuaded of it up to the screenings in New York. He said I was going to walk out of the cinema a star. And he believed it. But, of course, it was not the case. My name was known alright, but not as a star."

Seberg had met the young French lawyer François Moreuil while making *Bonjour Tristesse* on the French Riviera. They became engaged, and the couple felt that, for the sake of their future together and her career, the time had come for her to free herself from her mentor. Preminger had become accustomed to dominating her life, and, grateful as she was for all she owed to him, this could not continue. Moreuil arranged for Columbia Pictures to purchase Seberg's contract with Preminger.

After Seberg and Moreuil married, on September 5, 1958, in Marshalltown, they found themselves an apartment in Neuilly, northwest Paris. That autumn, Seberg signed to play in *The Mouse That Roared*, which was to be distributed by Columbia. The film was a hit, and marked the international breakthrough for Peter Sellers, already familiar to British radio audiences from *The Goon Show* and to British filmgoers for a string of comedy cameo roles.

In the spring of 1959 Columbia asked Seberg to attend acting classes taught by Payton Price in Los Angeles. Price was a former instructor at the American Academy in New York. He encouraged students to discover their own personalities by revealing and confronting their own anxieties, thus achieving the freedom needed for stage performance. Price had heard the Preminger stories and realized that, while Seberg had acquired some understanding of technique, a lot of her energy was absorbed by insecurities rather than being channeled into performance. Under his guidance she learned to relax, and she was generous in the credit she later gave him for helping her to develop her stagecraft.

This was a period of experimentation in France. Many young would-be film makers were finding ways of shooting films on a shoestring, even if only shorts, and often paid little heed to conventional "rules" of the craft. Moreuil had friends among them, and in the summer he learned that Jean-Luc Godard from the "*Cahiers*" group was planning to make a full-length feature set in Paris about a small-time crook and his girlfriend. Godard knew Seberg's work with Preminger, and he imagined her in the female role. Moreuil arranged a meeting between the two. Although Godard did not have a complete script, he had many ideas for the film that interested Seberg. She was not, however, used to working in this way. It took the persuasion of Moreuil, Godard, co-star Belmondo and Truffaut (who had written the treatment) before she finally agreed to join the project.

The issue of Seberg's contractual obligation to Columbia now arose. Godard sent a twelve-page telegram requesting Seberg's services for either $12,000 or half of the international profits from the film. Faced with the studio's refusal, Moreuil flew to New York as producer Beauregard's representative and confronted Columbia chief Harry Cohn. There he delivered an ultimatum: either they allow his wife to appear in the film or he would take her away from films forever. He had read how Nicky Hilton had used a similar ploy to win Elizabeth Taylor's freedom, and felt it was worth trying on Columbia. Unlike Hilton, Moreuil was not wealthy, but somehow the bluff worked. Columbia settled for $15,000, but in choosing the cash option it missed a deal which would have brought them millions in future revenues.

*Breathless*, as *À bout de souffle* came to be known in the English-speaking world, finally brought Seberg acceptance as an actress. The film was immediately hailed by many as a masterpiece, and even those who disliked it were unable to ignore it or to deny its challenging originality, both technical and conceptual. Not only was it a milestone in France's so-called New Wave, but it has remained a key document for the study of cinema, and has never ceased to provoke discussion and analysis in film schools around the world. Its image of Seberg, with her close-cropped hair, was not significantly different from her appearance in *Bonjour Tristesse*, but it was *Breathless* which gave Belmondo and Seberg lasting iconic status. Even now the Seberg "look" is regularly featured in the style pages of women's magazines.

From now on, and particularly in France, producers and directors began to look at her with more interest. In 1960 came a series of three films which built on her confirmed familiarity to French cinema-goers, including a critical favorite *Five-Day Lover* directed by Philippe de Broca and François Moreuil's *Playtime*. Seberg's characteristic Midwestern accent was sometimes an asset: as Nicolas Gessner put it, "[it] was deliberate and it reflected her intelligence ... it was with tongue in cheek, because it showed her superiority. When she spoke French she spoke it very well, with an accent ... not quite showing off with it, but taking away the criticism. She didn't want other people thinking 'oh, c'mon, she thinks she speaks French.' She went ahead of that criticism by conveying that she had this accent. Even today, so many years later, I can hear her speaking."

*Playtime* was Seberg's farewell present, as she put it, to her soon to be ex-husband. She had realized they had no future together, and events took a decisive turn when the couple visited Los Angeles in 1959. As a well-bred Frenchman, it seemed a natural thing to Moreuil to leave his card with the Consul General. Romain Gary held this post at the time, and he responded with a dinner invitation. When Moreuil found he needed to return to Paris, clearly unaware of the strong mutual attraction registered by the two, he asked Gary to take care of his wife: "and he did," he recalls in hindsight, "—he sure did."

Gary was a war hero and diplomat who had achieved international fame as a writer by winning the Prix Goncourt for his fifth published novel *The Roots of Heaven* (*Les Racines du ciel*) in 1956. His wife Lesley Blanch had achieved comparable fame two years earlier than her husband with the best-seller *The Wilder Shores of Love*. The couple had married in 1945 and had known difficult times in the post-war years, but the bond between them, never jealously possessive, had survived many strains. The entry of Jean Seberg into their lives was to prove one test too many for the marriage, although acrimony was not ultimately to destroy their friendship or respect for each other. Another consequence for Gary was that he soon realized he would be unable to continue a diplomatic career. He would henceforth devote himself to writing, but was also increasingly to be drawn into the world of cinema.

Late in 1961 Gary and Seberg moved into a spacious apartment at 108 rue du Bac in Paris. Seberg and Moreuil finalized their divorce in France in 1962, and they were subsequently to meet only once more. Lesley Blanch eventually accepted that her husband's relationship with the actress twenty-four years his junior was more than a passing fancy, and that her warnings to him were futile. They divorced in the spring of 1963, but it was not until October 16 that Seberg and Gary were married, in a ceremony in the little Corsican village of Sarrola-Carcopino.

By this stage in her career she was beginning to wonder whether she had reached a dead end. "The life of an actress is so uncertain," she confided to a journalist early in 1963, "—just like the movie business. You never know what happens to a career. Some actresses get trapped in the wrong kind of role. Some turn into successes, others just fade away. I think I've about exhausted the possibilities of work here. Whenever I'm given a role in a French film, they have to rewrite it to make the girl an American or something to account for my French accent, which is pretty flat." In any event, she was philosophical and, despite everything, seemed to have no regrets.

While Gary maintained his prolific literary output, publishing in both French and English, Seberg entered another interesting period in her screen career. Following the success of her unostentatiously produced European films, American film makers began to take a second look at an actress they had earlier written off. "I dreamed in Technicolor when I was a little girl," she quipped much later, "but it took five years to make it in low-budget black and white."

After her critically acclaimed performance in Robert Rossen's 1964 film *Lilith*, Seberg's American career seemed to flourish. Her name and box office status were now secure enough to permit her to alternate, if she wished, between big-budget Hollywood movies and smaller scale European productions. Between 1963 and 1969 she appeared in five American and six European made films, with an appearance in a British documentary. She really preferred the European method of film making: "I love working there," she told one interviewer. "There is a kind of group effort about it and much less pressure, like being one of a family. The pictures cost less, and often you don't even know if they will be distributed. But the fact that there is no great studio breathing down your neck relaxes everybody, and that is when the best happens."

Seberg appreciated the advantages of her new status, for, as she told *Radio France*'s Jacques Chancel in 1976, this brings the power to choose. Her name had been important in launching Godard's career, and she was happy to assist directors who were just starting out, whether in this way or as a silent investor. François Moreuil, Claude Berri, Joël Séria and Nicolas Gessner were among those who benefited from her support. "Directors are at their best when it's their first film," she told one. "They are fresh and innovative, and don't usually have the pressures of established directors." Nicolas Gessner remembers this helpfulness as one of her main characteristics, her attitude being typically one of "I trust this guy, so I will help him make his first movie breakthrough." This applied "all the way through." Where other actors would read their own lines and leave the director to give the lines to others, she would stay on, "always there, so very helpful in every respect, and in trying to arrange the shots. That's pretty consistent with her general behavior."

Frequent travel to the U.S. was a feature of her life, whether for family or career reasons. In the 1960s she made at least two trips a year to her childhood home in Iowa. On many occasions her parents joined her on location, both in Europe and America. The visits home were mostly quiet and unpublicized, leading some to claim that once she had "made the big time" she never went back to her hometown. Family tragedy brought inevitable publicity in May 1968, however, when her younger brother David was killed in an automobile accident outside Marshalltown. Seberg, who had been preparing to film *Pendulum* in Los Angeles, hastened home to her grieving parents. Romain Gary flew from Paris to join her, and the couple was photographed by the local press. Twelve months later her appearance at the dedication of the Martha Ellen Tye Playhouse in Marshalltown drew statewide coverage in newspapers and on television. Tye was the sister of the local millionaire Bill Fisher who had urged Seberg's nomination for the *Saint Joan* contest.

A strong sense of justice appears to have been an early trait. At fourteen she had subscribed to the NAACP, and it seemed entirely natural to her to support any campaign against racial inequality. In time youthful idealism became tempered with realism, but throughout her adult life Seberg gave financial or moral support to campaigning organizations of various kinds, including some which were considered politically radical. At one

1968 Hollywood fund-raiser she shocked some fellow celebrities when she asked "Exactly where is this money going to, and how will it be used?" On the other hand, her altruism sometimes made her too trusting of the motives of others.

After completing *Paint Your Wagon* in Los Angeles in 1969, Seberg gave her support to the Black Panther Party's Free Breakfast Program, which provided hot meals to under-privileged children. Subsequently her contributions to the Party increased, although she never joined it, nor ever, according to one senior member, provided funding which was subsequently used for the purchase of arms. She also became powerfully influenced by the charismatic founder of the Malcolm X Foundation, Hakim Jamal, who also established a Montessori school for poor black children. Jamal had contacts both with the Panthers and with liberal Hollywood celebrities, and used these to the full.

Official reaction to radical civil rights movements, like those movements themselves, is an important strand of the social history of the United States in the last century. At this time J. Edgar Hoover was Director of the FBI, and he deemed the Black Panthers "the biggest threat to the national security." It was Seberg's support of the organization which resulted in her being kept under surveillance from 1969 through 1971. A former FBI agent stated that "one of the worst things the FBI did was aimed at Jean Seberg." Celebrity involvement in radical politics was more than a source of irritation in the fraught atmosphere of the day, and in her case one method of countering the threat could be to attack her public image. A rumor was planted that the father of the child the actress was expecting was a "black militant." This surfaced as a "blind item" in *The Los Angeles Times* in the summer of 1970, but it was on August 24, when the story was printed explicitly in *Newsweek* magazine, followed by a hundred newspapers across the United States, that the main impact was felt.

The shock sent Seberg into labor three months prematurely. The child, Nina Hart Gary, lived for only two days. Seberg took her daughter's body to Marshalltown for burial, wishing her to rest in a place she always regarded as home—all who wished would be able to see that the story was a lie. Romain Gary had very publicly stated that the child was his own, and denounced the libel in the strongest terms in the press. Realizing the difficulties of legal action in the U.S., the couple sued *Newsweek* in France and won. Although the damages awarded amounted to less than $12,000 they both felt this was a vindication and moral victory.

The consequences of the smear story were profound, and the death of the child was only the most immediate of these. Added to her private grief was the shock of finding that she could be the object of such vindictive hostility. This seems to have had a generally de-stabilizing influence on her life which she was never to overcome in the following years.

Seberg and Gary had divorced in July 1970, but their bond remained strong, most importantly through their son Alexandre Diego. Gary's novel of the same year, *White Dog*, reveals, if one-sidedly, how Seberg's political involvements had come between them. Apart from this, the peripatetic life of a screen actor was hardly compatible with a writer's need for long spells of concentrated tranquility. Eventually he became weary of accompanying his wife from one film set to another. Perhaps, too, he had become more conscious of their age difference, which increasingly made him feel more of a father figure than a husband.

In March 1972 Seberg married, after a whirlwind romance, for a third and final time. Her new husband was aspiring film maker Dennis Berry, son of the director John Berry. The apartment at the rue du Bac was divided up, enabling Diego to move easily between his father, Romain Gary, and his mother, while also having his own quarters. Together

Seberg and Berry set up an informal acting group. Although she never again made a film in the United States, she pursued her career in France, Italy, Spain and England, making a total of eleven films in five years. In 1973 she became one of the first women to write, direct, produce, edit and star in her own film project, *Ballad for the Kid*. Her final completed film was, like her first, based on a classic play: a German production of Ibsen's *The Wild Duck*.

These years were marked by bouts of sickness and hospital care, growing dependence on prescription drugs and alcohol and episodes of mental instability. There were dubious "friends" and hangers-on who exploited her at times reckless generosity and further depleted the small fortune her films had brought her. In 1978 she separated from Berry, who relocated to Los Angeles for film work. During the following year she developed a relationship with a young Algerian of questionable past named Ahmed Hasni. That summer, under his influence and to the dismay of Gary, Seberg sold the apartment at the rear of 108 rue du Bac to which she had earlier moved. In early August she rented a small apartment in rue de Longchamp, which she would briefly share with Hasni. On the 29th she went with him to see the screen adaptation by Costa-Gavras of Romain Gary's novel *Clair de femme*. The purchaser of Seberg's apartment, Marie-Odile Bouilhet, reported having three telephone conversations with her that evening, but the following morning Hasni told her that Seberg and he had argued, and that his companion had left the flat in the early hours.

It was only ten days later, on September 8, that police finally located the missing actress. Her decomposing body was discovered in the back seat of her car, parked in the nearby rue du Général Appert. A note addressed to her son, asking for forgiveness, was also found at the scene. The autopsy, confirming the initial findings of the police pathologist, revealed that she had absorbed an overdose of barbiturates. More puzzlingly, it also showed a level of alcohol in her system which would rapidly have resulted in coma, making driving impossible. Police suspected that her body had been moved after her death, but were unable to prove the involvement of any other individual. Final cause of death was left as "probable suicide," and the re-examination of the case in June 1980 was no more conclusive. The circumstances surrounding her death remain a mystery never satisfactorily clarified.

On September 10, the day of the autopsy, Gary called a press conference at his publishers Gallimard, produced documents obtained through the American Embassy and made the startling claim that the FBI was responsible for Seberg's death. The action it had taken to discredit her because of her financial support for the Black Panthers had, he argued, caused her mental illness and repeated suicide attempts. No American media were represented, but the accusation received wide, if somewhat skeptical coverage. To his credit, four days later, FBI Director William H. Webster made a public statement admitting that the Bureau, while under Hoover's direction, had decided to "neutralize" her. "The days when the FBI used derogatory information to combat advocates of unpopular causes have long since passed. We are out of that business forever," he pledged. It was only years later that staff of *The Los Angeles Times* admitted that they had been under pressure to print the rumor.

Seberg's only surviving child Diego wished her to be buried in Paris. On the same day as Webster's story broke, September 14, the funeral took place at Montparnasse Cemetery, attended by Romain and Diego Gary, François Moreuil, Dennis Berry, Ahmed Hasni, Jean-Paul Belmondo and many friends. Simultaneously, a private service was held in Marshalltown by the Seberg family and friends from home.

Seberg had planned a trip home to Marshalltown in the autumn, and there had been other projects. There was a film in progress, *Operation Leopard* (*La Légion saute sur Kolwezi*) directed by Raoul Coutard, which she felt would revive her career. She had been due to resume shooting for this in September. There was also talk of a film with David Niven, her co-star in *Bonjour Tristesse*. There were also the books which she had talked of writing and planned in outline. Of these, few clues remain, although extracts from an autobiographical sketch were supplied to journalists by Ahmed Hasni and published in *Journal du dimanche* and the Italian weekly *Gente*. Coutard's film was later completed with Seberg's role recast, and the scenes she had shot remain unseen, by decision of producer Georges de Beauregard.

On the evening of December 2, 1980, after calm and careful planning, Romain Gary ended his life with a bullet through the head. Anticipating the facile explanations, his suicide note urged the "devotees of broken hearts" to look elsewhere. Those who knew him well seem, nevertheless, in little doubt about the profound psychological effect the death of his former wife the previous year had had.

If nothing else, Jean Seberg's debut in the film industry had taught her the insecurity of her chosen profession. It was a lesson she never forgot. In interviews she often speculated about other things she might do, such as floristry or secretarial work, or spoke of courses of study she wished to pursue. Sometimes she expressed general disenchantment with the whole film world, despite her enthusiasm for cinema as an art form. Yet for all that, as she made clear in an interview for *Seventeen* magazine in March 1963, it was acting which made her feel most alive: "I care about acting. I can't help it. You hear all these stories like the way Hitchcock keeps telling his actresses it's only a movie, but I can't feel that way. I do care. The thing about being in a movie is that you recognize that it's like a small immortality in a way, that whatever you do in a film is going to be seen by your children and grandchildren, maybe for a hundred years. When making a picture, you've got to believe in it."

In 1969 Seberg was asked what advice she would give a budding actor or actress. Her response hinted at the trials she herself had experienced at the same time as pointing out that "one successful actor out of ... maybe four or five thousand makes a sound living. I don't think anyone can advise young people. I don't think they listen. I know I certainly wouldn't have listened to anyone giving me advice. I would only ask someone wanting to follow an acting career to question their depth of need for it. Because if it isn't something you truly feel a need for, I think it's too tough. There are too many things to be sacrificed along the way to make it all worthwhile."

"[Seberg] was an emblem," says Gessner, "with the short cut hair, the tom-boyish thing she projected in *Breathless*. For people who perhaps don't remember *Breathless*, 'Jean Seberg'—that means something. She had this star quality. She was not superstar like, say, box office-wise, [but] she was on the marquee, and she was a quality name. And she was very significant."

# Part I

## *From Saint to Sinner, 1958–1963*

*Saint Joan* catapulted the unknown Jean Seberg to international "star" status, thanks to Otto Preminger and his publicity machine. This film was essentially a stage play adapted for the screen and not conceived as another *Gone with the Wind* epic, but the stories about its production which were constantly fed to the media inflated expectations beyond all reason. The reaction which followed its release was doubly severe as a consequence. Preminger was wise in not pushing his next Seberg vehicle, *Bonjour Tristesse*, to the same degree, although the notoriety of Sagan's story assured it much media attention. These two films were a world apart. The latter was a contemporary story, largely shot in Technicolor on the French Riviera, and the worldly-wise and amoral character of the scheming Cécile seemed the polar opposite of Joan. As Seberg herself expressed it during filming, "You might say I've gone from saint to sinner." Unfortunately for her, few at this stage, and very few American critics, seemed to feel that the sinner had redeemed the saint.

After breaking with Preminger, Seberg did retrieve some credit with a less prominent role in the highly successful comedy *The Mouse That Roared*. This was followed up by an insignificant part in the somber melodrama *Let No Man Write My Epitaph*, which did nothing to further her career. It did nevertheless give her an insight into the differences between Hollywood and European film production, and she noted the wastefulness of

With Jean-Pierre Cassel in Philippe de Broca's *The Five-Day Lover* (*L'Amant de cinq jours*) (**Kingsley International Pictures**).

11

the former as well as the friendlier atmosphere in the less lavish and formal conditions of British film making. For better or worse, she was not to return to California to make a film until 1965.

With the international success of Godard's *Breathless* came a lasting status as actress and icon. In France she became, almost like Brando or James Dean earlier, a glamorous emblem of free-spirited American youth, but at the same time, she and Belmondo seemed the heralds of an exciting rebirth of cinema. Her appearance in the French comedy *The Five-Day Lover* confirmed her popularity with French audiences, and it was this film which led to a star role in the American-produced *In the French Style*, also shot in Paris. The two other films made in the French capital and released in 1961, Moreuil's *Playtime* and Valère's *Time Out for Love*, had a more mixed reception, but nevertheless kept her very much in the public eye.

The Italian-made experimental film *Congo Vivo* showed Seberg was not afraid to try different film styles, although this was not counted a success and had limited distribution. Jean-Luc Godard persuaded her to revive the character she had played in *Breathless* for a short called *Le Grand Escroc*. Unfortunately this was dropped from the collaborative venture for which it was intended, and received very little exposure. Despite a rocky start, by this stage Seberg had gained acceptance among the general public and the critics alike.

Back home in Marshalltown all of these films were screened, with the exception of *Time Out for Love*, *Congo Vivo* and Godard's short. Seberg's English language films were popular, *Saint Joan* had its Western Hemisphere premiere here, and *Breathless* played in September 1961, but perhaps most favored and best remembered by locals was *The Five-Day Lover*. Despite the fact that it has never been seen there since its week-long run in May 1962, it made an impression which somehow stayed in the memory.

# *Saint Joan* (1957)

"There is one thing that I shall never forgive [Preminger] for:
he took away from me the one thing that is most essential to
an actress, and that is her self-confidence."—Jean Seberg

A Wheel Productions production; A United Artists release
Original release: in English
Also known as: *Sainte Jeanne* [France]; *Die heilige Johanna* [Germany]; *Giovanna d'Arco* [Italy]; *Santa Juana* [Spain]
Running Time: 110 minutes
Format: in Black and White

CAST: Richard Widmark (The Dauphin [Charles VII]); Richard Todd (Dunois); Anton Walbrook (Cauchon, Bishop of Beauvais); John Gielgud (Earl of Warwick); Felix Aylmer (The Inquisitor); Harry Andrews (John de Stogumber); Archie Duncan (Robert de Baudricourt); Barry Jones (de Courcelles); Finlay Currie (The Archbishop of Rheims); Bernard Miles (The Master Executioner); Patrick Barr (Captain La Hire); Kenneth Haigh (Brother Martin Ladvenu); Margot Grahame (Duchesse de la Trémouille); Francis de Wolff (La Trémouille, Lord Chamberlain); Victor Maddern (English soldier); David Oxley (Gilles de Rais); Sydney Bromley (Baudricourt's steward); David Langton (Captain of Warwick's Guard); Jean Seberg (Saint Joan of Arc); [uncredited: Thomas Gallagher (Foul-mouthed Frank); Norman Rossington (soldier); Richard Palmer (page); Mark Mileham (child);

David Hemmings (page); Tatiana Beesley, Simonne Cardon, John Freeman, Simone Harman, Michael Lewin, Eileen Norton, Susan Raie, Julie Rosson, Theone Sheriston, Kenneth Tarrant, Jenifer Wrathall]

PRODUCTION CREDITS: *Director and Producer:* Otto Preminger; *Screenplay:* Graham Greene, based on the play by George Bernard Shaw; *Music:* Mischa Spoliansky; *Camera Operator:* Denys Coop; *Production Design:* Roger Furse; *Sound:* Peter Handford, Red Law; *Wardrobe:* John McCorry; *Editor:* Helga Cranston; *Art Direction:* Ray Simm; *Photography:* Georges Périnal; *Still Photography:* Bob Willoughby, John Jay; *Scenic Artist:* Alexander Bilibin; *Technical Advisor:* Charles R. Beard; *Casting Director:* Lionel Larner; *Makeup:* Tony Sforzini; *Hairdressing:* Gordon Bond; *Titles:* Saul Bass; *Associate Producer:* Douglas Peirce; *Production Manager:* Laurie Laurence; *Assistant Director:* Peter Bolton; *Script Supervisor:* Doreen Francis; *Religious advisor:* Father Burke

## Synopsis

The ghostly Joan appears before Charles VII of France in a dream in the year 1456. In extended flashbacks we see how the country girl, convinced of her divine mission to drive out the English, had miraculously achieved his coronation at Rheims in 1429.

Regarded as an upstart and heretic by church authorities, Joan had soon lost royal support also. When she was captured in battle and sold to the English her enemies saw the opportunity to be rid of this idealist who challenged their power. The cynical Earl of Warwick was happy to see her condemned by her own countrymen, standing ready to execute the sentence of an ecclesiastical court. Even Joan's courage seemed to falter under inquisition, faced with an agonizing death. However, seeing that there was no chance of freedom, she had retracted her acceptance that her voices might have deceived her, and had steeled herself for martyrdom.

One after another, key participants in the Maid's fateful story materialize before the aged King and Joan. Each comments on his own role with rueful hindsight, though none desires her return. Joan asks God when the world will be ready for his saints: there is no answer.

## Reviews

"It is sure to encounter some hostility from those to whom the stage version is more or less sacrosanct ... Dramatically, Graham Greene's concise telescoping helps the superb playing of the British male cast ... Jean Seberg as the Maid stands up well among so many far more experienced actors."—*Today's Cinema*

"Preminger's ambitious film version of Shaw's *Saint Joan* is a curious and oddly unbalanced affair.... A main flaw lies in Graham Greene's adaptation and rearrangement of Shaw's play."—*Monthly Film Bulletin*

"In cutting George Bernard Shaw's incisive and barb-filled three-and-a-half hour study of the Maid of Orleans to its present one hour and fifty-minutes length, [Preminger and Greene] have come up with a series of vignettes full of declamations that rarely move a viewer."—*New York Times*

"[Seberg] makes a sincere effort, but her performance rarely rises above the level of the Iowa prairie. Her pale, somehow uninspired Joan rarely communicates the dramatic intensity and the magnetic, robust leadership qualities that the author had in mind.... There is no flame in Miss Seberg."—*Variety*

"Seberg, with the advantage of youth and the disadvantage of inexperience, is drastically miscast. Shaw's Joan is a chunk of hard bread, dipped in the red wine of battle and devoured by the ravenous angels. Actress Seberg ... is the sort of honey bun that drugstore desperadoes like to nibble with their milkshakes."—*Time*

"Miss Seberg acts with all the talent and sincerity at her command, make no mistake about that; and it is a talent and sincerity that will stand her in good stead in the future. ... if her burning zeal to come out top-of-the-class all prove her to be totally miscast as Joan, the fault is not hers."—*Films and Filming*

## Notes

By his own account, Preminger had harbored the ambition of screening Shaw's play for some twenty years before work on the film actually began. Few film directors could have better understood the challenge this would present than this man who had studied stagecraft alongside the renowned Max Reinhardt in Vienna. Negotiations to secure the rights had taken two years, so the gestation period for the project was an extended one. As an experienced theatre director with an enormous admiration for Shaw, Preminger was reluctant to tamper with the original text of "one of the greatest plays ever written." On two points he was clear: his star should be young and relatively unknown, and there would be no wide screen epic treatment. "I want to put the emphasis on people, on characterizations, on emotions, and on the words of Bernard Shaw," he explained in a Canadian broadcast. "Color, or too much spectacle added to it, would distract rather than help to give this play to the public."

Preminger was not initially aware that Shaw had made his own screen adaptation of the play, two versions of which are held in the British Library. It was in fact to novelist Graham Greene that the director turned for dialogue revision. Changes and substantial cuts clearly had to be made for the demands of cinema, and Greene, who was given six weeks in which to make them, was far less reverential than Preminger. Part of the Epilogue became a prologue, creating a frame for the action. Bold cut-and-paste editing allowed Greene to claim that the shrunken text was still "95% Shaw."

Preminger's obviously risky concept was to use an unknown actress of about Joan's actual age, supported by an all-star cast. Once committed to this course he was nothing if not organized, laying out a timetable for everything up to the premiere as if for his own military campaign. Indeed, at this stage in his career, with 22 films behind him, he was able to control every aspect of a production and fully appreciated the advantages such power delivered.

The publicity value of the search for a Joan was inestimable. A trailer shown in movie theatres in 1956 yielded some 18,000 applications, which could soon be filtered down to around 3,000. Preminger then embarked on a tour of audition venues covering the U.S., Canada, the UK, Ireland and Sweden. Once he had decided that Seberg had precisely the "strength and simplicity" called for, the PR machine swung into action in earnest, launching on *The Ed Sullivan Show* 21 October what would be an intensive schedule of broadcast and press interviews, generating worldwide interest.

On the eve of her eighteenth birthday, November 12, Seberg flew to New York, arriving in London on the 15th to begin preparatory work. Photo-opportunities at London landmarks were followed in December by a five-day pilgrimage to Domrémy, Vaucouleurs, Orléans, Rheims and Rouen. Ingrid Bergman, who had played Joan on screen in 1948, was performing *Tea and Sympathy* in Paris, an opportunity not to be missed. Preminger and Seberg visited her backstage, and the trusty "Hollywood special," cameraman Bob Willoughby, was again on hand to immortalize the moment.

Formal rehearsals began on 17 December and the nine week shoot initiated on January 8. Preminger defended his choice of Seberg to the press: "She has the looks, intelligence, feeling and just the right innocence.... She has shaped very well under instruction and she is doing very well on the set, though, of course, she was nervous and felt strange at first. She has never been near a film studio before. It's a gamble, of course, to play an unknown, and about that I can only hope." The risk element may have been played up for the press, but this director left little to chance. Feared for his sudden explosions of anger, he could also be a patiently relentless taskmaster in extracting the performance he was seeking. The former actor would personally school his star down to the smallest detail. Nevertheless, he politely deflected pointed references to the famous novel by Du Maurier: "I try to teach her to think. Surely that is the opposite of Svengali. His trick was to ensure that his 'victim' didn't think. I can't get out of Miss Seberg what isn't there." Two months had been spent perfecting the 20-odd sets, with historical advisors on hand to ensure authenticity. Composer Mischa Spoliansky had provided fitting royal fanfares and courtly dances as well as a haunting title theme. The brilliant young graphic artist Saul Bass, who had already worked with Preminger on two films, was commissioned to design the credits and publicity materials. Arrangements were even made for a documentary film to record the whole ambitious venture from start to finish.

For all the preparation, the shoot was not without mishaps. Cinematographer Georges Périnal had to take over with a day's notice as a result of disagreements with Desmond Dickinson, who had attended rehearsals. Kenneth Haigh was substituted as Brother Martin when Paul Scofield decided to withdraw. More seriously, on February 21 Seberg was literally burned at the stake when gas cylinders flared out of control. The terrified actress struggled to free herself and cover her face, surrounded by 1500 shocked extras, while the camera continued to roll. Luckily her burns were superficial, though the scars would never entirely fade. Newspapers around the world printed pictures of the drama or of the plucky actress with bandaged hand. "I smell just like a singed chicken," she joked with the journalists. Perhaps it was a portent. Preminger praised her courage, and despite the scare was not displeased to have the dramatic extra footage, though offended by the suggestion of another publicity stunt: "Would I risk burning the star of my picture?" he protested. The following day the car taking director and star to Shepperton Studios skidded on the icy road. Preminger suffered a cracked wrist and Bob Willoughby's cameras were a write-off, but Seberg escaped with a few bruises. On March 2 director and star were guests of The Shaw Society, and Seberg described how the moving experience of playing Joan had convinced her of the dramatist's greatness and humanity, whetting her appetite for further Shavian roles.

Despite the setbacks, the director would still be able to boast that he had completed filming a day ahead of the mid–March schedule. Cutting and dubbing were finalized within the following weeks. The film's release was to be the climax of Preminger's publicity campaign. A glittering premiere in aid of polio victims was planned to coincide with the French national holiday marking the Saint's day. The patients at the hospital at Garches had their own preview in the presence of the director and his discovery on May 10. *Paris Match* featured another Seberg visit to Orléans on May 9. It had been planned that a helicopter would take the saint between the simultaneous screenings at Orléans and Paris, but this stunt had to be called off. The premiere at the Paris Opéra on May 12, featuring a sketch by Bob Hope and Fernandel, received maximum attention, and was followed by a VIP supper at Maxim's. Over a million francs were raised for charity, but rarely, if ever, can there have been a tyro so deliberately spotlighted among so many established stars. The London Gala Premiere, in aid of the British Film Studio Workers' Benevolent Funds, was held in Leicester Square Theatre on June 20. Five days later the star's birthplace, Marshalltown, celebrated the "Western Hemisphere Premiere" with a capacity audience at the Orpheum Theater. The *Times-Republican* carried a full-page message of gratitude to the teenager who had given the town worldwide publicity. So far so good, notwithstanding the doubts expressed by some, but then the reviews began to appear.

Why was the film so badly received by so many? The reasons seem to have been of several distinct, but perhaps not unrelated kinds. Some will have had in mind one of the earlier classic treatments of the story which captured qualities lacking here, perhaps the intensity of Dreyer or the epic sweep of Marco de Gastyne, for example. Did some expect Preminger to open up the play in a style completely at variance with his stated intent? Was the quarrel with Shaw rather than with the director? In his Preface Shaw had anticipated some of the ways in which people would want to "improve" on his play, and it is certainly true that his view of Joan's story is highly personal. This was, for one thing, a sympathetic rationalist's take on sainthood, and a caustic view of clericalism even in the Catholic Greene's version. Shaw's satirical tone is if anything sharpened by Greene, who adds his own humorous details. Some felt that Widmark's Dauphin, added to this, brought the whole thing dangerously close to burlesque. This is, too, a wordy film even after Greene's pruning, and clearly reveals its theatrical origin. Ingrid Bergman recalled a conversation with Shaw in which she had challenged him for making Joan too clever and articulate, pointing out discrepancies between his play and transcripts of the trial. For Bergman, the words were "marvelous, but they're George Bernard Shaw's words, not Joan's."

To Shaw, Joan was a genius of a kind, but she was no divine mouthpiece. She is a naively idealistic country girl pitted against a motley collection of dogmatic, pragmatic or cynical individuals who find her baffling; and the incomprehension is mutual. Preminger senses that she must seem a misfit, and this is implicit in his casting. A more experienced actress might have given a more "knowing" performance at odds with this point. As it is, what Seberg gives us is a performance of warmth and total sincerity, a bumpy ride, perhaps, but with many moments which ring admirably true. In retrospect, *American Film* recalled: "[she] has a certain sparkle in her spunkiness, a certain erotic élan that one does not pick up in acting school. Shaw himself would have been fascinated by the poignant suggestion of regret in Seberg's Joan." For Preminger biographer Foster Hirsch, Seberg's totally committed performance at the climax of the trial scene is "thrilling"—"and it is possible, after all, to see why Preminger cast Jean Seberg, and what he saw in her."

We may question whether Preminger's selection of Seberg from so many hopefuls brought her the opportunity of a lifetime or a poisoned chalice. It was as though some of the critics felt compelled to punish the director's presumption in fashioning a star to order, Pygmalion-like, to take on this iconic role. Not only would she ultimately be judged by the severest standards, but in the process would be subjected to a notoriously bullying style of direction she was simply not equipped to deal with and against which she could have no defense. "He never stopped shouting and insulting me," she was to recall many years later; "I was a naïve young girl then, and at night I used to imagine ways of killing him." The importance of not damaging a young actor's confidence would be a key principle for her later, when she herself experimented with directing. Preminger probably overestimated her toughness, liking to recount to journalists how when taunted she had retorted defiantly that she would carry on rehearsing "until you drop dead." Bob Willoughby remembered her resilience: "I would see her get a tongue lashing from Preminger, swallow it, go off by herself and psych herself up. Then she'd come back and do the scene again.

She was no quitter under fire. If there were medals for courage, for bravery in the cinema world, Jean would have won them all."

Years later Preminger was to state that he alone had been to blame for the film's failure. This was indeed true, yet Seberg apparently never acquitted herself of blame. "I wanted everyone to be proud of me and I wanted everyone to justify their faith in me," she said. "I wasn't ready to do it. I simply didn't have what it takes to be a professional. I had to learn." Regarding the publicity excesses, she commented, "You can never force a new personality on any public. They have to select you. And all the publicity men and all the producers and all the talent of the best directors of the world are not going to make the public accept you if they don't choose to on their own."

To say expectations were high for this film would be an understatement, yet, because of original decisions Preminger had made about casting, Seberg was doomed to fail with all those who looked for an accomplished tour de force of stagecraft. Additionally, she was never going to satisfy the majority of those hoping to see their own conception of the historical "Jehanne" realized. Yet for others ready to approach the play with an open mind, without seeking a definitive reading, the film still has much to offer, if only as a view of Shaw's view of his problematic heroine, posing interesting questions rather than presenting

As St. Joan with director Otto Preminger. Both later regretted the misunderstood communication between actor and director (UA).

ready-made answers. Falconetti's Joan remains one of cinema's unforgettable images, but nothing could be further from Dreyer's expressionistic 1928 masterpiece than the humane intellectualism of the play Shaw had written five years earlier. If Seberg inhabits a wholly different, recognizably modern world of youthful conviction meeting the intricate compromises of adult society, this too is arguably a valid reading of a legend which is also human history. Did Preminger consciously use Seberg's own situation, floundering and fighting against all odds, as a way of portraying Joan's? Some perceptive critics seemed to sense this, but for at least one, Michel Mourlet, this screen version is in the end truer than all its illustrious predecessors. In any case, with half a century of hindsight, most critics would probably accept Chris Fujiwara's verdict that "*Saint Joan* is one of Preminger's most underrated films."

In the context of so much proven talent, blaming Seberg's inexperience was an all too convenient explanation for a very literary film's initial failure to please. The contrast was, of course, deliberate. The central performance we see on screen was the product of a merciless verbal pummeling which Widmark later summed up as "sadistic," and which could not fail to leave its mark. It's interesting to note that, five years later, Robert Bresson's completely different approach to Joan's trial dispensed with professional actors entirely, resulting in a classic which is eloquent in its austerity. Such public sneers as Seberg incurred can be tenacious and hard to live down. Jessica Lange's screen debut in the derided 1976 remake of *King Kong* is still cited by the media as an indicator of her talent, even after a notable career and two Academy Awards. In time Seberg was to show that Preminger's first instincts about her had not been wrong, as indeed he would later boast, but the public had yet to be convinced.

## References

Aubriant, Michel. *Cinémonde* 1174, 7 February 1957, pp. 8–9.

Baby, Yvonne. "Brève rencontre avec Otto Preminger." *Les Lettres françaises*, 671, 16–22 May 1957, p. 7.

Bergman, Ingrid, and Alan Burgess. *My story*. London: M. Joseph, 1980, pp. 183–5.

Brulé, Claude. *Ciné revue* 37:4, 25 January 1957, pp. 30–1.

Carluccio, Giulia, and Linda Cena. "Otto Preminger." *Il Castoro cinema*, 145 Jan./Feb. 1990, pp. 89–94.

*The Daily Express*, 10 January 1957. John Lambert. "The new St. Joan: First day's filming for the small town girl," p. 3.

*The Daily Mail*, 21 January 1957. "Trials and tribulations of the new St Joan," p. 8.

Delville, Olivier. "De la première mondiale de 'Sainte Jeanne,'" *Le Soir illustré* 1300, 23 May 1957, pp. 7–9, 13.

Devay, Jean-François. Le petit drame... *Paris-presse*, 16 May 1957, p. 2.

Falk, Quentin. *Travels in Greeneland: the complete guide to the cinema of Graham Greene*. 3d ed. London: Reynolds and Hearn, 2000, pp. 88–9.

Fujiwara, Chris. *The world and its double: the life and work of Otto Preminger*. New York: Faber and Faber, 2008. pp. 198–209.

Grob, Norbert, Rolf Aurich, and Wolfgang Jacobsen. *Otto Preminger*. Berlin: Jovis, 1999, pp. 118–20, 187, 275–6.

Hill, Derek. "Cameraman on the sidelines." *American Cinematographer*, 38:8 August 1957, pp. 510–11, 526.

Hirsch, Foster. *Otto Preminger: the man who would be king*. New York: Knopf, 2007, pp. 248–77.

*Hollywood Reporter*, 142:50, 3 January 1957, p. 8, 143:40, 28 February 1957, p. 3.

*Life*, 41:18, 29 October 1956. "Dragnet for a new Saint Joan," pp. 119–20.

*Life*, 42:10, 11 March 1957. "St. Joan really burns," p. 138.

Lisi, Umberto. "Dopo *Giovanna* Bonjour tristesse." *Cinema nuovo* 6:100, 15 February 1957, pp. 68, 70.

Mattern, Marjorie. *Saint Joan*. New York: Feature Books, 1957.

Mayersberg, Paul. "Saint Joan." *Movie*, 2: September 1962, p. 21.

Millstein, Gilbert. "Evolution of a new Saint Joan." *New York Times*, 7 April 1957, pp. 28, 56.

*Motion Picture Daily*, 81:91, 10 May 1957. "New idea in trailers launched for 'St. Joan.'"

Mourlet, Michel. "Jeanne d'Arc et le cinéma." *Le Spectacle du monde* 197 August 1978, pp. 75–80.

_____. "*Saint Joan* d'Otto Preminger." *Études cinématographiques* 18–19 Autumn 1962, pp. 79–82.

*Newsweek*, 49:14, 8 April 1957. "Charmer on the set," pp. 113–4.

Ott, Beverly. "The trials of Jean." *Photoplay* 51:6, June 1957, pp. 50–3, 104–7.

Pinel, Vincent. Filmographie: "Jeanne à l'écran." *Études cinématographiques* 18–19 Autumn 1962, pp. 131–4.

Preminger, Otto. *Preminger: an autobiography*. New York: Doubleday, 1977, pp. 152–3.

Preminger, Otto [quoted in *Times*, 22 November 1962, p. 15].

Sarris, Andrew. "Otto Preminger: Shattering taboos, he pointed the way to rebel filmmaking." *American Film*, 14:8, June 1989, pp. 69–71.

_____. "Preminger's two periods: studio and solo." *Film Comment*, 3:3 Summer 1965, pp. 12–17.

Seberg, Jean, and Terry Fincher. *Le Soir illustré* 2201, 29 August 1974, p. 29.

*The Shavian*, 9: May 1957, p. 16.

Shaw, George Bernard. *Saint Joan: a chronicle play in six scenes and an epilogue*. 1924.

_____, and Bernard Frank Dukore. *Saint Joan; a screenplay*. Seattle: University of Washington Press, 1968.

Watts, Stephen. "Screening Shaw's 'Saint Joan' on schedule." *New York Times*, 17 February 1957 (s.2 p. 7).

Widmark, Richard. "Lettre à Elia Kazan." *Positif* 519 May 2004, p. 45.

Wiener, Thomas J. *Otto Preminger: Anatomy of a Filmmaker* [documentary film by Valerie A. Robins, 1991].

Willoughby, Bob. *Hollywood, a Journey Through the Stars*. New York: Assouline, 2001, pp. 100–109.

## Reviews

*America*, vol. 97, 29 June 1957.

*Les Annales*, 64:81 July 1957. Jacques Nels, pp. 52–4.

*Arts*, 621, 29 May–4 June 1957. Eric Rohmer, p. 5.

*L'Aurore*, 18–19 May 1957. Claude Garson, p. 4.

*Bianco e nero*, 18:12 December 1957. Giuseppe Ferrara, pp. 66–8.

*Cahiers du cinéma*, 13:73 July 1957. Jacques Rivette, pp. 38–40.

*Le Canard enchaîné*, 38:1909, 12 May 1957. Donald Duck, p. 4.

*Chicago Sun-Times*, 28 June 1957. Doris Arden.

*Commonweal*, 66:16, 19 July 1957. Philip T. Hartung, pp. 400–1.

*Cosmopolitan*, 142 June 1957.

*La Croix*, 6 June 1957. Jean Rochereau.

*Cue*, 29 June 1957.

*The Daily Mirror*, 21 June 1957. Reg Whitley, p. 12.

*The Daily Telegraph*, 22 June 1957. Campbell Dixon, p. 9, profile p. 5.

*The Evening Standard*, 20 June 1957. Philip Oakes, p. 6.

*L'Express*, 308, 17 May 1957. J-P Vivet, p. 23.

*Le Figaro*, 22 May 1957. Louis Chauvet, p. 14.

*The Film Daily*, 8 May 1957, p. 11.

*Film-Dienst*, 43, 25 October 1957. Paul Sackarndt.

*Film-Echo*, 85, 23 October 1957. Georg Herzberg.

*Filmblätter*, no. 42, 18 October 1957. Ingeborg Donati, p. 1219.

*Filmforum*, vol. 6, June 1958. Dieter Krusche.

*Film-Kritik*, 16 November 1957.

*Filmkritik*, November 1957. Ulrich Gregor, p. 167.

*Films and Filming*, 3:10, July 1957. Paul Rotha, p. 21.

*Films in Review*, 8:6, June/July 1957. Ellen C. Kennedy, pp. 280–1.

*Filmwoche*, no. 45, 2 November 1957. Hellmut Stolp.

*Le Franc-tireur*, 23 May 1957. Denis Marion.

*France-soir*, 25 May 1957. André Lang, p. 10.

*Frankfurter allgemeine Zeitung*, 30 September 1957. Karl Korn.

*Frankfurter Rundschau*, 27 September 1957. Wolfgang Bartsch, p. 8.

*Glasgow Herald*, 14 October 1957. Molly Plowright, p. 5.
*The Hollywood Reporter*, 8 May 1957. James Powers, p. 3.
*Image et son*, 104 July 1957. Jacques Chevallier, p. 13.
*Index de la cinématographie française*, 1957B. Jean Houssaye, p. 170.
*Intermezzo*, 12:13, 15 July 1957, p. 12.
*Kinematograph Weekly*, 20 June 1957, p. 20.
*Les Lettres françaises*, 672, 23–29 May 1957. Christian Remédy, p. 7.
*Library Journal*, vol. 82, July 1957.
*Los Angeles Examiner*, 27 June 1957.
*Los Angeles Times*, 27 June 1957. Philip K. Scheuer, pt. 4 p. 9.
*The Manchester Guardian*, 22 June, p. 3 and 15 October 1957, p. 4.
*Le Monde*, 25 May 1957. Jean de Baroncelli, p. 12.
*Monthly Film Bulletin*, 24:282 July 1957. J.A.D.C., p. 98.
*Motion Picture Herald*, 11 May 1957, p. 369.
*The Nation*, vol. 185, 20 July 1957.
*Neue Zürcher Zeitung*, 2 June 1957, p. 1610/3.
*The New Republic*, 137:7–8, 12 August 1957. Janet Winn, p. 22.
*The New York Herald Tribune*, 27 June 1957. P.V. Beckley, p. 15.
*The New York Times*, 27 June, p. 21, 30 June 1957 (s.2 p. 1) A.H. Weiler.
*The New Yorker*, 33:20, 6 July 1957. John McCarten, p. 52.
*News of the World*, 23 June 1957. Peter Burnup, p. 13.
*Newsweek*, 49:25, 24 June 1957, p. 108.
*Paris-presse*, 23 May 1957. Claude Brulé, p. 10.
*Picturegoer*, 6 July 1957, p. 13.
*Positif*, 25–6, 1957, p. 95.
*Saturday Review*, 40:26, 29 June 1957. Hollis Alpert, p. 22.
*Sight and Sound*, 27:1 Summer 1957. Penelope Houston, p. 38.
*Süddeutsche Zeitung*, 12 November 1957. Franziska Violet, p. 7.
*The Sunday Express*, 23 June 1957. Peter Tudor, p. 12.
*Time*, 70:1, 1 July 1957, p. 80.
*The Times*, 13 May 1957 [Paris premiere], p. 14.
*The Times*, 20 June 1957, p. 3.
*Today's Cinema*, 20 June 1957. P.L.M., p. 8.
*Variety*, 8 May 1957, p. 6.
*Die Welt*, 9 October 1957. Willy Haas, p. 7.
*Die Zeit*, 12:19, 9 May 1957. Ludwig Ullmann, p. 21.

# *Bonjour Tristesse* (1958)

"My tension is apparent through much of the picture,
but I was not quite as bad as in *Joan*. As Preminger has said since,
he treated me all the wrong ways...."—Jean Seberg

A Wheel Production; Distributed by Columbia Pictures Corporation
Original release: in English
Also known as: *Buongiorno tristezza* [Italy]; *Buenos días tristeza* [Spain]
Running Time: 93 minutes
Format: in Technicolor, with black and white sequences; in Cinemascope

CAST: [* denotes above the title billing] Deborah Kerr* (Anne Larsen); David Niven* (Raymond); Jean Seberg* (Cécile); Mylène Demongeot* (Elsa Mackenbourg); Geoffrey Horne (Philippe); Juliette Gréco (nightclub singer); Walter Chiari (Pablo Villami); Martita Hunt (Philippe's Mother); Roland Culver (Henri Lombard); Jean Kent (Helen Lombard); David Oxley (Jacques); Elga Andersen (Denise); Jeremy Burnham (Hubert Duclos); Eveline Eyfel (maid); [Tutte Lemkow (Pierre Schube)]

PRODUCTION CREDITS: *Director and Producer:* Otto Preminger; *Screenplay:* Arthur Laurents, based on the novel by Françoise Sagan; *Photography:* Georges Périnal; *Production Design:* Roger Furse; *Sound:* David Hildyard, Red Law; *Art Direction:* Raymond Simm; *Set Direction:* Georges Petitot; *Editor:* Helga Cranston; *Music:* Georges Auric; *Conductor:* Lambert Williamson; *Wardrobe:* May Walding; *Gowns:* Givenchy; *Jewelry:* Cartier's; *Accessories:* Hermès; *Costume Coordinator:* Hope Bryce; *Script Supervisor:* Eileen Head; *Paintings:* Kumi Sugai; *Titles:* Saul Bass; *Camera Operator:* Denys Coop; *Sound Editor:* David Hawkins; *Hairdressing:* Gordon Bond, Janou Pottier; *Assistant Directors:* Adrian Pryce-Jones, Serge Friedman, Alain Gouze, Henri Valrude; *Associate Producer:* John Palmer; *Assistant to the Producer:* Maximilian Slater; *Production Managers:* Erica Masters, Philippe Senné; *Choreography:* Tutte Lemkow; *Chief Grip:* Pierre Cecchi; *Photography:* Germaine Kanova; *Makeup:* George Frost, Hagop Arakelian; *Recording:* Jacques Thibault; *Outdoor Direction:* Nady Chauviret, André Labussière; *Dressers:* Ginette Manzon, Clo Ramoin; *General Direction:* Georges Testard; *Production Secretary:* Anne-Marie Edmonds

## Synopsis

Pampered eighteen-year-old Cécile leads an apparently carefree existence in Paris with her father, playboy businessman Raymond, yet their hectic pursuit of pleasure has lost its savor. The reason for this becomes clear as she relives the events of their holiday on the Côte d'Azur the previous summer.

Father and daughter share their villa with Elsa, his latest conquest. The mood changes with the arrival of another guest, the serious-minded Anne, who feels slighted by the situation in which she finds herself. Soon Raymond switches his attentions to Anne and makes her believe he will mend his ways. They become engaged, but, when Anne tries to restrict Cécile's flirtation with Philippe and to force her to study, the teenager schemes with Elsa and Philippe to create a rift between Raymond and Anne. Cécile's plot, exploiting Raymond's fickleness, succeeds only too well. Anne is distraught and flees, suffering a fatal car crash which looks like suicide.

Looking back on her lost innocence, Cécile wonders whether her father is equally haunted by the tragedy which they cannot discuss, despite their interdependence. Both appear condemned to maintain their joyless façade, continuing with a sybaritic life which has lost all its meaning.

## Reviews

"Otto Preminger's latest film is just as curious, and misfires just as badly, as his *St Joan*. The emotional tones of the original were predominantly grey and black; Preminger's adaptation is a blaze of clashing colours ... it comes out as a heavy-weight *soufflé* whose sophistication lapses into boredom, with a lifeless pace and dull direction." — *Monthly Film Bulletin*

"[It is] excellently directed by Otto Preminger, who lovingly models his young discovery. Jean Seberg is for the spectator exactly the Cécile the reader had imagined." — *France-soir*

"... while honest, it doesn't rise above the level of fidelity to the text." — *Radio cinéma télévision*

"In its airy way, *Bonjour Tristesse* has a certain amount of charm although, of course, it seems likely that puritan circles will be heard from.... Strangely enough, Miss Seberg, while lacking necessary expression in the early reels, appears to achieve at least some professionalism.... Perhaps it's a matter of getting used to her." — *Variety*

"You may wonder how such a fragile sketch could be made into a full-length movie.

The answer is that it can't ... Jean Seberg is about as far from a French nymph as milk is from pernod."—*New York Herald Tribune*

"Almost everything about this picture ... manifests bad taste, poor judgment and plain deficiency of skill ... every one of the actors seems incompetent or uncomfortable ... Seberg ... reads her lines and takes her positions as if she were a misplaced amateur. David Niven is vapid as the father ... 'Bonjour Tristesse' is a bomb."—*New York Times*

"Preminger, apparently, has not yet succeeded in convincing Miss Seberg that she is an actress."—*Saturday Review*

"Jean Seberg blooms with the right suggestion of unhealthy freshness."—*Time*

"Suffice to say here that [Seberg] is basically better, more assured as an actress ... she still has things to learn, but her natural good looks and girlish ebullience stand her in good stead. You want to like her."—*New York Post*

"Miss Seberg is still an amateur actress."—*Newsweek*

"... when Jean Seberg is on the screen, which is all the time, you only look at her. ... her kind of sex appeal hasn't been seen on the screen: she is led, controlled, directed in the tiniest detail by her director... [Seberg] carries this whole film on her small shoulders...."—*Arts*

## Notes

The publication of *Bonjour Tristesse* in March 1954 caused ripples far beyond the French literary establishment. Françoise Quoirez had at eighteen years of age, under a pseudonym borrowed from a Proustian princess, published a slim first novel which was devastating in its frankness and lucidity. The book, which borrows its title from a poem by Paul Éluard, reads like a private diary. In this, Sagan's seventeen-year-old heroine Cécile shocked readers with her awareness of the adult world of relationships, power and sexual intrigue, minutely observed and recounted in a tone disturbingly close to moral neutrality. There was, too, this strange father-daughter relationship, almost conspiratorial and decidedly unhealthy. François Mauriac referred to "this charming monster" whose talent shone out from every page. The precocious author was already a best-selling celebrity.

No one could have anticipated the huge success of the book. Ray Ventura had promptly bought the film rights from Julliard for what later appeared a paltry sum, a twelfth of what the eventual director paid to secure them for Columbia, and so Sagan's enthusiasm for Preminger's venture was understandably qualified. Sagan reported how the director proposed that she should play her own heroine. "Are you kidding?" had been her response. Interest in the role was considerable, and *Elle* magazine ran a competition modestly foreshadowing the *Saint Joan* search, printing fifteen photos from the 1500 submitted. Audrey Hepburn had reportedly turned down the part on the grounds of its immorality. Nothing had been decided, but in the meantime a Shaw heroine had to be found. Either Otto or fate decreed the same solution to both problems. Some seven weeks into the *Saint Joan* shoot, on February 24, Preminger announced on *The Ed Sullivan Show* that Seberg would also play the part of Cécile, joining co-stars Kerr and Niven. Needless to say, he ensured that she was soon pictured with the fêted young author in the world's press.

Despite the hard time he had already given her, Seberg was grateful to Preminger for his confidence in entrusting to her this second role. "I love this book—the character is fantastic," she told the press. "Cécile is so much like all of us, today's young girls." There were problems, and the original screenplay by Sam Behrman was abandoned in favor of one by Arthur Laurents, who underscored the "moral" in a way Preminger thought would be acceptable. The villa belonging to Sagan's wealthy media friends Hélène and Pierre Lazareff, "La Fossette" at Le Lavendou, was found to be available for the Côte d'Azur location shoot. This seemed ideal, and a feature in Hélène Lazareff's *Elle* in August 1957 showed off the superb, magnificently situated residence which was to be the setting for Sagan's scandalous intrigues.

The shoot began in Paris, in black and white, on July 31, before production moved to the Riviera for the color sequences. Preminger again lived up to his reputation as an exacting taskmaster, and not simply with Seberg, although it was her career which was most in jeopardy. Journalist Geraldine Jones recognized the pressure she was under, but also witnessed the director's more patient side. Niven made light of the rumored clashes to *Hollywood Reporter* journalist Mike Connolly, explaining that "Otto's voice is like my mustache—it's part of him. But sometimes it grows too big and frightens the pigeons." David Niven and Deborah Kerr were well able to stand up for themselves but protested about his treatment of the young actress. "I formed a very deep respect for the quiet strength with which she had to put up with all the extravagant publicity that had been forced on her by her discovery, and the lashing she took from the critics," Kerr recalled. "This strength was also apparent in her coping with Otto, who as a friend and social companion is a charming and witty person, but who turns into a demon when directing."

Mylène Demongeot puts things more forcefully: "Otto Preminger was a nasty man. I didn't speak a word of English—only what I learned in school. The big scene when [my character is] in bed with David Niven was a one-shot scene—six minutes of speaking English. It was terrible. [Preminger] wasn't happy when he saw the rushes, and he re-shot the scene another time. So we did it two times. I worked as well as I could, but to do six minutes of English, which is not my language.... And he did that, I'm sure, on purpose because he was like that. He was terrible. I remember when Jean had the scene at the end of the movie ... [Preminger] decided on a very long travelling shot, and she had to look at herself in the mirror, and the tears were to come out like that. No movement in the face. Nothing. A face that was ice cold, tears coming out. He shot all day long. Twelve hours of shooting. He did it and did it and did it again until she could do it. When she cried, she moved her face, and he didn't want any movement. It was shot very well, but he was rude to her."

"I had Asiatic flu the day the scene was shot," Seberg recalled. "My temperature was somewhere near 102, and the light meter wasn't working right." When asked if the tears were real, she answered "Well, you think of your own isolation, your own hurts and fears. The tears keep coming, and I guess, in a way, they were real."

Preminger used basically the same device as has been employed with *Saint Joan*, framing the story as extended flashbacks, seen in painful hindsight, between scenes of a later period. This was the means by which elements of the book's retrospective running commentary could be incorporated without completely disrupting the on-screen narrative. An ingenious difference here is the use of monochrome to contrast the mood to which the title refers with the carefree hedonism which had gone before. "Glorious Technicolor" was certainly what was called for in the Côte d'Azur scenes. Perhaps the point about the grayness of the city seems a trifle unsubtle and contrived, like the moral lesson which is being simultaneously underscored for us, but in purely visual terms the film works well. The relaxed Riviera atmosphere is convincingly conjured up, with strong direction and assured camerawork from Georges Périnal and Denys Coop. Périnal, who had stepped in for *Saint Joan* at the last minute, seemed to understand instinctively not only what the director wanted, but also

In *Bonjour Tristesse* with David Oxley and David Niven (Columbia).

why, and Preminger was warm in his praise when interviewed by *Movie* in 1962. Imaginative mobile title credits were again supplied by Saul Bass, simple but expressive ideas such as a falling petal which becomes a teardrop. Preminger also had the advantage of the services of Georges Auric, one of the most gifted film score composers of his day, and his title song is rendered with just the right moody introspection by chanteuse Juliet Gréco.

Filming moved from France to Shepperton Studios at the start of October for its final ten day phase, and Preminger would return here in November for editing. On December 31 *Hollywood Reporter* announced that the film would premiere at New York's Capitol Theater in January, followed by screenings in Chicago, Los Angeles, Boston and Washington.

Prior to the film's release, Preminger joked about its award of the Production Code seal of approval. "Now I can walk unashamed again," he told a reporter from the *New York Herald Tribune*, with obvious allusion to the scandal provoked by *The Moon is Blue* and *The Man with the Golden Arm*. He recounted that a dress manufacturer had, all the same, declined a *Bonjour Tristesse* tie-in deal on the grounds that the film was immoral. A little controversy made good publicity, and he was again ready to defend the choice of his young star, regardless of the bad *Saint Joan* reviews:

"I think this girl has great talent, great poise. I watched her the other night on one of those tough television interview programs where they ask loaded questions. The way the girl stood up to it and answered them was admirable.... I think people here have a kind of inferiority complex about Marshalltown. Abroad, nobody asked me why I had not used a French actress for the part."

Although a less resounding critical flop and grossing higher takings than *Saint Joan*, *Bonjour Tristesse* too was considered a failure after its New York premiere on January 15,

1958. Preminger and Seberg were present to confront the journalists, but the representative from the French daily *Combat* ironically noted the untypical modesty of the occasion, as if the "great man" had foreseen the second total defeat awaiting him and his discovery. Now, in the face of American critical reactions, Preminger really began to question his faith in Seberg's "star" qualities. The quintessential "Englishness" of Niven and the Scottish-born Kerr left little of the story's Gallic flavor, despite the authentic setting. Sagan declared herself dismayed after the first viewing, and one French critic declared indignantly that this was "not Sagan at all" (*L'Express*). Some in France were not displeased, however. Preminger had admirers within the *Cahiers* group, and it was specifically Seberg who impressed Truffaut and Godard as refreshingly new and different.

Looking back, something he was usually reluctant to do, Preminger was to comment: "*Bonjour Tristesse* is a film I like. I rarely say this, but I really don't think the American critics did it justice. You know, it was a very big success in France, and in America the critics said it wasn't French enough, which is very funny." It seems nevertheless ironical that, just when he was ready to give up on Seberg, François Truffaut should be describing the picture as a "love poem" devoted to her, giving credence to the fanciful rumors that the two were now engaged. Truffaut brushed aside complaints that the film was not true to Sagan's book, preferring to see it as a remake of Preminger's 1953 film *Angel Face*. In any case, he seems to suggest, the true subject is Seberg herself, and this, her second film, is a kind of complement to *Saint Joan*. In his *Cahiers du cinéma* article, entitled *Sainte Cécile*, Jacques Rivette takes a similar view, praising the director's intelligent craftsmanship in taking what he needs from his source and recasting it with fresh authorial creativity and what Rivette saw as "the genius of the short cut." This is, of course, not Sagan's slender novel visually realized, but it could be seen as a very faithful Anglo-Saxon transposition, scrupulously plotting a parallel course as far as the difference in medium permits.

Seberg was learning to act on screen, although some critics refused to detect any progress. Would the same confident fluency of acting style called for in the roles of Raymond and Anne have been appropriate for the adolescent Cécile? Surely it would not, and that can hardly have been what Preminger wanted. The question must be whether Seberg is convincing as Preminger's Cécile rather than Sagan's, and the answer must be that she generally is, whatever view you take of his treatment of the story or indeed of the story itself. This is not a normal father-daughter relationship, for although there is no suggestion of incest, Cécile is at once daughter, confessor and co-conspirator to Raymond. She is approaching the transition to an adulthood which he will clearly never achieve. Anne is the intruding potential

In *Bonjour Tristesse*, 1958 (Columbia).

stepmother who threatens her power and their whole pattern of existence. The contrivance whereby Cécile disposes of the threat is not entirely convincing, but her motivation makes dramatic sense, and there is nothing in Seberg's performance which undermines this. Nor is she unconvincing at the end, as the child/woman who must somehow deal with the significance of the tragedy inwardly and alone because of her father's inadequacy. Seberg brings an odd but authentic mix of the graceful and the gauche to her role and seems to provide the perfect foil for both the carefree ingenuousness of Elsa and the cool intelligence of Anne. It is hard to imagine Sagan's Cécile plunging needles into her doll in a fit of petulance quite as Preminger's heroine does, yet here it seems right. Where in *Saint Joan* Seberg had seemed faltering in her search for her character, this time she seems on much firmer ground, bringing her own instinctive insights.

Preminger's copious output was uneven, like that of many directors, and reputations fluctuate as fashions change. Nevertheless, his standing, based on such films as *Laura*, *Anatomy of a Murder* and *Advise and Consent*, now looks very secure. *Bonjour Tristesse* must surely be counted among the best and most nuanced of his films, and many will recognize the touch of a master of cinematic craft in this stark tale of sun-drenched moral shipwreck.

## References

Cabrera Infante, G. *A twentieth century job*. London: Faber, 1991, pp. 238- 41.
Cameron, Ian. "Bonjour Tristesse." *Movie*, 2: September 1962, p. 22.
*Combat*, 17 January 1958, p. 3.
Demongeot, Mylène. *Tiroirs secrets*. Paris: Le Pré aux Clercs, 2001.
*Filmfacts*, 1:5, 5 March 1958, "Bonjour Tristesse," pp. 17–18.
*Les Films pour vous* 4:126, 11 May 1959, pp. 3–62.
Fougères, Roland. *Ciné revue* 38:36, 5 September 1958, pp. 22–3.
Fujiwara, Chris. *The World and its double*. New York: Faber and Faber, 2008, pp. 210–222.
Grob, Norbert, Rolf Aurich and Wolfgang Jacobsen. *Otto Preminger*. Berlin: Jovis, 1999, pp. 104–12, 276–8.
Hirsch, Foster. *Otto Preminger*. New York: Knopf, 2007, pp. 265–77.
*Hollywood Reporter*, 146:27, 12 September 1957, p. 2.
Jones, Geraldine R. "No price too high." *Hollywood Screen Parade* 12:2, March 1958, pp. 23, 68–72.
Lambert, Christian. "Estreno de 'Bonjour Tristesse' en las pantallas Parisienses." *Blanco y negro*, 68:2395.
Lamy, Jean-Claude. *Sagan*. Paris: Mercure de France, 1988, pp. 173–5.
*Motion Picture Daily*, 82:22, 1 August 1957, p. 2.
*Movie*, 4: November 1962. "Interview with Otto Preminger," p. 20.
Ott, Beverly. "Sprite with spunk." *Photoplay* 52:6 December 1957, pp. 32–5, 69–71.
Ross, Don. "Preminger Walks Unashamed with a Code-Approved Movie." *New York Herald Tribune*, 12 January 1958, s.4 p. 3.
Sagan, Françoise. *Bonjour tristesse*. Paris: Julliard, 1954, translated Irene Ash. New York: Dutton/London: Murray, 1955.
*Le Soir illustré* 1316, 12 September 1957, "La Cécile de *Bonjour Tristesse* aura désormais le visage de Jeanne d'Arc," pp. 22–3, 34.
Truffaut, François. *Les films de ma vie*. Paris: Flammarion, 1975 and 2007, pp. 163–7.
Whitecomb, Jon. *Bonjour Tristesse* on location. *Cosmopolitan*, March 1958.
Willoughby, Bob. *Hollywood, a Journey Through the Stars*. New York: Assouline, 2001, pp. 126–9.

## Reviews

*America*, vol. 98, 25 January 1958.
*Arts*, 661, 12 March 1958. François Truffaut, pp. 1, 7.
*L'Aurore*, 8–9 March 1958. Claude Garson, p. 4.
*Bianco e nero*, 20:1, January 1959. Morando Morandini, pp. 65–8.
*Cahiers du cinéma*, 82, April 1958. Jacques Rivette, pp. 52–4.

*Le Canard enchaîné*, 39:1951, 12 March 1958. Michel Duran, p. 5.
*Cinema nuovo*, no. 138, March–April 1959. Guido Fink, pp. 163–4.
*Combat*, 17 January 1958; 8 March 1958. R-M. Arlaud, p. 2.
*Commonweal*, 67:18, 31 January 1958. Philip T. Hartung, pp. 457–8.
*Cue*, 18 January 1958.
*The Daily Cinema*, 26 March 1958. F.J., p. 9.
*The Daily Mail*, 28 March 1958. Marshall Pugh, p. 10.
*The Daily Telegraph*, 29 March 1958. Campbell Dixon, p. 9.
*Éducation nationale*, 20 March 1958. André Bazin.
*L'Express*, 850, 6 March 1958. Denis Vincent, p. 22.
*Le Figaro*, 8 March 1958. Louis Chauvet, p. 18.
*Film Daily*, 16 January 1958, p. 6.
*Film-Dienst*, no. 38, 18 September 1958.
*Film-Echo*, no. 76, 20 September 1958. Bert Markus.
*Film Forum*, 7:3 March 1958. C. Boost, pp. 46–7.
*Le Film français*, 15:720, 14 March 1958. X, p. 25.
*Film-Kritik*, no. 300, 30 May 1959.
*Filmblätter*, no. 39, 26 September 1958. H.J. Helmers, p. 1175.
*Filmkritik*, June 1958. Dietrich Kuhlbrodt, p. 135.
*Films and Filming*, 4:7 April 1958. Peter J. Dyer, p. 23.
*Films in Review*, 9:2 February 1958. F.de St.É., pp. 87–8.
*Filmwoche*, 13:42, 18 October 1958, p. 8.
*France observateur*, 9:409, 13 March 1958. Louis Marcorelles, p. 17.
*France-soir*, 9 March 1958. Robert Chazal, p. 9.
*The Glasgow Herald*, 26 May 1958. Molly Plowright, p. 5.
*The Hollywood Reporter*, 15 January 1958. Jack Moffitt, pp. 3–4.
*Image et son*, no. 111 April 1958. F. Tranchant, p. 14.
*Index de la cinématographie française*, 1958B. Louis Gaumont, pp. 80–1.
*Intermezzo*, 13:3, 15 February 1958, p. 12, 13:18–19, 15 October 1958, p. 10.
*Kinematograph Weekly*, 2641, 27 March 1958, p. 16.
*Les Lettres françaises*, 713, 13 March 1958. Michel Capdenac, p. 5.
*Libération*, 11 March 1958. Simone Dubreuilh, p. 2.
*Library Journal*, vol. 83, 1 February 1958, p. 396.
*The Los Angeles Examiner*, 13 February 1958. Ruth Waterbury.
*The Los Angeles Times*, 13 February 1958. Philip K. Scheuer, pt. 4 p. 13.
*The Manchester Guardian*, 29 March 1958, p. 3.
*Le Monde*, 9 March 1958. Roger Dardenne, p. 10.
*Monthly Film Bulletin*, 25:292 May 1958. J.A.D.C., p. 55.
*Motion Picture Daily*, 15 January 1958. Richard Gertner, p. 4.
*The Nation*, vol. 186, 1 February 1958, p. 396.
*The New York Herald Tribune*, 16 January 1958. William K. Zinsser s.1: p. 13.
*The New York Times*, 16 January 1958. Bosley Crowther, p. 32.
*The New Yorker*, 33:49, 25 January 1958. John McCarten, p. 98.
*Newsweek*, 51:3, 20 January 1958, p. 89.
*Noir et blanc*, 14:680, 14 March 1958. Pierre Laroche, p. 182.
*Les Nouvelles littéraires*, 1593, 13 March 1958. G. Charensol, p. 10.
*Paris-presse*, 13 March 1958, Claude Brulé, p. 9.
*Picturegoer*, 29 March 1958, p. 27.
*Radio, cinéma, télévision*, 427, 23 March 1958. Claude-Marie Trémois, pp. 44–5.
*Revue des deux mondes*, 1 April 1958. Roger Régent.
*The Saturday Review*, 41:7, 15 February 1958. Arthur Knight, p. 30.
*Sight and Sound*, 27:4 Spring 1958. Peter John Dyer, p. 202.
*Süddeutsche Zeitung*, 16 October 1958. Franziska Violet, p. 11.
*Time*, 71:3, 20 January 1958, p. 86.
*The Times*, 31 March 1958, p. 3.
*Variety*, 15 January 1958. Gene., p. 6.
*Village Voice*, 3:14, 29 January 1958. Joseph K., pp. 8, 10.

# *The Mouse That Roared* (1959)

"It's nice to be playing a human being for a change."—Jean Seberg

An Open Road Films production; A Highroad Picture; A Columbia Pictures release
Original release: in English
Also known as: *La Souris qui rugissait* [France]; *Die Maus die brüllte* [Germany]; *Il Ruggito del topo* [Italy]; *Un Golpe de gracia* [Spain]
Running Time: 83 minutes
Format: in Eastmancolor

CAST: [* denotes above the title billing] Peter Sellers* (Tully Bascombe/Grand Duchess Gloriana XII/Prime Minister Count Mountjoy); Jean Seberg* (Helen); William Hartnell (Will); David Kossoff (Professor Kokintz); Leo McKern (Benter); MacDonald Parke (General Snippet); Austin Willis (U.S. Secretary of Defense); Timothy Bateson (Roger); Monty Landis (Cobbley); Harold Kasket (Pedro); Colin Gordon (BBC announcer); George Margo (O'Hara); Robin Gatehouse (Mulligan); Jacques Cey (ticket collector); Bill Nagy (U.S. policeman); Mavis Villiers (telephone operator); Charles Clay (British Ambassador); Harry de Bray (French Ambassador); Bill Edwards (army Captain); Guy Deghy (Soviet Ambassador); Robert O'Neill (reporter); Stuart Sanders (Cunard Captain); Ken Stanley (2nd officer); Alan Gifford

PRODUCTION CREDITS: *Director:* Jack Arnold; *Producer:* Walter Shenson; *Screenplay:* Roger MacDougall, Stanley Mann, from the novel *The Wrath of Grapes* by Leonard Wibberley; *Director of Photography:* John Wilcox; *Editor:* Raymond Poulton; *Sound:* Red Law, George Stephenson; *Music:* composed and conducted by Edwin Astley; *Art Director:* Geoffrey Drake; *Costume Design:* Anthony Mendleson; *Production Manager:* James Ware; *Titles:* Maurice Binder; *Hairdresser:* Joyce James; *Associate Producer:* Jon Penington; *Production Supervisor:* Leon Becker; *Camera Operator:* Austin Dempster; *Assistant Director:* Philip Shipway; *Continuity:* Pamela Davies; *Sound Editor:* Richard Marden; *Makeup:* Stuart Freeborn; *2nd Unit Cameraman:* John Wimbolt

## Synopsis

The tiny independent Duchy of Grand Fenwick is in economic crisis. The export market for its wine has collapsed, and Prime Minister Mountjoy can think of only one solution: by declaring war on the United States of America they can incur immediate defeat followed by reconstruction aid. Grand Duchess Gloriana gives her uneasy consent to the plan and Field Marshal Bascombe is dispatched with his bowmen by sea to New York. On arrival they come upon Q-bomb scientist Kokintz and his daughter Helen. Bascombe returns home with these hostages and the bomb, not realizing the international crisis he will thereby trigger. Disgraced, he is made Prime Minister to clear up the mess. Amid Cold War diplomatic moves, Mountjoy plots to seize and return the bomb, and a hectic chase ensues. It is Bascombe who eventually triumphs, however, when he obtains a favorable treaty with America and wins Helen's heart as well. What of the bomb? Fenwick can keep it as a guarantee of world peace. That the bomb is a dud after all can remain their little secret.

## Reviews

"[This] is the kind of irrepressible topical satire whose artistic flaws become increasingly apparent but whose merits outlast them. This is mainly because the script distributes its ironic, malicious, slightly gruesome humour with such vigour and naive impartiality that the film is certain, for at least part of the time, to be greatly enjoyed."—*Monthly Film Bulletin*

"A hilarious movie."—*Life*

"... funnier than the actors are the wisecracks and the situations."—*Commonweal*

"There are a few occasions when *The Mouse That Roared* gets over-smart and then some of its witty sallies, gimmicks and gags may go over the heads of the patrons. But on the whole it has kept its slight amusing idea bubbling happily in the realms of straight-forward comedy ... Jean Seberg is pretty, but makes little impact."—*Variety*

"But instead of mining the rich satire ... we are soon belabored with not too funny farce about a 'Q' bomb ... Sellers ... is especially good.... The rest of the cast is capable, with the exception of Jean Seberg, who still hasn't learned how to act."—*Films in Review*

"Original touches, charming backgrounds, and agreeable playing by Peter Sellers, Jean Seberg, William Hartnell."—*Daily Telegraph*

"*The Mouse That Roared* is our nominee for the funniest picture of the year!"—*New York World-Telegram*

"... social burlesque and sheer Mack Sennett farce ... Jean Seberg looks better than she's looked yet."—*New York Times*

## Notes

After Preminger sold the remaining five years of Seberg's contract to Columbia Pictures her first role was in this small-budgeted comedy. Leonard Wibberley's gentle Cold War satire had originally appeared in serialized form in *The Saturday Evening Post* under the title *The Day New York Was Invaded,* but neither this title nor the amusing twist on John Steinbeck's novel used for its reissue (*The Wrath of Grapes*) was found suitable for the film adaptation. Its idea was that little nations might save the world from the Great Powers as the world teetered on the brink of nuclear disaster: the mice could usurp the role of the lions. The imaginary alpine duchy of Grand Fenwick, a forgotten time capsule from the Fifteenth Century, is the mouse in question here who shows how it can be done.

Walter Shenson had bought the film rights for Wibberley's book, but he waited several years before turning to Carl Foreman's company High Road Productions for help. This, Foreman believed, could be the satire he was looking for, one which might even "beat the British at their own game." The "fresh talent" selected for the project was Jack Arnold, known for such SF products as *The Creature from the Black Lagoon* (1954) and the 1957 cult classic *The Incredible Shrinking Man.* Shenson's bosses at Columbia insisted on the casting of Seberg for this film because, despite the failures of her two previous films, she could provide a recognizable name. Among the largely British cast, no one, not even Peter Sellers at this stage, was really well known internationally. Arnold agreed to use Seberg in order to get the film made. "This film is without doubt just what I needed. A bit of success wouldn't go amiss," commented the actress, still smarting from her critics.

Arnold later remarked that the producers did not feel greatly involved in the project, and were actually planning to treat the film's expenses as a tax write-off. In the event it surprised everyone, rather like Mel Brooks' hit *The Producers* was to do in 1968, and *The Mouse* not only recouped its $450,000 production cost but earned more than a hundred times that amount, an estimated $50 million worldwide by the mid–1980s.

The production was based at Shepperton Studios, where *Saint Joan* and part of *Bonjour Tristesse* had been filmed, and lasted from late October until late December 1958. Suitable locations in London, Maidenhead and Southampton were found, with shots of New York edited in. In the novel the Fenwickians encounter the liner Queen Mary at sea and shower her with arrows. Quite by chance, the Queen Elizabeth appeared while they were filming this sequence at Southampton, a golden opportunity Arnold was quick to seize. Among the publicity shots, Columbia featured a studio party for Seberg's 20th birthday, with her husband, the director and Sellers dressed as Mountjoy in attendance.

The film has some highly original touches right from the start. The famous Columbia logo, featuring a woman holding a torch aloft like the Statue of Liberty, suddenly comes to life, hoists the hem of her dress and scurries off screen. The torch remains suspended behind, trailing an electric cable, while the cause of her panic is, of course, revealed to be just a mouse. This piece of fun, a joke Arnold played on the company and got away with, sets the teasing tone aptly, and in general it is well sustained.

The film's humor is decidedly of the tongue-in-cheek variety, much of it built on the scale and anachronistic character of the miniature nation with so much faded Ruritanian pomp. To underline the irony of its name, the paucity of its material and human resources is illustrated in comic detail: The mailed infantry change into civilian garb at the border and take the local bus to the tramp steamer chartered for their invasion of America. But the medieval broadsword is double-edged, and much play is made with the inability of the major powers to deal with an unforeseen challenge, locked as they are into the rigid Cold War mindset of nuclear standoff. Stereotypes abound, but there is just sufficient inventiveness throughout to avoid staleness. Perhaps as tellingly funny as anything here are the jokes built on cross-cultural incomprehension. When the glowering General Snippet is brought back as a prisoner he warns the benevolent Grand Duchess that he knows the Geneva Convention by heart. "How nice," she simpers. "You must recite it for me some evening. I play the harpsichord."

There is a scene in the film in which the bomb is tossed back and forth like a football among the world leaders who have descended upon Grand Fenwick. Suddenly a nuclear explosion, with a mushroom cloud, fills the screen—a shocking cut in what is essentially slapstick. A voice over then assures the audience that this is not "the end." "It was a way of making a social comment I felt was important," explained Arnold. "The most effective way to make a social comment is to do it by satire and comedy. Those who were sophisticated enough to get the meanings we were putting into the film got it.... If you're going to say something that ... has a message, I think you should do it satirically and do it in a way that audiences will get it even though they're not aware of it...."

Playing three different characters, Peter Sellers gives an impressive display of his protean talent in an evident bid to emulate the feat of Alec Guinness in *Kind Hearts and Coronets* from 1949. If *The Mouse That Roared* is in an inferior league of comedy to Hamer's film, Sellers matches Guinness in his ability to switch effortlessly from one well characterized persona to another. Unlike Guinness, Sellers attempts only three roles, but each is a leading character: Tully, the timid mother's boy who turns man of action, the finagling aristocrat Mountjoy and the delightfully dotty matriarch Gloriana. Already well known to and appreciated by British audiences through radio and film, Sellers had hitherto made little international impact. Columbia claimed that this was his first on-screen kiss, and trailed the Briton as a major discovery.

Clearly, this was very much Sellers' picture, but he is well supported by an able and experienced cast, including Kossoff, Willis and McKern, in the subsidiary roles. Wibberley's story had a teenage Gloriana paired with Tully for romantic interest, but the desire to provide Sellers with a comic transvestite role evidently took priority. For the film, the Duchess was matured and Professor Kokintz was given a daughter, thus meeting both these requirements and strengthening the American element Arnold wanted. A reporter asked the sensitive Sellers whether his love scene would be serious. "Quite serious," he

**In her first box office hit:** *The Mouse That Roared* with David Kossoff and Peter Sellers (Columbia).

replied, "Miss Seberg is charming, but I'm sure she would prefer the scene to be done by Gregory Peck. Though, of course, the Borgnines have done it, so why shouldn't I?"

Seberg told Elizabeth Hardie "I have played a French saint and a rather nasty little French girl: now I am playing an aggressive, healthy, extrovert American college girl—a comedy part that doesn't lend itself to much character development." Although she was right about the limitations of her role, essentially a foil to Sellers' Bascombe, she was able to show that she was improving technically and had an instinct for the special requirements of comedy. This first post–Preminger film also refurbished her wholesome, girl-next-door image, as when Helen protests against the theft of the Q-bomb: "Give it back! If you don't you'll live in terror the rest of your lives! It's the honest thing to do! It's the wise thing to do! It's ... it's the American thing to do!" When she is taken away, Sellers turns to a soldier and says "Now there goes a red-blooded American girl." Many moviegoers thought likewise. Apparently it took her some time to adjust to the easy-going directing style of Jack Arnold. She had not known that his was the antithesis of Preminger's method and had been prepared for similar procedures on this film.

*The Mouse That Roared* is a benign and unpretentious comedy in which the satire is arguably too generalized and comfortable (mushroom cloud excepted) to retain much of a bite. Despite this, Roger Lewis's description of it as "sentimentalising gibberish" seems excessively harsh, even if one has Kubrick's masterly *Dr. Strangelove*, which starred Sellers in 1964, in mind. Director Jack Arnold felt his film was "a little before its time" in 1959, and that it ought to have been made ten years later. Peter Sellers rated it as "quite a good picture," but remembered it without affection, feeling it had not been made as well as it could have been. Towards the end it descends into rather inept slapstick, reminiscent of the Keystone Kops on an off day, but repeated viewing reveals many nice details which could easily escape notice. The ditty which Gloriana sings at the keyboard is just such a moment, and there are many more.

Awareness that there was a serious message behind the gentle satire, not to mention sound promotional instincts, may have lain behind the haste made to complete the film for an early special screening in Geneva. Here the audience comprised diplomats and news reporters, for the occasion was the UN conference in late May 1959 at which the four major powers were to discuss the future of Berlin. The film officially premiered in London on July 16, 1959, and even if it failed to change the course of history, it was an immediate hit. An adaptation of Wibberley's sequel entitled *The Mouse on the Moon*, directed by Richard Lester, followed four years later from United Artists. Neither Sellers nor Seberg wished to be involved, and only David Kossoff from the original cast was featured. By this time the Grand Duchy and its famous vintage seemed to have lost their sparkle, the joke was wearing thin and the careers of its original stars had in any case moved on.

## References

*The Daily Cinema*, 8067, 15 October 1958. C.H. B-W., p. 11.
*Filmfacts*, 2:48, 30 December 1959. "The Mouse That Roared," pp. 291–2.
Fougères, Roland. "La Souris qui rugissait." *Ciné revue* 39:37, 11 September 1959, pp. 25–27.
Gris, Henry. "Seberg interview." *Moustique*, 34:1740, 31 May 1959, pp. 4–6.
Hardie, Elizabeth. "Jean Seberg tells her own story." *ABC Film Review*, 9:2 February 1959, pp. 4–5.
Ivers, James D. "Reverse Fillip Makes 'Mouse' Fiction Real." *Motion Picture Daily*, 86:80, 23 October 1959, pp. 1–2.
Letner, Kenneth J. "Films of Peter Sellers." *Film Quarterly*, 14:1 Fall 1960, pp. 51–4.
Lewis, Roger. *The life and death of Peter Sellers*. London: Century, 1994, pp. 536–45.
*Life*, 47:19, 9 November 1959. "When the US Lost a War," p. 91.
Mitchell, Robert. *Magill's Survey of Cinema*. English language films first series. Englewood Cliffs, NJ: Salem Press, 1980, vol. 3, pp. 1159–63.
Reemes, Dana M. *Directed by Jack Arnold*. Jefferson, NC: McFarland, 1988, pp. 122–35.
Starr, Michael. *Peter Sellers: a film history*. Jefferson, NC: McFarland, 1991, pp. 32–7.
Walker, Alexander. *Peter Sellers, the authorized biography*. London: Weidenfeld and Nicolson, 1981, pp. 93–4.
Wibberley, Leonard. *The Wrath of Grapes*. London: Hale, 1955.

## Reviews

*ABC* (Madrid), 7 August 1969. Antonio de Obregon, p. 58.
*America*, 102, 14 November 1959, p. 212.
*Amis du film et de la télévision*, 158/9 July/August 1969, p. 42.
*Le Canard enchaîné*, 41:2050, 3 February 1960. Michel Duran, p. 6.
*Commonweal*, 71:4, 23 October 1959. Philip T. Hartung, p. 106.
*The Daily Cinema*, 15 July 1959. F.J., p. 11.
*The Daily Mail*, 17 August 1966. Cecil Wilson, p. 6.
*The Daily Telegraph*, 18 July 1959. Campbell Dixon, p. 5.
*The Evening News*, 16 July 1959. Jympson Harman, p. 4.
*The Evening Standard*, 16 July 1959. Iain Crawford, p. 6.
*Le Figaro*, 26 January 1960. Louis Chauvet, p. 14.
*Film Daily*, 2 October 1959. Mandel Herbstman, p. 6.
*Le Film français*, 17:819, 5 February 1960. X., pp. 24, 26.
*Filmkritik*, March 1960. Dietrich Kuhlbrodt, p. 88.
*Films and Filming*, 5:11 August 1959. Peter G. Baker, p. 24.
*Films in Review*, 10:10 December 1959. Hartley Ramsay, p. 625.
*France-soir*, 22 January 1960. Robert Chazal, p. 9.
*The Hollywood Reporter*, 1 October 1959. Jack Moffitt, p. 3.
*Image et son* (*Saison cinématographique* 1960). François Chevassu, pp. 279–80.
*Index de la cinématographie française*, 1961. P.-A. Buisine, pp. 279–80.

*Intermezzo,* 14:21, 15 November 1959, p. 6.
*The Manchester Guardian,* 18 July 1959, p. 3.
*Le Monde,* 24–25 January 1960. Jean de Baroncelli, p. 15.
*Monthly Film Bulletin,* 26:307 August 1959. P.J.D., pp. 102–3.
*Motion Picture Herald,* 3 October 1959. Richard Gertner, pp. 436–7.
*The New York Herald Tribune,* 27 October 1959. Joe Pihodna, p. 23.
*The New York Times,* 27 October 1959. Bosley Crowther, p. 40.
*The New Yorker,* 35:38, 7 November 1959. John McCarten, p. 198.
*Newsweek,* 54:19, 9 November 1959, p. 120.
*Paris-presse,* 22 January 1960. Michel Aubriant, p. 13.
*Saturday Review,* 42:39, 26 September 1959. Arthur Knight, pp. 28, 36.
*Senior Scholastic,* 75, 28 October 1959, p. 29.
*Sight and Sound,* 28:3/4 Summer/Autumn 1959. Penelope Houston, pp. 162–3.
*Time,* 74:19, 9 November 1959, p. 84.
*The Times,* 20 July 1959, p. 8.
*Variety,* 5 August 1959. Rich., p. 6.

# *Breathless (À bout de souffle)* (1960)

"We knew when we saw the rushes that we were doing something very unusual, very new in its style."—Jean Seberg

An Impéria Filma/Productions Georges de Beauregard/Société nouvelle de cinématographie (SNC) production; A Films Around the World release
Original release: in French; released with English subtitles
Also known as: *Ausser Atem* [Germany]; *Fino all'ultimo respiro* [Italy]; *Al final de la escapade/Sin aliento* [Spain]
Running Time: 90 minutes
Format: in Black and White
[Opening caption: *Ce film est dédié à la Monogram Pictures*]

CAST: Jean Seberg (Patricia Franchini); Jean-Paul Belmondo (Michel Poiccard/Laszlo Kovacs); Daniel Boulanger (Inspector Vital); Jean-Pierre Melville (Parvulesco); Roger Hanin (Carl Zumbach/Zombart); Henri-Jacques Huet (Antonio Berruti); Claude Mansard (Claudius, the car dealer); Van Doude (himself); Liliane David ("Minouche"/Liliane); Michel Fabre (second detective); Jean-Luc Godard (informer); Richard Balducci (Luis Tolmatchoff); André S. Labarthe, Jacques Siclier, Jean-Louis Richard (journalists); François Moreuil (photographer); Virginie Ullman (Swedish photographic model); Michel Mourlet (studio photographer); Jean Domarchi (man mugged in toilet); Jean Herman (soldier who asks for light); Jacques Rivette (accident victim); with Jacques Serguine, Louigny, Guido Orlando, René Bernard, Philippe de Broca, Jean Douchet, Émile Villion, José Bénazéraf, Raymond Ravanbaz, Madame Paul, Jacques Lourcelles
PRODUCTION CREDITS: *Director:* Jean-Luc Godard; *Producer:* Georges de Beauregard; *Screenplay:* Jean-Luc Godard, based on an outline by François Truffaut; *Photography:* Raoul Coutard, Raymond Cauchetier; *Camera Operator:* Claude Beausoleil; *Makeup:* Phuong Maittret; *Script Girl:* Suzanne Faye; *Production:* Gaston Dona; *Assistant Director:* Pierre Rissient; *Sound:* Jacques-Maumont; *Editor:* Cécile Decugis; *Assistant Editor:* Lila Herman; *Technical Advisor:* Claude Chabrol; *Music:* Martial Solal; extracts from the Clarinet Concerto in A K.622 by Mozart and Waltz no. 4 in F op. 34 no. 3 by Chopin.

## Synopsis

Opportunist thief Michel steals a car in Marseille and heads north. His plan is to persuade Patricia, an American working in Paris, to go to Italy with him, but he shoots a pursuing policeman and is quickly a hunted fugitive. Finding Patricia proves easier than retrieving money owed to him by associate Berruti. Patricia vacillates, hesitating between this renewed affair and her own ambitions, unaware that the police are tracking her lover. Soon the two are linked and Patricia is warned by Inspector Vital to cooperate in the manhunt.

The couple eludes the detectives while Michel tries in vain to collect the cash needed for their getaway. Finally everything is arranged and they hide overnight in a borrowed apartment. The following morning Patricia resolves her dilemma by informing the police of Michel's whereabouts and confessing the tip-off to him. Disgusted by this betrayal, Michel refuses his last chance of escape. Berruti arrives with the money only moments before the police appear. They see Michel and open fire in the street, fatally wounding their quarry.

Patricia and the two policemen look down at the dying man as he makes pantomime faces at her: "C'est vraiment dégueulasse!" Patricia turns to Vital in puzzlement—"What did he say?" Vital maliciously alters Michel's last words: "Il a dit: vous êtes vraiment une dégueulasse!" "What is *dégueulasse*?" she asks, turning a blank gaze into the camera and instinctively mimicking Michel's Bogart mannerism, her thumb tracing the outline of her lip.

## Reviews

"It is far and away the most brilliant, most intelligent and most exciting movie I have encountered this season. ... it will be imitated endlessly and probably ineptly, by dozens of film-makers...."—*New Yorker*

"The deftness of Godard is visible in his having chosen the most classic and the most commercial of themes: a criminal in flight. Good strategy.... We joyfully salute the birth of the first cinéaste of the young school who brings us [a work] unlike anything made before him."—*Le Figaro littéraire*

"[Godard's] story has little more than twenty or thirty minutes of vitality in it."—*New York Herald Tribune*

"It is emphatically, unrestrainedly vicious, completely devoid of moral tone ... a chunk of raw drama, graphically and artfully torn with appropriately ragged edges out of the tough underbelly of modern metropolitan life."—*New York Times*

"My BW reprimands me for saying Jean's prettier than (Brigitte) Bardot or a better actress or that I'd rather watch Seberg. 'They're not the least bit alike,' she pouts. That's true. The greatest difference: Jean seems to have a brain and growth-potential."—*Des Moines Register*

"As Jean Seberg plays her—and that's exquisitely—Patricia is the most terrifyingly *simple* muse-goddess-bitch of modern movies."—Pauline Kael

"Miss Seberg lacks emotive projection but it helps in her role of a dreamy little Yank abroad playing at life. Her boyish prettiness is a real help."—*Variety*

"... let us not close without noting how much the pretty, touching and this time quite astonishing Jean Seberg contributes...."—*Le Figaro*

"Jean Seberg, who up to now had seemed to me devoid of interest, succeeds in being at the same time the most exquisite and most treacherous image of femininity."—*Libération*

## Notes

On November 24, 1952, at Pontoise, northwest of Paris, a young police motorcyclist called André Grimber was shot dead after chasing with a colleague what proved to be a stolen car. A major police operation was launched, and within days the fugitive gunman was identified from fingerprints as Michel Portail, a Frenchman who had just returned from the USA after serving a four-year prison sentence for extortion. Dramatic headlines appeared in the press as the story unfolded: "Hunted killer at large in Paris" and "An army of policemen search Paris," etc. According to a girlfriend, Portail liked to act the tough guy, but others found him charming. He had claimed to be working with an American woman journalist, and actually interviewed several well-known French film actresses. One man claimed to have been robbed by him. He eluded pursuit by changing hotels, leaving without paying, and would sometimes lie low in cinemas to avoid attention. When arrested in early December he had been stealing from cars and sleeping on a yacht on the Seine, close to the Champs-Élysées. More intense publicity followed his four-day trial at Versailles two years later. The whole tawdry, sad but sensational affair bore a strange resemblance to a story by Georges Simenon.

Portail's story caught the attention of François Truffaut and Claude Chabrol, who both saw the potential for a film here but had different ideas about how the narrative should be developed. Truffaut sketched out a fictionalized treatment in 1956, but eventually passed this on to his friend Jean-Luc Godard in view of his own commitments. The hand of fate might seem to have been at work in the metamorphosis of this plot into a milestone of cinema, a process amply documented by Godard scholars Michel Marie, Alain Bergala, Antoine de Baecque, Dudley Andrew and Colin MacCabe. The success of such films as *Les Quatre cent coups* and *Les Cousins* demonstrated that the radical approach of the young filmmakers from the *Cahiers du cinéma* circle, using low budget techniques, could be sound business. Distributor René Pignères was ready to finance a *nouvelle vague* film, and producer Georges de Beauregard was prepared to take a chance on the still unknown Godard, but recognized names were needed to reassure backers. The *Cahiers* "mafia" had the solution. Ostensibly, Truffaut would be the screenwriter and Chabrol the technical and artistic adviser for the project, on condition that Godard should direct. In fact these roles were completely fictitious, as Chabrol told Claude Ventura in 1993 with great amusement. If *À bout de souffle* was a ship which left harbor under false colors, this was simply consistent with the cheeky tone of the whole enterprise.

A star name was needed too, and this was where Jean Seberg fitted like a glove. Both Truffaut and Godard had been impressed with Seberg's Cécile in *Bonjour Tristesse*, despite the film's poor reception in the U.S. Godard conceived his film almost as a sequel to Preminger's, with Sagan's character recreated in a new setting. "I could have taken the final shot of the film and faded to a caption 'Three years later,'" he explained. His fascination with this actress had made him wish to direct her on camera, simply doing "many little things that pleased me," an impulse he would later ascribe to his former "movie fan" phase. Indeed, he would later define his film as a documentary about its principal actors. Seberg had the fame generated by Preminger's huge publicity drive, but she was a tarnished star associated with two flops, and might now be afforded even within Beauregard's tiny budget. It was her husband François Moreuil, familiar with the *Cahiers* set, who both persuaded Seberg that this was an offer to accept and negotiated her release by Columbia Pictures for a modest $15,000 (even so, a sixth of the budget for the entire film). Moreuil describes how this came about:

> We were married and lived in Neuilly, a suburb of Paris. Jean-Luc Godard got interested in Jean for a movie which was to be called *À bout de souffle*. Columbia did not want her to do the film, and she did not want to do the film. A producer friend of mine said

**With *Breathless* (*À bout de souffle*) director Jean-Luc Godard during production (courtesy Manoah Bowman, Independent Visions).**

"Since you speak English and you know the story, go to Columbia and try to get permission for her to do that movie." I wrote some of the dialogue with Godard, because there was no script.

Casting the male lead had been more simply resolved. After making the short *Charlotte et son Jules* in 1958 it was Godard's ambition to make a full-length feature using the same young actor, Jean-Paul Belmondo. In fact we already see the personality of Michel Poiccard emerging in this humorous sketch in which the lovelorn hero harangues his girlfriend without ever waiting for a response. The character of Michel Poiccard, though founded on Portail, was perhaps derived in part from Belmondo's own breezy confidence, in part from Godard's acquaintances such as Paul Gégauff. Other friends were persuaded to take some of the minor roles, notably Jean-Pierre Melville as the opinionated novelist Parvulesco and Daniel Boulanger as detective Vital. The director himself would make a Hitchcock-style appearance as a police informer.

Beauregard had enough confidence in his director to allow him considerable latitude, but he did insist on the cameraman who had worked on his recent projects, Raoul Coutard, in preference to Godard's own choice Michel Latouche. Godard chose Pierre Rissient as his assistant director, but was happy to work with several of the producer's existing team. One of these was the Vietnamese makeup artist Phuong Maittret, who was to form a close friendship with Seberg and work with her on many future films.

Seberg's contract was signed on June 12, 1959, and she arrived in Paris on July 16, one month ahead of the scheduled shoot. Godard had told her on the 5th that his scenario was complete, but this was misleading, for no screenplay yet existed. She was unprepared for what awaited her, for nothing could have been in starker contrast to Preminger's lavish Hollywood-style operations than this cheese-paring and apparently amateurish venture. François Moreuil remembers his wife's reaction:

> She was infuriated. The first day of shooting on the Champs-Élysées ... the camera was hidden in a small carriage, covered delivery carriage—at the time they had them like that.... The team gathered in a café, and Jean told me, "I am not going to work on that movie, they are not professionals, there's no script, there's nothing. I don't know what to do." So—I tried to be the go-between with Godard and her. I told Jean she should try, and she did, and it worked out.

On the first day of the shoot, August 17, Godard stopped work after two hours, explaining that he had run out of ideas. This kind of erratic approach by the director would so intensify the anxieties of a producer on the verge of personal bankruptcy that the two men reportedly came to blows. On the 3rd of September Beauregard wrote in bitter terms to Godard about the time wasted as a breach of trust, insisting on greater discipline. The worries of Seberg and the producer were understandable, arising as they did from a highly unorthodox and seemingly improvised style of filmmaking. Godard was in fact well prepared for *Breathless*, but the material was largely in his head or a personal notebook which he refused to show others. Comparison of the finished product with the detailed outline attributed to Truffaut in *L'Avant-scène* (Andrew pp. 153–60) may show how closely the director had decided to follow his friend's narrative, but Marie (p. 60) believes this version was written by Godard himself. It is true that he did not decide about the fate of Michel until a late stage, but his planning allowed scope for what he termed "last minute focusing."

While Seberg and Belmondo awaited instructions at a corner café, Godard would revise the dialogue prepared the night before for the day's filming. Since the sound was to be added later, the director would read out their lines to them, they would sometimes agree changes, and then the shoot would proceed. The tiny room in the Hôtel de Suède, setting for the film's long central section, barely allowed space for the two actors, the director and Coutard plus his assistant, leaving script supervisor Suzanne Faye and an electrician on the landing outside. Belmondo and Seberg "spent eight days in bed," as she told the journalist of *Cinémonde*, adding that "nothing is more tiring than that kind of work." This was certainly a far cry from Preminger, yet the spontaneity Godard encouraged in his actors was something both visibly responded to. Seberg did rebel, however, when Patricia was required to pick the pocket of the lover she had betrayed, and the director gave way.

One of Godard's early talents was his ability to turn constraints into strengths through sheer ingenuity, and in this respect he had found the ideal partner in Coutard. The former war zone cameraman was fast working and resourceful, anything but the old pro set in his ways. Apart from the mail cart referred to by Moreuil, from which he could operate his camera unseen in the street, a wheelchair was hired for the director to push him in for tracking shots. This proved far more maneuverable than a conventional dolly. The hand-held Caméflex brought great savings in time, and if its noise made simultaneous recording impracticable, there were advantages in that too. The absence of supplementary lighting could be compensated for where necessary by using highly sensitive film such as Agfa Record, Gevaert 36, or even manually adapted Ilford HPS, together with special processing techniques. For the young director, conscious that he was still leaning his craft but with the ambition to remake cinema, the only rule was that "anything goes." Rumors circulated about this eccentric and amateurish production, for which many predicted disaster. Belmondo's agent expressed the hope that this film might never be released, fearing it could end the actor's career. Nevertheless, thanks to Pierre Rissient's well prepared schedule, with locations indicated by the director in advance, the shoot proceeded with discipline which confounded doubters.

Even when the shoot was completed on September 19 the final form of *Breathless,* let alone its marketability, was highly uncertain. As Godard wrote to Pierre Braunberger, the crew, Coutard included, had been far from impressed by the rushes. The technical capacity of the film had been stretched to its limits, he noted with pride. Dubbing and mixing would be an arduous process. Before final editing, the film ran for at least two and a quarter hours, which meant that some forty five minutes would have to be cut to bring it within the contracted length. Seizing the initiative from editor Cécile Decugis, Godard set to work ruthlessly, ignoring conventional rules of continuity and systematically compressing his material with what came to be known as "jump cuts." Thus a key feature of *Breathless,* its audacious and provocative "trademark," was the product of duress rather than planning. The effect of this heretical technique was electrifying, giving the interplay of image and dialogue a snappy vitality which felt altogether new.

## *The Success and Legacy of* Breathless

The strong promotional campaign which led up to the premiere in Paris on March 16, 1960 paid dividends, boosted as it was by the award of the coveted Prix Jean Vigo and the Silver Bear at Berlin. Coutard won separate recognition from the German critics for his camerawork. Godard could well afford to shrug off the fact that his film, having already been released, was not selected as the French entry at Cannes. The four cinemas which initially screened it sold over 50,000 tickets in the first week alone, despite its restriction to over 18s, and ran it for a further six weeks. One factor in the film's instant success was that it was in tune with the moment and resonated especially with young people, as Jean-Pierre Esquenazi has shown. While Michel's colorful slang was frowned upon, many must have been amused to recognize the real language of the street (not least his insult to those who don't share his love of nature, addressed insolently to the camera) which is as integral to his persona as his lack of moral scruples. Seberg's androgynous coiffure featured on three different posters, two of them designed by C. Hurel, which captured a new look that would be emulated by a generation of young women. Here was a lesson in style to match that of Godard in technique, for it demonstrated the impact of a liberating simplicity which would not date and was accessible to all. The two stars, so unlike movie stereotypes, seemed in different ways to represent young people as they actually looked and behaved, and connected with audiences with an immediacy which both challenged and thrilled. The fine still photography of Raymond Cauchetier would crystallize key images of Seberg and Belmondo and give them an iconic status to rival any in cinema.

Much has been written attempting to explain why this has come to be regarded as a landmark in the development of cinema. One thing which seems clear is that it would be pointless trying to account for its unique character and tone without considering the interaction of key elements such as camerawork, music and editing. It had been Jean-Pierre Melville who had first enticed young jazz pianist Martial Solal into film score composition and brought him to Godard's attention. Now, in retrospect, it would be hard to isolate images of *Breathless* from their musical heartbeat. Solal can evoke the dangerous world of American noir which is seminal for the director, but connects instinctively with the peculiarly modern ambivalence of Godard's Gallic variation on the genre. The contrast of the two main themes associated with Michel and Patricia seems to echo the unbridgeable gulf between the two, omnipresent in the dialogue, but there is also an exciting tension between the fast pace of Godard's elliptical montage and Solal's often leisurely freewheeling score. Evidence of Godard's musical taste is as evident in his work as his literary or visual arts sympathies. In *Breathless* the tempo is constantly changing, but the essentially "real time" interlude between Patricia and Michel at the hotel may strike us rather like the slow movement of a classical structure. Dudley Andrew points out the opposition of jump cuts or quick cuts to elegant extended takes. There is an instinctive feel for what works in terms of pace, as in a musical composition. Recurrent motifs and symmetries are also striking.

No enumeration of American or European influences really helps to account for the phenomenon of *Breathless*, for these and other influences were so thoroughly assimilated that, as critic Claude Mauriac noted, his film in no respect resembled anything which had gone before. Even when most consciously emulating others, he remained more original than he knew. In hindsight, he told his *Cahiers* interviewer, "I see where it belongs—along with *Alice in Wonderland*. I thought it was *Scarface*."

In what sense does *Breathless* belong to the French noir tradition? The director's own statements make it clear that American gangster films were his conscious model, and the film's dedication to Monogram Pictures is also significant. Nevertheless, his first full-length feature feels much closer in spirit to the French thriller, whether to Carné's classics starring Gabin or to Melville's *Bob le flambeur*. Unlike these, though, there is a new kind of self-awareness, as if the characters feel themselves uneasily poised between reality and cinematic fiction. This manifests itself in a very deliberate breaking of the "fourth wall." The first words uttered by Michel ("After all … I'm an idiot") tell us he knows just how phony his Bogart act is. What is most authentically noir here is the sense of a hero trapped, forgoing his one escape route through a hopeless emotional attachment. Patricia, while enacting the treachery of the noir villainess, seems to be lost in existential confusion rather than ruthlessly calculating. In classic noir terms, Godard might appear to have lost the plot, allowing tension to dissipate by becoming too absorbed in the dynamics of his lovers' relationship and allowing the camera a lyrical celebration of the daylight city landscape.

In fact the range of Godard's interests could not allow him to confine himself to any established genre. For all the rich intertextuality and plethora of cultural references, all minutely analyzed in many published studies, here were both a summing up of and a rupture with the past. We can find evidence of nostalgia and the classical techniques he knew so well, but stylistically he was heading elsewhere. The private jokes and coded messages are signs of the irreverent Young Turk set on making a personal mark on a medium for which his feelings seem ambivalent (Adrian Martin's comments on the scene from *Westbound* furnish a nice example of this*). Godard's mind seems to have been a ferment of ideas on remaking the cinema, smashing outmoded convention at the same time as saluting worthy predecessors. As Truffaut recalled, there was a preoccupation with the theme of death, yet a fascination with gender psychology—where the barriers seem so much greater than merely cultural or linguistic ones—is surely no less evident. There is so much going on here that it is impossible to identify one single unifying thread, and it is this which makes the film an inexhaustible object of study and debate. If *Breathless* was identified as a manifesto film for the new wave, it was not because the *Cahiers* critic who had finally got his hands on his own train set had come up with a perfected new formula. This was not a demonstration of how films should or should not be made. Rather, like *Citizen Kane*, this was a brilliant exercise in proving the irrelevance of such rules in the face of sheer creative energy. To Godard it seemed that it was Bresson's Dostoyevsky-inspired *Pickpocket* or Resnais' *Hiroshima mon amour* rather than his own film which pointed the way forward to a new cinema

The accolades given to his first full-length feature took Godard by surprise. Its success would ensure him the opportunity to make more films, but each of these would demonstrate a restless desire to explore new areas. In 1963 he would again take up the character of Seberg's Patricia for the short *Le Grand Escroc*. While Godard's 1975 "remake" of *Breathless*, *Numéro deux*, financed by Georges de Beauregard in 1975, may have had no obvious connection with the original beyond its budget, Jim McBride's 1983 remake was a different matter. McBride transposed the action to Los Angeles, with an American hero and a French heroine, thus, whether intentionally or not, highlighting the chasm between the two cultures which Godard had seemingly wanted to draw together.

For Seberg, the legacy of *Breathless* was not only a career re-launch but also a kind of instant immortality as part of the Parisian landscape. There was, however, a downside. Identified by Godard with this quintessential ingénue transplanted from Middle America to this most worldly-wise of capitals, speaking faltering French with an engaging nasal accent, she had of course captured a very limited market. It is perhaps surprising that three more directors would ask her to reprise this role, with minor variations, before she was finally able to leave it behind her. Producer Georges de Beauregard would provide her with two further roles. The first of these would be the first of the two films she made with Claude Chabrol, *La Ligne de démarcation*. Her work on the second, *La Légion saute sur Kolwezi*, would remain uncompleted at her death. Whatever the stresses of Godard's collaboration with his producer on *Breathless*, he was to pay a generous and heartfelt tribute to the latter on his death in 1984.

## References

The literature on this film is huge. Particularly convenient for its study are the materials included with Michel Marie's masterly analysis, first published in 1999 and reissued in 2006, and in Dudley Andrew's translation of the continuity script. The release of Claude Ventura's documentary *Chambre 12, Hôtel de Suède* with interviews and other related material with the 2007 Criterion DVD transfer is especially welcome.

### Outlined and Transcribed Dialogue

Andrew, Dudley, ed. *Breathless*. New Brunswick: Rutgers University Press, 1987 [English translation with introduction and critical apparatus].

*L'Avant-scène du cinéma* 79, March 1968 [dialogue, "Truffaut" outline, reviews].

*Chez nous roman-film complet* 295, 15 January 1970, photo novel pp. 3–57.

Francolin, Claude. *À bout de souffle: roman, d'après le film de Jean-Luc Godard*. Paris: Seghers, 1960 [novelization].

*La Lettre du cinéma* 3, Autumn 1977. "Qu'est-ce qu'un scénario?" [Truffaut's outline], pp. 64–6.

Vaugeois, Gérard, ed. *À bout de souffle*. Balland, 1974 [complete dialogue with stills].

*Votre film* 1:2, 19 October 1962, photo novel pp. 3–56.

### General

Archer, Eugene. "Nonconformist on the crest of a 'New Wave.'" *The New York Times*, 5 February 1961 s.2 p. 7.

Baecque, Antoine de. *Godard: biographie*. Paris: Grasset, 2010, pp. 111–48.

\_\_\_\_\_, and Serge Toubiana. *Truffaut*. New York: Knopf, 1999.

Baurez, Thomas. "À bout de souffle; Raymond Cauchetier, le photographe de plateau se souvient...," *Studio* 215 September 2005, pp. 92–8.

Beauregard, Chantal de. *Georges de Beauregard*. Nîmes: Lacour, 1991, pp. 88–99.

Bechtold, Charles. *Cinématographie* 13 May/June 1975, pp. 40–2.

Bergala, Alain. "Godard au travail les années 60." Paris: Cahiers du cinéma, 2006.

Brody, Richard. *Everything is cinema: the working life of Jean-Luc Godard*. London: Faber and Faber, 2008.

Cauchetier, Raymond, and Marc Vernet. *Photos de cinéma: autour de la Nouvelle Vague 1958–1968*. Paris: Image France Editions, 2007.

Coutard, Raoul. "La forme du jour." *Le Nouvel observateur*, 45, 22 September 1965, pp. 36–7.

\_\_\_\_\_. *L'Impérial de Van Su*. Paris: Ramsay, 2007, pp. 63–71.

Durant, Philippe. *Belmondo*. Paris: Laffont, 1998, pp. 148–60.

Esquenazi, Jean-Pierre. *Godard et la société française des années 1960*. Paris: Armand Colin, 2004, "Le 'miracle' d'*À bout de souffle*," pp. 65–91.

*Le Film français*, 17:825, 18 March 1960. "Brillante réception à l'Élysées-Club pour la sortie de 'À Bout de souffle,'" p. 8.

*Filmfacts*, 4:7, 17 March 1961. "Breathless," pp. 35–7.

Godard, Jean-Luc. "Je ne suis pas à bout de souffle." *Arts*, 767, 23 March 1960, pp. 1– 4.

\_\_\_\_\_. "Mon film est un documentaire sur Jean Seberg et J.-P. Belmondo" [interview with Yvonne Baby] *Le Monde*, 18 March 1960, p. 12.

\_\_\_\_\_. Paroles... *Téléciné*, 202 September/October 1975, pp. 11–13.

\_\_\_\_\_, ed., and Alain Bergala. *Jean-Luc Godard par Jean-Luc Godard*. Vol. 1: 1958–84. Paris: Cahiers du cinéma, 1998.

Grenier, Alexandre. *Jean-Paul Belmondo*. Paris: Veyrier, 1985, pp. 64–8, 245.

Kael, Pauline. *I lost it at the movies*. London: Cape, 1966, pp. 127–32.

Lesage, Julia. *Jean-Luc Godard: a guide to references and resources*. Boston: G.K. Hall, 1979.

Lopate, Phillip. "'Breathless' turns 40, its youthful impudence intact." *New York Times*, 16 January 2000, s.2a p. 4.

MacCabe, Colin. *Godard: portrait of the artist at 70*. London: Bloomsbury, 2003.

Manceaux, Michèle. *L'Express* 445, 23 December 1959 [interview with Godard], p. 34.

Marie, Michel. *À bout de souffle, Jean-Luc Godard*. Paris: Nathan, 1999 [revised in *Comprendre Godard*. Paris: Armand Colin, 2006].

Marie, Michel. "It really makes you sick!" *The French Film: Texts and contexts*, ed. Susan Hayward and Ginette Vincendeau. London: Routledge, 1990, pp. 201–15.

Morrey, Douglas. *Jean-Luc Godard*. Manchester: Manchester University Press, 2005, pp. 8–15.

Moullet, Luc. "Jean-Luc Godard." *Cahiers du cinéma* 106 April 1960, pp. 25–36.

Narboni, Jean, and Tom Milne, eds. *Godard on Godard: Critical writings by Jean-Luc Godard*. New York: Da Capo, 1986.

Nemer, François. *Godard le cinéma*. Paris: Gallimard, 2006.

Pierret, Marc. "Carnet de bord d'un apprenti cinéaste." *France observateur* 10:459, 29 October 1959, pp. 14–5.

Riou, Alain. "Coup de poker les tournages de légende." *Le Nouvel observateur* 1814, 12–18 August 1999 *Téléobs* pp. 2–5.

Salachas, Gilbert. *Téléciné* 14:89 May/June 1960.

Seberg, Jean. *Films and Filming* 20:9 June 1974, pp. 15–6.

Smith, Steve. "Godard and *film noir*: a reading of *A Bout de Souffle*." *Nottingham French Studies* 32:1, Spring 1993, pp. 65–73.

Sterritt, David. *The films of Jean-Luc Godard: seeing the invisible*. Cambridge: Cambridge University Press, 1999, pp. 39–60, 267–8.

Temple, Michael, James S. Williams and Michael Witt. *For ever Godard*. London: Black Dog, 2004, A. Martin* pp. 255–62.

Trémois, Claude-Marie. "François Truffaut, scénariste du premier film de Jean-Luc Godard 'À bout de souffle' donne son avis." *Radio, cinéma, télévision*, 507, 4 October 1959, pp. 2–3, 54.

Ventura, Claude, and Xavier Villetard. *Chambre 12, Hôtel de Suède*. Studio Canal, 1993 [documentary film, reissued with the 2007 Criterion DVD of *Breathless*].

Warren, Jean-Paul and Raymond Lefèvre. *Image et son* 176/7 Sept./Oct. 1964, pp. 3–8.

## *Reviews*

*Amis du film et de la télévision*, 152 January 1969, p. 45.

*L'Aurore*, 17 March 1960. Claude Garson, p. 4.

*Le Canard enchaîné*, 23 March 1960. Michel Duran, p. 5.

*Chaplin*, 3:17 February 1961. Leif Krantz, pp. 33–5.

*Cinéma*, 46, May 1960. Marcel Martin, pp. 117–9.

*Cinema nuovo*, 10:149 Jan./Feb. 1961. L.P., pp. 60–1.

*Combat*, 19 March 1960. Pierre Marcabru, p. 3.

*Commentary*, 30 September 1960, pp. 230–2.

*Commonweal*, 73:21, 17 February 1961, p. 533.

*The Daily Cinema*, 26 June 1961. M.H., p. 7.

*The Daily Mail*, 6 July 1961. Barry Norman, p. 10.

*The Daily Telegraph*, 8 July 1961. Patrick Gibbs, p. 11.

*Des Moines Register*, 22 August 1961. Harlan Miller, p. 20.

*Esquire*, 56 July 1961, p. 20.

*The Evening News*, 6 July 1961. Ivon Adams, p. 4.

*The Evening Standard*, 6 July 1961. Alexander Walker, p. 10.

*L'Express*, 457, 17 March 1960. René Guyonnet, pp. 37–8.

*Le Figaro*, 18 March 1960. Louis Chauvet, p. 18.

*Le Figaro littéraire*, 15:726, 19 March 1960. Claude Mauriac, p. 16.

*Film*, 29 Summer 1961. Ian Cameron, p. 10.

*Film Daily*, 17 February 1961. M.H., p. 8.

*Film Quarterly*, 14:3 Spring 1961. Arlene Croce, pp. 54–6.

*Le Film français*, 25 March 1960. S, p. 21.

*Filmcritica*, 11:101 September 1960, pp. 660–1.

*Filmkritik*, June 1960. Enno Patalas, pp. 171–5.

*Films in Review*, 11:6 June/July 1960. Peter Lennon, pp. 367–8.

*Films in Review*, 12:3 March 1961. Henry Hart, pp. 175–7.

*France observateur*, 11:516, 24 March 1960. Claude Choublier, p. 22.

*France-soir*, 17 March 1960. France Roche, p. 11.

*The Glasgow Herald*, 7 August 1961. Molly Plowright, p. 5.

*The Guardian*, 8 July 1961. Isabel Quigly, p. 5.

*L'Humanité*, 19 March 1960. Samuel Lachize, p. 2.

*Index de la cinématographie française*, 1961. Gilberte Turquan, p. 76.

*Intermezzo*, 15:18–19, 15 October 1960, p. 10.

*Kinematograph Weekly*, 2803, 22 June 1961, p. 30.

*Les Lettres françaises*, 817, 24 March 1960. François Nourissier, pp. 1, 5; 818, 31 March 1960. Georges
     Sadoul, p. 7.

*Libération*, 23 March 1960. Simone Dubreuilh, p. 2.

*Le Monde*, 18 March 1960. Jean de Baroncelli, p. 12.

*Monthly Film Bulletin*, 28:330 July 1961. P.J.D., p. 90.

*The Nation*, 192, 11 March 1961, p. 223.

*The New Republic*, 144:7, 13 February 1961. Stanley Kauffmann, pp. 20–1.

*The New York Herald Tribune*, 8 February 1961. Paul V. Beckley, p. 12.

*The New York Times*, 8 February 1961. Bosley Crowther, p. 26.

*The New Yorker*, 11 February 1961. Roger Angell, p. 16.

*Newsweek*, 57:6, 6 February 1961, p. 84.

*Les Nouvelles littéraires*, 1699, 24 March 1960. G. Charensol, p. 10.

*Il Nuovo spettatore cinematografico*, 2:6 October 1960, pp. 53–7.

*Paris-presse*, 17 March 1960. Michel Aubriant, p. 14.

*Positif*, 33, April 1960. Louis Seguin, p. 49.

*Radio, cinéma, télévision*, 533, 3 April 1960. Gilbert Salachas, pp. 47–8.

*Revista internacional del cine*, 3:36–37 December 1960, p. 82.

*Saison cinématographique*, 1960. Jacques Chevallier, pp. 6–7.

*Saturday Review*, 11 March 1961. Hollis Alpert, p. 39.

*Schermi*, 3:27, November 1960. Morando Morandini, pp. 298–9.

*Sight and Sound*, 29:2 Spring 1960. Louis Marcorelles, pp. 84–5.

*Le Soir*, 2 September 1960. Yvon Toussaint, p. 24; 9 September 1960. André Thirifays, p. 24.
*Time*, 77:8, 17 February 1961, p. 62.
*The Times*, 7 July 1961, p. 15.
*Variety*, January 27, 1960. Gene Moskowitz, p. 6.

# *Let No Man Write My Epitaph* (1960)

"I wouldn't go see [the finished film]. I refuse to see it."—Jean Seberg

A Boris D. Kaplan Productions Picture; Released by Columbia Pictures
Original release: in English
Also known as: *Reach for Tomorrow*; *L'Étrange destin de Nicki Romano* [France]; *Die Saat bricht auf* [Germany]; *Che nessuno scriva il mio epitaffio* [Italy]; *Que nadie escribami epitafio* [Spain]
Running Time: 106 minutes
Format: in Black and White

CAST: [* denotes above the title billing] Burl Ives* (Judge Bruce Mallory Sullivan); Shelley Winters* (Nellie Romano); James Darren* (Nick Romano); Jean Seberg* (Barbara Holloway); Ricardo Montalban* (Louie Ramponi); Ella Fitzgerald* (Flora); Rudolph Acosta (Max); Philip Ober (Grant Holloway); Jeanne Cooper (Fran); Bernie Hamilton (Goodbye George); Walter Burke (Wart); Francis DeSales (Magistrate); Michael Davis (Young Nick); Dan Easton (Eddie); Nesdon Booth (Mike); Roy Jenson (Whitey); Joel Fricano (Barney); Joe Gallison (Lee)

PRODUCTION CREDITS: *Director:* Philip Leacock; *Produced by Boris D. Kaplan*; *Screenplay:* Robert Presnell, Jr., based on a novel by Willard Motley; *Director of Photography:* Burnett Guffey; *Music:* George Duning; *Editor:* Chester W. Schaeffer; *Art Director:* Robert Peterson; *Set Decorator:* Armor Goetten; *Sound:* Josh Westmoreland; *Recording Supervisor:* Charles J. Rice; *Assistant Director:* Sam Nelson; *Makeup:* Ben Lane; *Hairstyles:* Helen Hunt; *Orchestration:* Arthur Morton; *Song:* "Reach for Tomorrow" by Jimmy McHugh and Ned Washington [Ella Fitzgerald and Cliff Smalls also perform extracts from *I can't give you anything but love* and *Angel Eyes*]; extracts from Chopin Waltz no. 3 in a op. 34 no. 2; Brahms Rhapsody no. 2 in g op. 79

## Synopsis

Nick is a young pianist who has grown up in a deprived crime-ridden area of Chicago. His mother Nellie and her downtrodden friends, including alcoholic lawyer "Judge," have shielded him through childhood. They all dream of a better future for him. Despite his talent, his prospects look poor, and he must also be told that his father was executed for murder. Nick's hopes and ambitions are encouraged by an introduction to sympathetic attorney Holloway and his daughter Barbara. Meanwhile drug dealer Ramponi has become Nellie's lover and addicted her to heroin. Nick discovers his mother's secret too late. His furious confrontation of the pusher only results in Ramponi confining him and deciding to inject him too.

Judge eventually learns where Ramponi is keeping Nick and forces his way in. Ramponi shoots him, but the dying man chokes him with all his remaining strength.

Judge's sacrifice marks the beginning of a new life for Nick, together with Barbara, and another chance for Nellie. The task of Nick's group of protectors now seems completed.

## Reviews

"[A] powerful drama but the general subject, backgrounded against Skid Row and its seamy characters, lacks the appeal of a boxoffice hit. That it has been well produced and superbly enacted by a topflight cast there can be no question...."—*Variety*

"The saddest thing about this film is that the acting is good enough to induce one to sit through it. Burl Ives and Shelley Winters are as sincere as anyone could possibly be with dialogue of such high-corn content, and James Darren does well with the almost impossible part of the son."—*Glasgow Herald*

"A skilled cast, headed by Shelley Winters ... keep the film warm and affecting...."—*Saturday Review*

"Burl Ives as the Judge, Shelley Winters as the mother, Jeanne Cooper as the prostitute and James Darren as the unlikely Rubinstein of the slums, all survive in spite of the extreme banality of the material. Leacock's direction is as ponderous as the subject."—*Monthly Film Bulletin.*

"An occasionally moving but rather mild film.... This is not a bad picture, nor an especially good one...."—*New York Times*

"... aside from its sentimentality [the film] has a certain grainy honesty ... Jean Seberg plays with clean dispatch the not very demanding role of a wealthy lawyer's daughter...."—*New York Herald Tribune*

"It might have been wiser to entreat no critic to write its review."—*Evening Standard*

## Notes

The British director Philip Leacock had made a name with a series of films in the 50s, demonstrating with work such as *The Kidnappers* and *The Spanish Gardener* that he could handle potentially difficult themes with sensitivity and insight. *Let No Man Write My Epitaph* was a sequel to Willard Motley's earlier picture of life in the Chicago slums *Knock on Any Door*. This lengthy and predominantly downbeat novel meanders, but its passion and the authenticity of its background detail are evident. Motley's people and the hard times they experience have something of the feel of reportage. The taboo regarding drug abuse as a subject for cinema had already been defiantly breached by Preminger's 1955 picture *The Man with the Golden Arm*. Unfortunately, however, much of Motley's gritty realism and rough eloquence was lost in Presnell's adaptation, even after the rewrite the author demanded, and what remains is essentially a soft-centered melodrama which lacks some of the courage of its convictions.

Seberg recalled the film with a touch of pique, primarily because, despite her newfound success in France, she was required to test with two other actresses who had no film experience. This was for a small supporting role which required almost nothing in terms of interpretative skills. "I tested [for the role]," Seberg later said. "I should have said 'All right, I won the test, now I don't want the part.' I should have just gone away. I regret that I didn't." On the plus side, however, Seberg was pleased to have worked with Burl Ives, James Darren, Ella Fitzgerald and Shelley Winters. Whatever her reservations, the project had at least offered the chance of observing the different acting styles represented among the cast.

Shelley Winters had a personal commitment to this picture, established a good rapport with the director and insisted on a role in its artistic direction, casting included. She relates how she suggested George C. Scott for the part of Ramponi, eventually given to Montalban, but Columbia had felt Scott's was not a strong enough name. A few months later

Otto Preminger would cast him in *Anatomy of a Murder*, which amply vindicated Winters' instinct. "[Scott] proved that *I* should have been running Columbia," she wrote in her memoirs. She added: "I'm very proud of [it]. It was one of the first films to cast black actors as just human beings who happened to be black. The parts they played did not necessarily have to be black people, but when I had discussed the casting with Philip Leacock, he had eagerly accepted my suggestion about Ella Fitzgerald and Bernie Hamilton."

In leaping from Nick's early childhood to his latter school days the film is simply following the novel, but this is not the only hiatus which causes loss of momentum. In addition, Leacock's sometimes stilted direction and Presnell's frequently leaden dialog leave the actors painfully exposed at many points in the story. Montalban, taking his cue from the unsubtle script, turns in a caricature performance as the evil drug-pusher. The few weaknesses in acting are not serious, but they are most conspicuous in the clumsily staged climactic scene. Here the avenging figure of Judge advances on Louie golem-like, not succumbing to his bullet wounds before righteous rough justice has been executed.

Jean Seberg's slightly over bright performance as a rich daddy's girl seems cut-and-pasted in, but she is hardly to be blamed for this. Some dissonance is warranted where Nick encounters these alien beings, and in any case this is just one of the elements here which fail to gel. Shelley Winters gives a creditable performance as the downtrodden but susceptible single mother, but she cannot altogether dispel the sense that she is little more than a stock character. There is only a passing reference to the troubled childhood which Motley had elaborated, and we scarcely believe in the figure of Nick's executed father who continues to cast a shadow over their lives. It does nothing for credibility, either, that Nick's prodigious talent takes the form of full-blown keyboard virtuosity rather than the artistic gift which emerges in the novel.

George Duning provides a musical theme which, Chopinesque musings apart, sets the mood and hovers like a black cloud. If the film score is suitably noir, the photography of Burnett Guffey is an orchestration of grays which stresses the dismal environment of West Madison and its feel of hopelessness. Thus far the film is faithful to its source. There is a kind of heroism in the will to survive and to aid each other which these characters display, but it is a pity that the writing failed to invest them with a little more depth and individuality. This is a story which proceeds in fits and starts, containing moments of genuine drama but also offering us a deal of bathos and banality. Gordon Gow was surely right in pointing out

Seberg claims she never watched her film *Let No Man Write My Epitaph* with James Darren (Columbia).

that a "fresh, compelling approach" is needed when dealing with such themes, and he contrasted the sluggishness of Leacock's film to the vitality of Truffaut's *The 400 Blows*.

There is a particularly hollow ring to the final scene, in which the friends survey the pitiful items constituting the "estate" of Judge Sullivan. Nellie reads from a scrap of paper: "Let no man read my epitaph ... till other times and other men can do [me] justice," but the quotation from Robert Emmett's speech with which Motley prefaced his novel means little in this context. Max sums things up for them and provides the cue for the audience: "I think maybe it's finished now. Nick's grown up, he's going out on his own—maybe not down here with us, but somewhere...." Just as the characters are too neatly categorized—good or evil, weak or strong—the solution to Nick's problems is essentially simple. He must escape from the squalid environment in which he has been raised. A brilliant career and "good" marriage promise to take him away from all that, and we are not expected to trouble ourselves overmuch about the fate of his less conveniently gifted guardian angels.

Leacock's film probably went as far as then seemed commercially possible in showing the miseries of drug addiction depicted by Motley. Its focus is on the ruthlessness of the pusher rather than the suffering he causes, and here he takes the Mephistophelian form of Louie Ramponi. This is no Garden of Eden, but Louie is, as Fran puts it, "as smart as a snake." Despite the moral simplifications, the very real gulf between the bourgeois lifestyle of Barbara and her father and Nick's own world is clear enough, and this carries its own inbuilt message. At root, the struggling figures of West Madison's casualties and the stories behind them carry no less human truth than, say, Dostoyevsky's portraits in *From the House of the Dead*. The difference is that neither Motley nor Presnell could adequately voice their condition, but Ella Fitzgerald comes closest: in the words of Judge, "Flora sings like the whole world's weeping."

*Let No Man Write My Epitaph* was shot over some nine weeks from November 23, 1959. It appropriately enjoyed its "world premiere" (the prior British release apparently being discounted) in Chicago, October 12, 1960, with James Darren on hand to sign autographs. The Windy City welcomed the film, with the header "Film Set in Chicago's Skid Row Hits Home" in the *Daily Tribune*. Its own film critic declared that "in most respects the film is potent and penetrating," but elsewhere reviewers were not so kind. Overall, despite an interesting cast, its box office appeal proved disappointingly tepid, though it was entered in the Cartagena Film Festival in March 1961. Director Philip Leacock was to have a long and prolific career, primarily as television director and producer.

## References

*Ciné revue*, 40:45, 4 November 1960. Roland Fougères, pp. 25–7.
*Filmfacts*, 3:48, 30 December 1960, pp. 304–5.
Johnson, J. Wilfred. *Ella Fitzgerald: an annotated discography*. Jefferson, NC: McFarland, 2001, pp. 339–40.
*Motion Picture Guide, 1927–83*, p. 1656.
Motley, Willard. *Let no man write my epitaph*. New York: Random House, 1958.
*Screen Stories*, 59:10 October 1960, pp. 33–40.
Winters, Shelley. *Shelley II: the middle of my century*. New York: Simon & Schuster, 1989, pp. 268.

## Reviews

*The Chicago Daily Tribune*, 13 October 1960. Mae Tinee, pt. 5 p. 7.
*The Daily Cinema*, 17 August 1960. T.H., p. 5.
*The Daily Telegraph*, 20 August 1960. Patrick Gibbs, p. 11.
*The Evening News*, 18 August 1960. Jympson Harman, p. 6.

*The Evening Standard,* 18 August 1960. Alexander Walker, p. 12.
*Film Daily,* 21 September 1960. Mandel Herbstman, p. 6.
*Films and Filming,* 7:1 October 1960. Gordon Gow, pp. 26–7.
*The Glasgow Herald,* 20 August 1960, p. 11.
*The Guardian,* 20 August 1960, p. 3.
*The Hollywood Reporter,* 19 September 1960. James Powers, p. 3.
*Image et son* (*Saison cinématographique* 1961) Marcel Martin, p. 221.
*Kinematograph Weekly,* 2759, 18 August 1960, p. 10.
*Monthly Film Bulletin,* 27:321 October 1960, pp. 142–3.
*Motion Picture Daily,* 88:57, 21 September 1960. Sidney H. Rechetnik, p. 9.
*The New York Herald Tribune,* 11 November 1960. Paul V. Beckley, p. 11.
*The New York Times,* 11 November 1960. Howard Thompson, p. 36.
*Revista internacional del cine,* 3:39 June 1961, pp. 38–9.
*Saturday Review,* 43:43, 22 October 1960. Arthur Knight, p. 23.
*Schermi,* 28 December 1960, p. 360.
*Time,* 19 December 1960, p. 69.
*The Times,* 76:25, 22 August 1960, p. 3.
*Variety,* 21 September 1960. Whit., p. 6.
*What's on in London,* 1292, 19 August 1960. Maurice Speed, pp. 11–12.

# *Playtime* (*La Récréation*) (1961)

"François had the misfortune of coming in on the last crest of the new wave. The film had quite a few good reviews but unfortunately didn't make any money—and it's a merciless industry."—Jean Seberg

A General Productions film; An Elite Films production; An Audubon Films release (1963); A Columbia release (1961)
Original release: French; released with English dubbing
Also known as: *Love Play*; *Brennende Haut* [Germany]; *Appuntamento con la vita* [Italy]; *Diversión de amor* [Spain]
Running Time: 87 minutes
Format: in Black and White

CAST: [* denotes above the title billing] Jean Seberg* (Kate Hoover); Christian Marquand* (Philippe); Françoise Prévost (Anne de Limeuil); Evelyne Ker (Kate's friend Dominique); Paulette Dubost (Anne's maid); with Simone France, Robert Lefort, Joelle Latour, Michèle Lemoing, Agnès Rivière, Frédérique Villedent, Colette Colas
PRODUCTION CREDITS: *Director:* François Moreuil; *Producer/Production Supervisor:* Hervé Missir; *Screenplay:* François Moreuil, Daniel Boulanger, from a story by Françoise Sagan; *English Dialogue:* Laverne Owens; *Co-director:* Fabien Collin; *Photography:* Jean Penzer; *Camera:* Picon Borel, Jean Chaarvein; *Assistant Directors:* Georges Casati, Marc Simenon; *Music:* Georges Delerue; *Editors:* René Le Hénaff, Jean Reznikoff, Michel Leroy; *Sound:* Jean-Claude Marchetti, Jacques Bonpunt, Pierre-Henri Goumy; *Production Manager:* Paul de Saint-André; *Assistant:* Maurice Urbain; *Script Girl:* Andrée François; *Counselor:* Christian Stengel

## *Synopsis*

To the inmates of a girls' boarding school in Versailles the lives of neighbors Anne de Limeuil and her sculptor lover Philippe seem far more exciting than their own. A noisy party on a warm summer night is irresistible to American Kate Hoover. She climbs the wall for a closer look and mingles with guests, but her adventure is overshadowed when she witnesses a fatal hit-and-run-accident.

Anne and Philippe are amused by the trespasser. Initially irritated by Philippe's flirtation with the teenager, Anne soon decides that the cure is to let this adventure run its course. Her hasty business trip leaves him free to romance the increasingly infatuated Kate. Even the chilling realization that Philippe had been the guilty driver cannot break the spell for Kate, for she thinks he will confess his guilt to her once they have become lovers. Kate and Philippe do spend the night together, but this does not bring the new intimacy she had imagined. Her illusions shattered, she returns to the school from what she now feels has been a meaningless diversion.

## Reviews

"*La Récréation* must be seen, a brilliant début film, light, amusing, yet not lacking gravity or beauty, and where we find those two irreplaceable actresses Jean Seberg and Françoise Prévost. It allows us to welcome in François Moreuil a young creator full of promise."—*Le Figaro littéraire*

"Jean Seberg has not yet lost her exquisitely awkward sensitivity even in the most banal situation known to the 'continental' cinema. *Playtime* was directed by Francois Moreuil... and no von Sternberg he! ... I would say that such indifferent direction as this constitutes ample grounds for divorce."—*Village Voice*

"... it works, and the credit belongs to director and co-scenarist François Moreuil.... Obviously influenced by Jean-Luc Godard, he cuts his film as close as Miss Seberg's coiffeuse cuts hair. The effect ... is to offset the near sentimentality of the story."—*Newsweek*

"Chinks ... are filled by what amounts to a compendium of New Wave preoccupations...—all suffering from a tenuous overall conception and an inexperienced technical approach."—*Monthly Film Bulletin*

"Almost as though it were intended to kid [Sagan's] audacious trick of telling you practically nothing in a lot of pretty, fragile words, this arrogant little movie ... does the same thing in pictures.... [Moreuil's] pictorial narrative, embroidered with chic and modern atmosphere, is studiously disconnected, superficial and flat."—*New York Times*

"Moreuil has been content to let this simple tale amble along via the impetus of its actors which helps give it a feeling for incident and human relations.... It is good natured and even tender but its almost sentimental indulgence of whim and surface feelings does not give it the needed penetration...."—*Variety*

"Jean Seberg does nicely all that she can to enliven this hour of vacuity, but the male actor is one of those mistakes which are fatal."—*Le Canard enchaîné*

"Jean Seberg demonstrates undeniable spontaneity in this role which seems to replicate the one she had in *Les Grandes Personnes*."—*Les Lettres françaises*

"... the spectator is simultaneously delighted by the physical beauty and disgusted by the morbid decadence he sees. It's like being served a dead mouse *glacé*."—*Time*

"This is the lightest and most flexible of Gallic love encounters, so brief it is hardly an episode and conducted by Jean Seberg and Christian Marquand with style."—*Glasgow Herald*

"Miss Seberg, who can move like a dancer, makes Kate a good deal more than a creature of immature passions."—*Times*

## Notes

*Playtime* was based on a youthful story by Françoise Sagan which had appeared in a weekly magazine in 1953. François Moreuil knew Sagan, and she gave him permission to use it for his first and only experiment in making a full-length feature. Moreuil had appeared briefly as a photographer covering Patricia's interview with Parvulesco at Orly in *Breathless*. Now his wife, Preminger's saint and the screen incarnation of Sagan's scandalous heroine, with all the new fame Godard's hit had brought her, was to be the centerpiece of his own creation. Seberg and Moreuil had agreed to part, and were in divorce proceedings while the film was in the making. It was understood that this should not interfere with their working relationship, however, and in fact Seberg saw her participation as a kind of farewell gift and gesture of good will. The press had picked up the rumors, and seemed more interested in the dynamics between the couple than in the film. Seberg joked about Moreuil changing her lines constantly. It is clear from his own account that the shoot was an ordeal for the novice director, but Françoise Prévost did not remember the constant on-set arguments which he recalls.

The shoot commenced at Versailles on June 17, continuing throughout July. Other locations included the Forest of Saint-Germain-en-Laye and the girl's school l'Institut du Rond-Point, which could be utilized for the film's opening scenes in vacation time. On June 18, 1960 the throng of curious onlookers became so large that the police had to be called in to control things. Seberg's idolized grandmother, Frances Benson, had accompanied her on the return flight to France from Iowa at the end of May, and was able to witness much of the proceedings from a place of honor on the set. Never having visited Europe, she was enthralled by her eight week adventure and kept a detailed account of all she saw of her granddaughter's hectic film star life. In her memoirs, Benson described a scene of unscheduled drama in which Seberg and Marquand were riding together through the woods, at the gallop and down a winding road, as the script required. "The horses were nervous," she noted:

> It went well for a time, then Jean's horse sensed the fact that she was unable to handle her, and it started to buck going downhill. Jean was thrown off, landing on her head and shoulder. Help rushed to her side. She said that, at the short moment she lay there, her only thought was that the horse's hoof [which was shod] would crush her face ... I saw that she was not badly hurt. Jean was very nervous, but she wouldn't be bluffed. She was determined to try it again—and did.

As the scene proceeded, Seberg received a painful cut in the face from a branch. Rather than abandon the sequence, it was agreed that the ride would be completed at a walk and that the camera would be speeded up to achieve the desired effect.

The slender storyline betrays its origin as a short story, and the screenplay seems to add little of substance to what may have been rather sketched-in characters. Here, as in *Bonjour Tristesse*, Sagan is exploring a restless young girl's forays into an adult world which she is impatient to discover and sample at first hand. Kate, however, is just starting out, without the social experience and assurance of Cécile, whose playboy father treats her as an equal and accomplice. Literally confined as she is with her fellow pupils, Kate weaves romantic fantasies from the only material available to her, the smart and sophisticated world which she can glimpse from her window. The handsome, mysterious artist Philippe is the ideal figure to embody all the qualities of the knight errant. Although a witness to the hit-and-run incident, the girl cannot connect this ugliness to the hero of her imagination with the brow of Michelangelo's David. How is she to know that this god, who can render the beautiful features of Anne so sensitively in clay, has feet of the same material? Disillusionment waits in ambush.

Conscious of his own inexperience, Moreuil spent more than a year preparing his screenplay with Daniel Boulanger. Sagan's story supplied simply an outline which could be freely adapted. The rather down-at-heel school location felt authentic and preferable to studio conditions, but the debutant cineaste was eager to try out the techniques employed by the filmmakers he admired, not least Godard and the Young Turks of the New Wave. This implied the kind of spontaneity which he had witnessed on the *Breathless* shoot, improvising and filming stealthily on the street and allowing the camera to stray at will. Moreuil's lack of technique was, as observed during production by critic Trémois, in part made up by his collaborators. In addition, he was fortunate in having the gifted Georges Delerue to provide a musical setting. The slightly nervy pizzicato of the title music, accompanying the graphic images of a kaleidoscope, is immediately intriguing. For the most part the score is not obtrusive, setting a tone of gentle nostalgia which is probably more appropriate for this subdued drama, with only the occasional suggestion of gathering clouds.

The overall result, it must be admitted, is uneven and often lacking in assurance. Many of the shots seem arbitrary. At times the lively camera flits hither and thither, truncates bodies, alights on feet or finds significance in a doorframe; at others its positioning seems clumsy, as if simply forgotten. Likewise, editing often lacks the tautness which could have given us a more urgent and insightful narrative. Occasionally vapid dialogue is another problem. Despite these weaknesses, Kate's transforming adolescent experience, as imagined by Sagan and interpreted by Seberg, carries just enough conviction to hold the film together. Marquand and Prévost do not have much to work with as the pair of shallow sophisticates who represent a "grown-up" world so different from the girl's image of it, but Kate's gaucheness and ingenuous directness is well contrasted to the subtler arts and feline calculation of the equally purposeful Anne. Some may find Marquand a rather low-voltage philanderer, but perhaps that is the point. It is very much the girl who makes the running here, projecting her own fantasies onto the bored artist and goading him out

In *Playtime/Love Play* (*La Récréation*) with Evelyne Ker, directed by François Moreuil (Audubon Films/Columbia).

of his pampered ennui into a response. Seberg herself perfectly embodies the green fruit which dangles itself before him, combining a tomboy wantonness with moral naivety. Like a Cécile in embryo, Kate will not wait for experience to come to her, even if the risks are considerable. Obviously, in neither instance do we need to believe the disputed male worthy of the contest, simply that he can seem so to the female protagonists who embellish him in their imaginations. While the cynical Anne sees and accepts her lover as he is, Seberg's Kate is like an unsuspecting child confidently playing on the edge of the chasm which separates the worlds of reality and make-believe.

The accident is a time bomb carefully placed, lethally character-revealing but in itself an apparently unimportant detail which the narrative quickly dismisses. Philippe appears concerned only about the consequences of discovery, and we never learn Anne's view of her lover's conduct. The denouement comes, in effect, like a damp squib, or as if a sudden calm has brought a child's gaily painted kite crashing to the ground. A director with more experience than Moreuil might have brought this particular craft to earth with greater elegance and still made his point, but in any case a heavy sense of anticlimax is preordained. This is simply in keeping with the melancholy retrospection at the heart of Sagan's tale, a precociously knowing lesson in the school of life.

The film was released in Paris on February 22, 1961, and was distributed in the UK later that year, but it would be almost two years before the U.S. premiere. Selection for the Acapulco Film Festival was at least a modest triumph. It is striking that French reviewers were sharply divided in their responses. Some, such as Jean Domarchi and Claude Mauriac, saw talent and promise in this directorial debut which more than compensated for any technical deficiencies. Others found it derivative and saw little of merit in either the story or its treatment. With hindsight, Moreuil felt the end product was forgettable but "not so bad." He decided against pursuing a career as film maker after *Playtime*, but has enjoyed a successful television career and in the course of the ensuing years he wrote, directed and produced more than three hundred hours of programs.

## References

*Cinémonde*, 1376, 20 December 1960, pp. 34–5.
Deglin, Paul. *Ciné revue*, 41:42, 20 October 1961, p. 25.
*L'Exploitation cinématographique*, 13:272, 20 February 1961, p. 43.
*Festival film*, 2, 15 June 1961, pp. 44–60.
*Le Film français*, 17:855, 21 October 1960, p. 31.
*Filmfacts*, 6:7, 21 March 1963, *Playtime*, pp. 34–5.
*Jeunesse cinéma*, 30 November 1960, pp. 28–33.
Moreuil, François [interview with Garry McGee, 1999. See also: Moreuil, 2007, p. 148].
_____. *Flash back*. Chaintreaux: France-Empire Monde, 2007, pp. 155–63.
*Motion Picture Guide, 1927–83*, pp. 2417–8.
Trémois, Claude-Marie. *Radio, cinéma, télévision*, 550, 31 July 1960, pp. 2–3.

## Reviews

*Arts*, 810, 22 February 1961. Jean Domarchi, p. 7.
*L'Aurore*, 27 February 1961. Claude Garson, p. 10.
*Cahiers du cinéma*, 20:117 March 1961. Louis Marcorelles, pp. 50–2.
*Le Canard enchaîné*, 1 March 1961. Michel Duran, p. 5.
*Cinéma*, 56 May 1961. Jean Wagner, p. 108.
*Combat*, 24 February 1961. Pierre Marcabru, p. 8.
*The Daily Cinema*, 17 July 1961. S.S., p. 11.
*The Daily Telegraph*, 15 July 1961. Patrick Gibbs, p. 9.

*The Evening News*, 13 July 1961. Ivon Adams, p. 6.
*The Evening Standard*, 13 July 1961. Alexander Walker, p. 8.
*L'Express*, 507, 2 March 1961. Morvan Lebesque, pp. 33–4.
*Le Figaro*, 24 February 1961. Louis Chauvet, p. 20.
*Le Figaro littéraire*, 775, 25 February 1961. Claude Mauriac, p. 16.
*Le Film français*, 18:875, 3 March 1961. Z., p. 24.
*Filmkritik*, June 1962. Günther Rohrbach, pp. 279–80.
*France observateur*, 12:564, 23 February 1961. Louis Marcorelles, p. 22.
*The Glasgow Herald*, 23 October 1961. Molly Plowright, p. 13.
*Image et son*, 139 March 1961. François Chevassu, p. 21.
*Index de la cinématographie française*, 1962. Jacques Guillon, pp. 319–20.
*Les Lettres françaises*, 2 March 1961. Michel Capdenac, p. 6.
*Le Monde*, 3 March 1961. Jean de Baroncelli, p. 12.
*Monthly Film Bulletin*, 28:331 August 1961. P.J.D., p. 110.
*New York Times*, 16 January 1963. Bosley Crowther, p. 5.
*Newsweek*, 61:3, 21 January 1963, p. 91.
*Les Nouvelles littéraires*, 1748, 2 March 1961. G. Charensol, p. 10.
*Paris-presse*, 26 February 1961. Michel Aubriant, p. 10.
*Positif*, 39 May 1961. Louis Seguin, p. 77.
*Time*, 81:5, 1 February 1963, p.M19.
*The Times*, 14 July 1961, p. 5.
*Variety*, 8 March 1961. Jok., p. 7.
*Village Voice*, 8:13, 17 January 1963. Andrew Sarris, p. 19.

# Time Out for Love
# (*Les Grandes Personnes*) (1961)

"My bread and butter picture of 1960."—Jean Seberg

A Films Pomereu/International Productions/Films Fernand Rivers/P.E.G. Produzione
production; A Zenith International Release
Original release: in French; released with English subtitles
Also known as: *The Grown-Ups*; *A Taste of Love*; *The Adults*; *Die Erwachsenen* [Germany]; *Desideri proibiti* [Italy]; *Confidencias de una doncella* [Spain]
Running Time: 94 minutes
Format: in Black and White

CAST: [* denotes above the title billing] Jean Seberg* (Ann Westerling); Maurice Ronet* (Philippe Rochereau); Micheline Presle* (Michèle Vilmain); Françoise Prévost (Gladys); Annibale Ninchi (Dr. Séverin); Fernando Bruno (Bucchieri, the mechanic); with Jean Ozenne, Guarducci
PRODUCTION CREDITS: *Director:* Jean Valère; *Producer:* Yvon Guezel; *Screenplay:* Roger Nimier, Jean Valère, based on the novel *Histoire d'un amour* by Roger Nimier; *Photography:* Raoul Coutard; *Editors:* Léonide Azar, Claudine Bouché; *Sets:* Bernard Évein, Marc Frédérix; *Sound:* Guy Villette; *Music:* Germaine Tailleferre; *Conductor:* Georges Tzipine; *Dance Music:* Bill Byers; *Musical Director:* Henri Jaquillard; *Cameraman:* Jean Charvein; *Administration:* Paul LeMaire; *Makeup:* Phuong Maittret; *Hair:* Denise Lemoigne; *1st Assistant Producer:* Henri Toulout; *2nd Assistant Producer:* Geneviève Dormann; *Script Girl:* Lydie Doucet; *Still Photographs:* Roger Corbeau; *Executive Producer:* Bertrand Javal

## Synopsis

The infidelities of her lover Philippe drive couturier Michèle Vilmain to attempt suicide. She is saved by friend Dr. Séverin, who leaves his teenaged niece Ann to care for the recovering convalescent. Ann, a trained nurse from Nebraska, is impressed by Michèle's sophistication, while the older woman takes the inexperienced American under her wing. Michèle and her manipulative colleague Gladys resolve to turn Ann into a stylish Parisienne. The makeover succeeds, and playboy Philippe begins to take notice. His charm quickly prevails over Ann's moral disapproval when he reveals a more serious side of his nature. Michèle, leaving on a business trip, encourages their liaison, partly to spite Gladys. Ann is soon deeply in love, yet feels she has betrayed her friend. She is bewildered to find her lover's relationship with Michèle unaltered when the latter returns.

All the hopes Philippe had invested in reviving his father's racing car firm are dashed the next day, when he has to drop out of the Grand Prix. Ann rushes to console him, but he is scornful of her assumptions about their relationship. Michèle and Gladys show little sympathy for her artlessness in this "grown-up" game, although the former is touched by the girl's sincerity. Ann returns home to marry the childhood fiancé she now knows more surely she cannot love.

## Reviews

"The approach is elegant, consciously sophisticated and quite serious and this, perhaps, is the film's main weakness. The film's main virtues can be found in the playing and the locations. Jean Seberg ... exhibits a certain controlled charm and intelligence, and Micheline Presle suggests the older woman's more complex passions without overstatement."— *Monthly Film Bulletin*

"*Time Out for Love* is the absolutely minimal Seberg picture—and also the clearest for it relies entirely on the idiosyncrasies of the Marshalltown miss. There is no subtlety, no complication to cloud the issue. [The film] is absurd—but Seberg is not. She has an individual, unimpaired quality and it is enough to rescue even this ball of fluff."— *Newsweek*

"[Seberg and Ronet as a] couple falling coquettishly in love, are the trail-blazers on this tour of Paris, and they are distressingly dull ... Seberg reminds you of one of those youngsters who ... want to sell you Girl Scout cookies. And what she's selling is similarly saccharin."—*New York Times*

"Characters are futile and uninteresting. Director Valere and scripter Nimier have been unable to display an insight into what makes them tick. It is all handled in a glossy, conventional manner.... Acting alone cannot do much with the one dimensional characters."—*Variety*

"Jean Seberg, so perfectly pretty, surmounts the pitfalls of French pronunciation with exquisite grace."—*Le Figaro*

"Jean Seberg alone (remarkable) shows a touching fragility which makes her entry into the world of the 'grown-ups,' where you love and suffer, more painful."—*Cinéma*

"The three women are excellent ... Jean Seberg is delightful."—*Le Monde*

## Notes

This was only the second full-length feature by Valère, following *La Sentence* in 1959, starring Marina Vlady and Robert Hossein. Here he worked with Roger Nimier in a screen adaptation of Nimier's novel of the same name. Nimier had made a brilliant youthful entrance on the literary scene with a series of novels in the early 50s. He had already branched out into film, working with Louis Malle on the screenplay of *Lift to the Scaffold* (*Ascenseur pour l'échafaud*) from Noël Calef's novel.

Much is discarded from the novel, including its 20s setting, and there are substantial changes to the characters and situations. What Valère found interesting in Nimier's story were the relationships between the three women and the conflict between love and friendship. "I wanted to make a sober film," he told critic Trémois. "I tried to involve the camera with the characters, to make it move with them. But each image is stylized: it's the opposite of journalistic reportage as in *À bout de souffle*."

Valère was probably wise to follow his own instincts rather than to ape the mannerisms of his more experimental contemporaries, although there are certainly moments when the viewer longs for the flair and originality of a Truffaut or for Godard's daring. There are signs that he may have wished to relieve some of the book's fundamental pessimism for cinema audiences. Be that as it may, what this director gives us is a thoughtful treatment of Nimier's central situation, that of a trusting and inexperienced young woman introduced into a game with rules entirely alien to her. There is no heavy moralizing and there are no villains: people are what they are. Some, like Gladys, are protected by insensitivity, but all will suffer in some way or other because of their own nature. Ann's particular misfortune reflects the obvious universal truth, that her youth and ignorance of the world make her more emotionally susceptible and less prepared for the pain to come.

If much of the complexity and the undertones of the novel are jettisoned, Valère and Nimier do offer us a quartet of well-defined individuals. The most interesting of these is Michèle, and Presle is able to give a more nuanced performance than is possible for Ronet or Prévost. Ann is naïvely gullible in her unqualified admiration and trust she gives her patron, but there is a real ambivalence about Michèle's motives. We cannot say at what point gratitude and benevolence become corrupted into manipulation because the process is unconscious. In any case, the code of the society in which she shines sets dignity and style above kindness or sincerity. While in her case there is a suggestion of remorse, not least as she watches her friend's final departure at the station unobserved, there is no hint of such scruples in those of Gladys or Philippe. Gladys simply tempers revenge with the easy service of "opening the eyes" of this tiresome provincial interloper before sending her on her way. She is lucid—the function of girls like Ann is simply to divert the men for a while when they become bored. Philippe is almost the stereotype of the capricious playboy, one whose emotional lethargy in relation to anything lacking wheels makes it all the easier to slip into automatic as seducer. The woman who reclaims him has no illusions, but theirs is a pact which self-esteem is secondary provided that public humiliation can be avoided.

**With Maurice Ronet in *Time Out for Love* (*Les Grandes Personnes*) (Zenith International/Seven Arts).**

Seberg later regretted making *Les Grandes Personnes*, which she had agreed to do "for very base commercial reasons," as she put it. It is not hard to understand her dissatisfaction and her retrospectively apologetic dismissal of it. Not only was an original story reshaped to accommodate a heroine with the Midwestern background her accent could not hide, but it seemed that the central narrative of *La Récréation* was simply being retold in a slightly different setting, complete with echoes of the subsidiary characters. It hardly helped that both of the lovers were called Philippe, or that two of the rivals were played by Françoise Prévost. In fairness, this is in some respects a better film, but it gave the impression of a young actress stuck in a groove and unable to extend her range. While it might please her fans, it could do little to win round the doubters, something which would only be achieved through a very different kind of challenge.

The score for the film was composed by Germaine Tailleferre, the only female member of the celebrated "Six" which included Honegger, Poulenc and Milhaud. The less interesting dance music was composed for the film by Bill Byers and subsequently issued on an EP recording in France. Another asset for Valère was the service of *Breathless* cameraman Raoul Coutard. If the final result sometimes seems technically slacker, less consistent or more conventional than his work elsewhere, it is perhaps due to the lack of really purposeful direction. The camerawork seems at times to switch between a more studied or classical style and a certain quirkiness. Things begin with promise, however, as credits appear against the glass dome of the Galeries Lafayette and the camera tracks across the cathedral-like space to capture the bustle on the ground, while Tailleferre's vigorous score expresses all the boisterous energy of the city's commerce. Within a few moments there is a dramatic shift, as work ceases and shoppers depart, leaving Michèle a vulnerable and isolated figure. There are many scenes in which the veteran composer enhances mood or adds touches of color, such as the playful baroque cameo of Ann's transformation, or, combining with Coutard's photography, yields a moment of exhilaration, such as the boating trip taken by Ann and Michèle. The occasional false notes or scenes which lack conviction, critically some of those depicting the affair between Ann and Philippe, are all the more disappointing in view of these positive values. Ultimately, we may feel that there is much of interest here, but it is not the film it might have been, had it been bolder in its vision or deployed its strengths with more spontaneity. Françoise Prévost's verdict was that although the film was part of the New Wave movement, Jean Valère's direction was still of the old school style.

The six-week shoot of *Time Out for Love* at the Billancourt Studios and on location in Paris began on August 8, 1960. It premiered in Paris on February 3, 1961. In London too its release, under the title *A Taste of Love*, seemed purposely synchronized with that of *La Récréation*. *Daily Telegraph* critic Patrick Gibbs, noting the points of resemblance and regretting the "flotsam" of the new wave, could not resist skewering both with one thrust: "Identical conclusions: would-be *jeune fille en fleur* gets nipped in the bud. Goodness how sad—and bad."

## References

Barèges, Luc. *Ciné revue*, 41:8, 24 February 1961, pp. 12–3.
*Cinémonde*, 28:1367, 18 October 1960, pp. 24–5.
*L'Exploitation cinématographique*, 13:271, 5 February 1961, p. 30.
*Le Film français*, 17:855, 21 October 1960, p. 28.
*Filmfacts*, 6:33, 19 September 1963, pp. 189–90.
*Mon Film*, 689 June 1961, pp. 3–52.

Nimier, Roger. *Histoire d'un amour: roman.* Paris: Gallimard, 1953.
*Il Nuovo spettatore cinematografico,* 4:30–1 March/April 1962, p. 247.
Trémois, Claude-Marie. *Télérama,* 567, 27 November 1960, pp. 52–3.

### Reviews

*L'Aurore,* 8 February 1961. Claude Garson, p. 10.
*Le Canard enchaîné,* 42:2103, 8 February 1961. Michel Duran, p. 5.
*Le Cinéma,* 54 March 1961. Marcel Martin, pp. 99–100.
*Cinémonde,* 29:1384, 14 February 1961, p. 25.
*Combat,* 7 February 1961. Pierre Marcabru, p. 8.
*The Daily Cinema,* 10 April 1961. M.H., p. 5.
*The Daily Mail,* 14 July 1961. Barry Norman, p. 10.
*The Daily Telegraph,* 15 July 1961. Patrick Gibbs, p. 9.
*The Evening News,* 13 July 1961. Ivon Adams, p. 6.
*L'Express,* 8:503, 2 February 1961. Morvan Lebesque, p. 33.
*Le Figaro,* 6 February 1961. Louis Chauvet, p. 14.
*Le Film français,* 18:872, 10 February 1961. O., p. 44.
*Filmkritik,* April 1961. Dietrich Kuhlbrodt, p. 217.
*France observateur,* 12:562, 9 February 1961. Louis Marcorelles, p. 22.
*France-soir,* 8 February 1961. France Roche, p. 9.
*Image et son* (*Saison cinématographique* 1961). Guy Allombert, p. 135.
*Index de la cinématographie française,* 1962. Gilberte Turquan, pp. 209–10.
*Kinematograph Weekly,* 2807, 20 July 1961, p. 20.
*Le Monde,* 8 February 1961. Jean de Baroncelli, p. 12.
*Monthly Film Bulletin,* 28:328 May 1961. J.G., pp. 59–60.
*The New York Herald Tribune,* 23 April 1963. Judith Crist, p. 15.
*The New York Times,* 23 April 1963. Bosley Crowther, p. 31.
*Newsweek,* 61:18, 6 May 1963 (with interview), p. 95.
*Le Nouvel observateur,* 278, 9–15 March 1970, p. 8.
*Paris-jour,* 9 March 1970. Janine Merlin, p. 8.
*Paris-presse,* 10 February 1961. Michel Aubriant, p. 10.
*Positif,* 39 May 1961. Louis Seguin, p. 77.
*Variety,* 22 February 1961. Gene Moskowitz, p. 7.

# The Five-Day Lover
## (*L'Amant de cinq jours*) (1961)

"There are a lot of people who have talked to me about [*Five-Day Lover*]
and liked it. I like it. It's one of my favorite films."—Jean Seberg

A Films Ariane/Filmsonor/Mondex Films (Paris)/Cinériz (Rome) production; A Kings-
ley International Pictures release; Distribution: Cinédis
Original release: in French; released with English subtitles
Also known as: *Infidelity* [UK]; *Liebhaber für fünf Tage* [Germany]; *L'Amante di cinque
giorni* [Italy]; *El Amante de cinco días* [Spain]
Running Time: 86 minutes
Format: in Black and White

CAST: [* denotes above the title billing] Jean Seberg* (Claire Thiébault); Jean-Pierre
Cassel* (Antoine Chérier); François Périer* (Georges Thiébault); Micheline Presle*
(Madeleine de Saulieu); Albert Mouton (Halavoine); Gil Grossac (Taxi Driver); Jean Syl-
vain (maître d'hôtel); Pierre Repp (Pépère); Carlo Croccolo (Mario); Claude Mansard
(Paulin); Marcella Rovena (Madame Chanut); Albert Michel (Blanchet); Max Doria

(Tramp); Moïse Cohen (blind one-legged man); Alphonse Laurenty (Gros Pépère); David Tonelli (guest); Philippe de Broca (spectator at the racecourse); with Georges Douking and Philippe Prince

PRODUCTION CREDITS: *Director:* Philippe de Broca; *Producers:* Alexandre Mnouchkine, Georges Dancigers; *Director of Production:* Georges Dancigers; *Screenplay:* Daniel Boulanger, Philippe de Broca, based on the novel *Antoine* by Françoise Parturier; *Cameraman:* Pierre Goupil; *Photography:* Jean-Bernard Penzer; *Music:* Georges Delerue; *Art Director:* Bernard Evein; *Editor:* Laurence Méry; *Sound:* Jean Labussière; *Assistant Directors:* Louis Manella, Jean-Pierre Spiri Mercanton; *Production Assistants:* Georges Pellegrin and Robert Bober; *Assistant Editor:* Raymonde Guyot; *Assistant Sound Engineer:* Yves Dacquay; *Interior Designer:* Robert Christidès; *Makeup:* Marcel Bordenave; *Hairstyles:* Denise Lemoigne; *Scriptgirl:* Andrée François; *Press Attaché:* Georges Cravenne; *Photographer:* Silvère Pierre

## Synopsis

The pleasure-seeking Antoine is happy to be indulged by an older lover, wealthy businesswoman Madeleine. This does not curb his roving eye, which alights on Madeleine's young friend Claire. Claire has two small children by her archivist husband Georges, but her life lacks a certain something. Claire and Antoine find their secret assignations are the perfect solution to weekday tedium. All goes well until Madeleine detects the deception. She devises a fitting punishment for the guilty pair. Madeleine announces a soirée at which Claire, Georges and Antoine will be brought together.

At the reception the guests are at the mercy of the skillful hostess, who studies their reactions to each other and relishes their discomfort. Georges maintains his good humor, even suggesting to Antoine that they have something in common. It's clear he knew the truth already.

Antoine appeals to Claire to leave her husband, but it is Georges who had understood her, for she prefers things as they are. Madeleine will forgive Antoine, while Georges accepts his wife's need for romantic adventures: "I don't want to keep you in a cage—you are so beautiful when you come home."

## Reviews

"One of the Ten Best pictures of the year. An entertainment of outstanding quality ... it is indeed a rare thing to find a spirit so heartily joyous. Witty, light and passionate. A realistic and unshocked approach to adultery...."—*New York Post*

"[The film] moves with brisk detachment across a hurdle-like series of deliberately incongruous cuts, bouncing its facetious fancy man [Cassel] between the amoral young wife and the eccentric, elegant dressmaker who keeps him ... Presle is wickedly funny as the spiteful, demanding older woman, and Périer's even more substantial...."—*Monthly Film Bulletin*

"... for about an hour and a half, [it] is the year's funniest movie...."—*Time*

"I was happily swept off my feet by [de Broca's] first two comedies ... I consider his latest comedy, teasingly entitled *The Five Day Lover*, to be even better ... I was astonished by the tact and delicacy with which Miss Seberg played her tricky role. She, it turns out, is an actress, and, oh, how beautiful!"—*New Yorker*

"[De Broca's film] suggests that he is one of the most accomplished and individual French directors, with a wit, style and polish that rivals the early Clair."—*Financial Times*

"If [De Broca] keeps it up he'll be the new master of sophisticated comedy, for he has that rare thing that is needed, something known as 'the touch.'"—*Saturday Review*

"And finally, go see how pretty Jean Seberg is with her long hair. She is now also a very charming actress."—*Le Canard enchaîné*

"Pretty and gay as a lark, Miss Seberg has travelled a very long way from the cropped head and anguish of St. Joan, though her inquisitors might rightly claim the voices she hears on this occasion are the devil's.... Only puritans will frown."—*Evening News*

"Jean Seberg, looking quite different from what she has in previous films, is a bit too prosaic and posey—and immature, certainly—as the wife."—*New York Times*

## Notes

Several members of the crew who were working on *Playtime (La Récréation)* had previously worked with director De Broca, and some of them remarked to Seberg that they hoped she might work with him some time. "Philippe came out one day to meet me and asked me if I'd be interested in working on *The Five-Day Lover* which he was preparing," Seberg recalled. "I was delighted because it was a complete change of pace ... I learned a great deal from De Broca about comedy technique, about pace and rhythm and timing."

*The Five-Day Lover* was De Broca's third film, following quickly on from *The Love Game (Les Jeux de l'amour)* and *The Joker (Le Farceur)*, and his third success in a row. Each time he had featured leading man Jean-Pierre Cassel, whom he had discovered in the play *Oscar*, and he was to follow with international hits such as *That Man from Rio (L'Homme de Rio)*, starring Belmondo. At this stage in his career the director wanted to continue with the same leading man. The successful production company Ariane offered him this project working with Cassel, and agreed that De Broca's preferred screenwriter Daniel Boulanger should handle the screen adaptation of Françoise Parturier's novel. Seberg, in the wake of *Breathless*, was an obvious choice, and the leading quartet was completed with Périer and Presle, both stars whose acting the director admired.

De Broca believed that a director's job was to make the cast as comfortable as possible during filming, and that you should never berate actors for their performance, especially in comedy. Like most of Seberg's directors, he had a directing style which presented a total contrast to that of Preminger. De Broca gave Seberg credit not only for delicately balancing comedy and drama, but for doing both believably in different languages. "Humor is the hardest thing to understand in a foreign language," he remarked, "but Jean did. She was very gifted for comedy, and it's always surprised me she didn't do more."

The film was shot in Paris and at the Studios Épinay between 17 October and 29 November 1960. Part of the shoot, in the Ménilmontant district of Paris, was featured in *Le Soir illustré*, which made much of the transformation wrought by Seberg's brunette wig. The signs must have seemed auspicious when the film was selected as the French entry in the 1961 Berlin International Film Festival and nominated for the Golden Bear.

Surprisingly, despite positive reviews (especially in the U.S.), the film was not a success when it premiered in France on February 24, 1961, only a few days after the debut of Seberg's *Time Out for Love*. The director described the film as a "complete flop," adding that this is one of the rare occasions on which Ariane actually lost money. Seberg felt that one of the reasons for its failure in France was her own character Claire. "I'm sure if I had not had the two children they would have accepted [the lover]. But they felt it was outrageous. You would see me one second in the arms of my lover, and the next shot would be holding one of my children. It became a bit shocking ... [the film] was a bit flippant, almost a parody of a comedy about the husband with the cheating little wife. The Americans liked that a lot. I don't know why, especially."

Daniel Boulanger and Philippe De Broca based their screenplay on the amusingly cynical novel *Antoine* by Françoise Parturier. Parturier's first novel *Les Lions sont lâchés* was being filmed at this time by Verneuil, but De Broca knew of her only as a "fashionable author." Although collaborating with Boulanger on the screenplay, the director claimed that he did not read the novel until later. This book, with its conscious echoes of Laclos and awareness of sexual politics, cleverly portrays the pleasures and pangs of amorous intrigues among the bourgeoisie. Here, for the screen, the carefree and comic aspects of the story are developed rather than its telling insights and subtle spitefulness, and the relationships of its four main characters are freely adapted. Jean-Pierre Cassel recalled that the film was not to the liking of Parturier, and it is not hard to see why. The film in relation to the novel is rather like a frothy cappuccino compared to bracing espresso, more leisurely if perhaps less mentally stimulating. The froth, as administered by this quartet, is nevertheless a delight.

Evidently the director saw something poignant in the character of Georges, the bookish husband Claire loves but seems fated to betray if she is to live out her vital fantasies. This is a man to whom nature has assigned the role of buffoon, and he is too intelligent to imagine he can aspire to any other. His enthusiasms are absurd, but they give him an inner life which is touching and almost heroic. He cannot give his wife the element of romance she craves, but he constitutes the emotional anchorage without which her existence would be impossible.

There are many wonderfully absurd scenes, such as the Auvergnat clog dance spiritedly performed by Seberg and Cassel, or the collar adjustments by Cassel and Périer at Madeleine's soirée. François Périer is superb as the (un)deceived husband, and Cassel and

Dancing with Jean-Pierre Cassel in one of her favorite films, the comedy *The Five-Day Lover* (*L'Amant de cinq jours*) (Kingsley International).

Presle can scarcely be faulted as the pleasure-loving Antoine and the equally self-centered but more astute Madeleine. It is impressive that Seberg at twenty-two was already fully able to hold her own, with this accomplished trio, as the heartlessly romantic and devious Claire. The bitter-sweet atmosphere of the piece is greatly enhanced by the memorable musical score of Georges Delerue, one of France's most eminent composers for film, and who had also scored *La Récréation*. This may not be a great classic of French cinema, but it is certainly a forgotten gem of the era which well deserves to be rediscovered and cherished.

## References

B[enayoun?], R. *Positif,* 46 June 1962, pp. 21–2.

Bergan, Ronald. Philippe de Broca [obit.] *The Guardian,* 2 December 2004.

Cassel, Jean-Pierre. *À mes amours.* Paris: Stock, 2004, p. 43.

*Cinémonde,* 28:1385, 21 February 1961, p. 23.

Cohen, Joan. *Magill's survey of cinema. Foreign language films.* Englewood Cliffs, NJ: Salem Press, 1985, vol. 3, pp. 1114–16.

*Corail,* 2, March 1963, pp. 3–63.

*Le Film français,* 17:862, 9 December 1960, p. 24.

*Filmfacts,* 4:51, 19 January 1962, pp. 340–1.

Garel, Alain, et al. *Philippe de Broca.* Paris: Veyrier, 1990, pp. 86–7, 190.

Parturier, Françoise. *Antoine: ou L'amant de cinq jours, roman.* Paris: Julliard, 1959; new edition: Plon, 1971, translation Lowell Bair: *The Five Day Lover.* New York: Berkley, 1959.

*Le Soir illustré,* 1482, 17 November 1960, pp. 30–31.

## Reviews

*Arts,* 811, 1 March 1961. Jean Douchet, p. 7.

*L'Aurore,* 28 February 1961. Claude Garson, p. 12.

*Le Canard enchaîné,* 1 March 1961. Michel Duran, p. 5.

*Combat,* 28 February 1961. Pierre Marcabru, p. 8.

*The Daily Cinema,* 4 August 1961. M.H., p. 9.

*The Daily Mail,* 3 August 1961. Barry Norman, p. 4.

*The Daily Telegraph,* 5 August 1961. Eric Shorter, p. 9.

*The Evening News,* 3 August 1961. Felix Barker, p. 6.

*The Evening Standard,* 3 August 1961. Frank Entwisle, p. 8.

*L'Express,* 507, 2 March 1961. Morvan Lebesque, pp. 33–4.

*Le Figaro,* 1 March 1961. Louis Chauvet, p. 22.

*Le Figaro littéraire,* 776, 4 March 1961. Claude Mauriac, p. 16.

*Le Film français,* 3 March 1961. Y., p. 24.

*Films and Filming,* 7:12 September 1961. Gordon Gow, p. 31.

*The Financial Times,* 4 August 1961. David Robinson, p. 16.

*France-soir,* 1 March 1961. Robert Chazal, p. 10.

*The Glasgow Herald,* 6 August 1962. Molly Plowright, p. 5.

*The Guardian,* 5 August 1961. Isabel Quigly, p. 3.

*The Hollywood Reporter,* 6 June 1962. James Powers, p. 3.

*L'Humanité,* 28 February 1961. Armand Monjo, p. 2.

*Image et son,* 140/141 April/May 1961. François Chevassu, p. 34.

*Index de la cinématographie française,* 1962. Jean Houssaye, pp. 87–8.

*Kine Weekly,* 2810, 10 August 1961, pp. 19–20.

*Les Lettres françaises,* 865, 2 March 1961. P.L. Thirard, p. 6.

*Le Monde,* 28 February 1961. Jean de Baroncelli, p. 13.

*Monthly Film Bulletin,* 28:332 September 1961, p. 122.

*The New York Herald Tribune,* 14 December 1961. Paul V. Beckley, p. 17.

*The New York Times,* 14 December 1961. Bosley Crowther, p. 55.

*The New Yorker,* 37:44, 16 December 1961. Brendan Gill, pp. 111–2.

*Les Nouvelles littéraires,* 1748, 2 March 1961. G. Charensol, p. 10.

*Paris-presse,* 2 March 1961. Michel Aubriant, p. 10.

*Saturday Review,* 44:35, 2 September 1961. Hollis Alpert, pp. 27–8.
*Téléciné,* 15:96 May 1961. Gilbert Salachas.
*Time,* 24 November 1961, p. 66.
*The Times,* 4 August 1961, p. 3.
*Variety,* 5 April 1961. Gene Moskowitz, p. 6.

# *Congo Vivo* (1962)

"There are fascinating things in the film ... interviews with Mobutu and Kasavubu ... [but] it doesn't fit together at all."—Jean Seberg

A R.O.T.O.R. (Rome)/Orsay Films (Paris) co-production; A Dino De Laurentiis release; a Gala presentation; distributed through Columbia Pictures
Original release: in Italian and English; with English subtitles
Also known as: *Eruption* [UK]
Running Time: 107 minutes
Format: in Black and White

CAST: [* denotes above the title billing] Jean Seberg* (Annette); Gabriele Ferzetti* (Roberto Santi); Bachir Touré (Abbé); Frédérique Andrew (Eleonora, fiancée of Abbé); Alfredo Santagati (Michel Barrès); Carla Bizzarri (Marie Barrès); Italico Bertolini (Giorgio Cinotti); Ferruccio de Ceresa (Missionary); Dan Powell (American Journalist); Lynn Gordon (Edna); Rita Livesi (Nun)

PRODUCTION CREDITS: *Director:* Giuseppe Bennati; *Producer:* Carmine Bologna; *Screenplay:* Giuseppe Bennati, Paolo Levi, Lucia Drudi, William Demby, from a story by Giuseppe Bennati; *Dialogue:* Maurice Griffe; *Photography:* Giuseppe Aquari; *Cameraman:* Cesare Allione; *Music:* Piero Piccioni; *Editor:* Franco Fraticelli; *Art Director:* Pasquale Romano; *Sound:* Louis Hochet, Bruno Brunacci; *Production Manager:* Domenico Bologna; *Production Secretary:* Giorgio Zuccaro; *Assistant Directors:* Alain Roux, Ignazio Dolci; *Assistant Cameraman:* Giorgio Resis; *Assistant Editor:* Cesarina Casini; *Mixing:* Bruno Moreal; *Makeup:* Pauline [Phuong] Maittret; *Assistant Art Director:* Pietro Bologna; *Editing Secretary:* Francesco Bologna; *Music edition:* "DINO" Rome

## Synopsis

Correspondent Roberto returns to the Congo a year after the uprising he had personally witnessed in 1960. He is to interview leaders of the newly independent state, yet his thoughts return to the individuals he came to know who had been caught up in the violence.

There had been the Congolese soldier called Abbé who had demanded money at a road block and later become a friend. Abbé planned to study photography and marry his fiancée Eleonora, and had been eager to confide his hopes for the future to the sympathetic Italian. There had also been a young Belgian woman, Annette, who had been stranded at the Memling Hotel in Leopoldville when her husband needed to return home. He had been moved by both the beauty and the sadness of this fellow guest who turned to him for warmth. Her alternating moods baffled him.

Following an expedition with Abbé to aid victims of the conflict, Roberto persuaded Annette to accompany him to the more tranquil Brazzaville. Here she had seemed to master her anxieties, but her behavior had sparked his jealousy and a bitter quarrel. Only then had he learned about a rape she had suffered at her home, finally allowing the barrier separating them to fall away.

New riots had broken out in Leopoldville. He had found Abbé fatally injured by the mob and been forced to abandon his body by the river bank. At the hotel a note awaited him, telling him Annette had returned to Belgium.

Now, a year later, a chance encounter with Annette and her husband revives painful emotions. Roberto sees there is no longer a place for him in her life.

## Reviews

"It's a very interesting documentary, which blends into an imaginary story all the protagonists of the Congolese drama.... *Congo Vivo* deserves a quite particular mention. Here, at last, is a film whish doesn't seek refuge in the past, but wants to tackle the big problems of our time and our world."—*L'Aurore*

"There are obvious hazards about a film of this kind, notably the difficulty of getting at the truth of the matter ... however, it was an interesting attempt, and Jean Seberg's many admirers will doubtless be well enough pleased with it."—*Glasgow Herald*

"Producers and director deserve full credit for the job turned out under trying conditions.... Acting, with a few scenes between Seberg and Ferzetti, is only adequate, reflecting the rush job on the pic."—*Variety*

"The direction is undistinguished, newsreel shots being noticeably livelier than anything Bennati has to offer. ... the psychological motivation of Annette is so crude that one generously suspects large cuts. Technically, too, the film leaves much to be desired."—*Monthly Film Bulletin*

"The film wanted to say much more, and we glimpse something of this [but] the didactic tone and the accent of journalistic inquiry prevail over the good intentions of Bennati—who nevertheless, be it said, is good at times.... Gabriele Ferzetti and Jean Seberg, good actors, deserved more."—*Corriere della sera*

"Devoid of ideas, visual quality zero ... nevertheless let us congratulate the sensitive and charming Jean Seberg who succeeds in making a non-existent character moving."—*Le Figaro*

"Luckily there's Jean Seberg, whose seeming fragility, grace and emotion make the invented character she's required to play seem almost convincing."—*France-soir*

"Jean Seberg has perhaps never appeared as feminine and mysterious as in this role of the languishing, troubled and neurotic Annette. She plays this character with a naturalness and sincerity which seems almost brazen."—*Le Soir*

## Notes

The Congo's sudden transition from Belgian colony to independence in June 1960 threw the country into turmoil, with an army mutiny leading to the intervention of Belgian forces to protect civilians. The secession of Katanga under Moise Tshombe triggered the separation of other provinces from Leopoldville (now Kinshasa) and led to UN involvement, while exacerbating the conflict between President Kasavubu and Prime Minister Lumumba. Drastic action by military leader Colonel Mobutu tipped the balance against Lumumba, who was later executed by the forces of Tshombe. This was the dramatic and violent contemporary background against which Bennati decided to set his story.

Giuseppe Bennati began as a maker of documentaries in 1945, not turning to full-length feature films until 1951 with *Il Microfono è vostro*. Six further films preceded *Congo Vivo*, showing a mix of the overtly commercial, such as the light comedy *L'Amico del giaguaro*, and more personally engaged cinema. *Congo vivo* was a project which he had cherished for two years before it came to fruition. Seberg had turned down several offers from Italian filmmakers before 1962 because she felt they were unpromising. She agreed to appear in Bennati's film primarily because there was a temporary crisis in the French film industry, with a general slow-down in production. This time she decided to accept within 24 hours, on the basis of a treatment she described as "not very good" and an assurance from the producers that it would be improved. In late August 1961 she flew to Rome to begin work on the shoot, which would continue in the Congo in September.

The idea of location shooting in Africa strongly appealed to Seberg, although the filming coincided with the renewal of serious conflict. "This was a time when there were all kinds of excitement and agitation in Africa," she recalled. "In fact we were at the Leopoldville hotel, the Memling, when Hammarskjöld died [September 18]. In a sense it was a very frightening but impressive moment to be in Africa." In addition to Leopoldville, location work was done at a fishing village, Kinkole, and on the Angolan border. Eventually, as a result of the tensions in the country, the production crew retreated to Rome to complete filming. The Italian film journal *La Fiera del cinema* sent reporter Adele Cambria to report on the shoot, and in November 1961 she presented readers with a vivid account which included interviews with the director and stars. In December *Cinemundus Export* reported the return to Rome of Bennati's team. Despite the difficult conditions, requiring haste and continuous police protection, the director declared himself pleased with the results of the shoot.

Bennati's film is segmented by flashbacks of varying length, switching between the journalist's present visit and his vivid memories of his earlier assignment. However, it is not from this narrative structure as much as from the failure to incorporate the two contrasting elements that the main problem arises. The two interviews with key political figures are undoubtedly of interest, but they seem out of place here, and all the more so being in French with subtitles. Similarly, the newsreel footage is all too obviously such. The "voice over" observations by Roberto on the historical and political background are necessary, setting the context of the story, but they are not enough to marry together the fictional and documentary material convincingly and avoid the impression that we are seeing two films spliced together. Despite this, the suggestion by some critics that this is a dishonest film seems unjust. There could not be any analysis in depth of Congolese politics in a film of this nature, but the snapshot views it offers have their own validity and, while superficial, certainly do not lack compassion. Whether the backdrop of real violence and suffering is a

In *Congo Vivo* with **Gabriele Ferzetti** (Columbia).

fitting one for a rather sentimental love story is a different question, but one which could just as well be applied to *Gone with the Wind*.

*Congo Vivo* should be seen as a piece of fiction with an interesting historical setting, and one which touches on serious issues. The love stories of these two couples, one European and one African, would be of little appeal were it not for the quality of performance by the four principal players. The primary focus is on the journalist/narrator and the abandoned and traumatized young woman whose vulnerability ties him to her so powerfully. It is a chance encounter which links this pair to the other lovers, Abbé and Eleonora, whose playful courtship, more lightly sketched in, provides a nice foil to the anguish of Annette and Roberto. It is perhaps only justice that the story's real tragedy here belongs to the Congolese victim, rather than to the Europeans who are free to come and go. All four actors deserve credit for rendering sympathetic and believable roles which could very easily have seemed banal pulp fiction stereotypes. Aquari's fine monochrome photography is all too easy to distinguish from newsreel inserts, and the film is also well served by composer Piero Piccioni, whose swelling opening theme is redolent of film noir drama combined with romance, but who also employs African drums and jazz elements atmospherically.

There is enough genuine involvement with the plight of Congolese people here to dismiss the view that Bennati was just using an exotic setting to add color to a conventional love tale. In fact it is in part the director's very earnestness which draws attention to the film's uneasy balance. The points he makes are generally fair minded. It was the fatalism of the Africans which had allowed the colonialists to claim that they were less susceptible to suffering, but the Congolese troops had abused their suddenly acquired power. Bennati's main character feels shamed as a European by the villagers' trust, yet reveals that he too has prejudices. Although the chaos in which "sergeants and typists" were governing resulted from the uncontrolled pace of change, the main victims were the ordinary people who had greeted freedom with elation and extravagant and unrealistic hopes.

Critical reaction was very mixed. The general feeling about this unconventional film, half documentary and half fiction, was that it was an interesting experiment which failed to gel as a totality. Some critics were indignant at what they saw as a superficial and exploitative treatment of African politics, using the situation as a dramatic backdrop without seriously engaging with these events. Some, on the other hand, felt that the reportage elements and interviews with such leading figures as Mobutu and Kasavubu provide the most interesting scenes. The love interest introduced in the persons of Seberg and Ferzetti seemed to some grafted on and out of place, almost a kind of homage to 1930s Hollywood with an added touch of 60s psychological realism. The reference to Antonioni by one critic may refer in part to Ferzetti's role in *L'Avventura* the previous year. Jean Seberg admitted that she was mystified by this strange cocktail: "I'm not very happy with this film. There was no connection between the very strong documentary side and the love story between me and Gabriele Ferzetti. We could just as well have stayed in Cinecittà." Nevertheless, she praised the skill of the director and spoke appreciatively of Ferzetti.

The film premiered in Rome on March 30, 1962, with screenings in other Italian cities and a limited foreign distribution in the following months. A London premiere did not follow until January 1963, but the Congolese turmoil was then still very topical. The critical reception typically ranged between lukewarm and dismissive. Despite this, Seberg did not regret making it and did not believe it had been dishonorable. In a way, this was a precursor of the later experimental work in which she was happy to engage and which she believed important for the development of cinema.

Can *Congo Vivo* be dismissed as simply a piece of sentimental melodrama awkwardly interspersed with chunks of newsreel? This verdict is arguably fair, and yet the acting, backed by Piccioni's score, is good enough to evoke a haunting, indefinable sense of loss which suggests a little more.

## References

Benayoun, Robert. "Où commence le témoignage?" *Positif*, 49 December 1962, pp. 23- 28.

Cambria, Adele. *La Fiera del cinema*, 11 November 1961, pp. 38–41.

*Cinemundus Export*, 42:12 December 1961. "The company of *Congo Vivo* are back," p. 8.

Durieux, Gilles. [interview] *Cinémonde*, 1470 9 October 1962, p. 21.

*L'Exploitation cinématographique*, 14:304, 20 July 1962, p. 156.

*Le Film illustré*, 34, 15 August 1962. Congo Vivo, pp. 6–8.

Moccagatta, Franco. "Una giornata di fatica per un bacio di mezzo minuto." *Bolero film*, 15:754, pp. 36–7.

Montfort, Jacques. *Ciné télé-revue* 43:14, 4 April 1963, p. 43.

Poppi, Roberto, and M. Pecorari. *Dizionario del cinema italiano. vol. 3: I film 1960–9*. Rome: Gremese, 1992, p. 129.

*La Production italienne 1961*. Unitalia Film, 1961, pp. 92–3.

## Reviews

*Amis du film et de la télévision*, 86 April 1963. P.L., V.M., p. 23.

*Analyse générale des films*, 1963 (*Fiches du cinéma* 277, 6 October 1963), p. 180.

*L'Aurore*, 13 July 1962. Claude Garson, p. 10.

*Bianco e nero*, 4 April 1962. P. Valmarana.

*Le Canard enchaîné*, 18 July 1962. M.D., p. 5.

*Cinema nuovo*, 160 December 1962. Lorenzo Pellizzari, pp. 465–6.

*La Cinématographie française*, 1976, 21 July 1962. Jacques Guillon, p. 14.

*Combat*, 16 July 1962. Henry Chapier, p. 8.

*Corriere della sera*, 14 April 1962. G.Gr., p. 8.

*The Daily Cinema*, 12 November 1962. M.H., p. 10.

*Démocratie*, 19 July 1962. Gérard Devries.

*Le Figaro*, 19 July 1962. Louis Chauvet, p. 12.

*Films and Filming*, 9:4 January 1963. Raymond Durgnat, pp. 50–1.

*France-soir*, 18 July 1962. R.C., p. 6.

*The Glasgow Herald*, 19 August 1963, p. 5.

*Index cinéma*, 1963. J.G., pp. 131–2.

*Intermezzo*, 17:7/8, 30 April 1962, p. 4.

*Il Giornale d'Italia*, 31 March 1962. G.V., p. 3.

*Les Lettres françaises*, 936, 19 July 1962. M.C., p. 8.

*Monthly Film Bulletin*, 29:347 December 1962, p. 170.

*Il Nuovo spettatore cinematografico*, 4:30/31 March/April 1962. Maurizio Liverani, pp. 229–30.

*Paris jour*, 14 July 1962. Maurice Ciantar.

*Paris-presse*, 15 July 1962. Claude Veillot, p. 9.

*Le Soir*, 77:82, 5 April 1963. André Paris, p. 30.

*Télérama*, 29 July 1962. Jean d'Yvoire.

*Variety*, 16 May 1962. Hawk, p. 19.

# *In the French Style* (1963)

"[This] was an important step for me because it was my first film
[in English] in a long time. I was beginning to wonder if I wasn't some
kind of freak who could only act in a foreign language." —Jean Seberg

A Casanna Films Production/Orsay Films production; A Columbia Pictures release
Original release: in English
Also known as: *À la française* [France]; *Plaisir d'amour* [Germany]; *Amore alla francesa* [Italy]; *Al estilo francés* [Spain]
Running Time: 105 minutes
Format: in Black and White

CAST: [* denotes above the title billing] Jean Seberg* (Christina James); Stanley Baker* (Walter Beddoes); Philippe Forquet (Guy); Addison Powell (Mr. James); Jack Hedley (Bill Norton); Maurice Teynac (Baron Édouard de Chaziers); James Leo Herlihy (Dr. John Haislip); Ann Lewis (Stephanie Morell); Jacques Charon (Patrini); Claudine Auger (Clio); Barbara Somers (Madame Piguet); Moustache (Bistro Owner)

PRODUCTION CREDITS: *Director:* Robert Parrish; *Producers:* Irwin Shaw, Robert Parrish; *Screenplay:* Irwin Shaw, from Shaw's two short stories, "In the French Style" and "A Year to Learn the Language"; *Director of Photography:* Michel Kelber; *Cameraman:* Wladimir Ivanov; *Music:* Joseph Kosma; *Music Conductor:* Andre Girard; *Editor:* Renee Lichtig; *Art Director:* Rino Mondellini; *Miss Seberg's Wardrobe:* Philippe Venet; *Makeup:* Michel Deruelle, Phuong Maittret; *Hairstylist:* Jacques Dessange; *Sound:* Jean Monchablon; *Associate Producer:* Claude Ganz; *Director of Production:* Ludmilla Goulian; *Assistant Director:* Michel Wyn; *Assistant Editor:* Françoise London; *Continuity:* Marie-Jose Guissard; *Assistant Art Director:* Jacques Brizzio; *Assistant to the Producer:* Cathy Wyler; *Paintings:* Jane Eakin; *Production Assistant:* Suzanne Wiesenfeld; *Sound Effects Editor:* Denise Baby; *Music Publisher:* Manhattan Music; Extract from Schumann Piano Concerto in A minor

## Synopsis

Nineteen-year-old Christina James leaves her native Chicago for the chance to realize her great ambition, to become a painter. A year in Paris seems the ideal way to prove her talent, yet there are distractions. The youthful Guy singles her out and charms her by his earnestness. The interest of an aristocratic connoisseur raises false hopes. In contrast, Guy's overtures only reveal inexperience in love equal to Christina's own.

At twenty-two Christina is still in Paris, though now one of a circle of socialites and supporting herself by modeling. Her father visits, but he disapproves of her friends and lifestyle. Unconvinced by her work, he urges her to return home. By now she is involved with roving reporter Walter Beddoes. After a holiday on the Côte d'Azur Walter departs on a new assignment, leaving Christina again emotionally bruised and alone in Paris. Eventually she is coaxed out of seclusion by a former boyfriend. Unexpectedly Walter returns, pressing her to renew their relationship and this time offering greater commitment. He is too late, for Christina now knows what she really wants. She introduces Beddoes to her fiancé, an American doctor, with whom she will leave for San Francisco. The reporter finds her proof against all his appeals.

## Reviews

"... one of the best things to come my way this year ... Miss Seberg is something more than excellent. For the first time she is a star."—*Evening Standard*

"*In the French Style* is a delightful cruise along a romantic course. It is bright, gay and sometimes frivolous, yet a deep and moving drama, first-rate in all its facets."—*Daily Mirror*

"It's due to Jean Seberg, delicate and graceful, that the film partially avoids inanity and blandness."—*Paris-presse*

"[Seberg] is progressively more synthetic in the role, as she moves from the plausible stage of student to that of a brooding femme fatale. Her last big scene, in which she ticks off the things of which she has grown tired ... is just too utterly stagy, too romantically agonized."—*New York Times*

"This is a model case of film making. The partnership of Robert Parrish and Irwin Shaw has made a fine job of production, direction and writing ... *In the French Style* deserves to be everyone's style."—*Kinematograph Weekly*

"[Seberg's] performance indicates the judgement of Preminger [who] predicted she would become an important actress. She has arrived. She attains an emotional eloquence that is quite rare. Her performance here is so convincing it makes you share the bruises of her romantic encounters."—*Daily Mail*

"Jean Seberg is marvelous here, vivacious and pretty, demure too, emerging from the most delicate situations fresh and unsullied. Ravishing."—*La Croix*

"For those with preconceived notions of what Jean Seberg is like in motion pictures, *In the French Style* will come as a surprise. This is certainly the finest, the most moving performance the young lady from Iowa has ever given us, as real and truthful as the subject of the film itself."—*Morning Telegraph*

"... the work by Parrish can be seen with enjoyment, thanks above all to the graceful screen presence of Jean Seberg, whose acting has gained much maturity since her debut in *Saint Joan*, and who is completely inside the character she plays...."—*Le Soir*

"[The film] draws life from the personal development its performer experienced since *Breathless* and *Bonjour Tristesse*: we have come full circle in these three phases. You can, if you wish, see in the last scene filmed by Robert Parrish either a rebirth or a point of no return."—*Cahiers du cinéma*

"... the miracle of Jean Seberg's maturing in the right direction is worth observing."—*Films in Review*

"Its major asset, however, is Jean Seberg, whose progression from callow student from the Middle West to cosmopolitan sophisticate is managed with delicacy and judgment. ... she has now flowered into an intelligent actress of unusual charm."—*Glasgow Herald*

## Notes

Director Robert Parrish and writer Irwin Shaw were old friends, and, as Parrish recorded in his memoirs, he needed no persuasion when Shaw suggested they should make a film together. It was to be based on two of Shaw's stories, and it was Seberg's performance in *The Five-Day Lover* which led them to think of her for the role of American art student Christina James. Columbia proved amenable to the idea and willing to provide the finance. As Parrish saw it, it was "practically her own story" and ideal casting, but Jean herself had some initial reservations: would this just be a repetition of her post–Godard roles, and would she risk being typecast as a *Perils-of-Pauline*-type character? On the face of it, this could be *Groundhog Day* or a cameo from Dante's *Inferno*: fresh and innocent young American girl sheds her illusions along (modestly off-camera) with her clothes in the capital of sin, only to return home older and wiser to bake the pumpkin pies. Her doubts are easily imagined, but these were soon allayed after Parrish, armed with the screenplay, flew to Barcelona to convince her that this was a risk worth taking. The next day she told Parrish that she not only "loved" it, but declared she would never speak to either co-producer again if she didn't get the role.

At the end of July 1962 Seberg agreed to help test possible candidates for the male lead. Initially, an agent sent Shaw and Parrish a young, unknown actor named Robert Redford, but Columbia insisted that they cast an established actor. Shaw suggested an

ABC correspondent he knew socially. "He's on the television screen every night, so I know he's a good actor," Shaw reasoned. A screen test was arranged, and as the cameras rolled the correspondent froze, gripped the table as he delivered his lines, and nearly broke Seberg's neck as he bestowed a farewell "pat" on her head. Shaw did not feel the correspondent was bad, but Seberg flatly refused to play opposite him. In the end Shaw and Parrish decided to play safe and sign Stanley Baker for the role, a capable actor with a long list of screen appearances already to his credit.

The budget for *In the French Style* was set at a modest $557,000, despite the studio's willingness to provide three quarters of a million. The odd figure was arrived at by Shaw and Parrish by calculating the cost without the addition of unnecessary luxuries such as limousines and five-star hotels for the cast and crew. In exchange for the small budget the producers were guaranteed full artistic control, with no interference from Columbia, so that they could make the film they wanted. Production values were high despite the restraints, with location shoots on the Riviera (although little is made of these) as well as Paris and studio work at Billancourt. Filming began on August 27.

It was clear that the production would hinge entirely on Seberg's interpretation of Christina, who is present in every scene, but the two men had few doubts. Parrish recalled how: "Reading the screenplay, she found certain features of her own life as an American woman living in Europe ... Jean Seberg is an actress of amazing professional conscientiousness. As soon as she came on set she had several fully prepared interpretations. We understood each other perfectly." He later remembered the production as one of the best he had ever worked on. Prior to the release, Parrish tried to anticipate one possible line of attack: "Making this film in France has been a very great pleasure too. Nevertheless, I'm fearful of the reception from the French public, for I haven't tried to hide the fact that my point of view of Paris and the French is an American one. You can't be objective about this. Americans see Paris in their way, which is perhaps not that of the Parisians."

As so often the case, music gives the viewer some early clues about what is to come. The leisurely pace of the Joseph Kosma jazz theme which accompanies the opening credits points to a narrative which ambles good-naturedly. It knows where it is going, but there will be few moments of high drama and little by way of suspense. Shaw's tale can be seen as a kind of homely moral fable with modest aspirations, avoiding the kind of melodrama which depends on contrived situations, yet offering a good sprinkling of wry humor. In reality, of course, Christina James's story is anything but Seberg's own, but rather as it might have been. Here the heroine takes her voyage of self-discovery just so far, and then decides that she is an old-fashioned girl after all, and one who ultimately prefers a predictable and secure future to one of risk and excitement and potential unhappiness. *In the French Style* follows this learning process with some insight and sensitivity. Philippe Forquet gives a likeable performance as the proud but insecure Guy, desperate to maintain his façade as a man of the world, and this provides an effective foil to Christina's openness and lack of guile. The portrait of the relationship between these two mismatched youngsters is both amusing and touching. The miserable hotel room, complete with picture of Napoleon's retreat from Moscow and a window view of two swaying drunks beneath its beckoning neon, has the stamp of a lived experience.

Unfortunately the casting of Walter Beddoes, a role which called for just the kind of qualities Redford could have supplied, was to prove one of the film's flaws. The brooding intensity of Baker, which brings added weight to many of the "noir" roles he made his specialty, seems discordant in Christina's romantic counterpart. There are indeed moments

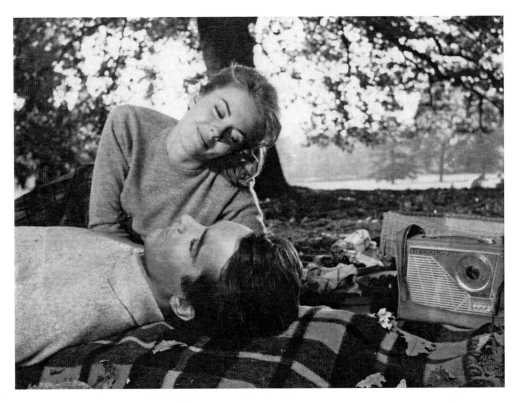

*In the French Style* with Philippe Forquet. It was the last of her American-girl-in-Paris films—
and the first filmed in English (Columbia).

when they seem less like lovers than a long-married couple who have grown slightly weary
of each other. In the important final scene, however, Baker does much to vindicate his
selection. Whereas earlier he seems to lack the charm and panache to sweep any girl off
her feet, qualities Jack Hedley far better suggests, now Baker leaves us in no doubt that
Walter has changed inwardly. The man who had been so assured and clear-headed about
his priorities is suddenly thrown off balance, and Baker ably projects his successive anger,
incredulity and crushing disappointment.

Construction is another problem. The fault line between the two stories is too great
to allow them to be simply bolted together with some voice over philosophizing. That
device is used at the Baron's party, but is not a consistent feature of the episodic but
carefully paced narrative, one which is never presented as a personal diary or reminiscence.
In any case, the gap is just too great and the point of resumption too arbitrary, as if an
impatient reader had skipped the middle of the book. Seberg herself felt in retrospect that
the two halves of the story did not "quite match together, unfortunately, which is why the
film doesn't really work," although conceding that it "had some nice scenes in it."

Viewed alongside the best films of its day, *In the French Style* now looks a little staid
and technically backward-looking. What is does offer beyond a snapshot in time is an
intelligent and unpretentiously thought-provoking screenplay with essentially believable
situations. Critic Bosley Crowther was surely wrong in his dismissal of the final confessional
scene as "stagy," as it could easily have been, for here it is precisely the truth of Seberg's
performance which saves it from being so. Crucially, Parrish and Shaw were proved correct

in their belief that Seberg now had the professional craft to carry their film. It is, without question, her sustained lead performance which raises this above the level of a forgettable B picture, captures and holds the audience's sympathies, and leaves it wondering about Christina's future. There is a real sense that she has progressed emotionally in the course of the story, even if, when it comes to the crunch, she chooses the more conventional path.

Can this be read as a moralistic tale, a case of the prodigal redeemed, having survived the pitfalls of decadence through the influence of a sound upbringing? Shaw and Parrish seem to have sensed this particular pitfall and adroitly avoided it. There is a light touch when Christina's father is introduced to the latter-day Sodom and Gomorrah of Bill's party, and the subsequent clash between father and daughter is balanced and believable. In the final reckoning it is the process of acquiring self-knowledge that matters in this story, and we are free to attach any more general message or none at all, unless it might be Polonius' famous maxim.

This was very much an American variation on the familiar Gallic theme, but the differences were important even if the transatlantic perspective of Parisian life did not please all French critics. This time, too, Seberg was released from her trademark accented French, the novelty of which had by now worn rather thin. These factors did much to acquit her from the charge of perpetually covering the same ground, tied to her real-life persona. The film was in fact considered a hit both financially and critically. It easily recouped its costs after the world premiere in London on the 21 September 1963, and despite Parrish's fears many of the French critics were generous. By consensus, they were impressed by the subtlety with which Seberg had depicted the development of her character in the film, seeing this as evidence of her own progress. Many thought she had never looked better on screen, but the changes, as some noted, went far beyond the new hairstyle: she had visibly matured as an actress, revealing the capacity to dig deeper into her own emotions and bring new insights to her roles.

There was much curiosity about her private life, and London's *Daily Mirror* seized the opportunity for an interview to coincide with the premiere. On September 23 it ran the front page story that "'Joan of Arc' plans to wed French writer." The marriage, she hoped, would be "very soon," though it might have to await the completion of Gary's current book. "I found happiness and love in Paris," she blithely told the reporter. Yet, as if to guard against naïve faith in happy endings, she added a caveat worthy of the pragmatism of Christina James: "My marriage to Romain is not going to be easy. Our lives are rather different. He tries to avoid the spotlight." Four days later the *Evening Standard* also ran a feature on the "three show business refugees" who had "found their freedom" and were now enjoying the film's success. The partnership between Shaw and Parrish had clearly worked well for both of them, and the author felt that at last there was a film version of one of his books which was true to the original: "I've written every word and it's filmed as I wrote it." When asked about the reversal of her own fortunes, Seberg smiled: "I don't want to sound pompous, but I find it very gratifying."

In 1963 a paperback edition of Shaw's screenplay was published, together with the two short stories from which it originated and an interesting account of the film project. It describes two scenes which both Parrish and Shaw liked but reluctantly decided to cut, feeling they would have been detrimental to suspense.

## References

Alpert, Hollis. "The joys of uncertainty." *Saturday Review* 45:51, 29 December 1962, pp. 16–17.
*The Daily Mirror*, 23 September 1963. "'Joan of Arc' plans to wed French writer," p. 1.

Deglin, Paul. *Ciné revue*, 44:11, 12 March 1964, pp. 18–9.

*L'Exploitation cinématographique*, 16:341, 5 April 1964, p. 79.

*Filmfacts*, 6:34, 26 September 1963, pp. 193–4.

Fougères, Roland. *Ciné revue*, 44:7, 13 February 1964, pp. 22–5.

Garrett, Gerard, and Maureen Cleave. "Mr. Shaw finds freedom." *The Evening Standard*, 27 September 1963, p. 8.

*Motion Picture Guide, 1927–83*, pp. 1374–5.

Parrish, Robert. *Hollywood doesn't live here any more*. Boston: Little, Brown, 1988, pp. 122–32.

Philippe, Claude-Jean. [interview with Parrish] *Télérama*, 715, 29 September 1963, pp. 62–3.

Shaw, Irwin. *In the French style*. New York: Macfadden, 1963 [screenplay and original stories].

_____. *Tip on a Dead Jockey, and other stories*. New York: Random House, 1957.

*Star ciné-roman*, 196 May 1965, pp. 11–65.

## Reviews

*America*, 109, 5 October 1963, p. 399.

*Amis du film et de la télévision*, 96 April 1964. J.Le., p. 22.

*Arts*, 956, 1 April 1964. Jean-Louis Bory, p. 7.

*Aux écoutes*, 3 April 1964. V. Volmane.

*Cahiers du cinéma*, 26:155 May 1964. M.M., p. 56.

*Le Canard enchaîné*, 1 April 1964. M.D., p. 5.

*Cinéma*, 86, May 1964. Y.B., p. 129.

*Cinema nuovo*, 13:170. U.F., pp. 282–3.

*La Cinématographie française Index*, 65. Ph. A., pp. 8–9.

*Combat*, 27 March 1964. Henry Chapier, p. 10.

*Commonweal*, 79:2, 4 October 1963. Philip T. Hartung, p. 46.

*La Croix*, 11 April 1964. H.R..

*The Daily Cinema*, 25 September 1963. M.H., p. 8.

*The Daily Mail*, 25 September 1963. Cecil Wilson, p. 3.

*The Daily Telegraph*, 27 September 1963. Patrick Gibbs, p. 13.

*The Evening News*, 26 September 1963. Felix Barker, p. 12.

*The Evening Standard*, 26 September 1963. Alexander Walker, p. 12.

*Le Figaro*, 31 March 1964. Louis Chauvet, p. 14.

*The Film Daily*, 17 September 1963. Mandel Herbstman, p. 7.

*Le Film français*, 21:1036, 3 April 1964. Y., p. 13.

*Film Quarterly*, 17:4 Summer 1964. Syney Field, pp. 48–51.

*Filmkritik*, December 1963. Dieter Kuhlbrodt, p. 585.

*Films and Filming*, 10:2 November 1963. Raymond Durgnat, p. 24.

*Films in Review*, 14:8 October 1963. Ellen Fitzpatrick, pp. 495–6.

*The Financial Times*, 27 September 1963. Penelope Houston, p. 28.

*France observateur*, 15:726, 2 April 1964.R.T., p. 19.

*The Glasgow Herald*, 20 January 1964. Molly Plowright, p. 11.

*The Guardian*, 27 September 1963. Ian Wright, p. 11.

*The Hollywood Reporter*, 17 September 1963. James Powers, p. 3.

*L'Humanité*, 1 April 1964. Samuel Lachize, p. 6.

*Image et son*, 180–1 Jan/Feb 1965, *Saison cinématographique* 1964. René Tabès, p. 11.

*Kinematograph Weekly*, 2921, 26 September 1963, p. 7.

*Les Lettres françaises*, 1023, 2 April 1964. Marcel Martin, p. 7.

*Libération*, 1 April 1964. Henry Magnan.

*Le Monde*, 31 March 1964. Jean de Baroncelli, p. 9.

*Monthly Film Bulletin*, 30:358 November 1963. E.S., p. 155.

*The Morning Telegraph*, 19 September 1963. Leo Mishkin, pp. 2, 9.

*Motion Picture Daily*, 18 September 1963. Charles S. Aaronson, p. 4.

*The New Statesman*, 66, 27 September 1963, p. 419.

*The New York Herald Tribune*, 19 September 1963. Judith Crist, p. 11.

*The New York Times*, 19 September 1963. Bosley Crowther, p. 23.

*The New Yorker*, 39:32, 28 September 1963. Brendan Gill, p. 106.

*Newsweek*, 62:18, 23 September 1963, pp. 101–2.

*Les Nouvelles littéraires*, 1910, 9 April 1964. G. Charensol, p. 10.
*Paris-presse*, 28 March 1964. Michel Aubriant, p. 13.
*Photoplay*, 64 September 1963, p. 13.
*Positif*, 1964–5, Rentrée 1964. Bertrand Tavernier, pp. 134–6.
*Saturday Review*, 46:39, 28 September 1963. Hollis Alpert, p. 44.
*Le Soir*, 78:63, 13 March 1964. Olivier Delville, p. 30.
*The Spectator*, 211, 4 October 1963, p. 415.
*The Sunday Express*, 29 September 1963. Thomas Wiseman, p. 23.
*Télérama*, 743, 12 April 1964. C.-J. Philippe, p. 65.
*Time*, 82:15, 11 October 1963, p.NY20.
*The Times*, 26 September 1963, p. 8.
*Variety*, 18 September 1963. Whit., pp. 6, 17.

# *The Big Swindler* (*Le Grand Escroc*) (1963)

"You have to let people live their lives and not look at them too long.
Otherwise you end up not understanding anything at all."—Jean-Luc Godard

Ulysse Productions (Pierre Roustang)—Paris, Primex Films—Marseille, Lux—CCF—
Paris, Vides Cinematografica—Rome, Toho-Towa—Tokyo, Caesar Film Produktie—
Amsterdam
Original release: in French and English
Also known as: *Beautiful Swindlers*; *Il Profeta falsario* [Italy]
Running Time: 20 minutes
Format: in black & white; Franscope

CAST: Jean Seberg (Patricia Leacock); Charles Denner (The Swindler); Laszlo Szabo
(Police Inspector); Jean-Luc Godard (Narrator and Man with Camera)
PRODUCTION CREDITS: *Director:* Jean-Luc Godard; *Producer:* Pierre Roustang;
*Screenplay:* Jean-Luc Godard; *Director of Photography:* Raoul Coutard; *Photography:* Claude
Beausoleil, Georges Liron; *Editors:* Agnès Guillemot, Lila Lakshmanan; *Music:* Michel
Legrand; *Sound:* André Hervé; *Production Management:* Philippe Dussart, Philippe Senné;
*Assistant Director:* Charles Bitsch; *Makeup:* Jackie Reynal; *Mixing:* Antoine Bonfanti

## Synopsis

American TV reporter Patricia Leacock is in Morocco for a *Reader's Digest* assignment.
She films a man distributing money in the medina and buys a djellaba from a trader. A
policeman interrogates her, suspecting she has paid with counterfeit notes. She explains
her project, *The Most Extraordinary Man I Ever Met*, is to make "cinéma vérité."

Disguised in her djellaba, Patricia follows the mysterious philanthropist and questions
him, receiving only enigmatic answers. Perhaps she too, in filming him, is stealing something
to give to others. She tells the police inspector of this inconclusive meeting, defending the
man as a sick and pitiful specimen. Her camera is turned on the viewer in the final frame.

## Notes

Just as he carried over the character of Seberg's Cécile in *Bonjour Tristesse* to *À bout
de souffle*, Godard returned to the character of Patricia Franchini, as realized by Seberg in
*Breathless*, in this short film. He imagines her to have evolved, four years on, into a roving
reporter and documentary film maker. As so often elsewhere, he plays on names and
identities: thus Patricia is here surnamed Leacock, a clear reference to the early exponent

of cinéma vérité Richard Leacock. His point here is not merely playful, for Patricia's character is a good illustration of Godard's simultaneous double role of critic and cineaste. The scathing entry on Leacock (contrast his view of Rouch*) which he contributed to a survey of American directors for *Cahiers du cinéma* later this year makes his point more directly. It is not enough, he argues, to attempt to capture reality simply by pointing a camera. However honest your intentions, you cannot be truly objective if you film indiscriminately, with neither understanding nor viewpoint. Anticipating the well-known dictum from *La Chinoise*, he points out that it is "useless to have clarity of image if the intentions are hazy." Godard's fascination with the no-man's-land between fiction and documentary comes very much into play in this short exercise piece. Patricia's/Seberg's mention of "Romain" (Seberg's second husband Romain Gary) signals that the borderline between actors and characters is deliberately blurred here. The jokes are characteristic of Godard, but the play on identities takes on a special meaning in the context of the literary source.

*Le Grand Escroc* is in part Godard's deference to the final great work of the author of *Moby-Dick*, whom a friend and fellow director had honored much earlier by adopting his name. *The Confidence-Man: his masquerade* is an extraordinary and challenging book which encompasses a disturbing universality within its apparently narrow focus. Its action, or more precisely talk, takes place on the river boat *Fidèle* in an era when "Mississippi operators" could find reasonable pickings among gullible fellow travelers. Setting out from St. Paul's definition of charity (I. Corinthians, 13), Melville explores the spectrum of trust and motivation and convinces us that our perceptions are indeed often received "through a glass, darkly." His characters are shrouded in mystery, often impossible to distinguish one from another, often studious to appear what they certainly are not, while his readers are compelled to question their own preconceptions about any essential identity at all.

Godard embarked on these deceptively deep waters as part of a compilation by five different directors under the title *Les Plus belles escroqueries du monde*, intended as an entertaining international look at different kinds of tricksters and crooks. The other contributions were Roman Polanski's *Amsterdam*, Ugo Gregoretti's *Naples*, Hiromichi Horikawa's *Tokyo* and Claude Chabrol's *Paris*. As cameraman Coutard noted, such collections of short films had become popular in the early 60s, and producer Roustang had involved Truffaut in a similar project, *Love at Twenty* (*L'Amour à vingt ans*, 1962). Godard had argued about the format of the film, which did not accord with his own doctrine. He had wanted to shoot in Marrakech primarily because his wife Anna Karina was there for a different production, but by the time the location had been agreed with all the collaborators her work was done, and he set out for Morocco in a thoroughly bad humor. Godard's sketch, he claimed, was based on a real story which Chaplin had considered using, of a man in Israel who had forged currency to give to beggars. This intrigued him as a particularly "fine" swindle in that it was apparently altruistic. This must have seemed to mesh quite well with the themes of philanthropy and moral ambivalence in Melville's novel.

Patricia, incessantly filming all that she observes, is Godard's satirical take on cinema as neutral reportage at this stage in his intellectual odyssey. She has no clear purpose other than to capture the "truth," naively supposing that appearances will yield that up spontaneously, whereas the book we see her reading tells her precisely the opposite. The later dialogues strike us as strange and disconnected, that is until we realize that they are largely composed of direct quotes from various parts of Melville's book. Thus the swindler's reference to amnesia caused by a head injury (chapter 4), his scheme of a global charity and the reference to early radical François Fourier (chapter 7) and Patricia's final exchange with

**The little-seen sequel to** *Breathless*: **the short** *Le Grand Escroc* **directed by Jean-Luc Godard (CCF).**

the inspector [chapter 41], ending in the famous quotation from Shakespeare's *As You Like It* [II, vii 140-], cannot fully make sense without reference to their original source. Nevertheless, the central point about the nature of reality is clear enough. As the director put it:

"The final moral is that Seberg continues to film, without quite knowing exactly why, but you have to carry on ... that's my personal moral. Maybe it's a difficult film to understand because it's purely didactic ... the distributors were very disappointed: they expected chases in Marrakech or that sort of thing, so they wanted to see the guy who made the banknotes.... It's not even that they didn't like it: the film really passed them by ... I don't know."

Godard's short was filmed in Marrakech over three days in mid–January 1963. After the compendium was premiered in Paris on August 14, 1964 the distributors decided to excise it. The reasons given were variously that it was "too philosophical" or that it would have made the total length excessive (hardly convincing, considering its 20 minute running time). It finally surfaced in Paris as an appendage to a screening of King Vidor's *Our Daily Bread*, at the *Studio Étoile* in September 1965, following on from a revival of *Breathless*. According to Lesage it was shown as a separate work at the London Film Festival on November 24, 1967 as well, though not officially scheduled, and it has since appeared at various Godard retrospectives.

The other four films under the title *The Beautiful Swindlers* received their first showing in the United States in 1967, with bookings at New York's Apollo Theater and Chicago's Monroe Theater. *Variety* was dismissive of the anthology: "For film buffs it has the dubious merit of displaying the worst work of noted directors Roman Polanski and Claude Chabrol." It called Polanski's work "shapeless," Chabrol's "silly," referred to Gregoretti's "drab visuals and ambling pace," and summed up Horikawa's contribution with "it takes a real directorial master to come up with something worse ... desperate humor [and] truly laughable serious moments."

In his book *Jean-Luc Godard*, author John Kreidl remarked: "The clearest intellectually self-defining film Godard ever made is *Le Grand Escroc*, which he calls didactic, and I would call highly poetic in its rhetoric as well. Since no one ever sees this film, the lack of its visibility hurts our clear understanding of Godard. As a presentation of Godard's methodology, *Le Grand Escroc* is a fully successful film. In the film, method and sentiment perfectly fuse. In all his other films, they are at loggerheads."

Another cri de cœur was heard from a critic in *Cinéma* in February 1964: "The distributors wanted to cut this last part because the entire film lasts 150 minutes [sic] and the Godard sketch seemed too philosophical to them. But the public can stand philosophy better than the distributors. Some decency, gentlemen, devil take it! ... stop swindling us and give us *Le Grand Escroc*."

In a Godard special published by *Cahiers du cinéma*, J.M. wrote: "Despite the light of Marrakech, the beauty of Coutard's images, the charm of Jean Seberg, *Le Grand Escroc* does not display great originality, and its main virtue is its subject matter."

It is hard to see why this interesting but frequently misunderstood short has still not been issued on DVD. A brief clip from *Le Grand Escroc* has, of course, long been accessible. This is the final exchange between Patricia and the inspector, which is viewed by Belmondo towards the end of Godard's *Pierrot le Fou* (1965).

*Jean Rouch, ethnographer and filmmaker who worked especially in West Africa. The documentary style of work such as the 1959 *Moi, un noir* were much admired by French critics, not least by Godard, who had heaped praise on Rouch in contributions to the weekly *Arts* and to *Cahiers du cinéma*.

## References

(see also *À bout de souffle*)

*L'Avant-scène du cinéma*, 46. March 1965, pp. 35–41 [screenplay].

Baecque, Antoine de. *Godard: biographie*. Paris: Grasset, 2010, pp. 223–4.

Brody, Richard. *Everything is cinema: the working life of Jean-Luc Godard*. New York: Henry Holt, 2008, pp. 154–5.

*Cahiers du cinéma*, 437 (Godard Supplement) November 1990. J.M., p. 115.

*Cinéma*, 83 February 1964, p. 14.

Coutard, Raoul. L'Impérial de Van Su. Paris: Ramsay, 2007, pp. 133–4.

*Le Film français*, 989–90 "Spécial Cannes, 1963," p. 55; 28 August 1964, p. 15.

*Filmfacts*, 11:24, 15 January 1969 "The Beautiful Swindlers," pp. 530–1.

Godard, Jean-Luc. "Le Grand Escroc." *Cinéma*, 94 (Godard Dossier) March 1965, p. 54.

_____. "Richard Leacock." *Cahiers du cinéma* 150–1 December 1963–January 1964 [reprinted in Bergala, A. *Jean-Luc Godard par Jean-Luc Godard*, pp. 250–1, translated: *Godard on Godard* pp. 202–3].

*Image et son* (Saison 1964) 180–1 January/February 1965. Raymond Lefèvre, p. 214.

*Intermezzo*, 19:18–19, 15 October 1964. "Le più belle truffe del mondo," p. 6.

Kreidl, John. *Jean-Luc Godard*. Boston: Twayne, 1980, p. 222.

Lesage, Julie. *Jean-Luc Godard: a guide to references and resources*. Boston: G.K. Hall, 1979, pp. 52–4.

Melville, Herman. *The Confidence-Man: his masquerade*. New York: Dix, Edwards, 1857, translated by Henri Thomas: *Le Grand Escroc*. Paris: Éditions de Minuit, 1950.

Morandini, Morando. "Les Plus Belles escroqueries du monde." *Bianco e nero*, 26:2 February 1965, pp. 76–8.

*Le Nouvel observateur*, 43, 8 September 1965, p. 31.

*Variety*, 1 November 1967. Beau., p. 7.

# Part II
## *The International Years, 1963–1969*

These were Seberg's zenith years, a period in which she alternated several American and French productions. She could shuttle between Europe and the U.S., going from one production to the next, enjoying what was perhaps a unique position at the time. Her international stature attracted European film makers not least because it could give them access to distribution in the U.S. and beyond. Conversely, her name would be sure to add interest to American productions outside the domestic market, regardless of the standing of her co-stars.

Perhaps the most distinctive film from this era is the drama *Lilith* by Robert Rossen. It became one of her favorites, and her widely praised performance still stands as one of which she could feel justly proud. "There were moments during the filming that I'd compare in a way to improvisational jazz," Seberg later recalled of this production. "It was as if we were moving around one another, and communicating and withdrawing. Rossen was very impressed by Godard. He pumped my brain constantly about how Godard used the camera."

It was her work on *In the French Style* which tipped the balance and won her the coveted title role in *Lilith*. This complex and demanding role was in its turn to earn her a Golden Globe nomination as "Best Actress in a Leading Role Drama" by the Hollywood Foreign Press Association.

Another American drama, though perhaps at the opposite end of the entertainment spectrum, was *Moment to Moment*. Here a contrived storyline is seductively decked out in glorious Technicolor, with a lush musical score, chic costumery and glamorous locations. It appears to have been the film's particular appeal to female audiences which brought it the success, albeit modest, that had eluded *Lilith*. Although partially filmed on the Côte d'Azur, most of *Moment to Moment* was shot in Los Angeles, where the news media made much of her heralded return to Hollywood. Five years had passed since she last set foot on a Hollywood sound stage, yet somehow in the intervening years she had achieved her ambition of becoming an actress of international standing.

Despite success in reclaiming her home ground, she continued to explore new avenues in the film industry of her adopted country, which still seemed to find good use for the fluent French and intriguing accent she added to a special kind of refined beauty and intelligence. There was *Backfire*, which reunited her with *Breathless* star Jean-Paul Belmondo for the part of a German photographer, and an underrated comedy *Diamonds are Brittle*, in which she played an alluring jewel thief. She also made two commercial films with New Wave exponent Claude Chabrol, the French Resistance drama *The Line of Demarcation* and the frivolously escapist *The Road to Corinth*.

Supporting roles in American products like *A Fine Madness* and *Pendulum* maintained her presence in the U.S. market, but without offering her the chance to prove herself capable of more. A leading role in the U.S. musical *Paint Your Wagon* did, though, bring her to the forefront, for this was seen by more people around the world than all of the other films Seberg made in this period.

One of the most talked about but rarely seen of her films is *Birds in Peru*, directed by her husband Romain Gary. At the time of its release its subject matter was found offensive by many, while others seemed disappointed to discover it was a serious experiment in film making rather than a piece of erotica. It is regrettable that critics and audiences have had few opportunities to revise the predominantly hostile first reactions.

Seberg also participated in the documentary *The Girls*, which also featured Joseph Janni, Susannah York and Jane Fonda. This film made by John Crome, though a revealing document of its time, has never had a public showing, and until recently was considered lost.

# *Lilith* (1964)

"Logically, I would not have progressed from
*The Mouse That Roared* to *Lilith*."—Jean Seberg

A Centaur Film; A Columbia Pictures release
Original release: in English
Also known as: *Lilith—la dea dell'amore* [Italy]
Running Time: 113 minutes
Format: in Black and White

CAST: [* denotes above the title billing] Warren Beatty* (Vincent Bruce); Jean Seberg* (Lilith Arthur); Peter Fonda (Stephen Evshevsky); Kim Hunter (Bea Brice); Anne Meacham (Mrs. Yvonne Meaghan); Jessica Walter (Laura); Gene Hackman (Norman); James Patterson (Dr. Lavrier); Robert Reilly (Bob Clayfield); Rene Auberjenois (Howie); Lucy Smith (Vincent's grandmother); Maurice Brenner (Mr. Gordon); Jeanne Barr (Miss Glassman); Richard Higgs (Mr. Palakis); Elizabeth Bader (Girl at bar); Robert and Jason Jolivette (elder and younger watermelon boys); Alice Spivak (lonely girl); Walter Arnold, Kathleen Phelan (lonely girl's parents); Cecilia Ray (Lilith's mother); Gunnar Peters (chauffeur); L. Jerome Offutt (tournament judge); W. Jerome Offutt (tournament announcer); Jeno Mate (Assistant to Dr. Lavrier); Ben Carruthers (dancer); Dina Paisner (psychodrama moderator); Pawnee Sills (receptionist);

PRODUCTION CREDITS: *Director and Producer:* Robert Rossen; *Screenplay:* Robert Rossen, based on the novel by J.R. Salamanca; *Director of Photography:* Eugen Shuftan; *Editor:* Aram Avakian; *Associate Editors:* Hugh A. Robertson, Robert Q. Lovett; *Production Designer:* Richard Sylbert; *Set Decorator:* Gene Callahan; *Costumes:* Ruth Morley; *Production Manager:* Jim Di Gangi; *Assistant Directors:* Larry Sturhahn, Bob Vietro; *2nd Assistant Director:* Allan Dennis; *Sound:* James Shields, Richard Vorisek; *Sound Editor:* Edward Beyer; *Assistant Editors:* Barry Malkin, Lynn Ratener; *Music:* Kenyon Hopkins; *Makeup:* Irving Buchman, Bill Herman, Bob Jiras; *Hair:* Frederic Jones; *Still Photographer:* Josh Weiner; *Titles:* Elinor Bunin; Camera Operator: Joe Coffey; *Assistant to the Producer:* Eleanor Wolquitt; *Optical Effects:* Film Opticals, Inc.; *Assistant Cameramen:* Bert Siegel, Tibor Sands; *Script Supervisor:* Dorothy Weshner Kanzer; *Wardrobe man:* George Newman; *Wardrobe woman:* Flo Transfield; Puppets by "the Zoo"; *additional music:* J.S. Bach. Concerto for two violins in d BWV 1043

## Synopsis

Vincent, returning from harrowing wartime service, seeks a worthy calling. He believes Poplar Lodge, a residential clinic for mental patients, can offer this, and he joins the staff for a trial period. Gaining the confidence of colleagues by his sensitivity, he is particularly entrusted with two young patients, Lilith and Stephen. Lilith is creative, inhabiting an imaginary world with its own language, yet seemingly with a firm grip on reality. Stephen, a withdrawn intellectual, is fascinated by Lilith and turns to Vincent as a go-between. As Vincent learns from Dr. Lavrier about the nature of mental illness he becomes increasingly committed to helping these patients. He believes he is making progress with Lilith despite Lavrier's pessimistic diagnosis, unconscious of his growing personal involvement.

An excursion culminates in Lilith and Vincent becoming lovers. She tests the power she has newly won over him by provoking his jealousy. His visit to local former girlfriend Laura, now unhappily married, only adds to Vincent's confusion and despair. Lilith's mental state worsens, with resurgent memories of childhood trauma. Stephen entrusts a box he has made for her to Vincent, who leads him to believe she has rejected it. Even the subsequent news of Stephen's suicide leaves him unmoved. The crisis in Lilith's condition coincides with Vincent's own psychological collapse.

## Reviews

"... one of the most hauntingly beautiful films this country has produced in recent years.... The film's major miracle is Jean Seberg.... A ripened, maturing actress of great personal magnetism ... [she] is exciting. As a witch who still sucks her thumb, she blossoms like a yellow-rayed sunflower in a black-and-white thorn patch...."—*Cosmopolitan*

"The success or failure of any film which tries to push mental illness into some metaphorical or allegorical meaning depends upon the tact of the screenwriter and the director. In both capacities, Rossen has been blunt where he should have been subtle, and timid where a truly subtle man might have dared to be blunt."—*Newsweek*

"Rossen delivers in extremis, with *Lilith*, his incontestable masterpiece.... *Lilith* is, with *Vertigo*, the most complete realization in cinematographic form of the indefinable, the inaccessible, which the conjoined power of beauty and of illusion shape into a sumptuous and fateful mirage."—*Cahiers du cinéma*

"The less said about *Lilith*, the better."—*New Yorker*

"Beatty ... is sorely miscast here. It isn't he who dominates the picture; it is actress Jean Seberg. Because Miss Seberg's performance is brilliant and Beatty's is lackluster, the whole film seems out of kilter. The film often seems to drag under the weight of its intentions."—*Chicago Sun-Times*

"What lifts this curious film out of the ordinary—and makes it worth a trip to the theater—is the lilting performance of Jean Seberg as Lilith.... Every nuance of her delicate interpretation—anger, love, laughter, bewilderment, pride, passion—is convincing. This is a revelation."—*Life*

"Jean Seberg, whose acting improves with every picture, gives Lilith a mad, haunting beauty and plays the role with great conviction."—*Commonweal*

"... despite the impossible role ... [Seberg] is interesting to watch. I doubt if anyone has ever embodied incest, lesbianism, and nymphomania so attractively—and so speciously." —*Films in Review*

*Notes*

Robert Rossen followed up his Oscar-winning film *The Hustler* with this screen adaptation of J.R. Salamanca's best-selling novel. Yvette Mimieux, Sarah Miles, Diane Cilento and Samantha Eggar were among a number of actresses considered for the title role. Columbia had been pleased with Seberg's work for *In the French Style* and wanted to retain her on its shrinking list of established stars. For these reasons, the studio wanted her name on the short list. After Warren Beatty had been signed for the male lead, he and Rossen met with Seberg to discuss the film. Rossen and Beatty both felt she was right for this challenging role. She quickly established a rapport with the director, and they discussed her role and the project in detail. "I wanted so badly to make an honest film," she later said. "All those movies in which the insane scream and yell and make wild faces—they're so ignoble and false. That's not madness at all. Madness is like a camera that goes in and out of focus—now sharp, now fuzzy. That's what hurts so much and makes for fascination. Here were all these lost, brilliant, sensitive, kind people, and suddenly they'd just go out of focus. There was this irrational violence just below the surface, and it was frightening—the way a high-strung horse is frightening when you know he can't control himself."

Seberg recalled feeling initially intimidated by co-star Beatty: "Not intimidated, really ... but he talked a different language than I did in his work." In mid-April 1963 Rossen and his two leading actors visited Maryland to scout the locations suitable for the shoot. Filming began on May 6 on the banks of the Chesapeake and Ohio Canal, moving between Maryland and Virginia and including the inauguration of the new studio facilities at Roosevelt Field, Long Island on June 24. Alarmed by rumors that she was to appear semi-naked in a love scene, Seberg assured a *Time* reporter that the stories were untrue. This was Beatty's fourth film, and here he was center stage throughout, yet he seemed fearful that Seberg or Peter Fonda might dominate the picture. His friendly relationship with the director quickly degenerated when he began to challenge Rossen's judgment, and he would later describe the shoot as "a very bad experience" and the film as "completely disorganized." Some of the clashes which made the shoot trying for both Beatty and Rossen seem to have arisen from the interpretation of Vincent's character. Rossen felt that Vincent's progression from "normality" into psychosis was unconvincing because Beatty's acting implied psychosis from the start. Rossen, who was suffering from terminal cancer, allegedly told friends that when he died it would be because working with Beatty had killed him.

In his long and wide-ranging career as screenwriter, director and producer, Rossen had never tried to stay within cinema's comfort zone, usually preferring difficult and challenging themes and focusing on troubled characters engaged in personal struggle of some kind. While a social critique is often implicit, it is the individual psychology of his characters which seems to interest him most, as in *All the King's Men*. These often appear to be searching for meaning and self knowledge through the medium of achievement, whether success takes the form of power or wealth or involves some self-imposed trial. From this point of view, *Lilith*, his last completed film, may be seen as less anomalous than it might at first appear. However remote Vincent Bruce may be from the pugnacious Willie Stark, *The Hustler's* Eddie Felson or from boxer Charley Davis in *Body and Soul*, *Lilith* too is about self-discovery. Like Stark, Vincent sets out with idealistic intentions but progressively betrays the trust reposed in him, bringing about the destruction of others and his own downfall.

Rossen showed his customary skill in adapting Salamanca's disquieting novel for the requirements of cinema. Although his approach required fidelity to the spirit rather than the letter, the quality and intelligence of the original writing persuaded him to use the original words in many scenes. No enthusiast for studio conditions, he also preferred authentic Maryland locations for much of the shoot. The house "Killingworth" in Locust Valley, Long Island served admirably for the Lodge. He omitted Salamanca's chapters on Vincent's earlier life for obvious reasons, leaving us clues to deduce the scars his mother's death and wartime experience have left on him.

It is Vincent's unconscious quest for self-healing through helping others which takes him to Poplar Lodge, and this soon focuses on two patients: Stephen and Lilith. The ease with which he gains Stephen's trust gives him confidence, but he soon begins to deceive himself about the nature of his interest in Lilith. In *The Hustler*, *All the King's Men* and *Alexander the Great* Rossen had reminded us of the human cost incurred where ambitions run out of control. *Lilith* pushes the lesson one step further, to a point of mental disintegration. Guilt feelings over the death of her brother have led Lilith to identify with her biblical namesake, an evil spirit with the need to "leave the mark of her desire on every living creature." Since she cannot, like Caesar, "do it with a sword," her weapon is sexual seduction. Vincent is drawn into the glittering web of her fantasy world until he is no longer able to separate the roles of patient and healer and becomes, in Lavrier's words, "dispossessed" by the "rapture" with which she has infected him. After her first unsuccessful attempt to seduce him, Vincent seems already to acknowledge her dominance: "I wish you would help me to do this one thing well. Honorably." When she does succeed, after the tournament, her power is total, and she taunts him and plays on his jealousy, knowing he must now lie to his colleagues and do whatever she demands. The extent of her schizophrenic delusions is finally matched by Vincent's own breakdown, after jealousy drives him to an act which precipitates Stephen's suicide. Again, the healer seeks help from the patient, as he begs: "Just say I did the right thing.... Say you wanted me to do it." Only at the end does Vincent recognize his transition from therapist to patient, which has now become complete.

The film's narrative technique is deliberately disjointed and elliptical at times, seeming to subvert conventional views of reality and normality. "What's so wonderful about reality?" one patient asks, and indeed all our assumptions are brought into question in the paradoxical caged world of Poplar Lodge. The patients are described by Dr. Lavrier as "destroyed ... by their own excellence ... heroes of the universe, its finest product and its noblest casualty," and yet Bea warns Vincent that his work will be "dirty, degrading— sometimes dangerous." The sickness which afflicts these "superior minds" is identical to that which causes spiders to spin out "fantastic, asymmetrical and rather nightmarish designs." Whereas the Lodge, with its romantic setting, seems to captivate Vincent like some kind of lost domain, the outside world of Stonemount and its inhabitants is made to appear banal and mean. The Barnsville Fair seems jarring, noisy and crass, but the tournament allows Lilith and Vincent to escape into a private medieval fantasy: "another time and place. Knights and lances," conducive to Lilith's magic. Vincent's visit to Laura's home reveals the depth of his alienation from the world of the "sane." He has by now effectively joined Lilith and the others on the inside of the web-like wire meshed windows, looking out. Yet Rossen is careful to avoid romanticizing mental illness and maintains a distance from the protagonists, even frequently positioning the camera as if we should not identify with them too closely.

**With Warren Beatty in *Lilith*. This was his fourth film, her twelfth (Columbia).**

Much could be said about the structure of the film and the echoed motifs used to tie together its diverse verbal and visual elements (water, reflected light, hands, the "crooked look" of asymmetry, and, of course, death among them), and Arthur Nolletti is one of those who have explored at length the symbolism and technique of Rossen's final work. Overall, what is striking is the artistic unity which the director achieved. Much is owed to the exceptionally fine and responsive photography and the mastery of its editing. Eugen Shuftan and his team create a whole gallery of images which contribute to the film's atmosphere of heightened reality and remain long in the mind. Composer Kenyon Hopkins had also written the score for Rossen's film *The Hustler*. Here the flute theme for Lilith conveys a childlike, almost saccharine innocence, but Hopkins mutates it in sudden transitions through strident and sophisticated jazz and lyrical orchestration, cleverly matching the shifting moods and visual imagery.

The casting of *Lilith* showed good judgment, with the arguable exception (in Rossen's own view) of Warren Beatty. The verdict on Beatty's performance ultimately depends on our reading of Salamanca's hero. His body language and delivery did not fit with the director's interpretation, and it is easy to see why. Peter Fonda gives a well-judged performance as the scholarly introvert Stephen, Anne Meacham seems ideal as the brittle aristocratic Yvonne and Gene Hackman, in this small early role, makes us wince with magisterial ease. Kim Hunter, Jessica Walter and James Patterson are also commendable. Kim Hunter had already received an Academy Award for her role in *A Streetcar Named Desire*. Beatty, Hackman and Dukakis, who plays a small non-speaking role as a patient, would all go on to win Oscars.

The term "rapture," with its multiple associations, reflects something of the challenge of the title role. Lilith is stricken, yet she is also the sorceress who binds Stephen and

Vincent. She is both victim and predator, a prisoner with delusions of divine powers. Seberg has an uncanny instinct for projecting this ambivalence, shifting convincingly from a knowing, amused superiority or calculating malevolence to childlike exuberance or sullen defiance. *Glamour* magazine confidently predicted that Seberg would get an Oscar nomination for *Lilith*. In the event, neither she nor anyone else was nominated for work on this remarkable and grossly underrated film.

In *Lilith*, 1964 (Columbia).

*Lilith* was in general poorly received in America. Although chosen to represent the U.S. at the 1964 Venice Film Festival, it was withdrawn as a result of highly critical comments made by the Festival's director Luigi Chiarini. Rossen had responded by describing Chiarini as tyrannical and called for his dismissal. Despite this, the prestigious *Cahiers du cinéma* selected it as sixth in its list of best films of the year, and one of its leading critics described it as an "incontestable masterpiece." In reviewing an edition of Rossen's screenplays, *Films in Review* noted in 1973 how "*Lilith*, which was either ignored or maligned by American critics at the time of its original release, now seems like one of the most important films of the Sixties in terms of both theme and technique."

Even if many critics completely failed to understand Rossen's intentions in this somber, multi-layered work, there were few who did not acknowledge the subtle and luminous performance of Seberg as its enigmatic central female figure. There were those who compared *Lilith* unfavorably with another film which dealt with mental illness, *David and Lisa* (1963, Frank Perry), failing to see that Rossen's treatment was both less guilty of stereotyping and creatively superior. Seberg was to look back on it as a kind of answer to those who persisted in doubting her credentials as a serious actress. In 1974 she told Susan d'Arcy, "I still think *Lilith* is the best work I've ever done. Rossen was a man who knew and felt my insecurities and helped me with them. I think that's why a kind of liberty came across that I haven't had in many other films."

## References

Appel, Kira. "On tourne au Maryland: les amours démentes de Warren Beatty et de Jean Seberg." *Cinémonde*, 31:1506, 18 June 1963, pp. 22–3.

Beatty, Warren. "Anything but passive, interview with Gordon Gow." *Films and Filming*, 21:11, August 1975, p. 10.

Broeske, Pat H. *Magill's survey of cinema: English language films*. Englewood Cliffs, NJ: Salem Press, 1981, second series, vol. 3, pp. 1377–81.

Casty, Alan. "The films of Robert Rossen." *Film Quarterly*, 20:2, Winter 1966–7, pp. 3–12.

\_\_\_\_\_. *The films of Robert Rossen*. New York: The Museum of Modern Art, 1969, pp. 46–54, etc.

\_\_\_\_\_. *Robert Rossen, 1908–1966*. Paris: Anthologie du Cinéma, 1967, pp. 430–6.

Cohen, Saul B. "Robert Rossen and the filming of 'Lilith.'" *Film Comment*, 3:2, Spring 1965, pp. 3–7.

Combs, Richard. "The beginner's Rossen." *Monthly Film Bulletin*, 53:624, January 1986, pp. 28–31.

Cook, Pam. Lilith. *Monthly Film Bulletin*, 53:624, January 1986, pp. 26–7.

Dark, Chris. "Reflections on Robert Rossen." *Cinema*, 6–7 August 1970, pp. 57–61.

Farber, Stephen. "New American Gothic." *Film Quarterly* 20:1, Fall 1966, pp. 22–7.

\_\_\_\_\_. "Stephen Farber on 'Lilith.'" *Film Comment*, Fall 1970, 6:3, pp. 51–4.

*Film Ideal*, 213, 1969. "En memoria Robert Rossen; Segismondo Molist: Trayectoria vital. Ramón Font: Lilith," pp. 64–78.

*Film Ideal*, 217–9, 1969. "Antonio Castro. Mas sobre: Robert Rossen y 'Lilith,'" pp. 51–9.

*Filmfacts*, 7:41, 13 November 1964, pp. 259–61.

*Films in Review*, 24:2, February 1973, p. 112.

Finstad, Suzanne. *Warren Beatty: a private man*. London: Aurum, 2005, pp. 296–308.

Fougères, Roland. *Ciné revue*, 44:35, 27 August 1964, pp. 22–5.

Gough-Yates, Kevin. "Private madness and public lunacy." *Films and Filming*, 18:5, February 1972, pp. 26–30.

Henry, Michael. "Lilith, ou le diamant fêlé." *Positif*, 581–2, July–August 2009, pp. 43–5.

Lloyd, Chris. Lilith. *The Brighton Film Review*, 15 December 1969, pp. 3–4.

*Motion Picture Daily*, 13, 18 and 26 August 1964, pp. 1, 3.

Munn, Michael. *Gene Hackman*. London: Robert Hale, 1997, pp. 21–2 [Seberg interview].

Nolletti, Art. "The fissure in the spider web: a reading of Rossen's 'Lilith.'" *Film Criticism*, Winter–Spring 1978, 2:2–3, pp. 90–103.

Paley, Stanley. "The shooting of 'Lilith.'" *Art Films*, 1:4, April–May 1964, pp. 10–14, 50–53.

Rossen, Robert. "Leçons de combat (interview with Jean-Louis Noames); Jean-André Fieschi. Le film unique; Jean Seberg. Lilith et moi." *Cahiers du cinéma* 177, April 1966, pp. 26–49. English translation: *Cahiers du cinéma in English* 7, January 1967, pp. 20–41.

\_\_\_\_\_. Robert Rossen's last interview in *Persistence of Vision*, ed. Joseph McBride, Wisconsin Film Society Press, 1968, pp. 207–19.

\_\_\_\_\_. *Three screenplays: All the King's Men, The Hustler, Lilith*. New York: Anchor Books, 1972.

Salamanca, J.R. *Lilith*. New York: Simon & Schuster, 1961.

Seberg, Jean. "Lilith and I." *Cahiers du cinéma in English* 7, January 1967, pp. 35–36.

Thomson, David. *Warren Beatty: a life and a story*. London: Secker & Warburg, 1987, pp. 201–7.

*Time*, 82:6, 9 August 1965, p. 35.

Van Ieperen, Ab. "Robert Rossen en de spelregels." *Skoop* 4:3, November 1966, pp. 34–41.

Walker, Janet. *Couching Resistance: Women, Film and Psychoanalytic Psychiatry*. Minneapolis: University of Minnesota Press, 1993, pp. 114–21.

## Reviews

*America*, 111, 10 October 1964, p. 423.

*Amis du film et de la télévision*, 122/3, July/August 1966. P.L., V.M., pp. 21, 28.

*Arts*, 990, 27 January 1965. Jean-Louis Bory, p. 11.

*Cahiers du cinéma*, 165, April 1965. Jean-André Fieschi, p. 70.

*Le Canard enchaîné*, 27 January 1965. M.D., p. 7.

*Chicago Sun-Times*, 26 October 1964. Eleanor Keen.

*Christian Century*, 81, 2 December 1964, pp. 1499–1500.

*Cinéma*, 94, March 1965. Claire Clouzot, pp. 121–3.

*Combat*, 20 January 1965. Henry Chapier, p. 8.

*Commonweal*, 81:4, 16 October 1964. Philip T. Hartung, pp. 101–2.

*Cosmopolitan*, 157:3, September 1964. Rex Reed, pp. 14–15.

*La Croix*, 6 February 1965. H.R.

*The Daily Mail*, 1 November 1966. Cecil Wilson, p. 12.

*The Daily News* (NY), 3 October 1964. Dorothy Masters, p. 22.

*The Evening News*, 3 November 1966. Felix Barker, p. 13.

*L'Express*, 710, 25 January 1965. Claude Tarare, p. 35.

*Le Figaro*, 26 January 1965. Louis Chauvet, p. 20.
*The Film Daily*, 21 September 1964. Mandel Herbstman, p. 8.
*Film Quarterly*, 18:2, Winter 1964. P.M. Hodgens, p. 58.
*Filmkritik*, June 1965. Heinz Ungureit, p. 337.
*Films and Filming*, August 1966. Allen Eyles, pp. 6–7.
*Films in Review*, 15:8, October 1964. Henry Hart, pp. 502–3.
*France-soir*, 26 January 1965. Robert Chazal, p. 10.
*The Guardian*, 4 November 1966. Richard Roud, p. 9.
*The Hollywood Reporter*, 21 September 1964. James Powers, p. 3.
*Image et son*, 190–1, Jan./Feb. 1966, *Saison cinématographique* 1965. Hubert Arnault, pp. 166–7.
*Intermezzo*, 20:1–2, 31 January 1965, p. 7.
*Kinematograph Weekly*, 3059, 19 May 1966. Graham Clarke, p. 12.
*Les Lettres françaises*, 1065, 28 January 1965, p. 8.
*Life*, 57:14, 2 October 1964. Richard Oulahan, p. 26.
*London Magazine*, 6:10, January 1967. James Price, pp. 77–80.
*Le Monde*, 23 January 1965. Yvonne Baby, p. 12.
*Monthly Film Bulletin*, 33:395, December 1966. T.M., pp. 179–80.
*Motion Picture Daily*, 96:57, 21 September 1964. Richard Gertner, pp. 1, 8.
*New Republic*, 22 August 1964. Stanley Kauffmann. World of shadows, pp. 35–6.
*New York Herald Tribune*, 3 October 1964. Judith Crist, p. 8.
*The New York Times*, 21 September 1964. Bosley Crowther, p. 37.
*The New Yorker*, 40, 10 October 1964. Brendan Gill, p. 202.
*Newsweek*, 64:15, 12 October 1964, pp. 116–7.
*Le Nouvel observateur*, 167, 24 January 1968. Michel Mardore, p. 41.
*Positif*, 69, 1965. Gérard Legrand, pp. 59–61.
*Saturday Review*, 47:42, 17 October 1964. Arthur Knight, p. 28.
*Seventh Art*, 5, Fall 1964. Gary Carey, pp. 20–1.
*Sight and Sound*, 35:3, Summer 1966. David Wilson, pp. 147–8.
*Téléciné*, 19:123, June 1965. Philippe Maillat, p. 39.
*Télérama*, 786, 7 February 1965. Jean Collet, p. 60.
*Time*, 84:14, 2 October 1964, p. 130.
*The Times*, 3 November 1966, p. 7.
*Variety*, 25 September 1964. Whit., p. 6.
*Village Voice*, 9:49, 24 September 1964. Andrew Sarris, p. 17.
*Vogue*, 144, 1 November 1964, p. 64.
*The Washington Post*, 15 October 1964. Richard L. Coe, p. C26.

# *Backfire (Échappement libre)* (1964)

A Sud-Pacifique Films / Capitole Films (Paris) / Benito Perojo Productions (Madrid) / Transmonde Film (Rome) / CCM/ CCFC production; a Royal Films International presentation [USA]; a CCCF release. Production at Paris-Studios-Cinéma
Original release: In French; released with English subtitles
Also known as: *Free Escape*; *Der Boss hat sich was ausgedacht* [Germany]; *Scappamento aperto* [Italy]; *A escape libre / Oro, brillantes y muerte* [Spain]
Running Time: 105 minutes
Format: in Black and White; in Franscope

CAST: [* denotes above the title billing] Jean-Paul Belmondo* (David Ladislas); Jean Seberg* (Olga Célan); Enrico Maria Salerno (Mario); Renate Ewert (The Countess); Jean-Pierre Marielle (Van Houde); Gert Fröbe (Fehrman); Wolfgang Preiss (Grenner); Roberto Camardiel (Stephanidès); Michel Beaune (Daniel); R.L. Calvo (fisherman Livanos); J. Mac (Hendrick); Fernando Rey (Police Inspector); with Diana Lorys, Xan Das Bolas, José Maria Caffarel, José Jaspe, Carmen de Lirio, Petar Martinovitch, Fernando Sancho, Margarita Gil (Seberg and Belmondo billing reversed in North America release)

PRODUCTION CREDITS: *Director:* Jean Becker; *Producer:* Paul-Edmond Decharme; *Screenplay:* Didier Goulard, Maurice Fabre, Jean Becker; *Dialogue:* Daniel Boulanger, from the novel by Clet Coroner; *Director of Photography:* Edmond Séchan; *Décor:* Georges Wakhevitch; *Chief Editor:* Monique Kirsanoff; *Production:* Paul-Edmond Decharme; *1st Assistant Director:* Costa Gavras; *Camera:* Jean-Paul Schwartz; *1st Assistant Operator:* Guy Delattre; *Photographer:* Jean Falloux; *Scriptgirl:* Annie Maurel; *Assistant Editor:* Chantal Delattre; *Makeup:* Phuong Maittret; *Hairdresser:* Danièle Lefort; *1st Assistant, Décor:* René Calviera; *Sound Engineer:* André Hervée; *Credits:* Jean Fouchet; *Props:* Robert Christidès; *Accessories:* Roger Bollengier; *Assistant Directors:* Alain Darbon, Alain Belmondo; *Production Secretary:* Gisèle Cornaud; *Administration:* Camille Lefrançois; Music by Martial Solal, Éditions Musicales Mondiamusic S.A.R.I.

## Synopsis

A criminal organization offers Parisian David Ladislas $10,000 for transporting a sports car to Lebanon. They will tell him little except that drugs are not involved, and he accepts. Glamorous Swedish-American photographer Olga, who is to accompany him, clearly knows more, but is uncommunicative. During their sea voyage she thaws towards him, but all he learns is that their vehicle contains 300 kilos of gold. When their ship arrives in Beirut Olga tricks customs authorities, and they continue to Damascus. David is convinced that they should keep the gold for themselves, aided by his friend Mario, and cannot be dissuaded. They fly to Athens. Olga's warning proves well-founded, for David has a narrow escape from gang boss Fehrman. Olga returns home to Bremen, while David bribes a fisherman to take him with the car to Italy. He leaves it in Genoa and, now penniless, hitches to Germany to find Olga.

Reunited with Olga, David foresees a golden future. Fehrman's reappearance dashes his hopes, but Olga has not betrayed him after all—simply saved his life at a high price. When the car arrives at the dockside the police and Fehrman are both waiting. One slip is enough for David's life of leisure to melt away before his eyes. After all, Olga consoles, money isn't everything.

## Reviews

"Let us salute a young director who, for his second major film, delivers a master stroke ... above all there is movement, development, an amusing script by Daniel Boulanger and lastly J-P Belmondo, always likeable."—*Le Canard enchaîné*

"Miss Seberg is enigmatic and very good to look at but she and Belmondo as a team don't work up a head of steam on their part or ours." *New York Herald Tribune*

"A pleasing mixture of romance, adventure and comedy.... *Backfire* doesn't exactly misfire, neither does it leave you *Breathless*."—*Los Angeles Times*

"[Like his father, Becker] possesses his profound feeling for his craft as director. He knows that cinema is above all an art of movement and rhythm. He gives his actors their head when he has confidence in them but also knows how to restrain their excesses."—*L'Humanité*

"The actors have the last word: Belmondo delights a public appreciative of his mannerisms (he doesn't stint), and once again Seberg acts with restraint and well."—*Cahiers du cinéma*

"Like *Goldfinger* ... high level tension and lively, suspenseful entertainment, intrigue, danger, willing sirens, road-racing and mayhem ... the danger-filled chase in high gear is fun."—*New York Review*

"Miss Seberg, whose French is still Iowa-accented, also speaks some German in this adventure. Dressed or in negligee, she is attractive to the eye, if not the ear, in a role that only calls for her to be either glum or laconic.... Lively, suspenseful entertainment" —*New York Times*

"Belmondo and Miss Seberg are a vibrant team to behold. Deft secondary characterizations are turned in by supporting players...." —*Film Daily*

"We remembered ... a charming little American girl with a boy's haircut and delightful accent, having at the same time a sweetness and acidity in her gaze.... But look how they've changed her! ... Hairdressers, makeup artists ... have given us a well-polished movie star...." —*Revue des deux mondes*

## Notes

This French-Spanish-Italian co-production was the second full-length feature for Jean Becker, son of the eminent French director Jacques Becker, again starring the by now hugely popular Belmondo. Jean-Louis Trintignant was to have taken the male lead, but theatre engagements had made him unavailable for the scheduled shoot in February and March 1964. The director initially hesitated about signing Seberg opposite Belmondo once more (shamelessly, as he later put it), foreseeing the inevitable comparisons which would be made with *Breathless*. Both of the stars of Godard's film were now established in France's A-list, and when their reunion for *Backfire* was announced the expectations for something equally exceptional were high. Clet Coroner's routine pulp story had appealed to Becker in its originality, but was skillfully filleted for the cinema in the knowledge that it would stand or fall by the style and flair its leading actors could bring to it. Once again, Belmondo would be a man on the run, torn between emotion and calculation as he eludes his pursuers. This time, though, the story would have an ending more to Seberg's taste. Could the two rediscover the instinctive rapport they had achieved for Godard, or would memories of the earlier pairing be just a distraction for audiences?

In fact, despite being another brisk crime story with a jazzy soundtrack from Martial Solal, *Backfire* is unlike *Breathless* in almost every other respect, storyline, characters, directorial style and editing included. For one thing, its higher production values gave the film a gloss quite alien to Godard's work. Seberg herself now appears chic, elegantly dressed and stylishly coiffed, far from the hesitant gamine the public remembered. Suddenly we find a composed, urbane professional who seems to know exactly what she wants. Her blonde sophistication counters interestingly with Belmondo's boyish version of masculine charm, at times a touch camp in its exuberance and spontaneous mimicry. Olga initially views David rather like a boisterous puppy, alternately tiresome and disarming, but which refuses either way to be ignored. Eventually, with a sigh, she will put her book aside and

In *Backfire* (*Échappement libre*), 1964 (CCFC).

give him her whole attention. Some may even find a more entertaining chemistry in this second partnership. If this is so, it is, of course, more to do with the screenplay itself than with directing technique. Where Godard chose not to make his characters sympathetic in the conventional sense, Becker wants us to like his reprobates and to feel they are not beyond redemption. Though a rogue, and outrageous in his male chauvinism, we sense that David might despise Michel Poiccard's sordid misdeeds. He was, we learn, a foundling, forced to live by his wits: allowances are called for. As for his more level-headed partner in crime, we feel confident that she will not betray him, however exasperated. Seberg's character has a strong element of feisty feminism to counterbalance the machismo of David. She does not spare him her irony ("how quick you are on the uptake!"), and seduces him just at the point when he has ceased trying to seduce her. Afterwards, seeing that even this was all about the gold on his part, she offers mock sympathy: "Poor David! So much trouble for nothing!" Whether or not Olga is the right guide to a future on the straight and narrow, we can be sure she will in time instill some balance in her hyperactive partner.

The final product is a fast moving adventure handled with a light touch, and which gains impetus from Solal's joyful and extrovert music. Camerawork is inventive and varied, making good use of the scenic opportunities. As we have seen, there is ample scope for Belmondo's physical style of acting and clowning, and this is well counterbalanced by Seberg's restrained role as the cool-headed half of the duo who can't help being amused as well as irritated by such nonsense. Her gradual transition from icy aloofness is far from the least effective element in this piece of escapism.

The two leads are supported by a series of colorful cameos, notably Gert Fröbe as the indefatigably menacing Fehrman, a pantomime heavy with a real zest for his work. Enrico

Reteaming with her *Breathless* co-star Jean-Paul Belmondo in the caper *Backfire* (*Échappement libre*) (CCFC).

Maria Salerno amuses as the indolent and generally horizontal mature toy boy Mario, a nicely realized specimen of the classic *cicisbeo*. Jean-Pierre Marielle makes a brief but memorable appearance as the louche harpsichord-playing Van Houde, a masterly thumbnail in decadence. Fernando Rey is the zealous scourge of smugglers who might well be mad enough to believe, as he claims, that he can smell gold through walls, while Wolfgang Preiss is suavely reptilian as The Organization's desk man Grenner. All in all, there is the sense that it was fun making this picture, and we share in much of that, without reproaching it for its undisguised frivolity. It never bores.

*Backfire* was released in the same year as a new offering from the director of *Five Day Lover*, Philippe De Broca. *That Man from Rio* (*L'Homme de Rio*) involves Belmondo in a hectic succession of chases, fights and death-defying stunts, all against a background of dramatic Brazilian scenery captured in Eastmancolor. This, rather than *Breathless*, was the film against which audiences would probably have measured Becker's action travelogue. The latter was shot in a large number of different locations including Geneva, Beirut, Damascus, Baalbek, Tripoli, Athens, Naples and Bremen, and even highly experienced designer Georges Wakhevitch found the succession of *Backfire*'s sets a challenge: "a huge and unusual task in a single film." Yet the absence of color often seems like an opportunity missed in Becker's otherwise lavish production. Both films highlight the flair and dynamism French audiences had come to expect from their male lead. Seberg's role was more of a novelty. As Olga she is required to speak German at times as well as French, though without needing to sound like a native speaker of either.

Becker's film does not attempt to match De Broca in thrills, but it does have some exciting moments (notably some stunt driving by Gilles Delamarre, to which the director gave special credit), and a broadly similar appeal. Rapid as the action is, space is given throughout for Belmondo and Seberg to develop their roles and to make their interaction a major strength. Of the two films, this is surely the less conventional and formulaic, yet it has been largely forgotten. Daniel Boulanger, who worked on both screenplays, recalled that this story had immediately attracted him, allowing humor to play off the elements of noir. As so often, the critics reacted to the film in quite different ways. Some drew inappropriate comparisons with *Breathless*, as Becker had predicted, while others deplored another addition to an overworked genre. The public, however, were receptive. Though failing to achieve the runaway international success Belmondo and Françoise Dorléac had had with De Broca's film, it did sell out many theatres in France after its opening in September 1964 and ranked a respectable fourteenth in Paris for that year.

One uncredited appearance in the film may be noticed by the sharp-eyed. When Seberg rejoins Belmondo at the bar of their Beirut hotel she passes a man sitting alone inside the entrance, smoking a cigar, who turns to look in her direction. It is the man she had married some four months earlier and who was present at much of the nine week shoot, Romain Gary.

## References

Becker, Geneviève, and Jean Becker. *Becker par Becker*. Paris: Éditions PC, 2004, pp. 99–105, 203.
Cebollada, Pascual. *Biografía y peliculas de Fernando Rey*. Barcelona: CILEH, 1992, p. 203.
Chazal, Robert. *Jean-Paul Belmondo*. Paris: Denoël, 1971, pp. 124–7.
*Cinémonde*, 32:1543, 3 March 1964. Gilles Durieux, pp. 2–3; 32:1555, 26 May 1964, pp. 14–15; 32:1569, 1 September 1964, pp. 24–25.
Coroner, Clet. *Échappement libre*. Paris: Librairie Plon, 1963.
Durant, Philippe. *Belmondo*. Paris: Laffont, 1998, pp. 217–8.

*Le Figaro*, 24 April 1964, interview, p. 26.
*Le Film français*, 22:1078–9, Winter 1964–65, p. 16.
*Filmfacts*, 8:20–21, 25 June 1965 "Backfire," pp. 117–8.
Grenier, Alexandre. *Jean-Paul Belmondo*. Paris: Veyrier, 1985, pp. 120, 250.
Guedj, Philippe. *Un nommé Jean Becker*. Fédération nationale des cinémas français, 59ème congrès 2004, pp. 9–71.
*Motion Picture Guide, 1927–83*, p. 122.
Sarlat, P. *Ciné revue*, 44:40, 1 October 1964, pp. 12–3.

## Reviews

*Amis du film et de la télévision*, 102, November 1964. P.L., p. 22.
*Arts*, 972, 16–22 September 1964. Pierre Marcabru, p. 14.
*Cahiers du cinéma*, 160, November 1964, p. 87.
*Le Canard enchaîné*, 9 September 1964, p. 5.
*Cinéma*, 90, November 1964. Patrick Bureau, p. 131.
*Cinématographie française*, Index, 1965. Guy Allombert, pp. 121–2.
*Combat*, 9 September 1964, p. 8.
*La Croix*, 19 September 1964. Henry Rabine.
*Le Figaro*, 10 September 1964. Pierre Mazars, p. 22.
*The Film Daily*, 26 April 1965. Mandel Herbstman, p. 4.
*Le Film français*, 25 September 1964, p. 23.
*Filmkritik*, November 1964. Enno Patalas, p. 594.
*Films*, 8, 1965, p. 117.
*France-soir*, 9 September 1964. Robert Chazal, p. 9.
*The Hollywood Reporter*, 10 June 1965. James Powers, p. 3.
*L'Humanité*, 9 September 1964. Samuel Lachize, p. 8.
*Image et son*, 180–1 (*Saison cinématographique* 1964), February 1965. Guy Gauthier, p. 99.
*Intermezzo*, 20:5–6, 31 March 1965 (*Scappamento aperto*), pp. 7–8.
*Les Lettres françaises*, 1046, 17 September 1964. Mic. M, p. 9; 1049, 8 October 1964. P.S., p. 9.
*Libération*, 7 September 1964. Jeander.
*The Los Angeles Times*, 10 June 1965. Kevin Thomas, pt. 5, p. 13.
*Minute*, 9 October 1964.
*Le Monde*, 12 September 1964. Nicole Zand, p. 17.
*Motion Picture Daily*, 97:80, 27 April 1965. Sy Oshinsky, p. 5.
*The New York Herald Tribune*, 27 April 1965. Judith Crist, p. 15.
*The New York Times*, 27 April 1965. A.H. Weiler, p. 27.
*The New Yorker*, 41:11, 1 May 1965. Brendan Gill, p. 120.
*Newsweek*, 65:19, 10 May 1965, pp. 118–118a.
*Paris-presse*, 10 September 1964. Patrick Thévenon, p. 10.
*Revue des deux mondes*, 15 October 1964. R. Régent.
*Saturday Review*, 48:20, 15 May 1965. Hollis Alpert, p. 34.
*Le Soir*, 2 October 1964. André Paris, p. 32.
*Le Spectacle du monde*, 31 October 1964. François Vinneuil, p. 87.
*Télérama*, 766, 20 September 1964. Gilbert Salachas, p. 55.
*Time*, 85:19, 7 May 1965, p. 107.
*Variety*, 7 October 1964. Gene Moskowitz, p. 6.

# *Moment to Moment* (1966)

"LeRoy is famous for coddling his leading ladies and I was no exception. The role was wonderful, sets fabulous and the gowns by Yves Saint Laurent were beautiful."—Jean Seberg

A Mervyn LeRoy Production; A Universal Pictures release
Original release: in English

Also known as: *Choc* [France]; *Der Schuss* [Germany]; *Da un momento all'altro* [Italy]; *Momento a momento / Pecado de amor* [Spain]
Running Time: 108 minutes
Format: in Technicolor

CAST: [* denotes above the title billing] Jean Seberg* (Kay Stanton); Honor Blackman* (Daphne Fields); Sean Garrison* (Mark Dominic); Arthur Hill (Neil Stanton); Grégoire Aslan (Inspector De Fargo); Peter Robbins (Timmy Stanton); Lomax Study (Albie); Donald Woods (Consul Robert Singer); Walter Reed (Hendricks); Albert Carrier (Travel Agent); Richard Angarola (Givet); Georgette Anys (Louise)

PRODUCTION CREDITS: *Director and Producer:* Mervyn LeRoy; *Screenplay:* John Lee Mahin, Alec Coppel, based on the story "Laughs With a Stranger" by Alec Coppel; *Music:* Henry Mancini; *Set Decorations:* John McCarthy, John Austin; *Editor:* Philip W. Anderson; *Sound:* Waldon O. Watson, David Moriarty; *Director of Photography:* Harry Stradling; *Art Direction:* Alexander Golitzen, Alfred Sweeney; *Titles:* Pacific Title; *Unit Production Manager:* Bob Larson; *Assistant Director:* Phil Bowles; *Miss Seberg's wardrobe:* Yves Saint Laurent; *Makeup:* Bud Westmore; *Honor Blackman's wardrobe:* Rosemary Odell; *Hairstylist:* Larry Germain; *Assistant Director:* Phil Bowles; *Music Supervision:* Joseph Gershenson; *Title song "Moment to Moment":* Music: Henry Mancini, Lyrics: Johnny Mercer

## Synopsis

Kay, her psychiatry professor husband Neil and their young son Timmy are an American family vacationing on the Côte d'Azur. When Neil leaves for a convention Kay has only party-loving neighbor Daphne for adult company. A chance encounter with naval officer Mark begins entirely innocently, but Daphne schemes to bring her friend and this attractive stranger together. Neil's return is delayed and Kay passes time showing Mark the local sights. Realizing her susceptibility, she tells him they shouldn't meet again. Nevertheless, a farewell visit ends in their spending the night together. Mark is bitter when he finds this has changed nothing. Drunk, he finds a gun and Kay shoots him accidentally in a struggle.

Daphne comes to the aid of her distraught friend. They dump the body, but soon the women come under scrutiny from detective De Fargo. When Neil returns the police seek his help in a case of amnesia. They study Kay's reaction when the amnesiac proves to be the man she supposed she had killed. Despite her skill in this cat and mouse game, everyone, including Mark, eventually deduces the truth. The police let matters rest and Neil forgives Kay.

## Reviews

"*Moment to Moment* is one of those medium-good suspense dramas that should have been something special. If only [it] had had Alfred Hitchcock instead of Mervyn LeRoy as director.... If only Mr. LeRoy had run a tight wire through his handsome production." —*New York Times*

"Mervyn LeRoy's directorial hand is so practiced in practically every film genre that even his soap opera is worth watching.. But if you concentrate on the scenery, on Seberg & Blackman, and on LeRoy's direction, *Moment to Moment* won't give you too bad a time."—*Films In Review*

"... Seberg shines with intelligence, charm and tenderness.... All that's lacking in the screenplay and direction we can find in the beautiful face of Jean Seberg."—*Télérama*

"This is a glossily mounted soap-opera cunningly concocted to appeal to housewives who have had more than enough of the kitchen sink. Nevertheless it could still provide a sunny piece of escapism for a wet afternoon."—*Monthly Film Bulletin*

"I suppose it has earned the label of a woman's picture because of the affluent background, its palpitations, and its remarkable silliness. That also makes it rather fun, if you are in that kind of mood."—*Glasgow Herald*

"Miss Seberg, looking maturely beautiful, gives an impressive performance...."—*Film Daily*

"Jean Seberg lacks dimension as the wife, even allowing for the script ... [she] often poses like Lana Turner, which isn't bad in one way, but further detracts from characterization. Sean Garrison is lifeless.... Honor Blackman ... gives the film some much needed zip as the neighbor, although, in context, it's occasionally overdone."—*Variety*

## Notes

Mervyn LeRoy was a Hollywood veteran who had begun as an actor, and he had been instrumental in bringing *Lilith* director Robert Rossen to Warner in 1937 as a young screenwriter. *Moment to Moment* was LeRoy's seventy-fifth and final picture, a feat that was celebrated when the cigar-puffing director, posing for the cameras with his stars, lit seventy five candles on a ceremonial cake. The opportunity of working with him was certainly something Seberg welcomed. Apart from that consideration, she liked the role, which seemed no stretch for her, and felt the script was an interesting one with possibilities. This was not, as suggested at the time, her Hollywood debut, for she had had the supporting role in *Let No Man Write My Epitaph* more than five years earlier. This, however, was a quite different proposition and would be a showcase for her, with top production values in terms of sets and art design, costumes designed by Yves Saint Laurent and location filming on the Riviera.

For the most part the filming, which began in France just after New Year 1965, went well. "In a scene we shot yesterday they had me stand on a box and I reached around a wide angle lens to find Sean Garrison's lips," Seberg laughed. "And all this time—for rehearsals and seven takes—I had to stand on my tip-toes. Don't make it read as though I'm complaining. Just say if anything better than kissing a nice-looking man comes along, I'd want to be the first to know about it!" As *Jours de France* reported, some supplementary acting was required, for on the beach at Le Dramont the two had to pretend to be basking in the summer sun rather than shivering in the actual midwinter temperature of the shoot. Privately, Seberg was doubtful about Garrison's adequacy for his role, and LeRoy later regretted his casting of a part which "cried out for somebody like Paul Newman."

Legendary cinematographer Harry Stradling, who did the camerawork for the film, paid his own tribute to the leading lady: "A cameraman never has to pose Jean Seberg. I'd certainly have to bracket her among the five most photogenic actresses I've caught in a camera. She has the greatest asset that any actress must have to become a big star—she projects from the screen at each male in the darkness of the theater, as if he alone is the object of her romantic intentions. It's an elusive, intangible chemistry that either comes out naturally or not at all. It can't be phonied up. Miss Seberg has it. That's why she is certainly slated to be one of the top female stars in the business."

Coppel's story starts out with the entirely plausible situation of a young wife left alone by her husband in a romantic setting and susceptible to entanglements she may live to regret. His plot device to create suspense, or what might be loosely termed the MacGuffin in a Hitchcock movie, is, alas, not nearly so convincing. We can only regret that the master of manipulation was not on hand to make all things credible and to surprise us with his cleverness. There are no small demands on the suspension of disbelief here, for the "corpse"

**Dancing with *Moment to Moment* and Hollywood veteran director Mervyn LeRoy, with new-comer Sean Garrison looking on (Universal).**

is miraculously raised from the dead, like Lazarus, with hardly a scratch to explain his mysterious temporary loss of memory. No real tension comes from the amnesia situation for the victim himself, as is the case in *Spellbound*. Here it is simply a means of producing the well-tried but effective tease in which the wily police inspector guesses the truth but needs to prove it. We see him set his snares and watch his equally quick-witted suspect skirt neatly round them. Credibility has been gravely compromised by this point, however, and the need to keep the audience fully involved presents the cast with something of an uphill task.

Author Coppel's impassioned hero had displayed a matching grasp of anatomy and psychology, shooting himself in the chest in despair after realizing that Kay does not plan to leave her husband, son and comfortable lifestyle on the strength of a romantic impulse. The screenplay, for which he had the collaboration of John Lee Mahin, helps plausibility a little. This provides for a struggle and accidental shooting with a gun belonging to Louise. It makes the action of Kay and Daphne in disposing of the body a shade less absurd, but it's not nearly enough. Once she discovers Mark is alive, the tension is generated by her fear that her husband will discover her infidelity and won't forgive her. In fact he does both, but it takes time and some highly contrived situations to get to this predictable outcome.

This film recalls both *Spellbound* and *Dial M for Murder* yet fails to rival either. Nevertheless, the remarkable thing is that *Moment to Moment* does succeed on some levels, despite the fatal weaknesses of its plot, and we do want to know how the story will end. Sean Garrison does not convince as the young officer Mark Dominic whose polite exterior supposedly conceals darker passions, but the fault is partly in the writing. Honor Blackman is excellent as the decisively worldly Daphne, a gold-digger with a sentimental side and a perfect foil to Kay's rather prim superiority. Arthur Hill seems right for the "dull but dependable" husband Neil, and Grégoire Aslan is well cast as the Inspector with a malicious relish in stalking his prey.

The challenge of holding this flawed enterprise together, however, falls chiefly to Seberg. She perfectly embodies the quality of poised insecurity called for by the character of Kay. Here she has all the schooled discipline of a tightrope walker whose nerve is failing, and who is suddenly all too conscious of the void beneath her feet. Whereas with Daphne all is displayed on the surface, Kay lacks her friend's self-knowledge. She clearly thinks of herself as a moral person, but does not know what she might do in an unprecedented situation, and neither do we. For Daphne, the appearance of Mark would only signify the opportunity for a spicy adventure. Kay, however, has at first no awareness of threat to the things she cherishes, being scarcely conscious of her own frailty, and the tension is real because we sense what is at stake for her. The correct aloofness with which she masks her vulnerability is also credibly tantalizing for a man who might be immune to her friend's overt flirtatiousness.

One of the film's strengths is the score by Henry Mancini, based on a haunting theme tune which is metamorphosed in subtle guises. Unapologetically lush in its treatment, with vocal backing, this gives the film a romantic gloss and "Hollywood" quality (in the positive sense) which does much to compensate for defects elsewhere. The color photography is excellent, as we would expect from Stradling, and the Riviera location sequences are a pleasure, even if we can sometimes too easily spot the back projection—something which, after all, we readily enough accept with Hitchcock. Similarly, the doves, presumably hand-colored, simply remind present day viewers of the technical sophistication we now take for granted. The studio interiors, however, which were shot back in California, have too much the feel of being just that, for all LeRoy's lavishness. Seberg had joked about having to travel 12,000 kilometers just to give the impression of standing still.

*Moment to Moment* received its world premiere in Miami on January 27, 1966, with LeRoy and Blackman in attendance. If it was to prove a modest success rather than the "sure fire hit" promised in Universal's publicity the following month, this was not due to half-hearted promotion. In July 1965 LeRoy and Stradling had filmed a 60-piece orchestra recording the film score under Mancini's direction. A full program of network television appearances and interviews was organized for LeRoy and his stars, and a feature was placed in *McCall's* to entice its 27 million readership. The studios persuaded Sean Garrison to undertake an exhausting 30-city promotional tour. The composer's recording of the title song was persuasively echoed in a version by Frank Sinatra. Department store buyers were entertained at the studio by the makers of the children's game "Blockhead" which was central to the plot. Universal quoted Hedda Hopper's glowing endorsement of a film which "has style, sophistication, beauty and four fine actors. Ladies will love it.... The song 'Moment to Moment' will haunt you. So will the story." Seberg's private verdict two months later was that it had done "pretty well," but that the lack of a well-known male partner had been a disadvantage which she would in future try to avoid. Garrison's debut as leading man in fact failed to propel him to stardom, notwithstanding a seven-year contract with Universal, though he would continue his acting career in television.

In summary, if *Moment to Moment* does not stand up to any rigorous scrutiny, it still offers much to enjoy for those who are in what the *Glasgow Herald* reviewer called "that kind of mood." The film provides eye-pleasing spectacle and enough twists and turns to sustain interest. Although this hardly qualifies as a thriller, it works well as a romantic drama with elements of suspense. The chief regret here is that so many opportunities were lost. A more fundamental rewrite could have helped, as a more experienced male lead would certainly have done.

## References

Canham, Kingsley. Mervyn LeRoy [pp. 133–89 in *The Hollywood Professionals*, vol. 5. London: Tantivy Press and New York: A.S. Barnes, 1976].
*Ciné revue*, 45:50, 9 December 1965. Roland Fougères, pp. 22–5.
Coppel, Alec. *Moment to Moment*. Greenwich, CT: Fawcett, 1966.
*Filmfacts*, 9:5, 1 April 1966, pp. 47–8.
*The Hollywood Reporter*, 184:46, 25 March 1965, p. 8.
LeRoy, Mervyn. *Mervyn LeRoy: take one*. New York: Hawthorn Books, 1974, pp. 214–5.
*Motion Picture Daily*, 99:15, 21 January 1966. "LeRoy to New York to boost his 'Moment,'" p. 2.
*Motion Picture Guide, 1927–83*, p. 2006.

## Reviews

*Amis du film et de la télévision*, 120/1, May/June 1966. J.D, V.M., p. 25.
*Cahiers du cinéma*, 178, May 1966. J.-P. B., pp. 80–1.
*Le Canard enchaîné*, 27 April 1966. Michel Duran, p. 7.
*Christian Science Monitor*, 6 May 1966. Alan N. Bunce, p. 6.
*Cineinforme*, 4:42, March 1966, p. 21.
*La Croix*, 7 May 1966. J. Ro.
*The Daily Cinema*, 4 May 1966. M.H., p. 8.
*The Daily Mail*, 12 May 1966. Cecil Wilson, p. 14.
*Evangelischer Film-Beobachter*, 18:11, 12 March 1966. A.W., p. 176.
*The Evening News*, 12 May 1966. Felix Barker, p. 8.
*The Evening Standard*, 12 May 1966. Alexander Walker, p. 10.
*The Film Daily*, 26 January 1966. Mandel Herbstman, p. 7.
*Le Film français*, 23:1153, 8 July 1966. P.A.B., p. 15.
*Films and Filming*, 12:10, July 1966. Mike Sarne, p. 56.
*Films in Review*, 17:4, April 1966. Eunice Sinkler, p. 249.
*The Glasgow Herald*, 25 July 1966. Molly Plowright, p. 8.
*The Guardian*, 13 May 1966. Ian Wright, p. 11.
*The Hollywood Reporter*, 26 January 1966. Don Carle Gillette, p. 3.
*Kinematograph Weekly*, 3057, 5 May 1966, pp. 16, 24.
*Monthly Film Bulletin*, 33:389, June 1966, p. 95.
*Motion Picture Daily*, 99:18, 26 January 1966. Richard Gertner, p. 3.
*The National Observer*, 5:6, 7 February 1966. Joseph N. Bell, p. 22.
*The New Statesman*, 71, 20 May 1966, p. 746.
*The New York Herald Tribune*, 3 March 1966. Judith Crist, p. 11.
*The New York Times*, 3 March 1966. Howard Thompson, p. 28.
*Le Soir*, 80:77, 1 April 1966. S., p. 32.
*Télérama*, 251, 8 May 1966. C.-M. Trémois.
*Time*, 87:11, 18 March 1966, p. 113.
*Variety*, 241:10, 26 January 1966. Murf., p. 6.
*Vogue*, 147, 1 February 1966, p. 101.

# Diamonds Are Brittle
# (Un Milliard dans un billard) (1965)

A Films Copernic / Filmédis (Paris) / Atlas Films (Munich) / Sancro Film Production (Rome); A Comacico release / Hanns Eckelkamp Filmproduktion
Original release: in French; released with German and English dubbing
Also known as: *Diamond Cue*; *Diamantenbillard* [Germany]; *Allarme in cinque banche* [Italy]; *Mil millones en un billar* [Spain]
Running Time: 93 minutes
Format: in Eastmancolor

CAST: [* denotes above the title billing] Jean Seberg* (Bettina Ralton); Claude Rich* (Bernard Noblet); Elsa Martinelli* (Juliette); Elisabeth Flickenschildt (Madame Ralton); Adi Berber (Max); Günther Ungeheuer (Professor Schmoll); Walter Roderer (Cuendet, the safe-breaker); Günter Lüdke (Marcellino); Günther Jerschke (Dr. Worms); Werner Schwier (Dr. Krautenbach-Levi); France Rumilly (woman with ring); Jacques Dynam (Superintendent); Jean-Paul Moulinot (jeweler Franck); Jacques Morel (Amédée de St Leu); Claude Darget (detective); Annette Poivre (cleaner); Pierre Vernier (Roger); Daniel Ceccaldi (captain); Jacques Balutin (agent); Henri Virlojeux (Picard); Pierre Mirat, Paul Pavel (sergeants); Jacques Santi (airport traveller); Bernard Musson, Louis Viret, Jean-Pierre Rambal, Marius Gaidon (policemen); Marcel Charvey (billiard player); Horst Pasderski, Jacques Préboist, Yves Elliot, Max Melder, André Dalibert, Gaston Meunier, Norma Dugo, Michel Danjou, Yves Acarnel, Marcel Gassouk, Laura Paillette, Anne-Marie Coffinet

PRODUCTION CREDITS: *Director:* Nicolas Gessner; *Producer:* Ernst Steinlechner; *Screenplay:* Charles Spaak, Nicolas Gessner; *Photography:* Claude Lecomte; *Editor:* Jean-Michel Gautier; *Production Manager:* Guy Lacourt; *Art Director:* Paul-Louis Boutié; *Music:* Georges Garvarentz; *Sound:* René Sarazin; *General Direction:* Ernst Liesenhaff, Raymond Danon; *Assistant Director:* Alain Gouze; *Titles:* Jean Fouchet; *Executive Producer:* Raymond Danon; *Direction Assistants:* Michel Lang, Marc Vaziaga; *Cameraman:* Guy Suzuki; *Assistants:* Roland Paillas, Armand Marco; *Script-girl:* Colette Robin; *Photography:* Leo Weiss, Jami Blanc; *Makeup:* Aïda Carange, Phuong Maittret; *Wardrobe:* Lily Caudrelier, Dora Balabanov; *Décor Assistants:* Jacques Douy, Jean Forestier; *Sound Assistants:* Jacques Gérardot, Paul Pauwels; *Admin:* Maurice Cadze, Paula Hayi; *Recording Engineers:* Pierre Cottance, Claude Huyard; *Secretariat:* Fanchette Brie; *Cutting Assistant:* Christiane Weil; *Props:* Robert Turelure, Claude Sune, Pierre Roudeix, Auguste Surin

## Synopsis

Bored bank teller Bernard divides his time between his schoolteacher girlfriend Juliette and the billiard hall run by inventor Roger. Roger's latest project is "the car of the future," but he has no money to build a prototype. Money is precisely the business of Madame Ralton, whose daughter Bettina is a bank customer. Bernard is intrigued, especially when he learns they are professional thieves and gets free coaching from the beguiling Bettina. Could the three friends scoop the proceeds from a jewelry robbery the Ralton gang is apparently planning? Roger is eager, while Juliette stipulates Bernard mustn't cheat on her. An ingenious device is to trigger alarms in five banks, throwing the police into confusion as the robbery occurs.

The plan works perfectly. Bernard sets off the jeweler's alarm at the critical moment, scattering the Ralton gang, and calmly helps himself to the loot. Unfortunately both robbers and police are soon hot on the trail, and Bernard weakens before Bettina's tears and Madame Ralton's colorful menaces. Bernard seems about to confess to the police, causing the gang to hasten to the airport. Juliette triumphs doubly, with the departure of her rival and a deal with the insurance company.

## Reviews

"A lively, light hearted caper that should amuse most audiences in search of cheerful, non-violent entertainment. An excellent choice for holiday periods."—*Today's Cinema*

"[Gessner's] story is diabolically ingenious. The humor of the situation and characters is well developed. The direction is alert and the color photography of Claude Lecomte is very fine.... The principals act in the relaxed style appropriate to this story.... This *billard* is decidedly worth its *milliard*."—*France-soir*

"Slight in substance but engaging in effect, this innocuous comedy of jewel thieves is pleasingly scripted but rather flatly directed. The performances, from a strong cast, are perfectly in keeping with the film's tone, absolutely straightforward and on this level quite enjoyable."—*Monthly Film Bulletin*

"[It] possesses both the charm of *Bande à part* and the elegant precision of the comedies of Blake Edwards. What a pretty trio [Rich, Martinelli and Vernier] make! And what a charming adventuress Jean Seberg is! ... Neither brawls nor vulgarity. The images are pleasing and colors felicitous. This is the realm of charm and imagination."—*Télérama*

"It's emptiness, emptiness in colors.... Accomplished photography, amusing moments, likeable actors (Jean Seberg and Elsa Martinelli), unfortunately can't save the direction from the clichés in which it gets bogged down and the childish nonsense."—*Les Lettres françaises*

"Miss Seberg is highly photogenic and walks through her role with ease with Rich a good foil. Others are okay in this pic that just misses."—*Variety*

"... the acting saves the film: Claude Rich, Jean Seberg ... seem to have a good time in this relatively banal adventure."—*L'Humanité*

"And if the diversion proceeds with some lightness of touch, this is due above all to the effervescent rascality of Claude Rich ... the silky charm of Jean Seberg and the sensuous grace of Elsa Martinelli."—*Le Figaro*

## Notes

Director Nicolas Gessner vividly recalls the making of *Un Milliard dans un billard*, his first film:

I had this project ... It was a good script, and the producer said, "I need names! I need names!" and I said, "OK," so we went to Jean Seberg, and she loved the script. I thanked her for trusting me as a first time director, and she said something that's very true: "That's when people are at their best, when they do their first movie." She was a specialist of people who do their first movies. She was well paid. The whole movie cost 2.5 million FF, which is nothing today. You can't shoot a TV movie for that.

Gessner had hoped to cast the popular Jean-Pierre Cassel as the male lead, but Cassel turned the offer down. Claude Rich seemed a highly acceptable substitute. Another problem arose, however, when it came to the sequence of the actors' billing.

We read the contract with Jean. She was to get above the title, first billing in the most favored lettering and in the first position. And then a couple of weeks later we made arrangements with Elsa Martinelli, who had the same agent as Jean. So I went to the agent and asked her about there being the same contract for the two actresses. She said, "That's for you to sort out." So in Italy we gave first position to Elsa Martinelli, and the rest of the world was Jean. Claude Rich was in second position since he didn't have an agent.

Shooting began on May 10, 1965. One of the first scenes took place on a boat. "The weather was rather damp—drizzle and rain," Gessner recalls.

> It was a very expensive shooting day with the boat and the extras. In one of the rehearsals on the boat's deck, which was soaked by the rain, Jean slipped and hurt her ankle. Very courageously she said, "No, it doesn't matter. Let's go on. Don't worry." They put a bandage on and I saw it was her [cue], so we finished the scene. The production manager heard about it, and he said, "Ah, you idiots! Of course she's hurt. Look at the poor girl!" Of course he wanted to put it on the insurance. "We can't go on shooting! It's an accident. We have to stop. We have to call the insurance." So we shot it the next day with the beautiful sunshine, and Jean was doing fine with her leg.
>   What I immediately recognized with her was this sort of professionalism, which I can say is a trademark of American actresses. They always know their lines, being on their marks, coming on time. And one shouldn't generalize, but French and Europeans are more—"I want to be spontaneous," and the result is they don't know their lines. How can you be spontaneous, how can you use your talent if you have to search your lines? Jean had learned the standard Hollywood acting, then European acting ... taking the best of both sides of the ocean.... She had gravity and seriousness and the wisdom. At the same time, that lightness—fun working with. She projected this American perfectionism.
>   In Europe, especially in France, the director is God—not the actor, and not the producer. Jean understood this, even though I was an unknown.

The neat rhyme of the French title means literally "a billion in a billiard table." This obviously doesn't work in translation, with or without the inflation, and so less inspired titles were accepted for the German, Italian and English-speaking markets. Gessner's belief in his screenplay seems fully justified. This is a warm, light-hearted comedy with enough sly observation and wit in its dialogue to allow the actors to show what they can do. They rise to the challenge commendably, and if the performances are unable to conceal the implausibility of the plot, they are engaging enough to make this feel unimportant. Any hint of film noir realism would in any case be out of place in a film which, although it pays a kind of cheeky homage to *Rififi* and the whole tradition of heist movies, is never for a moment in danger of taking itself seriously.

Bernard and Roger are anti-heroes who are well aware that they don't have what it takes to be successful robbers. They and Juliette prefer secure respectability, but are prepared to take a holiday from this just once if it will achieve their immediate goals. For cautious Roger this means the funding for an invention which he cannot obtain through conventional channels, for Bernard, escape from a hated routine and marriage with Juliette. Meeting Bettina opens a window onto a different world, with different values, for him. He is a dreamer, and it is perhaps this which charms Bettina, but the great thieves are like bankers—realists, she tells him laughingly. Despite her skepticism, he is ready to put himself to the test, but he inquires hesitantly whether Madame Ralton has killed anyone. Hardly at all, Bettina casually replies, adding in poker-faced explanation that it is against her principles.

There are times when Gessner allows the comedy to slide in the direction of outright farce, such as the scenes with the billiard table or the police visit to the malingering bank teller, and here the film is less effective. Far better are the moments when Seberg and Martinelli are allowed to tilt it towards romantic comedy. Here, when held in check, Rich is deft, Martinelli winning and Seberg shows the real talent for the genre which we had seen displayed earlier in De Broca's *Five-Day Lover*. One of the best scenes is the one on the lake, when Bettina puts Bernard through his instant criminal apprenticeship. The

In *Diamonds Are Brittle* (*Un milliard dans un billard*) with Elisabeth Flickenschildt and Jacques Santi (Comacico).

award-winning German actress Elisabeth Flickenschildt gives a nicely gauged performance in the key supporting role of the imperious mastermind Madame Ralton, and there is much to praise among the lesser players also.

A few critics saw this film as no more than a rehash of a worn-out formula, and there is certainly nothing novel in having amateurs outwit the professionals, nor indeed to see our heroes pursued by dangerous criminals, as in *Échappement libre* a year earlier. The modest originality this film does offer consists in its ability to incorporate some new twists, and above all in its freshness of characterization. Gessner and Spaak have a good deal of fun at the expense of Swiss banks, insurance companies and other easy targets, but it is all good-humored enough. Here the idea of scientific robbery goes one stage further, when Madame Ralton presides over a conference of "specialists" with academic titles, each presenting expert data in turn. There are many good throw-away lines and nice details, such as Cuendet pausing at the airport to collect the contents of a parking meter. The frothiness of this entertainment is well reflected in Georges Garvarentz's effervescent music. Nevertheless, those inclined to search a little deeper can find more substance, for this superficially amoral tale tenders food for thought in the questions it insinuates by slight of hand. We may ponder Bettina's ethical relativism or Juliette's pragmatism, and ask ourselves whether all property is, after all, theft. If, on the other hand, we prefer to let such things pass over us, we can relax and allow ourselves to be unpretentiously charmed.

The film premiered on November 17, 1965, in Paris. As Gessner recalls, "It was not a big, big hit in France, but did well enough. It was also a German-Swiss production and did very well in those countries. I wouldn't be [working today] if it had been a flop." A third of the production cost was recouped through sale to the USA alone, and it was Seberg's name on the billing which made this possible, though there was never a general release of the film in America or the UK.

## References

*Atlas Filmhefte*, 59. "Diamantenbillard." Frankfurt: Verlag Film-Kritik, 1965.
Buache, Freddy. *Le Cinéma suisse 1898–1998*. Lausanne: L'Age d'homme, 1998, pp. 111–12.
*Cinémonde*, 32:1628, 30 November 1965, p. 11.
Dumont, Hervé. *Histoire du cinéma suisse: films de fiction 1896–1965*. Lausanne: Cinémathèque Suisse, 1987, pp. 549–51.
*Le Film français*, 22:1119, 19 November 1965, p. 10.
Gessner, Nicolas. "J'ai voulu faire un Breughel" [interview with Jacques Scandelari], *Arts et loisirs*, 9, 24 November 1965, p. 40.
Gessner, Nicolas [unpublished interview].
*Intermezzo*, 20:11, 15 June 1965, p. 12.
*Jahrbuch der Filmkritik*, 7, 1967. Harry Rexin, Frauke Hanck, pp. 71–4.

## Reviews

*Amis du film et de la télévision*, 118, March 1966. P.L., V.M., p. 28.
*L'Aurore*, 19 November 1965. Claude Garson, p. 12.
*Cahiers du cinéma*, 173, December 1965. J.-A. F., p. 129.
*Le Canard enchaîné*, 24 November 1965. Michel Duran, p. 7.
*Cineinforme*, 4:39, December 1965, p. 33.
*Cinéma*, 102, January 1966, p. 135.
*Combat*, 18 November 1965. Henry Chapier, p. 8.
*La Croix*, 27 November 1965. H.R.
*Démocratie*, 25 November 1965. Guy Daussois.
*Evangelischer Film-Beobachter*, 17:42, 16 October 1965. Rex., pp. 698–9.
*L'Express*, 753, 22 November 1965. Pierre Billard, p. 69.
*Le Figaro*, 20 November 1965. Louis Chauvet, p. 20.
*Le Film français*, 3 December 1965. O., p. 15.
*Filmkritik*, November 1965. Dietrich Kuhlbrodt, p. 633.
*France-soir*, 18 November 1965. Robert Chazal, p. 17.
*L'Humanité*, 27 November 1965. Edmond Gilles, p. 8.
*Image et son* (*Saison cinématographique* 1968) C--- ^ ··
*Intermezzo*, 21:9–10 ?? ? ?
*Le Lettres fr*                                                          4.
*Le Monde*, 2
*Monthly Filh*
*Positif*, 75, N
*Télécine*, 20:1
*Télérama*, 82£
*Today's Cinem*
*Variety*, 12 Jan

"Tl                                                                  loved working
  v                                                                  Jean Seberg

A Pan Arts
Original reli

Also known as: *L'Homme à la tête fêlée* [France]; *Simson ist nicht zu schlagen* [Germany]; *Una splendida canaglia* [Italy]; *Sublime locura* [Spain]
Running Time: 105 minutes
Format: in Technicolor

CAST: [* denotes above the title billing] Sean Connery* (Samson Shillitoe); Joanne Woodward* (Rhoda); Jean Seberg* (Lydia West); Colleen Dewhurst (Dr. Vera Kropotkin); Patrick O'Neal (Dr. Oliver West); Clive Revill (Dr. Menken); Werner Peters (Dr. Frederick Vorbeck); John Fiedler (Daniel K. Papp); Kay Medford (Mrs. Fish); Jackie Coogan (Mr. Fitzgerald); Zohra Lampert (Mrs.Tupperman); Sorrell Booke (Leonard Tupperman); Sue Ane Langdon (Miss Walnicki); Bibi Osterwald (Mrs. Fitzgerald); Mabel Albertson (chairwoman); Gerald S. O'Loughlin (Chester Quirk); James Millhollin (Rollie Butter); Jon Lormer (Dr. Huddleson); Harry Bellaver (Knocker); Ayllene Gibbons (clubwoman); Richard Castellano (Albert); Renee Taylor (streetwalker); Bernie Meyer
PRODUCTION CREDITS:*Director:* Irvin Kershner; *Producer:* Jerome Hellman; *Screenplay:* Elliot Baker, based upon his novel; *Music:* John Addison; *Photography:* Ted McCord, Frank J. Calabria; *Art Director:* Jack Poplin; *Editor:* William Ziegler; *Sound:* Everett Hughes; *Music:* John Addison; *Set Designer:* Ward Preston; *Script Supervisor:* Doris DeHerdt; *Title Designer:* Wayne Fitzgerald; *Orchestration:* Billy May; *Score Mixer:* Dan Wallin; *Costumes:* Ann Roth; *Set Decorator:* Claude Carpenter; *Assistant Director:* Russell Llewellyn; *Makeup:* Gordon Bau; *Supervising Hairstylist:* Jean Burt Reilly; *Technical Adviser:* Jean Shepherd; *Stunts:* Ron Burke, Bill Hickman, Chuck Hicks, Fred Lerner, Harvey Parry, Jerry Vance

## Synopsis

Samson Shillitoe is a poet suffering from writer's block. His loyal and spirited wife Rhoda struggles to pay the bills from her earnings in a Lower East Side diner and gets to share Samson's suffering. A chaotic poetry reading for a women's cultural society brings Samson into the orbit of Lydia, the bored wife of prosperous psychiatrist Oliver West. Rhoda gives Samson's fee to West, insisting that he cure his problem. The enraged genius demands its return to no avail, for West's professional interest is sparked. West's clinic will at least provide sanctuary from creditors if not a wellspring of inspiration. Once installed there, Samson draws the attention of other staff. For one of these, Vera Kropotkin, his charms are irresistible, but for Dr. Menken he is a heaven-sent object for experimental brain surgery. West's refusal to sanction this is abruptly withdrawn after he finds the uninhibited poet sharing hydrotherapy with Lydia. Warned by Kropotkin, Samson takes flight, but has forgotten his precious manuscript and is forced to return. Although the outraged Lydia is too late to rescue him this time, even Menken's scalpel proves unable to curb Samson's excesses. Soon the unruly bard is back with Rhoda. Lydia's bid to "join Apollo" is doomed, it seems, but she helpfully clears his debts.

## Reviews

"[The film is] an odd one indeed, ranging from rich to raucous to plain fumbling. At times, it's funny as all get-out.... Seberg as the smitten spouse of a psychiatrist is pretty good. Give it A for effort and a brash B for impudence and originality. It flounders but it gleams...."—*New York Times*

"Although one never feels that Kershner is completely at ease with what he is doing (it is all rather too noisy, flurried and uncertain in mood for comfort), this remains an engaging oddball of a film, straddling a no-man's-land somewhere between the *Nouvelle Vague* and the crazy comedies of old Hollywood."—*Monthly Film Bulletin*

"*A Fine Madness* is offbeat, and downbeat, in many ways. Too heavyhanded to be comedy, yet too light to be called drama.... Fine direction and some good characterizations enhance negative script outlook."—*Variety*

"I am sorry Jean Seberg's role ... is so small. What little she has to do she does well, and it is a pleasure to watch her. It speaks well of her Iowa background that her experiences with Otto Preminger, and with the lunacies of the nouvelle vague, did not destroy her."—*Films in Review*

"*A Fine Madness* ... is also an elegant film, fluent, remarkably acted (marvelous Jean Seberg, brilliant Clive Revill, and look what Connery becomes under Kershner's direction), shot without any airs or affectations on the streets of New York...."—*Positif*

"It is interesting to notice the same talent for playing variations on a single mood.... But here all is lightness, accentuated by Ted McCord's pastel-shaded New York."—*Sight and Sound*

## Notes

Elliott Baker had had considerable experience writing for television when he embarked on his first lull-length feature, *A Fine Madness*, which was a close adaptation of his popular 1964 comic novel of the same name. For Sean Connery this was a surprising change of genre after four appearances as James Bond and the male lead in Hitchcock's *Marnie* had made him into a household name, with guaranteed box office appeal. The film was largely produced on the Warner Bros. lot in Hollywood, with some initial on-location shooting in New York City. At the time of production the Warner lot was practically deserted, with only *Who's Afraid of Virginia Woolf?* filming there concurrently. As a result of competition from television, the studio felt like a ghost town in 1965, although it would eventually recover and prosper. Seberg, Connery, Woodward and O'Neal were assembled in New York on September 13, 1965, to allow a week of location rehearsals before the shoot began.

Filming would finally wrap only a week before the Christmas vacation. During October the production team had had to cope with O'Neal's simultaneous commitment to Columbia's *Alvarez Kelly* and Woodward's illness with a viral infection. A more serious problem with the production of this film, however, was the repeated interference of Jack Warner, the studio's head. Warner demanded constant script rewrites during filming, and even after the film was completed and edited he insisted on a fresh edit. It is arguable that Baker tried to compress too much into his screenplay, and that cuts were inevitable. Seberg found working under these conditions trying, discovering changes made in her role as she went along which made little sense to her. At various times she threatened to quit the film, but the fear of being labeled as unprofessional dissuaded her, and she stayed with the project. Her feeling of frustration is understandable. Comparison of the script issued by MGM in October 1964 with the ultimate film edit shows her role to have been a prime victim of the cuts, making Lydia's behavior look completely incongruous. The final result, in the Warner edit, was not a product she felt happy about, and the director Irvin Kershner felt the same way about the film. To him, it was "beautifully cast, but nevertheless, a mess." For years he hoped to restore the picture to his original vision, but unfortunately that never happened, and we are still left with the confused and incoherent version released in May 1966.

Patrick O'Neal later remembered how Joanne Woodward organized a movie club for the cast, and how Paul Newman made popcorn for them: "Every Friday there was Sean Connery, Sean's wife, Diane, Paul, Joanne, Jean Seberg and Romain Gary.... It was just a social evening after work—we all felt very close ... Jean chose a Russian film about a little dog [presumably *Lady with a Dog*, directed by Josif Heifits in 1959, based on a Chekhov short story], which I thought was wonderfully appropriate—you know that Jean was a little girl from Iowa."

The choice of Connery as the incarnation of Baker's wild man of verse was shrewd, not merely in commercial terms. He hoped to break out of stereotype roles, and saw this one as worth doing even if it paid far less than a Bond movie. The raw energy he brings to this part gives the film an impetus which carries it through all its shakier moments, and if anyone could make this character halfway likeable or plausible as a seducer, then this is surely he. At times, in fact, we seem almost back in 007 territory, as when the amorous Dr. Kropotkin takes him under her wing. He is well partnered by Joanne Woodward as the pugnacious, strident but sympathetic Rhoda, Samson's chief mediator with the real world. Rhoda is the most believable of the characters here, but almost tips the comedy over into realistic drama when she appeals to West to accept her husband as a patient. Seasoned television actor O'Neal pitches his performance just right as the self-satisfied psychiatrist. West feels that only exceptional cases present a worthy challenge for him, but is disconcerted to find his professional ethics as insecure as everything else when he takes on this one. If O'Neal handles this joke rather well, there is little for Seberg to do beyond acting as the straight foil for him and the libidinous Freudian Vorbeck. Although Lydia's interaction with Samson is rendered nonsensical in the final cut, she projects effectively as the "bird in a gilded cage" in stark contrast to Rhoda. Untypically, as in *Five-Day Lover*, Seberg becomes a brunette pitted against a blond rival, but this time her character is almost unique in lacking any coloring of humor, and it is hardly her fault if it feels that she is out of place.

In *A Fine Madness* with Sean Connery (Warner Bros.).

Baker sidesteps any questions of taste in dealing with mental illness, for his satire is laser-guided onto the professionals. In any case, the film never claims to be more than a divertissement, and much of it works very well on the level of situational comedy. Here Kershner is well served by his supporting actors, notably Dewhurst, Booke, Albertson and Langdon. Clive Revill is memorably ghoulish as the scalpel-wielding egomaniac Menken, puffed up with the nobility of his calling, but to whom patients are simply fodder for self-glorification.

John Addison, whose scores have embellished so many British films, here provides a suitably opulent and brassy main theme for the Big Apple setting, perhaps playfully alluding to Connery's Bond film association, and with a passing nod to Cole Porter. At times Addison points up the comedy with tinkling harpsichord, ondes Martenot or similar effects suggestive of the weird world of psychoanalysis. Music supports characterization too, and Seberg is even provided with her own silky saxophone leitmotiv. Cinematographer Ted McCord, with laurels dating back to *The Treasure of the Sierra Madre* and *East of Eden,* came fresh from the hills of *The Sound of Music* to round off his long career with Kershner on the streets of Manhattan. Kershner and McCord are equally skillful in catching nuances of comedy in flight and in rooting the action in the reality of the city. A chase sequence on Brooklyn Bridge may seem superfluous and contrived, but here it is a visual bonus of which it would be churlish to complain. In summary, for all its confused plot and bouts of silliness, *A Fine Madness* is sufficiently well scripted and acted to make passable viewing even for audiences accustomed to a quite different style of comedy. As a window into the mid-60s, it is fascinating, but the formula failed to draw the crowds in the summer of 1966, notwithstanding the studio's guarantee of an "extrastrength laugh." In commercial terms the result was, by Connery's verdict, "highly unsuccessful."

Coincidentally, the Karel Reisz film *Morgan, a Suitable Case for Treatment* was also released in 1966. This low budget British production also took a whimsical look at the socially dysfunctional artist who leaves a trail of mayhem, and though the treatment is dissimilar, some reviewers noted the common theme. Kershner and Connery were to work together again seven years later, when the actor was lured back to the Bond series for *Never Say Never Again.*

## References

Baker, Elliott. *A Fine Madness.* New York: G.P. Putnams Sons and London: M. Joseph, 1964.

Berg, Herbert. "Stress feminine beauty in Warner 'Madness.'" *Motion Picture Daily,* 99:91, p. 4.

Ciment, Michel, et al. Irvin Kershner, interview. *Positif,* 148, March 1973, pp. 1–21.

*Filmfacts,* 9:15, 1 September 1966, pp. 176–7.

Huskins, D. Gail. *Magill's survey of cinema: English language films.* Englewood Cliffs, NJ: Salem Press, 1981, second series, vol. 2, pp. 781–3.

Morella, Joe, and Edward Z. Epstein. *Paul and Joanne: a biography of Paul Newman and Joanne Woodward.* New York: Delacorte Press, 1988, pp. 114–5.

*Motion Picture Herald,* 13 October 1965, p. 11-A.

Pfeiffer, Lee, and Philip Lisa. *The films of Sean Connery.* 3d ed. New York: Citadel Press, 2001, pp. 91–5.

Sellers, Robert. *Sean Connery: a celebration.* London: Robert Hale, 1999, pp. 87–8, 192.

## Reviews

*ABC Film Review,* 16:9, September 1966. Kevin McEgan, pp. 8–9.

*America,* 114, 18 June 1966, p. 861.

*Amis du film et de la télévision,* 129, February 1967. J.D., V.M., pp. 34–5.

*L'Aurore,* 31 December 1966. Robert Monange, p. 13.

*Cahiers du cinéma,* 186, January 1967. Jean Narboni, p. 72.

*Le Canard enchaîné,* 52:2411, 4 January 1967. Michel Duran, p. 7.

*Cinema,* 3:3, July 1966. Richard Whitehall, p. 48.

*Commonweal,* 84:10, 27 May 1966. Philip T. Hartung, pp. 284–5.

*The Daily Cinema*, 15 July 1966. M.H., p. 6.
*The Daily Mail*, 19 July 1966. Cecil Wilson, p. 10.
*The Daily Telegraph*, 22 July 1966. Patrick Gibbs, p. 17.
*The Evening Standard*, 21 July 1966. Alexander Walker, p. 10.
*Le Figaro*, 2 January 1967. Louis Chauvet, p. 10.
*The Film Daily*, 9 May 1966. Louis Pelegrine, p. 7.
*Film Quarterly*, 20:1, Fall 1966. R.M. Hodgens, p. 59.
*Filmkritik*, December 1966. Peter W. Jansen, p. 689.
*Films and Filming*, 12:12, September 1966. Mike Sarne, p. 10.
*Films in Review*, 17:6, June/July 1966. Adelaide Comerford, pp. 381–2.
*The Financial Times*, 22 July 1966. David Robinson, p. 24.
*France-soir*, 3 January 1967. Robert Chazal, p. 6.
*The Guardian*, 22 July 1966. Richard Roud, p. 11.
*The Hollywood Reporter*, 9 May 1966. James Powers, p. 3.
*Image et son*, 203, March 1967. René Tabès, p. 117.
*Kinematograph Weekly*, 3068, 21 July 1966. Graham Clarke, p. 10.
*Le Monde*, 1–2 January 1967. Yvonne Baby, p. 14.
*Monthly Film Bulletin*, 33:392, September 1966. T.M., pp. 136–7.
*Motion Picture Daily*, 99:90, 9 May 1966. Don Gordon, p. 8.
*The New Statesman*, 72, 22 July 1966, p. 141.
*The New York Times*, 30 June 1966. Howard Thompson, p. 28.
*The New Yorker*, 42:20, 9 July 1966. Susan Lardner, pp. 78–80.
*Newsweek*, 67:26, 27 June 1966, pp. 94–5.
*Le Nouvel observateur*, 113, 11 January 1967. Michel Mardore, p. 45.
*Positif*, 87 September 1967. Michel Ciment, pp. 52–3.
*Saturday Review*, 49:21, 21 May 1966. Arthur Knight, p. 49.
*Sight and Sound*, 35:4 Autumn 1966. Elizabeth Sussex, p. 201.
*Télérama*, 887, 15 January 1967. Claude-Marie Trémois, p. 57.
*Time*, 88:2, 8 July 1966, p. 84.
*The Times*, 21 July 1966, p. 17.
*Variety*, 4 May 1966. Murf., p. 6.
*Village Voice*, 18 August 1966. Andrew Sarris, p. 23.

# *The Line of Demarcation*
# *(La Ligne de démarcation)* (1966)

> "Chabrol is such a strange man. I think with *La Ligne de démarcation*
> he believed he was going to make almost a parody of the Resistance,
> and of that whole period of French life."—Jean Seberg

A Georges de Beauregard film / A Rome-Paris Films—Société Nouvelle de Ciné-
matographie co-production; A CCFC release
Original release: in French; released with English subtitles
Also known as: *La Linea di demarcazione* [Italy]
Running Time: 120 minutes
Format: in Black and White

CAST: [* denotes above the title billing] Jean Seberg* (Mary, comtesse de Damville);
Maurice Ronet* (Pierre, comte de Damville); Daniel Gélin* (Doctor Lafaye); Jacques Per-
rin* (Michel); Stéphane Audran* (Colette Lafaye); Claude Berri (Jewish refugee); Reinhard
Kolldehoff (Major von Pritsch); Claude Léveillé (Captain Duncan Presgrave); Roger
Dumas ('Le Chéti'); Mario David (Urbain); Jean Yanne (Tricot, the schoolteacher); Noël
Roquevert (Ménétru); Jean-Louis Maury, Paul Gégauff (Gestapo agents); Pierre Gualdi
(Curé); René Havard (Loiseau); Jean-Louis Le Goff (Tavier); Henri Attal (gendarme);

Dominique Zardi (German soldier); René Havard (Loiseau); Serge Bento (Siméon, the barber); R. Lenoir (German customs officer); M. Dacquin (German officer); J. Gerster (young German soldier); G. Bucchini (Jeanne, wife of Urbain); D. O'Brien (American airman); B. Curran (Scottish airman); J.-M. Arnoux (Belgian); G. Servien (carpenter); L. Palys (farmer); G. Kern, G. Outrey (patriots)

PRODUCTION CREDITS: *Director:* Claude Chabrol; *Producer:* Georges de Beauregard; *Screenplay:* Colonel Rémy, Claude Chabrol; *Director of Photography:* Jean Rabier; *Editors:* Jacques Gaillard, Monique Fardoulis; *Music:* Pierre Jansen; *Musical Director:* André Jouve; extract from Weber clarinet concerto op.73; song *Bel Ami* sung by Raoul Valmont, words and music by Mackeben & Beckman, publisher Méridian; *Sound:* Guy Chichignoud; *Production Design:* Guy Littaye; *Production Directors:* René Demoulin, Roger Scipion; *Assistant Directors:* Pierre Gauchet, Claude Bakka, Alexis Poliakoff; *Cameraman:* Claude Zidi; *1st Assistant Cameraman:* Paul Bonis; *Accessories:* Jean Brunet; *Costumes:* Dolly Cousteau; *Script Girl:* Annie Maurel; *[Still] Photographer:* Jean Klissak; *Continuity:* Aurore Paquiss; *Perchman:* Guy Odet; *Production Secretary:* Colette Roy

## Synopsis

Dôle is on the border between Nazi-occupied and Vichy France where this follows the course of the river Loue, and is a vital crossing point for fugitives. Among those who secretly help escapees is Mary, English-born wife of Pierre, Comte de Damville. In 1941 Pierre, an injured officer captured by the Germans, returns home convinced that further resistance is futile. Their friends Dr Lafaye and his wife Colette also assist refugees at great personal risk, while others exploit these for profit. German Commandant Von Pritsch seeks cordial relations with the aristocratic couple, but the situation changes when Gestapo officers learn of two agents parachuted into the area. One of these, radio operator Michel, is badly wounded and treated by Lafaye at the hospital. Fearing that the Germans will force Michel to betray the network, Resistance volunteers in German uniforms stage a daring rescue. The doctor and his wife pay dearly for their involvement. Michel is sheltered by the schoolteacher and nursed by Mary. Finally the curé plans to transport Michel safely across the river hidden in a coffin.

When his own wife is arrested Pierre realizes belatedly that it is the Gestapo which wields all the power. Pierre shoots down the two Germans who attempt to stop the hearse as it crosses the bridge, sacrificing his own life to save Michel.

## Reviews

"[The film] had the paradoxical effect of seeming almost too respectable, with its carefully judged atmosphere of wartime resistance and solidly restrained playing by Gélin and Seberg.... Though the film becomes rather silly towards the end, there is much to admire in the detailed clarity of its telling."—*Sight and Sound*

"You cannot but admire the way in which he places his characters, tells his story and handles the flow of the action.... For Claude Chabrol the age of creative maturity has arrived."—*Télérama*

"The intelligence and modernity of expression of Jean Seberg make her character as the Countess of English origin believable, just as the injured and demoralized tone of Maurice Ronet admirably reflects this aristocrat ... [but] Chabrol's film does not avoid tiresomeness."—*Combat*

"Chabrol ... here puts away many of his inside jokes, anarchic themes and characters to make a solid action drama on the divided France during the last World War. Jean Seberg etches a good picture of a dedicated woman ready to risk her life and yet accept her husband's weary resignation."—*Variety*

"The introduction of actors with a natural modern technique, such as Jacques Perrin and Jean Seberg, creates a discord. They, and particularly Seberg, make one forget the excessive characterization of their roles through their humanity, but that still prevents them from appearing as positive elements."—*Cahiers du cinéma*

"*Line of Demarcation* is proof that Chabrol can concern himself with the fate of many instead of his usual handful of characters. [It] is a must for admirers of this New Wave pioneer."—*Los Angeles Times*

## Notes

According to Chantal de Beauregard, the resistance hero Colonel Rémy was approached with the proposal for a film which would pay homage to the French resistance movement. The name of Anthony Mann was put forward for director, and there was talk of Montgomery Clift for the leading role. It was concluded, however, that this would be a less ambitious, national project. It was natural for Beauregard to turn to Claude Chabrol, and Rémy warmly endorsed this choice. Chabrol liked to work with people he knew, and Maurice Ronet was selected for the role envisaged for Clift. When Leslie Caron turned down the part of the Countess, the choice fell on Seberg.

The film was shot on location in the Dôle region of the Jura over seven weeks, from January 31, 1966. The story was based on real incidents which Colonel Rémy had incorporated in a series of books before working with Chabrol. Despite the director's genuine interest in the period, this must have been a slightly odd collaboration, and Chabrol described Rémy as an "old reactionary" and "one of the most appalling characters I know." He related with amusement to the journalists of *Positif* and again to François Guérif how he duped the veteran on set, pretending to shoot a scene which he had decided to cut. This was one in which Rémy heavy-handedly contrasts the "honorable" Wehrmacht and the ruthless Gestapo. It was Chabrol who insisted that if the *Marseillaise* featured in the final scene, so too should the *Internationale*.

The director often seems scrupulously detached from his narrative. Clearly he didn't take the film as solemnly as some would have wished, and while it honors the real courage of many of its characters (note the opening dedication to the heroic "passeurs"), there is an occasional hint of tongue-in-cheek about the moral demarcation line we are being offered. Chabrol told Claude Sartirano, "Let's say it's a realistic film, a film entirely at face value. There's no hidden message ... there is no point of view ... or rather there are sixty. I told each actor he had the principal role, and it's true." He likened the whole thing to a funnel in which all the action converged, and perhaps this throws light on his stance as a somewhat aloof and ironic, if not entirely unsympathetic puppet master.

There are obvious touches of Chabrolian malice. We note his treatment of certain stock characters, no doubt inescapable in such a real life situation. He evidently relishes, for example, the Gestapo man played by Jean-Louis Maury, the irascible Ménétru who preposterously launches into the *Internationale* for the benefit of an astonished German, and the *passeur* "Le Chéti" (an apt nickname, meaning shifty) who shrugs off the shameless exploitation of a Jewish family because he has "a family to feed." Some critics were offended by this tone, while others hardly seemed to notice. In any case, for Chabrol this was just representing human beings "as they are," telling the truth as he saw it. He tells it, indeed, with a certain technical mastery, deployed without ostentation.

If this was the director's farewell to black and white, the absence of color in this instance seems in no way a weakness. In fact the somber tones of Rabier's camerawork

In Claude Chabrol's period piece *The Line of Demarcation* (*La Ligne de démarcation*) with Daniel Gélin, Stéphane Audran and Maurice Ronet (CCFC).

build an atmosphere of hovering menace from the very outset. When the nerve-jangling musical score of Pierre Jansen, another Chabrol stalwart, is added to this the mood becomes doubly intense and oppressive.

The film was premiered in Paris on May 25, 1966, with many decorated war veterans making a show of the occasion. It seems to have been well received by the public at the time, and Chabrol recalled that it sold well, but it has not been highly rated among his large output over the years. In an interesting survey of films missed by British distributors, John Baxter attributed this film's failure to gain release to the perplexing changes in style between the director's films rather than to doubts about its quality. Its neglect certainly seems unwarranted, even if it cannot rival his greatest successes. *La Ligne de démarcation* has many good things to offer, not least of which are the well measured performances of the leading cast.

## References

Alexandre, Wilfrid. *Claude Chabrol, la traversée des apparences: biographie*. Paris: Éditions du Félin, 2003.

Baxter, John. "Unforthcoming attractions." *Sunday Times Magazine*, 13 May 1973, pp. 36–41, 83–4.

Beauregard, Chantal de. *Georges de Beauregard*. Nîmes: Lacour, 1991, pp. 207–9.

Chabrol, Claude. Interviews with Claude Sartirano and Anne Capelle. *Arts et loisirs*, 26, 23 March 1966, pp. 15–16, and 36, 1 June 1966, p. 63.

_____. Interview by Michel Ciment, Gérard Legrand, Jean-Paul Török. *Positif*, 115, translation Elisabeth Cameron: *Movie*, no. 18, Winter 1970–71, p. 6.

Delmas, Jean. 19440–44 à l'écran de 1966. *Jeune cinéma*, 20 February 1967, pp. 3–4.

*Le Film français*, 23:1130, 4 February 1966, p. 10.

Guérif, François. *Conversations avec ... Claude Chabrol: Un Jardin bien à moi*. Paris: Denoël, 1999, pp. 91–4, 172, 253.

*Image et Son*, 279, December 1973. Jacques Zimmer, pp. 60–61.

Le Fol, Sébastien. "Mon village à l'heure allemande." *Le Figaro*, 18627, 26 June 2004, pp. 76–7.

Rémy, Colonel. *Le Pont sur la ligne, d'après La Ligne de démarcation*. Paris: Solar, 1966.

Thomas, Kevin. "'Line' in weekend marathon." *Los Angeles Times*, 9 February 1973, s.4 p. 20.

Wood, Robin, and Michael Walker. *Claude Chabrol*. London: Studio Vista, 1970.

## Reviews

*Amis du film et de la télévision*, 126, November 1966, p. 36 [see also note in 127, December 1966, p. 36].
*L'Aurore*, 26 May 1966. Claude Garson, p. 9.
*Cahiers du cinéma*, 182, September 1966. Luc Moullet, pp. 72–3.
*Le Canard enchaîné*, 1 June 1966. M.D., p. 7.
*Cineinforme*, 4:46, 13 July 1966, p. 38.
*Cinéma*, 108, July/August 1966. G. Braucourt, pp. 104–6.
*Combat*, 27 May 1966. Henry Chapier, p. 10.
*La Croix*, 4 June 1966.
*Le Figaro*, 30 May 1966. Louis Chauvet, p. 8.
*Le Film français*, 1149, 10 June 1966. L.D., p. 11.
*France nouvelle*, 2076, 15 June 1966. Albert Cervoni.
*France-soir*, 29 May 1966. Robert Chazal, p. 7.
*Frankfurter Rundschau*, 4 May 1966. Felix Unruh, p. 14.
*Image et son*, 197–8, Sept./Oct. 1966 (*Saison cinématographique* 1966). Jacqueline Lajeunesse, p. 113.
*Les Lettres françaises*, 1134, 2 June 1966. Marcel Martin, pp. 19–20.
*Livres de France*, 17:7, August/September 1966. Marcel Lasseaux, p. 29.
*Le Monde*, 31 May 1966. Jean de Baroncelli, p. 21.
*Le Nouvel observateur*, 82, 8 June 1966. Michel Cournot, p. 40.
*Le Populaire de Paris*, 7 June 1966. Henri Marc, p. 6.
*Positif*, 80, December 1966. Albert Bolduc, pp. 140–1.
*Sight and Sound*, 35:4, Autumn 1966. John Gillett, p. 173.
*Téléciné*, 21:131, December 1966. C. Hermelin, p. 54.
*Télérama*, 856, 12 June 1966. Claude-Jean Philippe, p. 77.
*Variety*, 8 June 1966. Gene Moskowitz, p. 18.

# *Revolt in the Caribbean (Estouffade à la Caraïbe)* (1967)

A PAC (Paris) / CMV (Rome) co-production; A Valoria release
Original release: In French; Dubbed in English
Also known as: *The Looters*; *Stew in the Caribbean*; *The Gold Robbers*; *Haie bitten zu Tisch* [Germany]; *Avventurieri per una rivolta* [Italy]; *Bucaneros siglo XX* [Spain]
Running Time: 100 minutes
Format: in Eastmancolor, Franscope

CAST: [* denotes above the title billing] Jean Seberg* (Colleen O'Hara); Frederick Stafford* (Sam Morgan); Maria-Rosa Rodriguez (Estella); Fernand Bellan (Targo); Vittorio Sanipoli (Kosta); André Cagnard (soldier); Marco Guglielmi (Dietrich); Mario Pisu (Patrick O'Hara); Paul Crauchet (Valdes); Serge Gainsbourg (Joey Clyde); César Torrès (Miguel); Cissé Karamoko (Manolo); and José Noguero
PRODUCTION CREDITS: *Director:* Jacques Besnard; *Producer:* André Hunebelle; *Screenplay:* Pierre Foucaud, Michel Lebrun, from the book by Albert Conroy; *Photography:* Marcel Grignon; *Editor:* Gilbert Natot; *Music:* Michel Magne; *Art Director:* Henri Sonois; *Sound:* René Forget, Jacques Lebreton; *Production Manager:* Cyril Grize; *Assistant Director:* Michel Lang; *Still photography:* Roger Corbeau; *Décor:* Max Douy, Henri Sonois; *General production:* Jacques Pignier; *Assistant Producer:* Paul Cadéac; *Direction 2nd crew:* Pierre Cosson; *1st Assistant:* Michel Lang; *Script Girl:* Charlotte Lefèvre; *Cameramen:* Georges Pastier, Bernard Noisette; *Assistant Operator:* Robert Fraisse; *Décor Assistants:* Jacques Douy, Jean-Jacques Cadéac; *Assistant Editor:* Colette Lambert; *Sound effects:* Daniel Couteau; *Costumes:* Mireille Leydet, Jo Ranzato; *Makeup:* René Daudin, Denise Daudin; *Jean Seberg's hair:* Jacques Dessange; *Special effects:* Michel Durin; *Accessories:* François and Michel Sune; *Fights:* André Cagnard; *Photography:* Roger Corbeau; *Director's Assistants:* Ginette Bodin, Chantal Larouette; *Production administrator:* Bernard Artigues; *Press Assistant:* Paulette Andrieux

## Synopsis

Sam Morgan is a reformed safebreaker working for wealthy tourists in Miami. He is drugged and shanghaied by alluring stranger Colleen O'Hara and taken to the island of Caribo, ruled by dictator President Cuevas. Resistance to Cuevas is led by idealist Valdes and bandit chief Kosta. With the help of O'Hara, Colleen's gangster father, they hope to recover the island's gold reserves and topple the regime. O'Hara has already recruited Morgan's former partner Clyde, yet still needs Morgan's unique skills to get at bullion stored in the island's fortress. Morgan only agrees to help after he witnesses the brutality of police chief Targo's men at first hand.

Morgan and Clyde succeed in stealing the plans of the bullion vault from the Presidential Palace. Targo's soldiers ambush the rebels. Morgan rescues Colleen from them, but her father is killed in the fighting before help arrives. The insurgents succeed in entering the fortress and holding it until the gold can be secured. Targo is killed, the President resigns and a new government under Valdes is proclaimed. Morgan further redeems himself in Colleen's eyes when he persuades the others to restore all of the island's treasure to the people.

## Reviews

"Attractive location work is the best feature of this rather old-fashioned Caribbean adventure, which has the benefit of a convincing general setting and an authentic-looking fortress citadel. The action, quite lively from the start, builds up to a nicely timed climax, even if some of the development is a little sluggish."—*Monthly Film Bulletin*

"There are some fair battle scenes and the obvious suspense of the safe cracking ploy. But this rather turgid tale neither reaches the heights of a gutsy tongue-in-cheek actioner or a melodramatic politico adventure opus."—*Variety*

"One imagines that this blend of gangsterism and revolution isn't easy to make work on the screen. The director doesn't entirely succeed, but improves in the action scenes, which are generally well handled. Jacques Besnard handles crowds skillfully, which is something not all directors can do."—*Le Soir*

"Besnard and his team have tried to produce an American-style film: adventure, love scenes, scraps, suspense.... They have succeeded in doing that. The screenplay is just a conventional vehicle for introducing fights and suspense, but the production is attractive and the pace dynamic. Interest is sustained, which is the important thing...."—*Analyse générale des films*

"Frederick Stafford has very well filmed pectorals and Jean Seberg has recalled her *Saint Joan* role in playing a Passionaria of charm."—*France-soir*

"Jean Seberg attractively does all that is necessary with the part of Colleen, and there is a strong and active supporting cast."—*Kinematograph Weekly*

## Notes

Jacques Besnard had worked as an assistant to director André Hunebelle on *Furia à Bahia Pour OSS 117* (*Mission for a Killer*, 1965), which had starred the muscular Czech-born actor Frederick Stafford. This time Hunebelle was producer and Besnard took over as director for an adaptation of an action adventure called *The Looters*. Its author Albert Conroy (a pseudonym used by Marvin H. Albert) had set his adventure on a fictitious small Caribbean island named Caribo, and it was decided that the shoot should take place in northern Colombia. For Stafford, who would again star, this was no more than a variation on the kind of James Bond-style roles for which he had already proved his aptitude. In Jean Seberg's case the "carrot," as she referred to it, which induced her to accept the female lead was the unusual location setting. As she explained to Claude-Marie Tré-mois, "I play a quite complex character who interested me, the daughter of a gangster. I'm torn between an almost tribal loyalty to my father and the contempt I feel for his source of income." The inclusion of hugely popular singer Serge Gainsbourg in the casting could only add to box office appeal. Production began on August 8, 1966, and was concluded at the Studios St-Maurice by the end of October. Seberg, Stafford and Gainsbourg posed for publicity shots designed to exploit the colorful Cartagena background. Behind the smiles, Seberg was said to have been appalled by the extreme poverty she witnessed around her. In an interview six years later she would also recall the overwhelming heat which dissolved makeup, and that she had to be protected from the sharks while swimming in Santa Marta Bay.

Conroy's book and its adaptation by Foucaud and Lebrun are conceived in terms of action and adventure, and there is little investment in the development of characters beyond the requirements of spectacle. Thus, apart from the love interest provided by Seberg and Stafford, everything serves the creation of situations of danger, pursuits and fights which comprise the major sections of the film. Morgan is immediately drawn to Colleen, but has to overcome her assumption that he is like the other criminal types her father employs. In her eyes he is a "cheap thief," not to be trusted and "capable of anything." He finds such disapproval odd, coming from a gangster's daughter, but she points out that parentage, unlike a profession, isn't a matter of choice. She seems to protest too much in declaring her loathing for "you and everything you represent," and her sudden conversion comes as little surprise after he has proved his essential integrity and heroism.

There is no time here for much moral complexity. Targo is sadistic and his men child-killers and would-be rapists, whereas Valdes is an idealist who works with bandits only for pragmatic reasons. Colleen instinctively sides with justice in spite of her upbringing. With her father's self-sacrificial death and Morgan's vindication her conflicts are resolved. That the hero Morgan will henceforth choose the path of virtue has been made clear from the outset. Dietrich is "a rat," but has helped good to prevail despite his intentions, and

In *Revolt in the Caribbean* (*Estouffade à la Caraïbe*) with **Daniel Crauchet, Cissé Karamoko, Frederick Stafford, Serge Gainsbourg, Vittorio Sanipoli.**

it is implied that Clyde can be excused a little larceny on the same grounds. Dialogue is used chiefly to move the story along, and we learn what we need to know about the characters more from their behavior than from their words. The action sequences are generally well handled, if occasionally a little confused, and although the story is conventional enough it has a well sustained pace which hides most of its weaknesses.

An *estouffade* is a kind of beef stew. No dish can please everyone, but this is wholesome enough fare made all the more palatable by the contributions from Seberg and Stafford. This is a Robin Hood world in which villainy is thwarted and nobody (intellectual film devotees excepted) suffers very much. Besnard's film is ultimately a forgettable piece of escapism without pretensions, as conventional in point of view as in its characters and formula, rather like an adventure holiday expertly shot in Eastmancolor. When the film premiered in Paris on August 9, 1967, the critics generally appeared to accept it on these terms, perhaps noting the weak script yet simultaneously appreciating its visual qualities.

Stafford was to have a leading part in Hitchcock's *Topaz* in 1969 and was, as we shall see, to be reunited with Seberg in 1975 for a very different kind of role.

## References

Conroy, Albert. *The Looters*. New York: Fawcett, 1961.
Deglin, Paul. *Ciné revue* 47:33, 17 August 1967, p. 27.
*Le Film français*, 23:1156, 26 August 1966, p. 14.
*Intermezzo*, 22:18, 30 September 1967, p. 10.
Samadiegos, Luiz. *Le Nouveau cinémonde*, 32:1662, 11 October 1966, pp. 17–19.

## Reviews

*Amis du film et de la télévision*, 137, October 1967. J.D., V.M., p. 26.
*Analyse générale des films*, 1968. F.B., pp. 157–8.
*Cahiers du cinéma*, 194, October 1967. Jean Narboni, p. 71.
*Le Canard enchaîné*, 16 August 1967. R.B., p. 7.
*Cineinforme*, 5:59/60, August/September 1967, p. 70.
*Le Figaro*, 14 August 1967. Pierre Mazars, p. 8.
*Le Film français*, 1 September 1967. J.G., p. 13.
*France-soir*, 11 August 1967. Jean Macabies, p. 6.
*Image et son*, 219–20 Sept./Oct. 1968, *Saison cinématographique* 1968. René Tabiès, pp. 219–20.
*Kinematograph Weekly*, 3247, 3 January 1970. Graham Clarke, pp. 10, 16.
*Le Monde*, 13–14 August 1967. Yvonne Baby, p. 13.
*Monthly Film Bulletin*, 37:433, February 1970, p. 33.
*Le Soir*, 18 August 1967. Synchro., p. 20.
*Télérama*, 919, 27 August 1967. Claude-Marie Trémois, p. 48.
*Télérama*, 2472, 28 May 1997, p. 123.
*Today's Cinema*, 9769, 9 January 1970. Marjorie Bilbow, p. 12.
*Variety*, 8 November 1967. Gene Moskowitz, p. 24.

# *The Road to Corinth*
# *(La Route de Corinthe)* (1967)

"[Chabrol] tries a bit of everything. He plays in the best sense: the kind
of make-believe you find in children. He enjoys what he does, and he
always does it with incredible gusto."—Jean Seberg

A Films de Boétie (Paris) / Compagnia Generale Finanzaria Cinematografica (Rome) / Orion Films (Athens) co-production; A CCFC release
Original release: in French; English dubbed
Also known as: *Who's Got the Black Box?*; *Criminal Story* [Italy]; *Die Strasse von Korinth* [Germany]; *La Ruta de Corinto* [Spain]
Running Time: 90 minutes; [85 minutes English version]
Format: in Cinemascope, Eastmancolor

CAST: [* denotes above the title billing] Jean Seberg* (Shanny); Maurice Ronet* (Dex); Christian Marquand* (Robert Ford); Michel Bouquet (Sharps); Saro Urzzi [elsewhere Urzì] (Khalides/Skolikidis); Antonio Passalia (Killer); Paolo Giusti (Josio); Claude Chabrol (Alcibiades); Stève Eckardt (Socrate); with Max Roman, Artemis Matsas Zannino, Vassili Diamantopoulos
PRODUCTION CREDITS: *Director:* Claude Chabrol; *Producer:* André Génovès; *Screenplay:* Claude Brulé, Daniel Boulanger; *Dialogue:* Daniel Boulanger; Based on the novel by Claude Rank; *Music:* Pierre Jansen; *Music Director:* André Jouve; *Photography:* Jean Rabier; *Editors:* Jacques Gaillard, Monique Fardoulis; *Art Design:* Mariléna Aravantinou; *Sound:* Guy Chichignoud; *Production Managers:* Alain Quefféléan, Stefanos Vlachos; *Assistant Directors:* Pierre Gauchet, Michel Grégoriou; *Script Girl:* Denise Gaillard; *Cameraman:* Claude Zidi; *Assistant Operators:* Paul Bonis, Janine Rabier; *Still Photographs:* Pierre Zucca; *Chief Costumer:* Maurice Albray; *Costumes:* Arlette Nastat Réal; *Hairstylist:* Jacques Dessange; *Grip:* Jean Gimello; *Accessories:* André Davalan; *Administration:* Paul Maigret, Gérard Espinet; *Production Team:* Gérard Crosnier, Patrick Delaunaux, Max Roman

## *Synopsis*

A plot to disable NATO's radar defense system in Greece is detected. Undercover agents Robert and Dex are to investigate and report to their untrustworthy boss Sharps. Robert learns only of a link to Khalides Marble Industry before his informant Alcibiades is shot. Robert is assassinated and his wife Shanny arrested as a suspect. Sharps wants the widow quickly out of the way. She dupes him, determined to avenge Robert's murder. Alcibiades, still alive, offers information if she will bring payment to the cemetery in two days. Shanny eludes Dex, charged by Sharps to ensure she leaves Greece, and uses her wits to find the money needed.

Shanny is followed to the rendezvous by Sharps and Dex, who see Alcibiades knifed by assailants disguised as priests. She continues to spy on the marble works and hides in a truck visiting the quarry at Corinth. Khalides' men interrogate her, but with help from truck driver Josio she escapes. Dex reluctantly accompanies Shanny to the factory, where they see electronic devices hidden in marble blocks. Shanny evades her protector only to be captured again by Khalides. The timely arrival of Dex ensures the spectacular end intended for her is Khalides' own fate.

## *Reviews*

"... The banal and mechanical plot was never intended as anything more than a transparent thread on which to string a succession of hallucinatingly beautiful images.... But by the end of the film one has come to savor the sheer sensuality of Chabrol's playful Greek tragedy...."—*Monthly Film Bulletin*

"Whereas spy films are usually ugly, boring and mediocre, this one by Claude Chabrol is quite the contrary. There is just enough mystery and drollery here to make the story's twists and turns captivating and amusing. ... it shows how you can be 'commercial' with talent."—*Le Monde*

"*La Route de Corinthe* is a pastiche of all the 'James Bond' movies known, past, present and to come, showing the public that, if it lets itself be gulled elsewhere, it can come here for a laugh, with a story at least as 'serious' as the others it is offered every week." —*L'Humanité*

"The plot, however, is hardly up to the same standard and its somewhat jerky progression is largely predictable and careless of probability. There is, however, a fair enough ration of excitement in the shape of the villain's sinister hired killers and some chases." —*Kinematograph Weekly*

"Jean Seberg is too scatterbrained and her protector, Maurice Ronet, too occupied by the lovely eyes of his partner, Michel Bouquet too much caricatured.... And yet ... the director doesn't lack imagination, and the hiding-place of the 'radar-jammer' will amuse you, like us, when you discover it." —*L'Aurore*

"This golden role—or at least a gold-plated one—is played with conquering charm by Jean Seberg." —*France-soir*

"Let's not forget to mention, among the favorable factors: Jean Seberg and her graceful liveliness...." —*Le Figaro*

## Notes

Claude Rank's 1966 spy thriller *La Route de Corinthe* is a competent but routine pulp offering, with little to differentiate it from the 60s spate of James Bond-style adventures other than having a female protagonist. André Génovès was the producer invited by the distributors to turn the book into a film, and apparently felt no great enthusiasm for the project, which was seen as purely commercial. Claude Chabrol's was not the first name considered when looking for a director, as Nicolas Gessner reveals:

The script was so stupid I turned it down despite the fact that Jean would star. Do you know why Chabrol did it? Because I withdrew. When I told the producer I didn't want to do it, I suggested Chabrol. "Ah, Chabrol. Great idea!" Chabrol was in a very bad period—silly spy spoof movies. So I feel I'm the Godfather to the comeback of Chabrol." When Génovès contacted Chabrol about *The Road to Corinth* he found him also lukewarm, but he agreed to direct it provided he could also direct a second film of his own choice. "He got a double contract," as Gessner recalls, "and his second movie was *Les Biches*, which was a big, big hit. He then made all of the big shot movies after *La Route de Corinthe*. [He] did the film as well as he could—probably better than I would have done, because I would have been worried about all the weakness of it. Chabrol didn't mind and just went along. Perhaps that was the best thing to do.

In fact this was a good deal for the director, relieving him of immediate money problems and financing the making of a film he had just written, with a major role for Stéphane Audran. It also marked the beginning of his fruitful partnership with Génovès and an important friendship and collaboration with the actor Michel Bouquet. He was happy to work for a second time with Seberg and Ronet because, as he told François Guérif, they had become great friends making *La Ligne de démarcation*. Génovès was, in the event, let down by the distributors, so that the production ran out of money during the seven-week shoot. Chabrol nevertheless managed to finish the picture, which cemented his relationship with the producer in a partnership which would produce a dozen further films.

Rank's plot involves a conspiracy to conceal electronic devices to disable NATO radar missile defenses in the pylons bordering the Corinth Canal. On arriving on location, however, Chabrol was dismayed to find there were no such pylons. Some hasty rewriting was called for, involving Claude Brulé, Daniel Boulanger and the director himself.

What would a director like Chabrol do when stuck with a story too silly to believe in? His response has to be to make it even sillier, but to have as much fun as possible on the way. Little of the original narrative survives in the screenplay, but the elements with the greatest entertainment potential have been freely cannibalized. Villainous plots, disguised assassins, abduction, hidden passages—we might wonder whether we haven't strayed into the world of Louis Feuillade. Wisely, Chabrol allowed himself to be guided by his own sense of humor and penchant for off-beat characters. Admittedly, he often over-eggs the pudding, but by entering into the spirit of his story in this way he avoids the tedium which might have resulted from a more literal treatment. What he finally offers us are the picaresque adventures of Shanny, a wide-eyed but resourceful innocent, who somehow survives the perils of a world where "nothing is quite what it seems."

There was no reason to resist the odd private joke or Godard-style self-indulgence in a piece of genial nonsense like this. Accordingly, Chabrol too dons various false whiskers to play the ill-fated informer Alcibiades, whose appearances seem to mimic the solemnity of Greek tragedy. Romain Gary accompanied his wife during the shoot, so the bronzed and bearded writer is predictably on screen too as an Orthodox priest in the final moments. We are not told whether he had any other input. This, at any rate, was the tone of the film, but Jean Seberg plays it "straight," with an instinctive understanding of what this playful confection needed from her own role.

Whatever else might be lacking, Chabrol could rely on cameraman Jean Rabier to capitalize on the photogenic locations and stars. He does this excellently, in glowing color. Pierre Jansen supplies more local color with some hectic bouzouki accompaniment, perhaps sensing the need to keep things moving.

With a disguised *Road to Corinth/Who's Got the Black Box?* (*La route de Corinthe*) director Claude Chabrol (CCFC).

One of the most absurd sequences involved dangling Seberg over the edge of the Corinth Canal suspended from the jib of a crane—a sheer, vertiginous drop. There was no stunt person, and her stand-in wouldn't even consider it. Though terrified, Seberg insisted she could do it, and later told Gordon Gow how foolishly proud she had felt in going through with it: "French TV had flown out to the location, and their sports program did a half-hour documentary about this feat, saying it was more daring than anything trapezists do." So much the greater had been her disappointment at seeing the end product: "But for the film itself Claude had used two cameras, and for once in his life—because, heaven knows, he's clever with cameras—he placed them very clumsily. And I don't think you really get the sense of the danger of it ... if I was going to do something that show-offy and breakneck, I wanted it to look super."

In some English language versions the prelude to the film, featuring the arrest and interrogation of a magician smuggling one of the black boxes, is cut. According to the director, the point of this scene was to overturn the Aristotelian principle that the action was to be predictable. There are, of course, other clear indicators that we are not dealing with everyday reality, not least the apologetic admonition which follows the credits: "I do not ask you to believe in it, I offer it to you as a dream."

Ironically, *The Road to Corinth* failed to be the money-spinner intended, as Génovès was wryly to recall. Chabrol too remembered it as a "big flop" and admitted its unevenness, going so far as to describe it as "completely empty." As he observed, this film went furthest among his studies of human folly ('connerie'), but this is a theme which he tackled, through an output of nearly sixty films, with far more zest, intelligence and inventive artistry than most. In this case it's also often very good fun.

Shooting on location lasted from May 8, until the end of June 1967. On July 28, Seberg and Ronet were returning from final dubbing for the film at the Boulogne studio when they were involved in a road accident. Her car was struck in the side at a crossroad and spun round, throwing her passenger onto the pavement. Ronet, who suffered two broken ribs and feared lasting disfigurement, was pictured in hospital on the front pages. Seberg was badly shaken but was, as she explained to *Paris-presse*, amazed to have escaped injury. The film opened in five Paris cinemas in late October 1967.

## References

*Art et essai*, Dossier 69, 19 October 1967, issue 32, pp. 35–40.
Blanchet, Christian. *Claude Chabrol*. Paris: Rivages, 1989, pp. 46–8.
Braucourt, Guy. *Claude Chabrol*. Paris: Seghers, 1971, pp. 114, 153.
Chabrol, Claude. [int. by Michel Ciment, Gérard Legrand, Jean-Paul Török]. *Positif*, 115, translated by Elisabeth Cameron: *Movie*, 18 Winter, 1970–71.
Gow, Gordon. "Re-birth." *Films and Filming*, 20:9, June 1974, p. 18.
Guérif, François. *Conversations avec ... Claude Chabrol: Un Jardin bien à moi*. Paris: Denoël, 1999, pp. 89–91, 254.
Julien, Pierre. "Jean Seberg: 'Vive la Grèce!'" *L'Aurore*, 29 June 1967, p. 10.
*Motion Picture Guide, 1927–83*, p. 3839.
Rank, Claude. "La Route de Corinthe: roman d'espionnage." Paris: Éditions Fleuve Noir, 1966.
Wood, Michael, and Robin Walker. *Claude Chabrol*. London: Studio Vista, 1970, pp. 98–102.

## Reviews

*Amis du film et de la télévision*, 143, April 1968. P.L., p. 38.
*L'Aurore*, 31 October 1967. Claude Garson, p. 10.
*Cahiers du cinéma*, 196, December 1967. S.D., pp. 71–2, 211, April 1969. Pascal Kane, pp. 53–5.

*Le Canard enchaîné,* 8 November 1967. M.D., p. 7.
*Ciné revue,* 48:6, 8 February 1968. Luc Barèges, p. 35.
*Cineinforme,* 6:63, December 1967, p. 38.
*Cinéma,* 121, December 1967. Philippe Defrance, p. 119.
*Combat,* 30 October 1967. Henry Chapier, p. 13.
*L'Express,* 23 October 1967. Pierre Billard, pp. 44–6.
*Le Figaro,* 3 November 1967. Louis Chauvet, p. 30.
*Le Film français,* 17 November 1967, p. 12.
*Filmkritik,* May 1968. Peter W. Jansen, p. 349.
*France nouvelle,* 8 November 1967. A. Cervoni.
*France-soir,* 1 November 1967. Robert Chazal, p. 11.
*Frankfurter allgemeine Zeitung,* 13 August 1968. Wa., p. 2.
*The Guardian,* 31 January 1969. Richard Roud, p. 8.
*L'Humanité,* 2 November 1967. Samuel Lachize, p. 8.
*Image et son,* 215, March 1968. Hubert Arnault, p. 154.
*Kinematograph Weekly,* 3199, 1 February 1969, p. 20.
*Les Lettres françaises,* 1208, 15 November 1967. T.R., p. 27.
*Le Monde,* 2 November 1967. Yvonne Baby, p. 19.
*Monthly Film Bulletin,* 36:422, March 1969. Jan Dawson, pp. 53–4.
*Le Nouvel observateur,* 152, 11–17 October 1967. Michel Cournot, pp. 48–9.
*Positif,* 93 March 1968. Laurent Leverrier, p. 63.
*Süddeutsche Zeitung,* 27 June 1968. Florian Fricke, p. 26.
*Der Tagesspiegel,* 11 August 1968. Karena Niehoff, p. 4.
*Télérama,* 930, 12 November 1967. Claude-Jean Philippe, p. 58.
*Today's Cinema,* 31 January 1969, p. 9.
*Variety,* 25 October 1967. Gene Moskowitz, p. 20.

# *The Girls* (1968)

"I was excited to work on it with [Seberg]. ...One would think of Jane Fonda
as a much bigger star, but at that time, in my view at least and many
others, Seberg was the bigger star."—director John Crome

A Silverscreen Tomasso presentation; Filmcenter Europe
Also known as: *Filmcenter Europe—The Girls*
Documentary
Original release: in English
Running Time: 25 minutes
Format: in color

CAST: Jane Fonda, Anita Pallenberg, Joanna Shimkus, Macha Méril, Jane Birkin, Jean Seberg, May Spils, Susannah York [uncredited interviews: Roger Vadim, Joseph Janni]
PRODUCTION CREDITS: *Director:* John Crome; *Producer:* Tom Parkinson; *Associate Producer:* D. Imrie Swainston; *Camera:* Nic Knowland; *Music:* Tony Hazzard; *Editor:* John Jeremy; *Created and devised by:* Malcolm J. Thomson.

## Notes

*The Girls* was never shown commercially and remains almost unknown and forgotten. In an interview in 2003 director John Crome revealed the genesis of the project and Jean Seberg's involvement:

There was a chap called Malcolm Thomson who was a publicist. He brought the idea to a producer called Tom Parkinson, who subsequently became a very major producer with a Paramount company in Australia. Tom had a little company called Silverscreen with other people. This young chap put the money up on the basis that we would make a series about European cinema which would be in English but would be sold worldwide, and *The Girls* was the pilot for that series, and it was a sort of obvious.

We were all very young at the time. I had been working at the BBC making a program for the youth market. This was "swinging London," and I had made film interviews with most of the rock, pop stars at the time and the fashion people, so I was an obvious choice to do the sort of thing.

The premise was that in Europe ... there was a different attitude in the cinema toward women and sex than in the Unites States. It was, in effect, comparing Europe with America, and it wasn't just about actors; it also included interviews with film directors and producers who were women, and with some eminent producers who were male as well.

We filmed [the interviews] primarily in London and Paris. One was with a woman called Joanna Shimkus, who subsequently married Sidney Poitier. She was a Canadian actress, extremely beautiful, and she was on the set of a film that Robert Enrico was shooting [*Ho!*] with Jean-Paul Belmondo and others.... There was Macha Méril, who also made a Godard film, a great actress but who was by then producing a couple of films, and Jane Fonda was the last one. Jane Fonda was married at that time to Vadim, and we filmed her at the farm she and Vadim had together just outside Paris, and they were doing some inserts there for a film. Anita Pallenberg, who was the sort of girlfriend of various Rolling Stones.... Joe Janni, who produced *Darling*, was interviewed about Julie Christie because she was unavailable.

[The interview with Seberg] was shot in Paris in the salon of fashion designer Ungaro. He claimed to have designed the miniskirt, and Jean knew him well. It was her suggestion that we went there to film because she was being measured for a dress, and basically he was her designer. She bought top range clothes designed by him for her, and that would have been extremely expensive at the time.

The interview was very superficial. We didn't get into anything terribly deep. It was basically about her feeling of freedom in Europe ... [that] the films were more intelligent. Essentially we were talking about differences between the Hollywood life and the European life, and the sensibility, and so forth.

She saw herself as a European, and she was very happy to promote the thesis ... that in Europe there was a greater freedom for women to express themselves [in film]. The irony of course was the thing was called *The Girls*, which is a completely stupid title for a film. Today you couldn't possibly call a film about women *The Girls*—that would be a sort of sexist appellation, completely daft. But at that time there was no sense of irony about it. That was considered a good and snappy title. I sort of cringe when I hear it now.

The film was made and cut and I had absolutely no more to do with it in terms of selling it, and shortly after the actual company that made it went into liquidation, and the thing died. Now I managed to get a copy of it so many years later. I thought this is too interesting a document to leave languishing, [so] I gave it to the film archives, the British Film Institute.

It's a typical story of films at that time, of things getting made and then never getting shown. There's an awful lot of material shot in the 60s, a burst of activity of people doing things, but without the knowledge, if you like, or the industry backing to actually do much with this material.

*The Girls*, whose title was captioned "From the motion picture capitals of a continent," is, as director Crome put it, very much a product of its time. The erratic camerawork, wild editing, and catchy music are all consistent with a style of filmmaking of the late 1960s and reinvented in the 1990s by certain directors such as Tarantino, not to mention innumerable music videos around the world. Some of these features now strike us as self-consciously quirky, if only because of mannerisms differing from those currently prevalent. This example of film reportage is fascinating to view today, especially in the knowledge that it never had a public showing and that *The Girls* could so easily have been destroyed in the ensuing years. It is significant as a document of its time in that it records the experience, opinions and ambitions of prominent women working in European films, accompanied by comments from men with whom they worked in the industry. Their candid and insightful views help to explain how and why European films continued to be groundbreaking in the 1960s, while a majority of the products coming from Hollywood in that decade remained essentially conservative.

After viewing this work one may wonder just how much similar material is now lost to us forever. It seems likely that *The Girls* would still find an audience in an age of reality television and growing acceptance of documentaries in the mainstream of filmmaking. The subjects form an interesting group, even if connected to one another solely by their chosen occupation. Most of the views expressed now seem to state the obvious, but in the context of the time they reflected a thoughtful and realistic view of the prospects for women interested in trying new things in cinema. There is certainly no sense of this being just another exercise in self-promotion or a "kissy-kissy" put on for the benefit of the camera.

*The Girls* scarcely strays from its focus of interest. There is, for example, neither mention of the Vietnam War nor of civil unrest in the U.S. and elsewhere. Virtually no political issues are discussed, although there are references to social values and mores. Attitudes towards eroticism and censorship are repeatedly mentioned, and the difficulties facing women in the film world are highlighted, but larger questions of equality are hardly touched on. The film is like a time capsule, preserving a small yet poignant moment in film history. It is noteworthy—and disturbing—that the subjects' comments on their struggles and aspirations seem almost as relevant to today's women in film as they were in 1967: the difficulty of competing in a male-dominated environment, the desire to direct and/or produce, and the wish not to be exploited. The thoughts of the women interviewed coincide on many topics. They are in favor of the new directness with which European cinema approaches sex. They welcome the move away from gender stereotypes but are concerned not to lose their femininity. The freedom and informal style of European filmmaking are seen as positive even if Hollywood offers greater financial rewards. There are few illusions about how hard production and direction are. Spils did not expect to make many films, adding the observation that "it's work for men." Film production had left Méril sleep deprived, broke yet "very happy" despite her pessimism about the future. Among points of incidental interest are the clips of Richard Attenborough directing Susannah York and Dirk Bogarde in *Oh! What a Lovely War*.

Apart from her contribution to the collective thoughts of the subjects, Jean Seberg's involvement provides one of the relatively few filmed interviews she gave which still survive. Unlike today, when actors promote their movies endlessly on morning "news" shows, late night talk shows, and syndicated gossip features, back then it was not a common practice to flood the television media. This was primarily due to the fact there were only four networks in the U.S. (ABC, CBS, NBC and PBS), and three channels in the UK. Also, few shows from that era retained all of their episodes. Seberg's U.S. appearances on *The Tonight Show* and *The Dick Cavett Show* no longer exist. Lacking foresight, the networks destroyed them, along with several thousand hours of other taped material throughout the years.

Seberg admitted in *The Girls* that she would like to direct (a wish not realized until *Ballad for the Kid* some six years later), "which I guess is what everybody goes through sooner or later who works around films ... the whole technical-visual thing is exciting." She declared herself pleased with the way her career had evolved and to have been part of the French New Wave: "I've had a much more exciting life, certainly, living in Europe ... than had I had ... a typical Hollywood career." She felt she was not and never would be a "star" in the California sense, and also disputed conventional ideas of what constitutes masculinity and femininity: "What does it mean any more, the whole business of ... what is womanly and what is manly ... those are late Victorian questions."

Perhaps, like the director, viewers may now wince or simply laugh at the patronizing tone of both commentary and title. Hindsight notwithstanding, Crome's documentary remains an honest open-minded attempt to offer at first hand a female perspective of European film at this point. A new feeling of freedom and opportunity emerges, despite the qualified expectations in what is still seen as "a man's world." All too many of the hopes expressed would remain unrealized, but these voices have much to tell us about the atmosphere, sexual politics and creative energy of the late 60s.

# Birds in Peru (Les Oiseaux vont mourir au Pérou) (1968)

"In Paris [*Birds in Peru*] has been damned as the worst film ever made, and praised as an outstanding work of art."—Jean Seberg

A Universal Productions France film; A film by Romain Gary; A Regional Film release
Original release: in French; released with English subtitles
Also known as: *The Birds Come to Die in Peru*; *Vögel sterben in Peru* [Germany]; *Gli uccelli vanno a morire in Perù* [Italy]; *Insaciable en el amor* [Spain]
Running Time: 96 minutes
Format: in Eastmancolor; in Dyaliscope

CAST: Jean Seberg* (Adriana); Maurice Ronet* (Rainier); Pierre Brasseur* (the husband); Henry Czarniak (Truck driver); Michel Buades (Alejo); Pierre Koulak (Jacques, the bouncer); Danielle Darrieux (Madame Fernande); Jean-Pierre Kalfon (Alberto, the chauffeur); Jackie Lombard (Rita); and Jacqueline Jacques
PRODUCTION CREDITS: *Director:* Romain Gary; *Producer:* Jacques Natteau; *Screenplay:* Romain Gary, based on his short story; *Director of Photography:* Christian Matras; *Cameraman:* Alain Douarinou; [*Still photography:* Pierre Zucca]; *Editors:* Denise Charvein, Raymonde Guyot; *Music:* Kenton Coe; *Production Manager:* Fred Surin; *Assistant Directors:* Michel Wynn, Pierre Cottance; *Art Director:* Jacques Brizzio; *Sound Engineer:* Guy Chichignoux; *Set decoration:* Fernand Chauviret; *Wardrobe:* Jacques Dessange; *Script Girl:* Denise Gaillard; *Makeup:* Phuong Maittret; *Hairstyles:* Valentine Montero; *Music Publisher:* Éditions Société Générale de Musique; *Décor from* maquettes by Rino Mondellini; Laboratoires Éclair, Centrique FL Jean Fouchet

## Synopsis

Sunrise reveals a young woman, Adriana, lying on a shore. Nearby are bodies and masks remaining from a night of carnival celebrations. The Rolls Royce limousine of

Adriana's husband cruises the coastal roads in search of the missing woman. Uniformed chauffeur Alberto tries to assuage his employer's anxieties as he drives. Adriana seeks refuge in a bordello close by, hinting she has been attacked. The sympathetic owner, Fernande, turns away the husband and Alberto when they ask after her. They soon return, even more threateningly. Adriana has left, but the misogynistic Alberto only awaits his employer's permission to kill the woman whose sexual cravings have plagued their wanderings.

Adriana comes upon a café owned by Rainier, a rootless ex-soldier who, aided by the youth Alejo, nurses the sickly birds littering the shore. Rainier is moved by the suffering of this beautiful stranger who seems strangely resigned to her fate. He begs her to stay with him and is determined to confront her pursuers. They soon appear, and the husband caustically mocks Adriana and her impotent protector. When Alberto raises his gun to execute Adriana, Alejo stabs him and then plunges into the sea. Rainier gathers up the chauffeur's jacket, recognizing his own fate is now inseparably linked to Adriana's.

## Reviews

"Miss Seberg tries valiantly to give her role some life but her very state makes her unreal from the beginning.... Pic is reminiscent of early Hollywood films about femme fatales but here her illness is named. But it does seem somewhat overdone and overemphasized for today's forthright sex attitudes."—*Variety*

"Each image here is admirably composed, while a tragic grandeur unfolds at a deliberately slow pace ... the film is [that] of an aesthete, even in the love scenes, sublime and thus not shocking despite their frankness."—*Le Film français*

"Gary has directed his principals well, but Miss Seberg can do little with her role except to look good.... The film's structure and purity of line impresses for its economy but also destroys the generation of any life force. We don't feel the loss of anything because we never had it in the first place.... Altogether it's a cold film...."—*Hollywood Reporter*

"Seberg is a lovely but not very interesting Adriana. ... she doesn't resemble a woman lost to an empty passion as much as a little girl about to lose a spelling bee. The picture does contain some heated love scenes, but it is neither trashy nor vulgar...."—*New York Times*

"*Birds in Peru* is the kind of movie I find infinitely more entertaining than overrated limburger like *The Lion in Winter*.... Despite the transparency of the personal allegory and the obviousness of the winged metaphors, *Birds in Peru* is blessed with an authentic personal signature...."—*Village Voice*

"It is, in fact, a daring and accomplished work, and I'd find it difficult to name another writer who has changed media so effectively in a first try."—*Films and Filming*

"*Birds in Peru* is about as self-indulgent as a movie can get ... [it] has most of the defects of a very bad home movie: it is unintentionally funny where it is not flat.... The scenes are not remotely erotic."—*Time*

"Jean Seberg interprets the role of the woman whose desires disturb her sanity with a sincerity which is sometimes very moving."—*Le Figaro*

## Notes

Romain Gary recorded some of the severe technical problems encountered during the shoot in Mazagón, on the Gulf of Cadiz, and Mauritania, which followed the initial studio

**Surrounded by fans during a break filming *Birds in Peru* (*Les Oiseaux vont mourir au Pérou*).**

work at Billancourt from October 2, 1967. The first twelve days' location work was largely wasted because the rushes could not be processed locally. It was only discovered that the hired Mitchell cine camera was defective when the results were reported back from France. Gary had complained to a journalist from *Paris Match* that his producer had only allowed him, a beginner, five weeks for filming, less time than any experienced director would have been given (in the event he would have nine weeks). On the other hand, he tended to play down his inexperience in film making and the leap between writing and directing. He recalled his previous involvement in screenwriting and Hollywood contacts from his years as Consul General in Los Angeles. In any case, as he had written in an article in *Show* and underlined in interviews, the new wave radicals had demystified filmmaking, proving that a long technical apprenticeship is not an indispensable requirement for directing. After all, he pointed out, "talent is the only know-how that matters even in such a supposedly very technical art form." He had always conceived his books in visual terms, and was to find the process of editing the film not unlike the final shaping of a text. One painful lesson he did learn from this production, he later revealed, was that constraints imposed by a cheese-paring producer could seriously compromise artistic freedom.

Gary had felt confident that the experienced cast assembled for the project would be able to realize his vision, praising Brasseur in particular. His claim that Jean Seberg's performance as Adriana was by far her career best may well be considered biased, but it is clear that their professional partnership and mutual rapport served the film well: without that, in fact, it could hardly have been possible at all. If she found this role challenging in some ways, it seems unlikely that any other actress could have given greater conviction to her character. Evidently she had revised her view, expressed to Léon Zitrone in January 1967, that she would not take the risk of working with Gary as director. For him, he claimed, it was possible to forget completely that he was directing his own wife. Seberg saw things differently. It affected her deeply to be part of her husband's new venture. As she told the *Elle* journalist, her faith in him would surmount any problems: she would allow him to "recreate" her. Shooting the scenes in which Adriana appears virtually naked on the beach was nevertheless a trial for her, despite Gary's readiness to declare a "closed set." Considering the sensitivity of the theme, she could not but be uneasy about the inevitable gossip. Gary had used elements of her identity in his novels. Some would naively speculate whether he hadn't depicted aspects of his own marriage through the on-screen characters. This would perhaps take a toll on their personal relationship. On the other hand, as Seberg later told a television interviewer, her private qualms about Gary's inexperience in directing would prove unfounded. On seeing the rushes, she had been amazed by the novelist's sure visual instincts.

As a writer, Gary seldom operated on the level of simple realism, and it is not surprising that he did not choose to do so in his first essay in cinema. The film is based on a short but very characteristic fable which blends his distinctive romanticism with a total rejection of conventional romantic illusion, and indeed the tone of this whole group of stories is one of mordant irony. An experience while traveling near Lima had provided the title and atmosphere which especially appealed to Gary's visual imagination. The author

**With co-star Maurice Ronet and director Romain Gary in *Birds in Peru* (*Les Oiseaux vont mourir au Pérou*) (Universal/Regional Films).**

explained that the story had been entirely reshaped in its screen version, retaining only the husband and wife situation essentially unaltered. He wished to avoid a typically modern psychoanalytical approach to Adriana's mental illness: "What I wanted to show was, on the contrary, how a certain type of dementia may not be perceived and understood by others as such ... and I wanted to treat this clinical theme in a poetic and almost mythological way...." It is revealing that the sole literary influence he admitted awareness of in this film was Joseph Conrad, and this only in terms of general atmosphere. The allusion to Shakespeare's *Othello* is overt, coming from the lips of the jealous husband himself. It is true that Alberto plays, to some extent, an Iago-like role, but this is really as far as the parallel goes. It is worth noting that the character of Jacques Rainier, played here with distinction by Maurice Ronet (in his fourth collaboration with Seberg), also appears in two of Gary's longer literary works. He is a central figure in the highly satirical novel *The Colors of the Day* (*Les Couleurs du jour*, published 1952 and rewritten in 1979), and would be the protagonist of *Your Ticket Is No Longer Valid* (from the 1975 French original). In *Les Oiseaux*, as in the early novel, Gary employs a quartet of wife, jealous husband, lover and hired assassin to produce a characteristic mix of the romantic and the acidly comic.

Some thought the tale distasteful, but Gary never shrank from challenging conventional moral attitudes in advancing his own strongly held values. Opposites grapple, and vaudeville comedy coexists with tragedy in his fiction. Exploration of the human condition must include even the most ludicrous aspects of behavior, for rather than diminishing man's aspirations, for him they add a kind of poignancy and heroism. From this viewpoint, no form of mental disturbance should be off-limits, either to writer or film maker. Why should the subject of nymphomania be taboo if it is, in Rainier's words, a sickness "like any other"? Whether the audiences could be induced to take it seriously in a dramatic context was, of course, another question. In any case, the problems of censorship encountered at the time seem nonsensical by present day standards. Despite having earlier approved the screenplay for adult audiences, in April 1968 the Commission for Film Censorship had recommended a complete ban by ten votes to nine. The Minister for Information Georges Gorse, for whom Gary had been working since April 1967, was not bound by this and was more sympathetic. He approved the film's release with two small cuts and a restriction to over-eighteens. According to Gary, the Commission had not judged the film obscene, but had favored a ban on the grounds that it might lead vulnerable women to suicide. Would they have liked to ban *Anna Karenina* too, the author wondered.

The critic of *Time* commented on the film's lack of eroticism, as if this were evidence of the director's incompetence. This is surely a misreading of intent, for there is a studiously detached and aesthetically refined treatment of the opening scenes, with no sense of voyeurism. The film's daring consists in its subject matter rather than visual interpretation. Danielle Darrieux looked back on her role as Madame Fernande:

> I appeared in *Les Oiseaux vont mourir au Pérou* out of friendship with Romain Gary, another intellectual turned film director. There I embody a homosexual hotel keeper. Precisely that! But as we were very modest in those days; the consuming love I'm supposed to feel for the touching Jean Seberg is expressed only by my hand placed on her bare shoulder....

Nicolas Gessner's comments on the film echo some of the critical response at the time of its release:

> Romain Gary wanted to get onto the bandwagon of those crazy movies which didn't require logical progression. It was a bit wild, but I think in those times it worked on its own merits.... Jean again was marvelous. I remember very interesting shots, with an extreme

close-up of [Jean] lying on the sand, and then suddenly [it] opened up and we'd see the sea and the birds. It was interesting, but not my kind of movie. *Birds in Peru* had a marvelous look, but I didn't like the story. I thought Jean with her super talent and her super beauty and her super radiance [was] still best held with a good director. But on the other hand you could feel that they did this together.

*Birds in Peru* might very well be read as a tragicomedy on love, a view which would shift the focus away from the torment of Adriana, who serves primarily as a catalyst (and we might note the contrast between the highly manipulative Lilith and the more introverted Adriana, well differentiated by Seberg in these two films). The husband and Alberto, exemplifying possessiveness and masculine ego, are opposed to the idealism of Rainier and Alejo. Madame Fernande, another whose desire is kindled by Adriana's beauty, stands somewhere between these poles. Her reaction to Alberto, like her borrowing of the celebrated quip by Arletty, locates her as a pragmatist who knows how the world works. The passion of the mute Alejo is the more intense and explodes more violently because it cannot be expressed. Like his namesake in *The Colors of the Day*, Rainier is the "professional" idealist, quixotic espouser of lost causes, a melancholy knight errant ready to embrace failure or death because declaration of allegiance is more important than either of these. The central metaphor is clear enough. It is Fernande who addresses Adriana as "my little bird." Rainier and Alejo rescue the ailing birds from the vandals whose sport it is to kick them to death, even if Adriana thinks it might be more merciful to let them do their work. For Adriana's husband no less than for her, death might offer release from suffering, but is elusive. Humor distinguishes the mocking cynic from the romantic defender of beauty. The misogynistic hired killer Alberto declares himself "a great sentimentalist." There is a heavy sarcasm in the exchanges between Alberto and his employer, and this is a currency Fernande too understands, whereas Rainier's wistful irony is gentler and generally self-directed. Unable to heal Adriana's sickness or the self-loathing it generates, he becomes her accomplice in denial and deception. The ultimate logic of his fidelity is the crowning irony, for it requires him to make up the empty place in this doomed trio.

The first class photography and the musical score by Kenton Coe both deserve mention, adding luster to the mise en scène and complementing the quality of the performances. Coe uses full orchestral resources for dramatic effect, but more often Andean folk music provides the rather surreal aural backdrop to the measured action of the story. As many of the reviews reveal, Gary's mythic treatment of a peculiarly modern form of angst, unfolding as it does at the solemn pace of Greek tragedy, did not meet with universal comprehension or sympathy. He must have known that the very selection of such a theme would be condemned in advance by many as tasteless, even if they were prepared to take it seriously.

Much publicity had preceded the film's Paris premier on June 19, 1968, and the critical backlash was immediate. Some columnists found it ponderous, pretentious or simply laughable, and there were also those who deplored Gary's use of his wife in a role they found degrading. In an interview with André Bourin for *France Culture* broadcast the following year, the director appeared to have few regrets, pointing out that his film had run for three months and brought overwhelmingly favorable letters from the public. In November *Birds* evoked an equally mixed response from American critics. *New York Times* critic Vincent Canby noted that it was the first film to carry the new Production Code "X" rating. The Motion Picture Association of America intended this to exclude children under 16, but, as reported by *Newsweek*, at least one major theatre chain was challenging the classification and disregarding this restriction. Ray Loynd, writing in *The Hollywood Reporter*, like Canby found the "X" unwarranted. He speculated that "the only reason for its X marks the spot is because it would totally bore those in puberty." In Italy the film trade journal *Intermezzo* complained in December 1968 of the film's seizure and of inconsistent regulation, but here, as in France, the fuss was temporary and simply provided additional publicity.

Despite the widely hostile critical response at the time of its release, it does seem surprising that such a bold experiment by a significant European creative figure has so long been neither accessible to the general public nor subjected to critical re-evaluation. Whatever its arguable weaknesses as a literary adaptation, this is memorable, visually dazzling cinema and must surely count as a remarkable achievement for a novice director. If any scandal still attaches to this film, it is that it remains locked away and denied to students of both cinema history and the work of Romain Gary.

## References

Assouline, Pierre, et al. *Lectures de Romain Gary*, Paris: Gallimard, 2010, pp. 196–200.

Badder, David J. "Romain Gary." *Film Dope*, 19 December 1979, pp. 2–3.

Bostel, Honoré. "Romain Gary: sa femme, le temps d'un film, n'est plus qu'une actrice." *Paris match*, 966, 14 October 1967, p. 116.

Cohn, Bernard. "Romain Gary à l'américaine." *Les Nouvelles littéraires*, 45:2096, 2 November 1967, interview, p. 14.

Darrieux, Danielle. *Danielle Darrieux: filmographie commentée par elle-même*. Paris: Ramsay, 1995, pp. 137–8, 143, 210.

*Elle*, 1139, 19 October 1967, "Pour Jean Seberg Romain Gary devient metteur en scène," pp. 92–3.

*Le Figaro*, 28 July, p. 10; 11 October, 21 September 1967, p. 28, 5 April 1968.

*Le Film français*, 24:1216, 3 November 1967, p. 15.

*Filmfacts*, 11:24, 15 January 1969, "Birds in Peru," pp. 438–40.

*France-soir*, 4, p. 13, 5, p. 10, April 1968 [censorship].

Gary, Romain. "The foamy edge of the Wave." *Show*, 4:4, April 1964, pp. 75–6.

_____. *Gloire à nos illustres pionniers: nouvelles*. Paris: Gallimard, 1962 [reprinted in 1975 as *Les Oiseaux vont mourir au Pérou*; translated as *Hissing Tales*. New York: Harper & Row, 1964].

*Hollywood Reporter*, 202:34, 16 September 1968. "Birds in Peru": Even the French are shocked and business sensational [advertisement], pp. 8–9.

*Intermezzo*, 23:24, 31 December 1968, p. 4.

Lentz, Serge. "Tête-à-tête avec Romain Gary," 1968, reprinted in *Romain Gary. L'affaire homme*. Paris: Gallimard, 2005, pp. 181–5.

Lévy, Bernard-Henri. "L'avantage, pour un écrivain, du cinéma ? Le corps de ses acteurs." *Le Magazine littéraire*, 354, May 1997, pp. 46–8.

Mann, Roderick. "Quand un grand romancier fait tourner sa femme" [interviews]. *Le Nouveau Candide*, 342, 13 November 1967, pp. 38–40.

*Le Monde*, 5 April 1968. "Le film *Les Oiseaux vont mourir au Pérou* est autorisé," p. 24.

Montfort, Jacques. *Ciné revue*, 49:12, 20 March 1969, p. 21.

*Newsweek*, 72:23, 2 December 1968. "X marks the spot," pp. 96–7.

*Le Nouveau cinémonde*, 1721, 28 November 1967, p. 36.

*La Règle du jeu*, 20:42, January 2010. "Hommage au film ... de Romain Gary," pp. 297–329.

"Romain Gary." Interview published by Universal Film, Service de Presse [1967, reprinted in *Romain Gary*. Paris: l'Herne, 2005, pp. 183–5. See also ibid. pp. 181–2].

"Romain Gary, le nomade multiple: entretiens avec André Bourin." INA, Radio France, 2006, 2xCD Harmonia Mundi 211876.

Santerre, François de. "Fauteuil à bascule et confettis pour Romain Gary cinéaste." *Le Figaro*, 11 October 1967, p. 31.

Swamp, J.M. "Romain Gary: Comment bien diriger sa femme?" *Ciné revue*, 47:41, 12 October 1967.

Tillier, Maurice. "Romain pris en traître par Gary." *Le Figaro littéraire*, 1123, 23 October 1967, interview, p. 36.

## Reviews

*Amis du film et de la télévision,* 156/7, May/June 1969. J.B., V.M., pp. 26–7.
*L'Aurore,* 20 June 1968. Claude Garson, p. 9.
*Bianco e nero,* 30:1–2, January/February 1969. Fabio Rinaudo, pp. 105–6.
*Le Canard enchaîné,* 3 July 1968. Michel Duran, p. 7.
*Cineinforme,* 6:71/72, August/September 1968, p. 70.
*Cineforum,* 9:84, April 1969. Ermanno Comuzio, p. 291.
*Cinéma,* 130, November 1968. Daniel Urbain, p. 142.
*Combat,* 17 June 1968. René Quinson, p. 13. 24 June 1968. Henry Chapier, p. 13.
*The Daily Cinema,* 9562, 16 August 1968. Marjorie Bilbow, pp. 4–5.
*The Daily News* (NY), 7 November 1968. Kathleen Carroll, p. 90.
*The Daily Telegraph,* 30 August 1968. Sean Day-Lewis, p. 17.
*The Evening News,* 29 August 1968. Felix Barker, p. 3.
*The Evening Standard,* 29 August 1968. Alexander Walker, p. 8.
*L'Express,* 886, 1 July 1968. Pierre Billard, p. 24.
*Le Figaro,* 2 July 1968. Louis Chauvet, p. 24.
*Le Film français,* 25:1250, 5 July 1968. A.M., p. 15.
*Film Quarterly,* 22:2 Winter 1968–9. William Johnson, pp. 52–5.
*Films and Filming,* 15:1, October 1968. Gordon Gow, pp. 37–8.
*France-soir,* 21 June 1968. Robert Chazal, p. 9.
*The Guardian,* 30 August 1968. David Wilson, p. 6.
*The Hollywood Reporter,* 7 November 1968. Ray Loynd, p. 3.
*Image et son,* Sept./Oct. 1968 (*Saison cinématographique* 1968). Jacqueline Lajeunesse, pp. 144–5.
*Intermezzo,* 24:9–10, 31 May 1969, p. 4.
*Le Journal du dimanche,* 23 June 1968. Michel Aubriant, p. 14.
*Kinematograph Weekly,* 3176, 24 August 1968, p. 21.
*Les Lettres françaises,* 24 June 1968. Marcel Martin, pp. 16–7.
*Liberté,* 152, 1 October 1968. Michelle Delcombre, p. 6.
*Le Monde,* 23 June 1968. Jean de Baroncelli, p. 15.
*Monthly Film Bulletin,* 35:417, October 1968. Jan Dawson, p. 149.
*Motion Picture Daily,* 104:89, 11 November 1968. Tony Vellela, p. 22.
*The New York Post,* 7 November 1968. Frances Herridge, p. 67.
*The New York Times,* 7 November 1968. Vincent Canby, s.7 p. 51.
*Nord éclair,* 4 September 1968. Jean Leroy, p. 8.
*Le Nouvel observateur,* 189, 26 June 1968, p. 45.
*Les Nouvelles littéraires,* 2127, 27 June 1968. Gilles Jacob, p. 14.
*Positif,* 98 October 1968. Albert Bolduc, p. 66.
*Time,* 92:23, 6 December 1968, pp. 110, 113.
*The Times,* 29 August 1968. John Russell Taylor, p. 9.
*Variety,* 251:10, 24 July 1968. Gene Moskowitz, p. 24.
*Village Voice,* 12 October 1968. Andrew Sarris, p. 58.

# *Pendulum* (1969)

"It touched on an important issue and I thought the
performances were rather good."—director George Schaefer

A Pendulum Production; A Columbia Pictures release
Original release: in English
Also known as: *La Nuit sans témoin* [France]; *Nacht ohne Zeugen* [Germany]; *Péndulo*
    [Spain]
Running Time: 106 minutes
Format: in Technicolor

CAST: [* denotes above the title billing] George Peppard* (Captain Frank Matthews); Jean Seberg* (Adele Matthews); Richard Kiley* (Woodrow Wilson King); Charles McGraw (Chief Hildebrand); Madeleine Sherwood (Mrs. Eileen Sanderson); Robert F. Lyons (Paul Sanderson); Frank Marth (Lt. Smithson); Marj Dusay (Liz Tennant); Paul McGrath (Senator Augustus Cole); Stewart Moss (Richard D'Angelo); Isabel Sanford (Effie); Dana Elcar (Detective "Red" Thornton); Harry Lewis (Brooks Elliot); Mildred Trares (Mary Schumacher); Robin Raymond (Myra); Phyllis Hill (Mrs. Wilma Elliot); S. John Launer (Judge Kinsella); Richard Guizon (Deputy Marshal Jack Barnes); Jack Grimes (Artie); Logan Ramsey (Sergeant Jelinek); Douglas Henderson (Detective Hanauer); Gene Boland (Garland); Jock MacKelvie (U.S. Attorney Grady Butler)

PRODUCTION CREDITS: *Director:* George Schaefer; *Producer:* Stanley Niss; *Screenplay:* Stanley Niss; *Photography:* Lionel Lindon; *Editor:* Hugh S. Fowler; *Production Designer:* Walter M. Simonds; *Set Decorator:* Maury Hoffman; *Assistant Director:* David Salven; *Sound:* Charles J. Rice, William Randall, Jr., Arthur Piantadosi; *Music:* Walter Scharf; *Makeup:* Ben Lane; *Hairstyles:* Virginia Jones; *Title song "The Pendulum Swings Both Ways":* *Lyrics:* Mack David, Music: Walter Scharf, sung by The Lettermen

## Synopsis

Washington, D.C., detective Frank Matthews, newly praised for work leading to the conviction of murderer Paul Sanderson, is among many disgusted to hear that the verdict has been quashed on a technicality. Sanderson's attorney King has misgivings and arranges for his client to stay with his mother in McKeesport, Pennsylvania to receive psychiatric treatment.

Matthews fears that his wife Adele has renewed her former relationship with businessman Brooks Elliot. He plans to return covertly from a lecture trip to Baltimore to test his suspicions. When Adele and Eliot are found shot dead, all the circumstantial evidence points to the jealous husband. Matthews believes he was himself the intended victim of a revenge killing by Sanderson. Giving his colleagues the slip before he can be charged, he makes for McKeesport in the hope of proving his innocence. Under pressure, Mrs. Sanderson admits the alibi she gave her son was false. The son returns home and attempts to kill Matthews, who is only saved by his mother's violent intervention.

The experience leaves the detective's view of the justice system soured. This time the balance between the rights of victim and accused has clearly proved wanting.

## Reviews

"Although the end result is a somewhat routine crime meller, *Pendulum* attacks head-on a major contemporary domestic problem: individual liberties under the U.S. Constitution vs. society as a whole. An excellent basic plot strain has been weakened by potboiler elements.... Performances, given the script, are good."—*Variety*

"... the movie's real novelty and worth is its flavor of healthily cynical realism combined with an entirely credible flow of humanity ... this is one of those careful projects where every performer counts, down to the smallest bit player.... Seberg is silkenly impressive ... *Pendulum* swings wisely, well and says something worth hearing."—*New York Times*

"The script fails to integrate its very disparate elements (love triangle, psychological thriller, chase story), while it effectively weights the film on the side of law and order by characterizing the murder as a brutal and unrepentant psychopath who can only respond to violence."—*Monthly Film Bulletin*

"The picture falls apart—but not before it has entertained you and made you think. It has an unfashionable 'uncinematic' look—but then it has an unfashionable amount of substance, too."—*Los Angeles Times*

"George Schaefer directs in an efficient, teleseries style, and even an intermittent rattle of messages ... does not distract too much."—*Times*

## Notes

George Schaefer had already had a highly successful career as television director when he took on *Pendulum*. This included a number of productions for *Hallmark Hall of Fame* series such as *Victoria Regina*, *Inherit the Wind*, *Green Pastures* and *Pygmalion*, and his *Macbeth* had won five Emmy awards. "Columbia Pictures wanted a new look director," he recalled. "George Peppard was the one who was instrumental in persuading them [to hire me]. It was the first feature film that I ever made. As I recall it was George Peppard who was particularly keen on [Seberg] for the role, which I thought was fine. I was more than happy to go along with him. I admired Jean and her pictures." On February 29, 1968, Columbia announced that she would co-star with Peppard and Richard Kiley in the Niss production. Producer/writer Stanley Niss thought highly of Schaefer's work and saw him as someone capable of handling the "delicate nuances of drama" in his screenplay. Niss had wanted to address a subject which he felt was topical, but to do this in a balanced way, without "preaching."

Filming began on April 1, 1968, with a week on location in Washington, D.C. Since Seberg's parents were present they were able to appear as extras in the opening scenes. As publicity would note, exterior sequences were a virtual tour of the city's landmarks. "We had shot one day, and the next day [April 4] Martin Luther King was assassinated," Schaefer remembered. "It was dangerous in a way, in that we had a lot of extras dressed in police uniforms. We had to call off the shooting because the extras ... were attacked by black youths. Fortunately no one was seriously hurt. It was a very tense time. We did those taxi scenes. If you look ... you can see in the background parts of Washington going up in smoke. You couldn't go down the street without seeing large columns of black smoke. We were all confined to our hotels, and waited two more days, then just gave up on it and came back to California."

Schaefer also recalled Seberg and Peppard discussing the love scene. Peppard worked out a system of signals: "he said 'When I'm holding you, I'll touch you down at your ankle with my third finger, at which time you'll break away.' I don't remember the exact details, but I do remember the two of them sort of saying 'that'll be great. That'll give everyone a feeling that will be right for that scene.'" Seberg's childhood friend Lynda Haupert recalls that Peppard was interested in more than acting the scene. After Seberg rejected Peppard's off-camera advances they were to film a scene which required him to slap her. Rather than fake the blow he actually slapped her, and so hard that she said she literally saw stars.

Tom Gray watched Schaefer rehearsing the interior scenes at Columbia Studios and reported on his rigorous and energetic style of working in *Motion Picture Herald*. Marj Dusay, who played Richard Kiley's secretary, later achieved success in daytime dramas, including the pivotal role of Alexandra Spaulding in CBS-TV's *Guiding Light*. Isabel Sanford (misspelled in the credits), who was new to Hollywood after working on Broadway and who was full of praise for the director, went on to win an Emmy as Louise Jefferson in the long running television comedy *The Jeffersons*.

*Pendulum* is a well constructed and intelligently scripted suspense story, and one which succeeds in exploring a serious perennial theme in an interesting way without forgetting for a moment that it is a product for popular entertainment. The moral issues involved in the balancing of justice for the victim against the rights of the accused receive a less facile treatment here than cinema often gives them. A convicted murderer is freed on procedural grounds, but the circumstances of a single case, as the judge points out, cannot invalidate the sound legal principles protecting individual liberties. It is the zealous detective who has defeated his own impatient pursuit of justice, but the clever defense counsel also feels a responsibility for the injustice of the outcome. Less sympathetic is the politician, Senator Cole, who appears to be exploiting the issue and specific situation for political advantage.

Is Matthews, whose personal dislike of Sanderson is so intense, capable of murder himself? We are left unsure whether he has killed his wife and her lover when we see him telephone Sanderson's mother from Washington on the night of the crime. As the obvious prime suspect, he depends on an alibi which we know will soon be exposed as false. Now all his sense of security has vanished, and, as King points out to him, he can more easily imagine the feelings of the crime suspect. This irony is neatly handled by Niss, although the resolution, when it comes, is predictable and engineered hastily.

The sudden exit of the silkily duplicitous Adele some forty minutes into the story is central to the plot, but with it one intriguing strand of the narrative is abruptly lost, together with the glamour Seberg contributes to the early scenes. It might have been interesting to explore this marital relationship further, which could have added depth to the rather one-dimensional detective, but that would have been a different movie. As it is, Peppard is sound in a leading role very similar to that of the *Banacek* television series of the early seventies. There is very little to quibble about in any of the supporting performances, many of which are excellent. Richard Kiley is entirely convincing as the smoothly confident attorney King, uneasily trying to reconcile conscience and ambition. Equally effective is the creepy performance by Lyons as the young psychopath. Even the tail-end cameo of his booze-dependent, loose-living mother by Madeleine Sherwood is far less of a caricature than it might have been, and it is not her fault if the attempt to account for his misogyny in terms of bargain basement Freudian psychology seems hackneyed.

Good camerawork and the fluent editing which mark the expansive lead-in views of the capital give promise of generous production values. In most respects the promise is fulfilled. A strong musical score and a catchy

With George Peppard in *Pendulum*. Location filming in Washington, D.C., was cut short after rioting threatened the safety of the production crew (Columbia).

theme, provided with 60s-style vocal backing (though with lyrics better overlooked), reinforce this impression of a quality production. Some critics felt that Schaefer's inexperience in the big screen medium showed at times, but the direction is smoothly professional, and we are seldom aware of being on a film set. In addition, there is a strong enough storyline to keep us involved even after the film's sharp change of direction. Ultimately, Schaefer does disappoint, with an anticlimactic ending which offers no surprises or strokes of originality, but we may still feel that this was an entertaining journey.

Columbia's promotional campaign for the film included television trailers and radio spots, with interviews by Peppard and Seberg and a 45rpm Capitol single of the movie's catchy theme song. The film was released on May 4, 1969, and received qualified approval from the majority of the American and foreign press.

## References

Appel, Kira. *Le Nouveau cinémonde,* 1748, 25 June 1968, pp. 8–10.
Deglin, Paul. *Ciné revue,* 49:15, 10 April 1969, pp. 6–7.
*Filmfacts,* 12:6, 1969, pp. 141–3.
Fougères, Roland. *Ciné revue,* 49:8, 20 February 1969, pp. 17–9.
Gray, Tom. "On the set of 'Pendulum.'" *Motion Picture Herald,* 15 May 1968, pp. 4–5.
*The Hollywood Reporter,* 200:16, 29 March 1968, p. 12.
*Motion Picture Daily,* 103:64, 2 April 1968, p. 2.
*Motion Picture Guide, 1927–83,* pp. 2365–6.

## Reviews

*Amis du film et de la télévision,* 158/9, July/August 1969. P.L., p. 12.
*L'Aurore,* 11 April 1969. Robert Monange, p. 16.
*Cahiers du cinéma,* 212, May 1969. M.D., pp. 64–5.
*Le Canard enchaîné,* 16 April 1969. Michel Duran, p. 7.
*Chicago Sun-Times,* 10 February 1969. Roger Ebert.
*Cineinforme,* 7:78, March 1969, p. 26.
*Cinéma,* 138, July/August 1969. Marcel Martin, p. 140.
*The Daily Telegraph,* 18 April 1969. Patrick Gibbs, p. 16.
*The Evening News,* 17 April 1969. Felix Barker, p. 11.
*The Evening Standard,* 17 April 1969. Alexander Walker, p. 14.
*Le Figaro,* 14 April 1969. Louis Chauvet, p. 26.
*Films and Filming,* 15:9, June 1969. David Rider, p. 50.
*Films in Review,* 20:4, April 1969. Flavia Wharton, pp. 252–3.
*The Guardian,* 18 April 1969. Derek Malcolm, p. 8.
*The Hollywood Reporter,* 15 January 1969. John Mahoney, pp. 3–4.
*Image et son, Saison cinématographique* 1969. 230–31 Sept./Oct. 1969. Guy Allombert, pp. 219–20.
*Intermezzo,* 24:5–6, 31 March 1969, p. 7.
*Kinematograph Weekly,* 3209, 12 April 1969, pp. 8, 21.
*Los Angeles Times,* 7 February 1969. Kevin Thomas, IV, p. 12.
*Monthly Film Bulletin,* 36:424, May 1969, pp. 106–7.
*Motion Picture Daily,* 105:10, 15 January 1969. Richard Gertner, p. 4.
*New York,* 14 April 1969. Judith Crist.
*The New York Times,* 22 March 1969. Howard Thompson, p. 24.
*Le Nouvel observateur,* 232, 21 April 1969. Michel Mardore, p. 55.
*Paris-presse,* 17 April 1969. Michel Aubriant, p. 2.
*Rivista del cinematografo,* 7 July 1969. Sergio Raffaelli, pp. 355–6.
*The Times,* 17 April 1969. John Russell Taylor, p. 14.
*Today's Cinema,* 18 April 1969. Marjorie Bilbow, p. 13.
*Variety,* 15 January 1969. Murf., p. 6.

# *Paint Your Wagon* (1969)

"[Elizabeth is] the best woman's role I have ever read. She is a 19th century
'flower child.' It's like a dream come true—something totally new for me."—Jean Seberg

An Alan Jay Lerner Production; A Paramount Pictures release
Original release: in English
Also known as: *La Kermesse de l'Ouest* [France]; *Westwärts zieht der Wind* [Germany]; *La Ballata della città senza nome* [Italy]; *La Leyenda de la ciudad sin nombre* [Spain]; *Oregon* [Belgium]
Running Time: 164 minutes [cut to 137 minutes for later general release]
Format: in Technicolor; in Panavision

CAST: [* denotes above the title billing] Lee Marvin* (Ben Rumson); Clint Eastwood* (Pardner); Jean Seberg* (Elizabeth Woodling); Ray Walston (Mad Jack Duncan); Harve Presnell (Rotten Luck Willie); Tom Ligon (Horton Fenty); Alan Dexter (Parson); William O'Connell (Horace Tabor); Ben Baker (Haywood Holbrook); Alan Baxter (Mr. Fenty); Paula Trueman (Mrs. Fenty); Robert Easton (Ezra Atwell); Geoffrey Norman (Foster); H.B. Haggerty (Steve Bull); Terry Jenkins (Joe Mooney); Karl Bruck (Schermerhorn); John Mitchum (Jacob Woodling); Sue Casey (Sarah Woodling); Eddie Little Sky (Indian); Harvey Parry (Higgins); H.W. Gim (Wong); William Mims (Frock-coated man); Roy Jenson (Hennessey); Pat Hawley (Clendennon); The Nitty Gritty Dirt Band
PRODUCTION CREDITS: *Director:* Joshua Logan; *Producer:* Alan Jay Lerner; *Screenplay:* Alan Jay Lerner; Adaptation by Paddy Chayefsky; Based on the play by Alan Jay Lerner and Frederick Loewe; *Director of Photography:* William A. Fraker; *2nd Unit Photography:* Loyal Griggs; *Aerial Photography:* Nelson Tyler; *Editor:* Robert Jones; *Costumes and Production Design:* John Truscott; *Art Director:* Carl Braunger; *Set Decorator:* James I. Berkey; *Sound:* William Randall; *1st Assistant Director:* Jack Roe; *Production Managers:* Carl Beringer, Fred Lemoine; *Special Effects:* Maurice Ayers, Larry Hampton; *Makeup:* Frank McCoy; *Choreography:* Jack Baker; *Costume Supervisor:* Bill Jobe; *Costume Coordinator:* Anne Laune; *Hairdresser:* Vivian Zavitz; *Camera Operator:* David Walsh; *1st Assistant Director:* Jack Roe; *Choral Music Conductor:* Roger Wagner; *Associate Producer:* Tom Shaw; *Choral Arrangements:* Joseph J. Lilley; Jonas Halperin; *Titles:* David Stone Martin; *Production Coordinator:* Gene Levy; *Dialogue Coach:* Joseph Curtis; *Script Supervisor:* Marshall Wolins; *Camera Assistant:* Bob Byrne; *Stereo Supervisor:* Fred Hynes; *Gaffer:* Joe Smith; *Key Grip:* Tom May; *Property:* Bob Eaton; *1st Assistant Director, 2nd Unit:* Al Murphy; *Music:* Frederick Loewe; *Additional music:* Andre Previn; *Lyrics:* Alan Jay Lerner; *Orchestral music score and conductor:* Nelson Riddle; *Songs:* I'm on My Way, I Still See Elisa, The First Thing You Know, Hand Me Down That Can o' Beans, They Call the Wind Maria, A Million Miles Away Behind the Door, I Talk to the Trees, There's a Coach Comin' In, Whoop-Ti-Ay!, The Gospel of No Name City, The Best Things in Life Are Dirty, Wand'rin Star, Gold Fever

## Synopsis

The Gold Rush adds new impetus to the stream of hopeful settlers heading west. Grizzled Ben Rumson is among these, a restless spirit who readily teams up with the young stranger he dubs "Pardner." They soon find themselves in the exclusively male No Name City, whose rough citizens are scandalized by the arrival of a Mormon with two wives. The younger one, Elizabeth, ventures being auctioned, even if the winner is the drunken Ben rather than Pardner.

Eventually the area's gold deposits dwindle, presenting the partners with a dilemma. Elizabeth won't abandon her cherished home, nor does she want either of the men to leave. The ménage à trois in Elizabeth's cabin seemed a perfect solution—that is, until the devoutly proper Fenty family arrives. Elizabeth's domestic arrangements become an embarrassment to her, and Ben's corrupting influence on the young Horton is the last straw. Pardner feels he can no longer share the woman he loves.

Tunnels have been dug to harvest the gold dust beneath the town's buildings. It takes only a rampaging bull to achieve the spectacular collapse of No Name City. This is the moment for Ben to move on, leaving Elizabeth and Pardner to each other.

## Reviews

"*Paint Your Wagon* is an expensive U.S. film musical, and a very typical one. That it is not an unusually good film musical is chiefly due to a witless handling of a puerile story.... Lee Marvin, Clint Eastwood and Jean Seberg are not singers, they get by."—*Films in Review*

"Even without good reviews, the film still has enough going for it—star names, bigness, a fine score and good production values. Any large budgeted film is up for close scrutiny.... Strongly in its favor is that the money spent can be seen on the screen. It's a visually beautiful film...."—*Variety*

"... the film, like all too many musicals, cries out to be pruned."—*Daily Mail*

"[Logan] directs in with his usual stage bound reliance on pretty, static compositions so that the film looks like a series of picture-postcards dissolving into each other ... [Marvin] does his stuff quite nicely, as do Clint Eastwood and Jean Seberg in an appropriately subdued manner, but without ever managing to get the action going."—*Monthly Film Bulletin*

"Its three stars ... are appealing performers ... age is giving [Seberg] a kind of gutsy quality that only makes her beauty more interesting. It's somewhat startling to hear the waif of *Breathless* break into song in a clearly cultivated voice, but she lip-syncs the lyrics with intelligence."—*New York Times*

"[Seberg's] just barely alive in a musical: she can't sing or dance; she can hardly *move*. Her eyes are as coolly blank toward Eastwood as toward everyone else. Why should we care if these two get together?"—*New Yorker*

"As directed by Joshua Logan it's entertaining enough, hilarious enough and poignant enough to keep Marvin, Clint Eastwood and Jean Seberg on the movie star map.... Seberg is beautiful as always and much more mature as an actress."—*Los Angeles Times* (*Haber*)

## Notes

Paradoxically, although Seberg was to look back on making this film as one of the happiest experiences of her career, its production was certainly one of the most troubled. It augured well enough when Paramount decided to draw on the talents of director Joshua Logan to bring the Lerner and Loewe stage musical *Paint Your Wagon* to the screen. Logan had *Picnic*, *Bus Stop* and *South Pacific* to his credit and was a Pulitzer Prize winner, while composer and writer Alan Jay Lerner, who was now producer for the first time, was considered second to none in his own field. The two had worked together harmoniously on *Camelot*, and both were enthusiastic at the studio's proposal to cast Lee Marvin as drunken prospector Ben Rumson, even if Logan thought Marvin's million dollar fee (plus a percentage) exorbitant. Charles Bluhdorn, head of Gulf +Western, the new owners of Paramount, indicated that money would not be a problem. With Seberg and Eastwood signed, things looked good. Seberg had been nettled at being asked to test for her part, but mollified when Marvin agreed to test with her, especially since, as she told *Hollywood Citizen News*, "it was the best commercial script I'd ever read."

**With 1969's *Paint Your Wagon* co-stars Clint Eastwood and Lee Marvin (Paramount).**

The script was in fact a complete rewrite by Paddy Chayefsky, since Lerner had not cared for the original. As Logan explained to Gordon Gow, "It's a preposterous story. Lusty. A mixture of Mark Twain, shall we say, and Bret Harte ... and Paddy Chayefsky and Alan J. Lerner. It's not anything like the original stage show, except for its background and a lot of the songs that have been saved. There are moments that show loneliness, but most of it is laughter: that's the feeling."

Unfortunately, differences between director and producer started to appear early on. Their partnership on *Camelot* had worked because Lerner had given Logan carte blanche, making only social appearances during the production. This time he would be constantly on set, instructing the cast and at times overruling the director's decisions. The anarchic style of Marvin did not help, although Logan regarded his bouts of drinking as a manageable problem. The good-natured if somewhat unpredictable ex–Marine could generally be relied on when it counted. According to actor Ray Walston, when the studio chiefs saw the first dailies [unedited film footage], "they—Gulf +Western, Bob Evans—were all up in arms. They didn't like what they saw. They began to look around for a new director, and Josh knew about it." Associate Producer Tom Shaw contacted Richard Brooks (director of *Elmer Gantry* and *The Professionals*) to sound him out about taking over. When Brooks proved reluctant, Lerner, seconded by Marvin, pressed him further. The atmosphere became far worse when gossip columnist Joyce Haber broke the story of Logan's impending replacement in *The Los Angeles Times*. In the view of writer Richard Schickel, the leak was "obviously not accidental. Haber was being used by Lerner to provoke Logan into quitting."

It is clear from Logan's account of the production that it was soured for him by what had happened, but that his good relations with the cast and camera crew made things bearable. He found Eastwood "warm and decent," Seberg "lovable and beautiful" and "liked Marvin enormously from the beginning." When the *New York Daily News* later ran the fanciful gossip story that Marvin ended an argument by using Logan's boots "like a dog uses a fire hydrant" he penned an amusing knock-down refutation. He pointed out that such behavior would be totally out of character with this southern gentleman when sober, "and when he is drunk ... he is *really* drunk. He staggers and careens in such a way that he wouldn't have the aim."

The sheer scale of the project threw up many problems and fostered anxiety that it was getting dangerously out of hand. Instead of constructing the set on Paramount's back lot, as Logan suggested, it had been decided to build the entire gold rush towns on location in Baker, Oregon. The choice of location had to be made in the winter so that preparations could be made for the shoot. There was no doubt about the beauty of the setting shrouded in snow. They would just have to hope that the valley looked equally spectacular in the spring. Helicopters could be used to ferry people quickly to and from the town, someone helpfully threw in. To add to the cost and complexity, No Name City had to be constructed so that it could be made to collapse repeatedly for shooting the final scenes. Looking back, Logan felt the decision to make (effectively) the entire picture on location had been a "crazy expense" and regretted the choice of John Truscott, who cared more for realism than for economy. The need for bearded extras generated its own minor gold rush, with long-haired hippies from far and wide descending on the set, at times creating logistical problems for the studio.

Seberg rented a house in Baker, entertained and had family visits. She enjoyed the setting and the holiday mood, and was photographed dandling babies among the beaded flower children. Logan, the three stars and The Nitty Gritty Dirt Band all attended the wedding of one young couple. Jean was full of admiration for Marvin, and shrugged off gossip about her friendship with Eastwood. The strains in her marriage to Romain Gary were nevertheless real, and in time it became evident that she was now deeply involved emotionally with Eastwood. Gary flew from Paris to make a dramatic appearance at which he challenged his rival to a duel. Fortunately good sense prevailed, and the couple announced their formal but amicable separation in mid–September.

After Brooks made it clear he thought it would be unethical to take over from Logan, who was backed by most of the crew and cast, Paramount patched up the quarrel. Logan, still smarting from what he regarded as a stab in the back, was then free to struggle with the multiple practical difficulties. One of these was the fact that none of the three leads was a trained singer. Seberg had been taking singing lessons specifically for the film, so it was a blow when it was finally decided that her songs, unlike Marvin's and Eastwood's, would be dubbed by a professional. Perhaps the large crew, the Hollywood film making method and the lagging production schedule contributed to her nervousness. For some reason, whereas her male co-stars were recorded later in a studio and deemed acceptable, she was not.

Although Carol Hollingsworth, Seberg's high school drama teacher, later vouched for her "lovely singing voice," André Previn, who wrote additional songs for the film, was frank: "It became mercilessly clear that Jean Seberg could not do her own singing. Her speaking voice was soft and modulated, her laugh was like the tinkle of a gamelan orchestra, but her singing was hopeless." He quickly auditioned several standby vocal doubles but dismissed them as unsuitable. Then he happened to find the voice he wanted in an old film on television, and was able to identify the singer as Anita Conroy. By the weirdest of chances it was Conroy, now working in a Western Union office in Los Angeles, who took Previn's dictated telegram addressed to herself. Within days Conroy was signed to dub Seberg's voice for *A Million Miles Away*, and, according to Previn, was handsomely paid for doing it.

The production ran on with escalating costs from mid–June 1968 almost to the end of the year, when the entire set of the Grizzly Bear dance hall was trucked from Oregon to Los Angeles for some final shots. When Logan had almost finished supervision of the editing, a task for which he was contracted, a studio executive informed him that Lerner intended to work on the final cut alone. The producer made many changes, but when this version was also found unsatisfactory, the studio's own personnel took control and produced a final edit in the form which was ultimately released. Clint Eastwood compared the three versions and pronounced Logan's original one as actually the best. Thus it is that this film, like *A Fine Madness*, has never been seen by the public in a form fairly reflecting the director's concept.

The decision to cast three non-singers in the leading roles was a gamble which failed to pay off. On the one hand, the dubbing of Seberg in her solo doesn't entirely convince, but on the other hand Eastwood and Marvin clearly lack the voice and musicality to make theirs work well either. The most successful musical numbers are the ensemble pieces, where there is a lusty invisible chorus to provide background. It was Marvin who was given top billing and allowed to dominate, and he does not hold back, offering a reprise of his *Cat Ballou* performance which sometimes makes Kid Shelleen appear almost sedate. An outlandish figure, he clowns extravagantly and often is extremely funny, but there is eventually rather too much of his act. Eastwood and Seberg seem conscious of their straight role as foils to their other third, giving good but slightly inhibited performances. Any element of psychological realism seems to rest almost entirely on their shoulders in what is a determinedly over-the-top piece which never asks to be taken seriously. The characters of Pardner and Elizabeth are all the more certain to look colorless when there are others such as Ray Walston and Alan Dexter attempting to vie with Marvin's excesses. There is a strange blend of accents too, but of these Walston's is by far the most bizarre.

This is a handsome outdoor musical, and the lavishness of the production and meticulous sets complement the natural beauty of the location setting. Good camerawork exploits these advantages well. Although the uneven musical material excludes it from the first rank of film musicals, there are enough memorable tunes to satisfy on this front too. Its weaknesses are mainly due to the overworking of relatively few ideas, and in this respect the length of the film, even after the cuts, becomes a liability. "How can a gold rush be slow?" asked *Newsweek*'s Joseph Morgenstern plaintively. He had a point, but for those with time to spare who appreci- ate spectacle, like their comedy broad and can stand to hear a joke twice over, *Paint Your Wagon* still has some harmless fun to offer its audiences.

*Paint Your Wagon* pre- miered on October 15, 1969, in New York City and played road show engagements followed by a general release well into 1970. *Time* chronicled Marvin's con- tribution to the promotional campaign together with its review, showing Paramount's determination to recoup its inflated investment. Three months later there was another fanfare when in London the Astoria cinema proclaimed the "Royal European Premiere," to be held on January 14 in the presence of Princess Anne. The soundtrack album peaked at 28th on the Billboard album

In *Paint Your Wagon*, 1969 (Paramount).

charts, and earned a golden record award for selling more than half a million copies. The film received an Oscar nomination for Best Score of a Musical Picture.

*Paint Your Wagon* has been depicted as one of the costliest failures ever to come out of Hollywood. This myth is largely the creation of critics who hated the film and reporters who failed to analyze the gross receipts adequately. Admittedly, this was a project char- acterized by serious financial mismanagement and indiscipline. Paramount had, moreover, been disappointed by the "M" classification resulting from the film's risqué storyline, feeling this would narrow its audience and make it that much harder to recoup the studio's invest- ment. The MPAA's Code and Rating Appeals Board could not be swayed. The film cost approximately $20 million in 1968, around $6 million in excess of the original estimate, but comparable to the budget for other major musicals of that era. At the 20th Century- Fox studio alone there had been three expensive flops: the $31 million *Dr. Doolittle*, the $40.8 million *Hello Dolly!* and Julie Andrews' $31.5 million *Star!* had yielded $16.3 million, $24.8 million and $7.6 million respectively in film rentals.

*The New York Times* reported on Paramount's lavish advertising campaign for the picture, which, with an estimated $2.5 million budget, included four different promotional films. *Paint Your Wagon* earned at least $15 million from its first run in North America, while it was a much bigger hit in the overseas markets, bringing the balance sheet into the black. Domestic receipts would attain $32 million. Despite this, it fell far short of the triumph that Paramount was hoping for and needed at the time. Its reputation as a famous movie disaster really reflects the imbalance between ambition and expenditure on one hand and, on the other, a finished product which often misfires and needlessly outstays its welcome.

## References

Appel, Kira. *Le Nouveau cinémonde*, 1759, 8 October 1968, pp. 19–23.

Cook, David A. *Lost Illusions: American cinema in the shadow of Watergate and Vietnam, 1970–1979*. New York: Scribner, 2000, pp. 181, 209.

*Film and Television Daily*, 16 October 1969, pp. 1, 7.

Gow, Gordon. "Gold diggers of 1969: Joshua Logan talks to Gordon Gow." *Films and Filming*, 16:3, December 1969, pp. 12–16.

Haber, Joyce. "*Paint Your Wagon*: director change." *Los Angeles Times*, 22 July 1968.

*The Hollywood Reporter*, 22 October 1969, pp. 7–22.

Kael, Pauline. "Somebody else's success," *Deeper into Movies*. Boston: Little, Brown, 1973, pp. 26–30.

Lentz, Robert J. *Lee Marvin: his films and career*. Jefferson, NC: McFarland, 2000, pp. 125–9, 214.

Leogrande, Ernest. "Real hippies—like 1853." *Sunday News*, 20 October 1968, pp. 29–30.

Lerner, Alan J. *Paint your wagon*. New York: Coward-McCann, 1952.

Logan, Joshua. *Movie stars, real people and me*. New York: Delacorte Press, 1978, pp. 211–25.

Montfort, Jacques. "Paint Your Wagon." *Ciné revue*, 50:5, 29 January 1970, pp. 18–9.

*The New York Times*, 8 August, p. 44, 31 October, p. 37, 7 November, p. 41, 8 November, p. 36, 1969.

Raft, Roberta. "Clint Eastwood." *Modern Movies*, March 1970, pp. 44, 89–91.

Sauter, Michael. *The Worst Movies of All Time, or What were they thinking?* Secaucus, NJ: Citadel Press, 1999, pp. 126–9.

Scott, Vernon. "'Paint Your Wagon' fits Jean Seberg." *Hollywood Citizen News*, 6 July 1968.

Scullin, George. *Paint Your Wagon*. New York: Macfadden, 1969.

_____. *Paint Your Wagon* [souvenir booklet with artwork by Peter Max]. New York: National, 1969.

Tanitch, Robert. *Eastwood*. London: Cassell, 2005, pp. 54–6.

*Time*, 94:17, 24 October 1969. "Fool's gold," pp. 100, 102.

*The Times*, 28 January 1970. "The friendly fight to publicize movies," p. 21.

Zec, Donald. *Marvin: the story of Lee Marvin*. London: New English Library, 1979, pp. 161–74.

Zmijewsky, Boris, and Lee Pfeiffer. *The films of Clint Eastwood*. Secaucus, NJ: Citadel Press / Carol Publications, revised 1993, pp. 94–103.

## Reviews

*ABC* (Madrid), 24 November 1970. Antonio de Obregon, p. 84.

*ABC Film Review*, 20:9, September 1970. Peter S. Haigh, pp. 6–7.

*America*, 121, 15 November 1969, pp. 474–5.

*Amis du film et de la télévision*, 166, March 1970. J.D., p. 30.

*L'Aurore*, 17 September 1970. Claude Garson, p. 13.

*Bianco e nero*, 31:5/6, May/June 1970. G.T., pp. 123–4.

*Le Canard enchaîné*, 23 September 1970. J.-P. G., p. 7.

*Cineinforme*, 8:91, November 1969, p. 15.

*Combat*, 21 September 1970. Henry Chapier.

*La Croix*, 19 September 1970. Henry Rabine.

*Daily Mail*, 14 January 1970. Cecil Wilson, p. 12.

*The Daily Telegraph*, 16 January 1970. Eric Shorter, p. 16.

*Dance Magazine*, 43:12, December 1969. Maria Harriton, p. 31.

*The Evening News*, 15 January 1970. Felix Barker, p. 2.

*The Evening Standard*, 15 January 1970. Alexander Walker, p. 19.

*L'Express*, 1001, 14 September 1970. Pierre Billard, p. 26.

*Le Figaro*, 19–20 September 1970. Louis Chauvet, p. 28.

*Film and Television Daily*, 15 October 1969. Edward Lipton, p. 3.

*Le Film français*, 1358, 9 October 1970. P.A.B., p. 15.

*Films and Filming*, 16:6, March 1970. Gordon Gow, pp. 46, 51.

*Films in Review*, 20:9, November 1969. Eunice Sinkler, pp. 571–2.

*The Financial Times*, 16 January 1970. Philip French, p. 3.

*France-soir*, 22 September 1970. Robert Chazal, p. 13.

*The Guardian*, 16 January 1970. Derek Malcolm, p. 8.

*The Hollywood Reporter*, 15 October 1969. John Mahoney, pp. 3, 13.

*Image et son,* (*Saison cinématographique* 1971), 252–3 Sept./Oct. 1971, Claude Ganne, pp. 149–50.
*Kinematograph Weekly,* 3249, 17 January 1970. Graham Clarke, p. 18.
*Les Lettres françaises,* 23 September 1970. Marcel Martin.
*The Los Angeles Times,* 21 October 1969. Joyce Haber, s.4 p. 1.
*The Los Angeles Times,* 23 October 1969. Charles Champlin, s.4 pp. 1, 7.
*Le Monde,* 23 September 1970. Jean de Baroncelli, p. 21.
*Monthly Film Bulletin,* 37:434, March 1970. Tom Milne, p. 50.
*Motion Picture Daily,* 106:72, 15 October 1969. Richard Gertner, pp. 1, 4.
*The New York Times,* Vincent Canby: 16 October 1969, p. 56, 26 October 1969, s.2 pp. 1, 33.
*The New Yorker,* 45:36, 25 October 1969. Pauline Kael, pp. 176–9.
*Newsweek,* 74:17, 27 October 1969. Joseph Morgenstern, pp. 124–5.
*Le Nouvel observateur,* 306, 21 September 1970, p. 9.
*The Observer,* 18 January 1970. Penelope Mortimer, p. 32.
*Positif,* 124, February 1971. Jean-Paul Török, p. 73.
*Saturday Review,* 52:46, 15 November 1969. Arthur Knight, p. 64.
*Téléciné,* 24:168, March/April 1971. G.L., p. 30.
*Télérama,* 1081, 4 October 1970. Stanislas Gregeois.
*The Times,* 15 January 1970. John Russell Taylor, p. 8.
*Today's Cinema,* 16 January 1970. Marjorie Bilbow, p. 9.
*Valeurs actuelles,* 5 October 1970. Jean Limousin.
*Variety,* 15 October 1969. Rela., p. 15.
*Village Voice,* 14:54, 23 October 1969. Andrew Sarris, p. 55.

# Part III

## *From Commercial to the Avant-garde, 1970–1979*

Seberg's work in the new decade started out well commercially. After *Paint Your Wagon's* Autumn 1969 road show engagements, its general release in 1970 resulted in a long run in theatres. Following release in the summer of 1970, *Airport* became the top grossing film in the U.S. For several weeks both films were playing simultaneously in medium and larger markets.

Contrary to the prediction of Paramount's head Robert Evans, Seberg was not voted one of the top box office personalities of 1970. Those listed included (in descending order): Paul Newman (*Butch Cassidy and the Sundance Kid* and *Winning*), Clint Eastwood (*Paint Your Wagon*), Steve McQueen (*The Reivers*), John Wayne (*True Grit* and *Chisum*), Elliott Gould (*M\*A\*S\*H* and *Bob and Carol and Ted and Alice*), Dustin Hoffman (*Midnight Cowboy*), Lee Marvin (*Paint Your Wagon*), Jack Lemmon (*The Out-of-Towners*), Barbra Streisand (*Hello Dolly!* and *On a Clear Day You Can See Forever*) and Walter Matthau (*Hello Dolly!* and *Cactus Flower*).

The combined box office gross of *Paint Your Wagon* and *Airport* easily exceeded the total gross for each of the above names, a fact which might have been expected to bring Seberg some acknowledgment. Simply in terms of box office performance, the films of Barbra Streisand grossed less than half of the sum realized by Seberg's movies. It is also striking that her two co-stars from *Paint Your Wagon* were singled out, while she was pointedly ignored.

1970 was easily Seberg's best year in commercial terms, and, despite the snub from America's film industry, it was not devoid of artistic recognition for her. When Nelo Risi's *Ondata di calore* was screened in February the same year many critics were impressed by her central performance. None of her films hitherto had depended so entirely on her interpretation of a role as this almost clinical psychiatric study. When this won Risi the Concha d'Oro for best film at that year's San Sebastian Film Festival, rather than the award for "Best Actress" for Seberg, her share in the honor was implicit.

*Airport* was to prove the last film Jean Seberg would make in her native country. From 1971 through 1976 she made eleven films, one of which (*Mousey*) was an American production, but filmed outside the U.S. She accepted roles in Spanish (*The Corruption of Chris Miller*), Italian (*Dead of Summer*, *This Kind of Love*, etc.), German (the critically praised *The Wild Duck*), as well as French productions, including a second film with Romain Gary (*Kill*) and a film directed by her third husband Dennis Berry (*Le Grand Délire*). Few of these achieved great critical and commercial success, but collectively they demonstrate continuing development, culminating in an understated style and maturity of interpretation capable of adding depth even to insubstantial roles.

In the film *The French Conspiracy*, as was noticed in *France-soir* in February 1972, she was the sole female star to appear alongside Trintignant, Volonte, Piccoli, Noiret, Bouquet and Périer—an extraordinary lineup of France's screen talent by any standard. This highly-publicized film was, however, the exception to the rule. In general she was happy to receive offers of work which interested her and presented a new challenge. Thus it was that she worked with Philippe Garrel on *Les Hautes Solitudes*, an experimental film virtually without funding, and ventured a project of her own, *Ballad for the Kid*, a short for which she starred, directed and oversaw almost every aspect.

In 1972, in collaboration with exiled Cuban director Fausto Canel, she wrote the screenplay for a gentle, bitter-sweet comedy called *Frontière palace*. Seberg received a grant from the French government to defray a portion of the cost of its production as a full-length feature, and there was interest from Paramount in the U.S. Seberg, however, stipulated that Canel should be allowed to direct. The American studio baulked at this, since Canel's work had been confiscated by the Cuban government and was unavailable for viewing. For several years the pair tried to secure funding from other sources, until finally compelled to admit defeat. This film was never made. To have agreed to an alternative director would have seemed to Seberg a betrayal of Canel. Nothing could have been more characteristic of the actress than to take this stand.

As she observed in a radio interview with Jacques Chancel in 1976, an actor or actress always feels "on a slope, upwards or downwards." Well aware that the days of offers in super-productions were over, she could be philosophical. She felt that different opportunities would come along. When asked whether she planned to write her own story, she was hesitant—"How far can you really tell the truth without hurting others: that's the problem."

Jean Seberg's final completed film was a German-Austrian screen adaptation of Ibsen's *The Wild Duck*. Unlike her debut in *Saint Joan*, this was a modest production which attracted little media attention before its release in 1976 and wider distribution the following year. Such notice as it did receive was for the most part complimentary to both the film in general and to Seberg.

# *Airport* (1970)

"In a Ross Hunter production, you are guaranteed there will be a certain polish—which is a contradiction to many of my European films."—Jean Seberg

A Ross Hunter Production; A Universal Pictures release Original release: in English
Also known as: *Aeropuerto* [Spain]
Running Time: 137 minutes
Format: in Technicolor, Todd-AO; in Cinemascope

CAST: Burt Lancaster (Mel Bakersfeld); Dean Martin (Vernon Demerest); Jean Seberg (Tanya Livingston); Jacqueline Bisset (Gwen Meighen); George Kennedy (Joe Patroni); Helen Hayes (Ada Quonsett); Van Heflin (D.O. Guerrero); Maureen Stapleton (Inez Guerrero); Barry Nelson (Lt. Anson Harris); Dana Wynter (Cindy Bakersfeld); Lloyd Nolan (Harry Standish); Barbara Hale (Sarah Demerest); Gary Collins (Cy Jordon); John Findlater (Peter Coakley); Jessie Royce Landis (Mrs. Harriet DuBarry Mossman); Larry

Gates (Commissioner Ackerman); Peter Turgeon (Marcus Rathbone); Whit Bissell (Mr. Davidson); Virginia Grey (Mrs. Schultz); Eileen Wesson (Judy Barton); Paul Picerni (Dr. Compagno); Robert Patten (Captain Benson); Clark Howat (Bert Weatherby); Lew Brown (Reynolds); Ilana Dowding (Roberta Bakersfeld); Lisa Gerritson (Libby Bakersfeld); Patty Poulsen (Joan); Jim Nolan (Father Lonigan); Malila Saint Duval (Maria); Ena Hartman (Ruth); Jodean Russo (Marie Patroni); Albert Reed (Lt. Ordway); Sharon Harvey (Sally); Dick Winslow (Mr. Schultz); Nancy Ann Nelson (Bunnie); Mary Jackson (Sister Felice); Janis Hansen (Sister Katherine Grace); Lou Wagner (Schuyler Schultz); Chuck Daniel (Parks); Shelly Novack (Rollings); Charles Brewer (Diller); Benny Rubin (passenger)

PRODUCTION CREDITS: *Director:* George Seaton; additional sequences directed by Henry Hathaway; *Producer:* Ross Hunter; *Screenplay:* George Seaton, based upon the book by Arthur Hailey; *Music:* Alfred Newman; *Editor:* Stuart Gilmore; *Assistant Director:* Donald Roberts; *Associate Producer:* Jacque Mapes; *Director of Photography:* Ernest Laszlo; *Special Effects:* Film Effects Hollywood, Don W. Weed, James B. Gordon; *Art Directors:* Alexander Golitzen, E. Preston Ames; *Set Decorators:* Jack D. Moore, Mickey S. Michaels; *Costumes:* Edith Head; *Makeup:* Bud Westmore; *Sound:* Waldon O. Watson, David H. Moriarty, Ronald Pierce; *Unit Production Manager:* Raymond Gosnell; *Hairstylist:* Larry Germain; *Technical Advisor:* John N. Denend; *Air Traffic Control:* Captain Lee Danielson; *Music Direction:* Arnold Schwarzwald; *Script Supervisor:* Betty Abbott

## Synopsis

Severe Midwest blizzards threaten to close Lincoln International Airport. Administrator Mel Bakersfeld calls on maintenance chief Patroni to clear a blocked runway. Extreme weather

The cast of *Airport*, the top grossing film of 1970. Front: Dean Martin and Jacqueline Bisset, Jean Seberg and Burt Lancaster; middle: Lloyd Nolan and Maureen Stapleton, Helen Hayes and Van Heflin; back: Barry Nelson, Barbara Hale (Universal/courtesy Manoah Bowman, Independent Visions).

simply adds to Bakersfeld's other problems, including his own marital crisis and tension with his philandering pilot brother-in-law Vernon Demerest. Wily senior Ada Quonsett gives public relation head Tanya further headaches through persistent unpaid flights.

Desperate unemployed construction worker D.O. Guerrero resolves to kill himself, but wants his suicide to appear an accident and to provide his wife Inez with a large insurance payout. Before she can raise the alarm he succeeds in boarding Demerest's flight to Rome with a home-made bomb concealed in his cabin luggage. On the same flight are Ada Quonsett and attendant Gwen Meighen, who is pregnant with Demerest's child. The flight is airborne before the crew can be alerted to the danger. Some quick thinking averts the worst, but cannot prevent Guerrero from detonating the bomb and killing himself. Only through a supreme effort in the air and on the ground is it finally possible to land the badly damaged aircraft without disaster. The impact of the drama brings resolution to some personal dilemmas, not least for Bakersfeld and Tanya.

## Reviews

"Place *Airport* on your must-see list! If you enjoy suspense, fine dramatic performances and top quality entertainment, it's a film you simply can't miss!"—Marilyn Beck, Bell-McClure syndicated columnist

"[*Airport*] is the sort of movie most people mean when they say Hollywood doesn't make movies like they used to ... [it] has an interior clock that came to a stop—I'd estimate—about 1939.... [It] is an immensely silly film—and it will probably entertain millions of people who no longer care very much about movies."—*New York Times*

"The acting in *Airport* is a pleasure to watch, for *all* the players seem to be *enjoying* their roles and to be trying to give good performances, *and succeeding* ... [Seberg] continues to show she is learning how to act."—*Films in Review*

"*Airport* is about four times better than the novel ... completely engrossing ... completely captivating!"—John B. Tucker, ABC-TV

"*Airport* is a handsome, often dramatically involving epitaph to a bygone brand of film making. This jet age *Grand Hotel* might do good business, but it's doubtful there will be the kind of stampede necessary to bail out Universal's investment of around $10,000,000. The sum of *Airport* is less than its high-priced parts."—*Variety*

"... despite some attempt at modernity by the use of multi-screen effects ... it seems, rather, to belong to the 'thirties, but with a curious difference. Then the centre would have been some monstrous part for a Joan Crawford or Kay Francis; now it is the men who are prominent."—*Daily Telegraph*

"Produced by Ross Hunter, fearless champion of the industry's *arrière-garde* (*Pillow Talk* and *Thoroughly Modern Millie*), the movie spends over two hours proving what every seasoned traveler already knows: waiting around airports can be a drag."—*Time*

"... In between Seberg is wasted...."—*Village Voice*

## Notes

*Airport*, based on the phenomenal bestselling 1968 novel by Arthur Hailey, appeared to rediscover and enhance a winning formula for lavish Hollywood productions. The string of star-studded disaster movies which followed in the 1970s included *The Poseidon Adventure*, *Towering Inferno* and *Earthquake*, perhaps representing three sub-genres, and of course three sequels of its own over the next decade. This film, with its all-star cast and multiple story lines, was considered "the granddaddy of them all" and might still serve as a blueprint for study by film makers, students and anthropologists alike.

Producer Ross Hunter, who began as an actor, had established himself with many hit films, among them *Magnificent Obsession*, *Pillow Talk* and *Thoroughly Modern Millie*. The director George Seaton was also highly experienced, having won Oscars for his screen writing. While used to the dual role, he was respectful of Hailey's minutely-researched blockbuster: there would be little rewriting and few changes. As Hunter saw it, this could be the *Grand Hotel* of the air.

Although the airport described in the novel resembled Chicago's O'Hare, filming at one of the world's busiest airports wasn't feasible. Instead, location filming took place at the Minneapolis-St. Paul International Airport in Minnesota, primarily at night when the facility was closed. Exterior scenes were filmed on the snow-covered runways in temperatures plunging to a wind chill of 43F degrees below zero. At times, film literally froze in the cameras, slowing the schedule.

Money was almost no object for the $10 million production. In order to achieve authenticity, Hunter rented a $7.5 million Boeing 707 at $18,000 a day from Flying Tigers Lines for the on-location scenes. Five weeks of filming were spent on scenes inside a mockup jet which stretched 145 feet, with 110 seats, combining components from seven different jets. "We tried to create an atmosphere of a jetliner in flight as much as possible within the confines of a film studio sound stage," Hunter explained, adding that "every one of our passengers was given an individual biographical sketch so they knew why they were on this jet." Authenticity of detail, from cockpit controls to food and beverage carts, was a major concern for Director Seaton. He used the largest portable refrigeration unit available to Universal in order to reduce temperatures to a level which would result from a mid-air explosion. "I wanted them to be cold as well as look cold with fear," he said, "and I wanted to help them all I could. It was a hard scene to sweat out in the 80-degree Hollywood weather."

That the casting for the picture would reflect Universal's investment in the project was a given from the outset. Dean Martin had been the first big name to be signed. Burt Lancaster would be right for the airport's manager Bakersfeld, Hunter felt, having "both the macho and the sensitivity that the role needed." Ross's first choice for the role of Tanya Livingston had been Angie Dickinson, but Universal had a "pay-or-play" two-picture contract with Seberg, and insisted that she should play the public relations manager and Lancaster's romantic partner. Universal calculated that Seberg's name would be a greater asset for the international market, and she would receive third billing. Lancaster was enthusiastic neither about the picture nor about his screen partner, and, despite his high level of professionalism, this shows. He was prepared to make a film which he regarded as a "piece of junk" but which would make a lot of money, because this enabled him to take chances with movies he actually believed in. If ever he made a movie on automatic pilot, *Airport* was it. Hunter remembered him as pleasant but aloof, while Seberg recalled him as uncommunicative and a somewhat cold personality. In fairness, not all of the cast shared Lancaster's evaluation of the project. Dean Martin thought it had "a lot of depth and a lot of emotion" and was "the most interesting film I've done in years." Helen Hayes had been impressed by Hailey's novel and felt the role she was offered was too good to turn down.

The very efficiency with which every element of *Airport* was put in place seems to lend it all the ponderousness of a Boeing 707. Critics picked up on the tempting metaphors and certainly did not need any cue from Ross Hunter to spot the formula of portmanteau drama à la *Grand Hotel*. For some of them it became almost a game of "spot the cliché." Hunter and Seaton deprived them of one target when they decided to eliminate Bakersfeld's emotionally disturbed brother Keith from the adaptation, but there were plenty left to go round. Though far from devoid of entertainment value, the film is a prime example of the triumph of technique and resources over content. Whatever life some of the cast manage to breathe into their soap opera characters is quickly overwhelmed by the pretensions of the contrived melodrama. Rather like an airframe, credibility is tested to the point at which alarming cracks begin to appear, while crisis is piled upon crisis and tension is ratcheted up with every musical crescendo. Guerrero is little more than a sketchily motivated human bomb, primed to detonate the dramatic climax. Once he is disposed of, all can resume the struggle with the problems we are expected to find more interesting and reassuring. Perhaps Maureen Stapleton brings us closest to convincing human reality as Inez Guerrero, but almost as a disoriented refugee from a different movie.

In sum, many in the audience may well feel no more passionately involved than Lancaster and Seberg appear to be, as they drive away together beyond the rolling final credits. It is hardly surprising that Jim Abrahams and David and Jerry Zucker, the creators of *Airplane!* (1980), realized that huge fun might be had at the expense of such solemn, gold-plated vacuity. It even appeared that there was air mileage for a sequel to their hilarious spoof. In its day, *Airport* set the standard for a whole class of popcorn melodrama, and it feels somehow unfair that imitators have made it seem even more cliché-ridden now than it actually was at the time. Maurice Yacowar, in his typology of the disaster genre, placed *Airport* in "The Ship of Fools" category, which typically plays on the dangers of an isolated

At the *Airport* wrap party with producer Ross Hunter, Jacqueline Bisset and Helen Hayes (Universal).

journey, noting the particular anxieties associated with flying. As Stephen Keane has pointed out, however, tension is derived from a whole set of circumstances. It is the elaborate combination of all these which gives the more skeptical viewer a sense of manipulation and particularly leaves the film wide open to satirical attack.

*Airport* opened at Radio City Music Hall on March 5, 1970, and took $500,000 in two weeks. Throughout March and April *The Hollywood Reporter* announced box office records in the U.S., Canada and Europe, and this became the biggest grossing movie of the year, topping $40 million. For the film's European launch, as part of what *The Times* described as "an unusually complex promotional package," Universal's London office had devised a "Miss World Airport" competition, with televised finals to precede the royal premiere. "In the depressed state of the traditional studio-based business this kind of glamour publicity is not now so common," the newspaper noted, explaining that the studio believed commercial sponsorship and merchandising would recoup much of its costs. The eventual gross would reach $100 million, with $45 million from rentals.

To cap its commercial success at home and abroad, *Airport* was nominated for ten Academy Awards (winners in parentheses): Picture (*Patton*), Supporting Actress, Screenplay based on material from another medium (*M\*A\*S\*H\**), Cinematography (*Ryan's Daughter*), Art Direction and Set Direction (*Patton*), Sound (*Patton*), Original Score (*Love Story*), Film Editing (*Patton*), and Costume Design (*Cromwell*). Maureen Stapleton and Helen Hayes were both nominated for Supporting Actress. In the event, Hayes received the film's only Oscar for her mildly amusing portrait of senior serial joy rider, Ada Quonsett. *Airport* was Van Heflin's last motion picture role, and here once again he adds a distinctive personal ballast to a supporting role.

## References

Canby, Vincent. "Can 'bombs' still make money?" *The New York Times*, 8 March 1970, s.2 pp. 1, 18, 23.

Cook, David A. *Lost Illusions: American cinema in the shadow of Watergate and Vietnam, 1970–1979*. New York: Scribner, 2000, pp. 251–2, 312.

Deglin, Paul. "Airport." *Ciné revue*, 50:15, 9 April 1970, pp. 8–9.

Fishgall, Gary. *Against type: a biography of Burt Lancaster*. New York: Scribner, 1995, pp. 261–4.

Godard, Colette. "Le petit chômeur à la mallette." *Le Monde*, 6 July 1986 (radio tv: p. 9).

Hailey, Arthur. *Airport*. New York: Doubleday, 1968.

Hayes, Helen. *My Life in Three Acts*. New York: Harcourt, Brace Jovanovich, 1990, pp. 226–9.

*The Hollywood Reporter*, 18 June 1970, p. 1.

Hunter, Allan. *Burt Lancaster, the Man and his Movies*. Edinburgh: P. Harris, 1984, pp. 114–5.

Kael, Pauline. *Deeper into Movies*. Boston: Little, Brown, 1973, pp. 136–7.

Keane, Stephen. *Disaster Movies: the Cinema of Catastrophe*. 2d ed., London: Wallflower Press, 2006, pp. 18–27.

Lacourbe, Roland. *Burt Lancaster*. Paris: Edilig, 1987, pp. 158–60.

Taubman, Leslie J. *Magill's survey of cinema: English language films* (Englewood Cliffs, NJ: Salem Press, 1981) second series, vol. 1, pp. 27–9.

*The Times*, 25 March 1970. "Up and away with Miss World Airport," p. 29.

Yacowar, Maurice. "The Bug in the Rug: Notes on the Disaster Genre," *Film Genre Reader III*, ed. Barry Keith Grant. Austin: University. of Texas Press, 2003, pp. 277–95.

## Reviews

*America*, 122, 21 March 1970, p. 312.

*Amis du film et de la télévision*, 170/1, July/August 1970. P.L., p. 23.

*L'Aurore*, 10 April 1970. Robert Monange, p. 18.

*Le Canard enchaîné*, 8 April 1970. Jean-Paul Grousset, p. 7.

*Cineinforme*, 8:98/99, March 1970, p. 42.

*Cinema d'oggi*, 14 September 1970, p. 10.
*Combat*, 4 April 1970. Jean Bourdon, p. 13.
*The Daily Telegraph*, 24 April 1970. Patrick Gibbs, p. 13.
*The Evening News*, 23 April 1970. Felix Barker, p. 2.
*The Evening Standard*, 23 April 1970. Alexander Walker, p. 25.
*Le Figaro*, 7 April 1970. Louis Chauvet, p. 30.
*Film and Television Daily*, 136:60, 17 February 1970. Mandel Herbstman, p. 3.
*Le Film français*, 1346, 19 June 1970. F.B., p. 10.
*Films and Filming*, 16:9, June 1970. Gordon Gow, pp. 84–5.
*Films in Review*, 21:4, April 1970. Harrison Hughes, pp. 243–4.
*The Guardian*, 23 April 1970. Derek Malcolm, p. 10.
*The Hollywood Reporter*, 16 February 1970. John Goff, p. 3.
*L'Humanité*, 4 April 1970. François Maurin, p. 8.
*Image et son* (*Saison cinématographique* 1970), 241–2 Sept./Oct. 1970, Guy Allombert, pp. 4–5.
*Intermezzo*, 25:20–21, 15 November 1970, p. 5.
*Kinematograph Weekly*, 3263, 25 April 1970. Graham Clarke, p. 16.
*Les Lettres françaises*, 1329, 8 April 1970. Marcel Martin, p. 19.
*Le Monde*, 5 April 1970. Jean de Baroncelli, p. 17.
*Monthly Film Bulletin*, 37:437, June 1970, pp. 126–7.
*Motion Picture Daily*, 107:30, 16 February 1970. Richard Gertner, p. 6.
*The New York Times*, 6 March 1970. Vincent Canby, p. 34.
*The New Yorker*, 46:5, 21 March 1970. Pauline Kael, pp. 165–6.
*Newsweek*, 75:11, 16 March 1970. Joseph Morgenstern, pp. 103–4.
*Le Nouvelles littéraires*, 2220, 9 April 1970, p. 14.
*Positif*, 117, June 1970. Jean-Paul Török, p. 68.
*Rivista del cinematografo*, 11 November 1970, pp. 561–2.
*Senior Scholastic*, 96, 13 April 1970, pp. 20–21.
*Sight and Sound*, 39:3 Summer 1970, p. 170.
*Time*, 95:12, 23 March 1970, p. 87.
*The Times*, 24 April 1970. John Russell Taylor, p. 15.
*Today's Cinema*, 28 April 1970. Marjorie Bilbow, p. 6.
*Variety*, 18 February 1970. Rick., p. 17.
*Village Voice*, 16 April 1970. Michael McKegney, p. 59.

# *Dead of Summer (Ondata di calore)* (1970)

> "It is the kind of role that I came back to Europe for. [At] thirty-years-old, one is not an ingénue anymore."—Jean Seberg

A Giorgio Venturini for Filmes Cinematografica (Rome) / Les Films Pomereu—Les Films Corona (Paris) co-production, Centro Cinematografico e Televisione, Rome; A Plaza Pictures and Titanus release

Original release: in Italian

Also known as: *Heatwave*; *Vague de chaleur* [France]; *Onda de calor* [Spain]

Running Time: 105 minutes [Italian version]; 91 minutes [English version]

Format: in Technicolor, Techniscope

CAST: [* denotes above the title billing] Jean Seberg* (Joyce Grasse); Luigi Pistilli (Doctor Volterra); Lilia Nguyen (the maid Nejla); Gianni Belfiore (Ali); Paolo Modugno (Chérif); Franco Acampora (Bianchi); Stefano Oppedisano (Consul Mayer); with Andrea Bosic, Armando Francioli, Massimo Pompili

PRODUCTION CREDITS: *Director:* Nelo Risi; *Producer:* Giorgio Venturini; *Screenplay:* Anna Gobbi, Nelo Risi with Roger Mauge; Based on the novel by Dana Moseley; *Photography:* Giulio Albonico; *Music:* Peppino De Luca, Carlo Pes; *Editor:* Gianmaria

Messeri; *Art Direction:* Giuseppe Bassan; *Set design:* Mario Ambrosino, Antonino Occhiuto; *Costumes:* Paola Nardi; *Assistant Director:* Monica Felt; *Cameraman:* Sebastiano Celeste; *Sound:* Massimo Iaboni, Franco Bassi; *Assistant Cameraman:* Enrico Fontana; *Inspector of Production:* Cecilia Bigazzi; *Script supervisor:* Vittoria Vigorelli; *Makeup:* Phuong Maittret; *Hairstyles:* Enriqueta Montero, Jacques Dessange; *Scene Photography:* Francesco Narducci; *Editing Assistant:* Mario Cinotti; *General [Production] Manager:* Solly V. Bianco; *Cosmetics:* Zasmin; *Synchronization:* Fono Roma; *Fashions:* Sartoria Mayer; *Music publisher:* Ariete Edizioni Musicali

## Synopsis

Joyce is the American wife of a German architect, Alexander Grasse, employed on the reconstruction of earthquake-stricken Agadir. Their spacious apartment is part of the unfinished development. She awakes alone, with only confused dreamlike memories of the previous day. A sandstorm rages, and the failed air conditioning makes the stifling heat unbearable. At her window she is conscious of watching eyes. Indoors the dominating reminders of Alexander, like his recorded messages, simply irritate. A bizarre inflatable doll brings fleeting amusement until the maid and a delivery boy arrive.

Driving to the airport, Joyce finds all flights are grounded. She shrinks from the familiar faces at the consulate, walking and driving aimlessly in a disturbingly surreal landscape. Alexander's hunting companion Ali is waiting at the apartment on her return. Impulsively, she tries to seduce the youth. Infuriated by his frightened reaction, she throws him out. Now at breakdown point, she persuades trusted friend Dr. Volterra to admit her to his clinic. Here her improvement is brief. Returning home on a new impulse, she finds detectives reconstructing Alexander's murder. In a trancelike state she mimes her confession to the shooting. Volterra escorts her away through the excited throng of newsmen.

## Reviews

"*Dead of Summer* provides an almost hypnotic pull upon the viewer; the slightest resistance will, however, break the spell and provide tedium for the action-oriented viewer. It is a movie for a special taste, one that has to be met willingly. Yield, however, and the experience is rewarding." —*New York*

"*Ondata di Calore* is a comparatively rare example of analytical cinema which is at the same time a study of human behavior seen objectively from the outside. The result is work of remarkable dramatic substance, stylistically perfect.... It must be added that great credit goes to Jean Seberg...." —*Rivista del cinematografo*

"*Ondata di Calore* proves a quite fascinating film ... which maintains a strong emotive charge and unusual cadence from start to finish, all the more so since everything is borne the shoulders of one character (Jean Seberg, outstanding as well as beautiful)." —*Oggi*

"... nothing could be deadlier than an hour and a half of watching Jean Seberg." —*New York Daily News*

"... Luigi Pistilli deserves credit in his smaller role. How much the film owes to the luminous photography of Giulio Albonico, to the lyrical settings ... of Giuseppe Bassan, also to the music of Peppino De Luca and Carlo Pas, informed viewers can see for themselves." —*Corriere della sera*

"... halfway between a crime story and a clinical case study, between thriller and a psychological tale, Risi, especially skillful with complex female portraits, has left his personal seal on this challenging narrative." —*Cineinforme*

"[The film contains] the tour-de-force performance of Jean Seberg upon which the entire film hangs.... On screen without respite from beginning to end, Miss Seberg thesps in virtuoso style. [Her] grandslam performance should not overshadow Risi's skillful direction ... for maximum mood and suspense."—*Variety*

"There's a further paradox in that the thing that sustains our (at least, my) interest in the film is the physical presence of Miss Seberg, who is hardly the world's most interesting actress, even in the best of circumstances.... [But] behind that extraordinary mask, there is real intelligence. *Dead of Summer* is a one-woman show, a Seberg celebration...."—*New York Times*

"An authentic 'performance,' a great trial of skill, by the beautiful Jean Seberg, who carries almost the entire weight of the film ... with supple intelligence."—*La Stampa*

## Notes

Nelo Risi, younger brother of the better known Italian director Dino Risi, trained in medicine before making a career in literature, notably as a poet, and in film. Beginning with documentaries and television work, he established a reputation with a series of more ambitious features in the late 60s and early 70s. *Ondata di calore* followed the success of *Diary of a Schizophrenic Girl* (*Diario di una schizofrenica*) of 1968 and was followed by the lavish *Una Stagione all'inferno*, based on the life of the poet Rimbaud, in 1971. The *Diary* adopted a semi-documentary style in what is almost a case history of the ultimately successful treatment of a young schizophrenic patient. The tone is compassionate but sober and clinical in its detachment. There are some similarities of approach in Risi's next study of psychological disturbance, but the situation was to be very dissimilar.

*Ondata* is loosely based on, or rather suggested by, the 1955 novel of Dana Moseley *Dead of Summer*, but has been deliberately transposed to a setting entirely different from Moseley's small Midwestern town. Morocco's 1960 earthquake had virtually destroyed Agadir, claiming many lives, and the skeletal modern city beginning to rise up in its place struck Risi as an ideal setting for the claustrophobic drama he envisaged. The entire action of the story would take place within some twenty hours, between a Saturday night and the evening of the next day. It would be seen almost exclusively through the eyes of the central character, Joyce, the younger American wife of a wealthy German architect. Risi explained that he wanted his film to be "analytical" rather than "psychological." He shows us a woman suffering from neuroses which have been aggravated by an alien environment, one in which she feels isolated and abandoned. Her state of mind is revealed through her behavior, "with keen and minute observation—every gesture, every expression, every look has its meaning. Finally a complete, reliable portrait should emerge."

The most important difference between *Dead of Summer* and its predecessor is that it would follow the "classic thriller formula." The audience is mystified, but is provided with a series of clues to assemble in order to make sense of what is happening on screen. Whether or not we succeed in piecing the jigsaw together, the final scene should make sense of the total narrative. Risi's formula is far from classic in some respects, however. To begin with, we are not even sure whether a crime has been committed, since we have no means of telling whether the images with which the film begins are dream or reality. When Joyce wakes on Sunday morning, she is disoriented, confused and seemingly aware only of the physical discomfort she feels. She has no recollection of the previous day. She is alone, and since she is accustomed to depend on her husband for advice, she plays tape recordings he has made for her. These, together with Alexander's possessions, provide the framework of her reality, even though she now rebels against it as a child against a parent. There are almost subliminal flashbacks, triggered by association, which hint at a different

truth which her mind rejects even
more violently. She is unable to
communicate with most of the people around her, who therefore
appear hostile and threatening even
when they try to help her. Even the
weather conditions seem to intensify
her paranoia. These are some of the
elements which we are left to
decode, and we can only do this by
understanding the distorting lens
through which everything around
her is perceived. Risi helps us to do
this by a host of different details and
devices which seem insignificant
individually, but which build cumu-
latively.

The director clearly felt freer in
relation to his source with *Dead of
Summer* than he had with the earlier
film, regarding this one as purely
fictional. Thus he did not feel the
need to consult specialists in psychoanalysis, as he had done for
*Diary*. Also, this time he did not
need to give the detailed direction

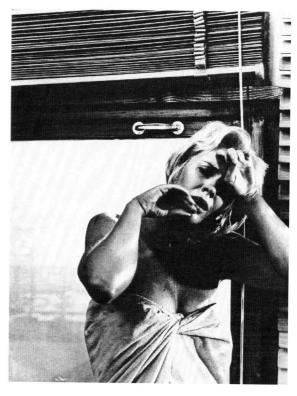

A "tour-de-force" performance in *Dead of Summer*
(*Ondata di calore*) (Plaza Pictures/Titanus).

necessary for an inexperienced young lead. In Seberg, whose signing for the project was
announced March 24, 1969, he saw a "consummate actress" with whom the interpretation
of a scene could be resolved through discussion of psychology and emotions as well as of
behavior. In the opinion of some Freudian specialists, he recalled, this freedom had resulted
in an even truer portrait of obsessive neurosis.

Some critics invoked comparisons with other works of literature or film making such
as Camus' *The Outsider*, Bergman's *The Silence* or Polanski's *Repulsion*, but the bold originality of Risi's concept and execution were generally acknowledged. Whereas *Repulsion*
builds up to the crisis of mental breakdown, here the director took the risk of founding
his drama on its aftermath. In this case the suspense is of a different and perhaps more
detached and intellectual kind, with no sensational effects, and within a relatively narrow
compass. Risi's suggestion of his heroine's altered state of consciousness, using surreal
imagery, seems, in fact, far subtler. The success of the whole enterprise clearly depended
on Seberg, her instinctive understanding of the director's objectives and her mastery of
mime. Despite a few dissenting voices, the consensus, not least in Italy, was that that this
was an impressive solo achievement on her part. Giulio Albonico's vibrant color photography is a definite asset, and the unobtrusive score by Peppino De Luca reinforces mood
at key points with a varied palette of instrumental effects. Leo Pestelli of Turin's *La Stampa*
praised these features in addition to Seberg's feat of solo acting. While finding Risi's film
slightly confined by its own excessive bravura, he wrote of its "figurative virtuosity, rendered
with exemplary clarity" and summed it up as a "refined thriller."

This joint Italian-French production began filming on location in Agadir in June 1969 and was completed in Rome in August. *Dead of Summer* won the Concha d' Oro (Golden Shell) for Best Feature Film at the 1970 San Sebastian International Film Festival, and it was Seberg who, as special guest, happily presented Risi with his award. It was premiered in Rome in February 1970, but received only a limited distribution, perhaps because it was seen as a specialist art house product with little commercial appeal.

In retrospect, Risi spoke appreciatively of Seberg's insight, professionalism and tact: "Jean Seberg is highly disciplined: she never creates a conflict or provokes friction with any part of the team, artistic or technical. She understands it all immediately. She can see what the director wants. And she really gets inside the skin of her character."

## References

Borsellino, Nino, and Walter Pedulla. "Storia generale della letteratura italiana." *Motta*, 1999, vol. 2, pp. 399–401.

*Cinema d'oggi*, 31 March 1970, p. 10.

*Cinestop*, 2:7, 21 March 1971, pp. 15–70.

De Bernardinis, Flavio. *Storia del cinema italiano*. Vol. XII, 1970–1976. Marsilio: Edizioni di Bianco & Nero, 2008.

Delroy, Gérard. "À Agadir Jean Seberg a vécu un cauchemar atroce." *Le nouveau Cinémonde*, 1817, 6 January 1970, p. 25.

Donald. "Panoramica de un Festival (San Sebastián, 1970)." *Blanco y negro*, 3039, 1 August 1970, pp. 70–74; "Jean Seberg (el porqué de una estrella)." *Blanco y negro*, 3042, 22 August 1970, pp. 66–8.

*Filmfacts*, 14:13, 1971, pp. 306–8.

Meccoli, D. *Epoca*, 1015, 8 March 1970.

*Motion Picture Guide, 1927–83*, p. 593.

Poppi, Roberto, and M. Pecorari. *Dizionario del cinema italiano vol. 3: I film 1960–9*. Rome: Gremese, 1992, p. 374.

*La Production italienne 1969*. Unitalia Film, 1970, pp. 90–91.

Risi, Nelo. "Il mio rapporto ambivalente col cinema e la poesia: colloquio con Nelo Risi a cura di Franca Durazzo Baker." *Cinema nuovo*, 28:262, December 1979, pp. 20–3.

## Reviews

*ABC*, 11:13, 27 March 1970. Callisto Cosulich, p. 49.

*Bianco e nero*, 31:7/8, July/August 1970, p. 133.

*Box Office*, 8 February 1971.

*Cineforum*, 10:94, September 1970. Elio Maraone, pp. 263–4.

*Cineinforme*, 8:103, May 1970, p. 16.

*Cinema nuovo*, 19:205, May/June 1970, p. 219.

*Corriere della sera*, 26 February 1970. Giovanni Grazzini, p. 15.

*Intermezzo*, 25:7–8, April 1970, p. 10.

*New York*, 15 March 1971. Judith Crist.

*New York Daily News*, 10 March 1971. Kathleen Carroll.

*The New York Times*, 10 March 1971. Vincent Canby, p. 32.

*Oggi*, 17 March 1970. Angelo Solmi, pp. 95, 97.

*Positif*, 120, October 1970. Colette Borde, p. 46.

*Rivista del cinematografo*, 6, June 1970. Mario Foglietti, p. 295.

*Saturday Review*, 44:10, 13 March 1971. Hollis Alpert, p. 80.

*La Stampa*, 28 May 1970. Leo Pestelli, p. 7.

*Tempo*, 15, 11 April 1970. M. Morandini.

*Variety*, 1 April 1970. Werb., p. 26.

# *Macho Callahan* (1970)

"The extraordinary thing is that when I work in America...
I let them do things to me—put me in silly wigs and treat me in a way
I wouldn't allow in any other country."—Jean Seberg

A Joseph E. Levine presentation; A Felicidad Films Inc. production; An Avco Embassy film
Original release: in English
Running Time: 100 minutes
Format: in Movielabcolor; in Panavision

CAST: David Janssen (Diego "Macho" Callahan); Jean Seberg (Alexandra Mountford); Lee J. Cobb (Duffy); James Booth ("King Harry" Wheeler); Pedro Armendariz, Jr. (Juan Fernandez); David Carradine (Col. David Mountford); Bo Hopkins (Yancy); Anne Revere (Crystal); Richard Anderson (senior officer); Diane Ladd (bar room girl); Matt Clark (jailer); Richard Evans (Mulvey); Jim Gammon (first cowboy); Gene Shane (second cowboy); Cyril Delevanti (old man); Willliam Bryant (dealer); Bob Morgan (McIntire); Buckland Beery (young man); Mike Masters (guard); Steve Raines (bartender); Ivan Scott (sheriff); David Carlile (horseshoe player); Bill Catching (Gruber); Jim Gurley (first player); Larry Finley (second player); Marco Antonio Arzate (Indian); Wallace Brooks (dog handler); John McKee (farmer); Hugo Stigliz (first man); Gene Shane (second man)

PRODUCTION CREDITS: *Director:* Bernard L. Kowalski; *Producers:* Martin C. Schute, Bernard L. Kowalski; *Screenplay:* Clifford Newton Gould, based on a story by Richard Carr; *Executive Producer:* Joseph E. Levine; *Photography:* Gerry Fisher; *Music:* Pat Williams; *Production Design:* Ted Marshall; *Editors:* Fabien Tordjmann, Jerry Taylor, Frank Mazzola; *Sound:* Jose B. Carles, Glen Glenn Sound Co.; *Production Design:* Ted Marshall; *Art Director:* Jose Rodriguez Granada; *Set Decorator:* Ernesto Carrasco; *Costume Designer:* Barbara Rosenquest; *Costumes:* David Berman; *Wardrobe Master:* Eddie Boyce; *Chief Electrician:* Luis Garcia; *Assistant Director:* Gordon Webb; *Makeup:* Sara Mateos; *Hairdressing:* Kathy Blondell; *Special Effects:* Leon Ortega; *Financial Controller:* Len Barnard; *Actors' Delegate:* Armando Velasco; *Head Grips:* Len Bukey, Jesus Beltran; *Chief Wrangler:* Jay Fishburn; *Head of Production:* Alberto Ferrer Alarcon; *Associate Producer:* Clifford Newton Gould; *Production Supervisor:* Alfonso Sanchez Tello; *Assistant Editors:* Arthur Schmidt, Richard Hiscott; *Sound Editor:* Michael Colgan; *Music Editor:* Robert Tracy; *2nd Unit Director:* Robert Buzz Henry; *Camera Operator:* Bernard Ford; *1st Assistant Director:* Manuel Munoz, Jesus Marin; *Assistant to the Art Director:* Javier Rodriguez; *Assistant to the Producer:* Patrick O'Brien; *Dialogue Director:* Manuel Escamilla; *Re-recording Mixer:* Gordon L. Day; *Titles and Opticals:* Modern Film Effects; Color prints by Movielab

## Synopsis

After escaping from a brutal Confederate prison camp, outlaw Callahan rejoins his partner Juan in Junction City. He has a score to settle, but before he can find his enemy, the trickster Duffy, he shoots a newly-married Confederate officer in a bar squabble. The widow Alexandra vainly appeals to the law for justice. Bent on revenge, she offers a reward for Callahan's killing. In turn Duffy and two hired gunfighters become further Callahan victims in their bid for this bounty.

Undeterred in her quest for vengeance, Alexandra raises the price on Callahan's head. She sees him in a casino where she works, although he slips away in the general confusion. The two fugitives head for safe haven in Felicidad and are overtaken by Alexandra. Her planned attack on the unwary killer only results in her rape by him. A band of bounty hunters led by her admirer Wheeler now closes in. By now Alexandra's hatred has turned to forgiveness and love, but it is already too late to halt the nemesis she has set in motion.

## Reviews

"It doesn't have enough laughs (unintentional) in it to be ludicrous; it's just an incredible western which can't defend its bloody brutality by striving toward 'realism' anywhere in the plot.... Direction by Bernard Kowalski wanders aimlessly, except he apparently concentrates on getting wooden portrayals from David Janssen and Jean Seberg."—*Variety*

"Though made by a predominantly American team ... *Macho Callahan* exhibits all the worst features of the European western. ...Not surprisingly, these limitations tend to swamp such conviction as the performances might carry.... Jean Seberg struggles with a part that is too ill-defined to make sense."—*Monthly Film Bulletin*

"David Janssen, scruffy and unshaven throughout, plays the part of Macho with almost unbroken impassiveness, and most of the histrionics are left to Jean Seberg as Alexandra. The talents of excellent supporting stars such as Lee J. Cobb (Duffy) and James Booth are hardly stretched."—*Kinematograph Weekly*

"Bernard L. Kowalski directed, and he handles the violent action sequences very well.... Otherwise, it appears that Kowalski merely devoted his time to staging his actors to form pretty pictures for Gerald Fisher's color cameras. Fisher provides some beautiful photography, but much of his work, like the script, doesn't make sense."—*Motion Picture Herald*

"If director Kowalski had been thinking, he might have used.... Miss Seberg, the way that Godard did—long, long ago—in *Breathless*. But then that presumes that an audience would want to know more about her, when the way the rest of the movie has been written, structured, even scored, negates that presumption."—*Hollywood Reporter*

"How, you ask yourself, did the nice, sophisticated, Paris-based Miss Seberg ever *hear* of a sadistic mishmash of a movie like *Macho Callahan*—much less get into it?"—*Evening Standard*

"Little to admire here either in the big opening crowd scenes in the prison, or the intimate threesome of the trail, and David Janssen makes an awfully dull dog of the killer."—*Daily Telegraph*

## Notes

Bernard L. Kowalski was a director who worked primarily in television but had made several feature films before this one, including the delightfully named *Attack of the Giant Leeches* and *Night of the Blood Beast* (1958) and the famously relocated *Krakatoa—East of Java* (1969). David Janssen was already familiar to television audiences before the long-running series *The Fugitive* made him one of America's best known screen actors. Jean Seberg was offered a generous $100,000 to co-star in this Joseph Levine western, which would also feature the respected Lee J. Cobb in a supporting role. The location work in Mexico for *Macho Callahan* began on December 1, 1969. Following a brief interruption for Christmas, there were two more weeks of interior work at Mexico City's Churubusco studios before resumption of exterior shooting in Durango. Seberg admitted to France Roche that she had expected to find the star of *The Fugitive* a rather dull or melancholy character, but that he had proved very amusing company. "I'd never ridden before the shoot," she told journalist Marc Hérisse (momentarily forgetting *Joan* and *La Récréation*). "But by the end of the filming I slept on horseback, I ate on horseback. What a marvelous country! I could already see myself buying a ranch there with loads of horses."

Janssen and Seberg sustained more than the usual quota of bumps and abrasions in making *Macho Callahan*. So realistic was the scene in which she attacks him that both were given three days to recover. In an earlier sequence three hundred men and women fight in a gambling casino, and Jean was caught up in the brawl as she escaped. She counted more than a dozen bruises. A week later she had to walk into a stinging sandstorm. After several retakes, both she and Janssen spent an hour removing layers of sand from their hair and clothing. Despite all the hardships, she claimed to have enjoyed the challenge of an adventure film. "I like them," she declared, "and if I get the chance, I'll do more of them." There was a reunion with an old friend in Cuautla when photographer Bob Willoughby joined the crew. More significantly, the Spanish-speaking actress soon became caught up in the welling political disturbances after production shifted north to Durango.

Despite Seberg's upbeat account of the production to the press, it was evident from the story line that this would be a particularly dark-hued western. Its late Civil War setting is significant only in the first scene, but this sets a grim tone which dominates the whole film. This portion lasts some twenty minutes. We see bodies being loaded onto a cart, cockroaches and rats even before the doom-laden title music cuts in. This set piece, culminating in almost orgiastic violence, is the most firmly controlled segment of the film. The low level of lighting and grainy color reveal more than enough of the degradation and suffering, which may not far exceed the historical reality. This background, we must suppose, has played its part in making the film's eponymous "hero" what he is.

*Macho Callahan* might have been a tale of personal redemption despite the tragic denouement it seems to aim at from the outset. The main problems are the limitations of the writing and the director's own apparent lack of conviction. Newton Gould's dialogue is as sparse and careless as his characterization. When the emphasis remains on action and imagery Kowalski carries the story forward passably well. The awkward blanks in the narrative which we are left to fill present no great challenge, and there are some effective scenes. The characters are the film's pivotal weakness. It is hard to believe in the transformation through love of this cold and vindictive central figure. It is one hour into the film before Callahan even starts on his journey to emotional literacy. By this point he has a hopelessly long road to travel, with or without the "First Eclectic Reader" which he presumably carries for sentimental rather than practical reasons. In a final flood of eloquence he reminds Alexandra that she "said something about finding happiness. Well I guess that's what Felicidad is. It's a good place, Felicidad."

Things are not much better in Alexandra's case. Her sudden bereavement changes her instantly from loving wife to ruthless avenger. It is even harder to swallow her further conversion from bitterness to love for her husband's killer, especially when it is the beating and implied rape she suffers from Callahan which reveal her true feelings to her. The fight scene between them is particularly crudely handled and unpleasant. Here, as in the scene at the prison, the cinematography of Gerry Fisher is edited into an almost subliminally rapid succession of shots, but the technique works far less well. Seberg was not well served by the costume department, and endures a terrible wig. Nevertheless, despite the various handicaps, it might be hard to suggest an actress who could have injected more warmth into this bleak western than Seberg manages to do. The supporting actors are not called upon to project much complexity. Cobb effortlessly combines avarice, lechery and general turpitude until meeting his amply deserved fate, whereas Carradine briefly embodies dignified gentility. Armendariz is everything the conventional sidekick should be, thankfully without caricature.

In short, the actors are left to flounder as the film's direction gets progressively weaker. Fumbling attempts at lyricism in the final scenes can do little to relieve the generally nihilistic tone of the film. It is hard to believe that the often muddy and erratic camerawork

**In *Macho Callahan* with James Booth (Avco Embassy).**

was supervised by the man who shot Losey's *Accident*. The gravitas of Pat Williams' score is overdone and out of place in a film which hints at a tragic dimension it is unable to deliver. The advent of the spaghetti western had done much to revive a genre which had grown stale, rejecting the old romanticized conception of the American West in favor of a darker, more violent and more cynical view. This shift was paralleled in Hollywood, and *Macho Callahan* is an interesting example of how far it could go. Unfortunately it lacked the stylistic elegance and wit which Leone, for example, had combined with the classic strengths of western noir. Straight drama was chosen over irony in this case, but if Kowalski was aiming at a kind of *High Sierra* finale for his film, it has to be said that he fails signally. The fate of his hero may be preordained, but he can invest neither tragic grandeur nor pathos into it.

It should be noted here that events during the making of the film form much of the narrative of Carlos Fuentes' novel *Diana* [*Diana, o la cazadora solitaria*]. Readers of the novel will have no difficulty in identifying the real people behind the names used by Fuentes, but are free to speculate where the borderline between fact and creative fiction lies. The novelist confided to a *Daily Telegraph* reviewer that "only about 70 per cent of *Diana* is Jean Seberg, which is a lot, I know. The other 30 per cent comes from other women I have known, or more important, invented. I couldn't call her Seberg because I am putting thoughts and words into her mind which never happened ... if you want to know all about the true Seberg, you can go to an archive, or watch her films." This seems an all too convenient let-out, given that the actress had no opportunity to challenge any part of the one-sided novelized memoir which would appear fifteen years after her death.

She left no account of her acquaintance with the Mexican novelist during this emotionally turbulent period of her life. At the conclusion of a radio interview in 1976 she spoke of the scruples which made her hesitant to "tell the truth" about her own story. Defenders of Fuentes will doubtless insist that other writers of less talent, fascinated by the Seberg legend, have presumed to weave her into far more extravagant fiction.

## References

*Daily Telegraph Magazine,* 23 September 1995. "The man who loved Jean Seberg," pp. 22–9.

Fuentes, Carlos. *Diana, the goddess who hunts alone.* New York: Farrar, Strauss and Giroux, 1995, translated by Alfred Macadam.

Hérisse, Marc. *France-soir,* 24–25 May 1970. "Jean Seberg: 'J'en ai assez des superproductions, je voudrais tourner avec Ingmar Bergman,'" p. 15.

*Hollywood Reporter,* 209:6, 19 December 1969, p. 16.

*Intermezzo,* 26:9–10, May 1971, p. 28.

Meyhöfer, Annette. "Machos Katzenjammer." *Der Spiegel,* 11 March 1996, pp. 140–147.

*Motion Picture Guide, 1927–83,* p. 1787.

Roche, France. *Paris-presse,* 14 April 1970. "Jean Seberg: 'Le cinéma de papa c'est confortable, mais je reviens en Europe chercher un vrai rôle pour mes 32 ans,'" p. 29.

## Reviews

*Amis du film et de la télévision,* 184, September 1971. J.B, p. 28.

*Le Canard enchaîné,* 56:2646, 14 July 1971. Michel Duran, p. 7.

*Cineinforme,* 9:115, November 1970, p. 18.

*The Daily Mail,* 12 June 1971, p. 15.

*The Daily Telegraph,* 11 June 1971. Patrick Gibbs, p. 14.

*The Evening News,* 11 June 1971. Felix Barker, p. 3.

*The Evening Standard,* 10 June 1971. Alexander Walker, p. 20.

*Le Figaro,* 11 July 1971. Pierre Mazars, p. 18.

*The Guardian,* 10 June 1971. Derek Malcolm, p. 10.

*The Hollywood Reporter,* 19 August 1970. Craig Fisher, p. 3.

*Image et son,* 263–4 Sept./Oct. 1972, *Saison cinématographique* 1972. Noël Simsolo, pp. 169–70.

*Kinematograph Weekly,* 3319, 22 May 1971, pp. 10, 18.

*Monthly Film Bulletin,* 38:450, July 1971. Allen Eyles, p. 144.

*Motion Picture Herald,* 9 September 1970. Ron Pennington, p. 503.

*The Times,* 11 June 1971. John Russell Taylor, p. 8.

*Today's Cinema,* 11 June 1971. Marjorie Bilbow, p. 15.

*Variety,* 19 August 1970. Har., p. 16.

# *Kill!* (1972)

An Alexander and Ilya Salkind / PROCINEX-BARNABÉ (Paris), ESTE FILM (Madrid), I.C.A.R. (Rome), DIETER GEISSLER (Munich) / Almos Mezo / Cocinor co-production; A Cinerama Release
Original release: in English
Also known as: *Kill Kill Kill* and *Police Magnum*; *Kill! (matar!)* [Spain]
Running Time: 110 minutes
Format: in Eastmancolor, Panavision

CAST: [* denotes above the title billing] Stephen Boyd* (Brad Killian); Jean Seberg* (Emily Hamilton); James Mason* (Alan Hamilton); Curd Jürgens* (Chief Inspector Grüningen); Daniel Emilfork (Inspector Mejid); Mauro Parenti (Cremona); Jose M. Caffarell (Algate); Carlos Montoya (Ahmed); Henri Garcin (Lou Krassavetz); Memphis Slim (vocalist); Victor Israel (Baron); Aldo Sambrel (Michelangelo Carcopino); Alan Collins (Medina); Chris Huertas (Nico Bizanthios); Tito García (Spyros Bizanthios); Tony Cyrus (Roberto); Willy Robke (radio operator); Maurice de Canonge (client); Albert Ruepprecht (chauffeur); Agostino de Simone (helicopter pilot); Walter Davis (black agent); Richard Santis (Karl); Simon Wilson, Dan van Husen (bodyguards); Ly Letrong, Dominique Niel ('porno girls'); Frank Fantasia (camel driver); Jose Maria (crippled man)

PRODUCTION CREDITS: *Director:* Romain Gary; *Producer:* Alexander Salkind; *Screenplay:* Romain Gary; *Director of Photography:* Edmond Richard; *Executive Producer:* Ilya Salkind; *Film Editor:* Roger Dwyre; *Associate Producers:* Almos Mezo, Daniel Carrillo; *Executive Assistant to the Producer:* Pierre Spengler; *Jean Seberg's Wardrobe:* Louis Féraud; *Costumes:* Cornejo; *Special Effects:* Manuel Barquero; *Production Supervisors:* Enrique Alarcon Jr., Hans Brockman; *Art Director:* Enrique Alarcon; *Production Managers:* Frank Bellot, J. Philippe Mérand; *Sound Engineer:* William Daniels; *Boom Operator:* Gus Lloyd; *Publicist:* Promo-Flash; *Camera Operators:* Bernard Sury, José G. Galisteo, Hans Burman; *Assistant Director:* James Bayarri; *Unit Manager:* Senny Marugan; *Administration:* J.A. Santos, Anthony del Toro; *Dialogue Coach:* Norman Enfield; *Mixing:* Jean Nény; *Production Secretary:* Carmen Moreno; *1st Assistant Director:* Henry Bellot; *2nd Assistant Director:* Michael Rubin; *Technical Advisor:* Frank Fantasia; *Script Girl:* Mary Manzano; *Set Dresser:* Louis Arguello; *Assistant Art Director:* Anthony de Miguel; *Makeup:* Adolfo Ponte, Phuong Maittret; *Hairdresser:* Manuela Castro, Daniele Schwartz; *Still Photography:* Cesar Cruz; *Sound Editor:* Anny Charvein; *Assistant Editors:* Catherine Ganz, Feliza Rueda, Angel Serrano; *Stunt Car Races:* Remy Julienne; *[Race] Director:* Rinaldo Bassi; *Props:* Luna, Mateos, Menjibar; *Main Titles:* Lax; *Music orchestrator and director:* Berto Pisano; *Songs: Kill:* written, composed and sung by Memphis Slim; *Kill 'Em All: Music:* Berto Pisano, Jacques Chaumont; Lyrics: Romain Gary, Jacques Chaumont; *Vocalist:* Doris Troy

## Synopsis

The battle to stem international narcotics trafficking is being lost through the corruption of law enforcement. Only a mysterious assassin challenges this criminal network. Interpol chief Grüningen wants his best agent Hamilton to cover a rumored meeting of five drug syndicate bosses in Pakistan. The identification of the shadowy "Coordinator" is a priority. Hamilton's wife Emily is bored with her dull life in Geneva and wants to accompany him. When he refuses she simply precedes him independently, asking directions to the hotel booked for him. Her delight in the exotic surroundings soon turns to fear in a nightmarish world of violence. Who is the terrifying stranger who suddenly appears and interrogates her?

With Hamilton's arrival the mystery only deepens. Before long it becomes clear that the stranger Killian and his young assistant Ahmed are waging war against Cremona's drug syndicate, whereas Hamilton is corrupt. Grüningen turns up to head the operation together with local police chief Mejid, and Hamilton agrees to help to ensnare the criminals. With Hamilton's help, Killian exposes Grüningen as the Coordinator. The police delay their trap to enable Killian, now joined by Emily, to exact merciless vigilante justice on the traffickers. Hamilton keeps his redemptive bargain and shares their fate. For Killian this is no more than a beginning.

## Reviews

"Gary's direction is sometimes flagging, but good in action scenes and film has a sense of humor that keeps it from falling into coyness and viciousness for its own sake."—*Variety*

"It's almost a call to murder drug traffickers on the grounds that there are no effective legal means against this scum ... the film is surprising in a degree of naivety, some excesses and a certain number of improbabilities.... Jean Seberg, Stephen Boyd, James Mason, perfect."—*L'Humanité*

"If it were a question of some little film from one of these 'sub' directors, purveyors of scandal, exploiters of eroticism and sadistic violence, one would pass it by in silence. But *Kill* has been written and directed by one of our best writers, Romain Gary.... And yet the result is a film full of mad ideas, incredible scenes, crazy images, extravagant characters."—*France-soir*

"Romain Gary, writer of repute and budding film maker, has surpassed himself. *Les Oiseaux vont mourir au Pérou* was already a work amusing in its pretentious pointlessness. With *Kill* all the records have been broken; the film is so absurd it's hilarious."—*La Revue du cinéma*

"Admittedly, there's the excellent Jean Seberg, and a remarkable contribution from Stephen Boyd, which save the day to some extent.... When will we get the first real film by Romain Gary?"—*Combat*

"Gary's direction is often lurid, focusing on cripples, beggars, blood and ugliness. His staging of action is confusing while his arty cutaways to associative images don't succeed in supplying psychological complexity.... Seberg is always credible, but her character is hardly an engaging one."—*Hollywood Reporter*

## Notes

This was Romain Gary's second and final venture into film making. Considering the generally adverse reaction to *Birds*, such a successful and prolific writer might have concluded that he was safer with a medium totally under his own control. Again, however, a primary motivation seems to have been to give a boost to Seberg's career through a major new film role, something a letter she wrote to him at the time of the launch clearly and movingly acknowledges. After the ordeals of 1970 she had begun to doubt whether she could ever find the psychological and physical strength to work again, and she had felt her very survival was at stake. This lifeline was, as she saw it, inspired by love. James Mason, who knew Gary, had originally agreed to appear in *Birds in Peru*. Having later dropped out, he settled the debt of honor by signing for this second project.

Gary's motivation in his choice of subject was very different, as he made clear in various articles and interviews: "My hatred for drug traffickers is boundless," he declared. He recalled seeing schoolchildren in New York queuing for heroin and a child of twelve die from injecting. Around 1969 he had begun a novel on this theme, but this had been abandoned. Now his film, both propagandist and personally cathartic, would be the product of a year's intensive research, which had taken him to the USA, Afghanistan and Turkey to ensure that all its details were accurate and well documented. He claimed even to have experimented with drugs personally, under medical supervision, to discover their effects. Having so clearly set out his honorable intentions in public, he must have anticipated a degree of sympathy for a film which looked so much like a personal crusade. Yet, despite its avowed message, he clearly believed it could work on the level of sheer entertainment: "It's an artistic thriller in the sense that I aim to raise the level of the genre. It's also an action film set in a strange, almost poetic environment. Action plus atmosphere, and all at a cracking pace."

In an interview Seberg and Gary gave on set to *Elle*'s Catherine Laporte they were evidently in good spirits, judging from his teasing remarks about Nixon and Sade which were calculated to provoke his star into a playful squabble. He wasn't above employing such ruses on camera:

"You see, just now I wanted a strong reaction from Jean. I went up to her and said very seriously 'I'd like you to concentrate a bit more.' For thirty seconds she had the expression of a wounded bird, until she realized I was winding her up. It was superb, exactly the expression I was looking for. To me, Jean is a true professional, with extraordinary photogenic quality and screen presence." Later, borrowing some of her ex-husband's phrases, she told Guy Farner how fully she shared Gary's repugnance for drug trafficking: "Romain and I love life too much not to hate everything which can destroy or corrupt it, whether it be pollution, safaris and other slaughter of animals, racial intolerance.... Drugs are the most appalling of modern forms of degradation." She added that hers was "an extraordinary action role unlike any I'd ever had before."

The shoot began on March 15, 1971, and was to involve location filming in Elche in south eastern Spain, Switzerland, Tunisia, Afghanistan and Yemen, in addition to work at the Studio Verona S.A. in Madrid. In retrospect he thought it was a "miracle," considering the complexity of the plot, that they had shot the film in ten weeks.

This time a completely different style from that of *Les Oiseaux* was adopted. *Kill* is perhaps more akin to the novel *Direct Flight to Allah* (*Les Têtes de Stéphanie*) which he would publish under the pseudonym of Shatan Bogat in 1974, an experiment in the pulp fiction genre. In *Kill* he offers a classic brain-teaser which is intricately plotted, taking us down a trail littered with clues, riddles, shocks and false leads. Its stylized and highly dramatized visual treatment, capitalizing to the full on the exotic features of the location, seems calculated and almost imitative of *bande dessinée* comic strip. The scene shifts constantly between the different characters, with stark, even lurid images and clipped dialogue. The episode in which Emily arrives in Pakistan alone and wanders in search of the hotel builds a dream-like atmosphere. The strangeness of the countryside and its inhabitants entrance her at first, but the delight and wonder turn to terror as darkness falls, bringing bizarre visions of violence. As in a nightmare, the sense of danger is as overwhelming as it is irrational and non-specific.

The English title for the film was to have been *Total Danger* before this was supplanted by the abbreviation of the avenging hero's name. Both titles are revealing, for Gary's ambition was to create a thriller with a message, and it is above all the conflict between the two objectives which led to its critical failure. This is not quite a satirical pastiche of the genre, but it comes confusingly close to that with its succession of ketchup-spattered cadavers, nudity and cardboard cutout villains. Although the film begins with images of drug victims, it almost immediately loses touch with the reality of narcotics. Instead we have a fanciful narrative in which those who trade in them and their corrupt accessories are brought to summary, vigilante-style justice. We may laugh at the bloodthirstiness of Killian's young helper Ahmed ("Bang! Bang! I like Americans!"), whom he affectionately dubs Che Guevara, but the humor is uneasy. Again, Gary's zeal in keeping his audience entertained leads him to overload the narrative with incident, such as a five-minute car chase, complete with crashes and explosions, or the attempted rape of Emily by Cremona's chauffeur Karl, neither of which is necessary to the central plot.

It is chiefly through Emily's eyes that the story unfolds, as she plunges blindly into this forbidden adventure, preferring danger to Swiss domesticity and life with a husband she does not love. The audience shares her fear and perplexity in a weird environment populated by assassins and spies. The cardinal principle is that nothing must be what it seems. She takes a lover, but which side is he on? Her husband Alan Hamilton is a man condemned in his own eyes, who has sold out to the people he despises through cynicism.

In Romain Gary's second film *Kill!*, Seberg was teamed with James Mason (Cinerama).

He wavers between the instinct for self preservation and self-hatred, finally preferring the "clean" death he is offered. If it is in Alan's words a "rotten, corrupt, criminal world," it is the "innocent" Emily who stands for life here, though paradoxically paired with a man who defends life by dispensing death on a prodigal scale. Perhaps more troubling than Killian is the boy warrior Ahmed, who is enlisted on the side of the angels, but who caresses his guns lovingly nonetheless. Readers of Gary's fiction will appreciate the appearance here too of the monocled Baron, an enigmatic protean figure who encapsulates so much of the director's love of the offbeat and quirky.

There is little realism in the love scenes between Emily and Brad, which seem almost as stylized as the violence. A body double was provided for Seberg, perhaps so that the erotic element required by distributors could be satisfied. Considering all the degrees of terror or astonishment she has to register here, her performance is commendable and seldom falters. Emily, true to the tradition of imperiled heroines, emerges from her adventures looking cool, poised and beautiful. Mason, haunted and world-weary, gives substance to the near-tragic role of the embittered renegade. By contrast, Boyd exudes testosterone as Emily's fantasy lover made real, and the nine-year-old Montoya gives a pleasing performance as the exterminator's apprentice.

Much of the dialogue is like a parody of the tough thriller idiom, but there are typical Gary touches. "What's the Afro wig about? Are we on a new protest kick?" sneers the cynic Hamilton. "For your information, the world was already saved 2000 years ago—and look at it!" Gary saves his most explicit satirical comment to the end, as the drug bosses debate their marketing strategy. Krassavetz urges caution in view of public opinion, but Medina is for "creativity": "You can't be a conservative in this business today ... I told my son, 'No kid, you ain't goin' to any goddamn college. That's where they put all kinds of subversive, antisocial, anti–American ideas into your head.'"

It was Gary the storyteller rather than the polemicist who finally dominated in the ambivalent conception of *Kill*. No doubt this liberated his imagination for the better, for despite all the excesses there are few scenes without visual interest. The leaping figures in the medina are a recurring image, exercising an hypnotic power on Hamilton, but there are other examples of arresting or disturbing visual effects. Edmond Richard's cinematography is generally outstanding, with sonorous coloring appropriate to the location backdrops. Viewers will judge whether scenes such as Cremona's slave market tableau are simply tasteless or there to make a legitimate point, albeit heavy-handedly. Gary reminds us of the voyeurism of the medium in any case, since "film within film" is a recurrent device here. The film score by Pisano and Chaumont has the right kind of hard edge to it, with jabbing rhythms to accompany Doris Troy's harshly delivered title lyrics. The composers are adept in changing mood, shifting between snarling brass and sighing strings or matching Middle Eastern instrumentation to scene and character, as with the cheeky signature tune which pipes in every appearance of Ahmed.

The film was released in Paris on January 21, 1972, the same week as *The French Connection*, as James Mason was to remember with a grimace two years later. The similar subject matter invited unfavorable comparisons. Compared with the tough realism of William Friedkin's outstanding thriller, *Kill!* struck many as outlandish, a technically clumsy extravaganza of lurid effects and images which veers too close to caricature in its villains and heroes. The American director was undoubtedly more in tune with popular taste, and critics were certainly not disposed to enter into the surreal world of mystification Gary conjured up for them. Gary received no credit for the bold originality of his treatment, his eye for the picturesque and flair for mystery, nor was there any recognition of his play with cliché, stereotypes and archetypes of fiction as a vehicle for irony or subversion. *Kill!* was taken, and almost universally dismissed, at face value. It was hardly seen in the U.S. and not approved for British distribution.

## *References*

Alameda, Sol. "3 famosos bajo las palmeras de Elche" [interviews with Seberg, Gary and Mason]. *Nuevo fotogramas*, 1178, 14 May 1971, pp. 19–21.

Assouline, Pierre, et al. *Lectures de Romain Gary*. Paris: Gallimard, 2010, pp. 186–8.

Chapier, Henri. "Lettre ouverte à Romain Gary à propos de *Kill*." *Combat*, 25 January 1972, p. 13.

*Cine en 7 dias*, 10:515, 20 February 1971. M.H.E. Romain Gary, autor y director: otra vez el mundo terrible de las drogas, pp. 8–9.

Duran, J. "Le Monde de la drogue et de l'érotisme vu par Romain Gary." *Playcinema*, 12, 1971, pp. 58–62.

*L'Est républicain*, 28 January 1972. "Tuez les trafiquants."

Farner, Guy. "Jean Seberg et Romain Gary ont réussi ... leur divorce." *Le Soir illustré*, 2070, 24 February 1972, pp. 20–3.

*Le Film français*, 1381:2399, 19 March 1971, p. 7.

Fougères, Roland. *Ciné revue*, 51:39, 30 September 1971, pp. 12–5.

Gary, Romain. "Faux romantisme et avenir: la drogue, ses adeptes et ses myths." *Le Monde*, 11 December 1971, p. 23.

_____. Film et roman: problèmes du récit. *Cahiers du cinéma*, 185, December 1966, pp. 85, 91–2.

_____. Ma haine des trafiquants. *Le Figaro*, 27 January 1972, p. 25.

_____. "'Kill: Romain Gary part en guerre contre les trafiquants de drogue" [interview by Mario Beunat]. *Le Figaro littéraire*, 30 April 1971, p. 32.

_____. "Vedette des deux prochains films de Romain Gary: Jean Seberg son ex-épouse" [interview by France Roche]. *France-soir*, 2 July 1970, p. 9.

Hirschhorn, Clive. *The films of James Mason.* London: LSP, 1975, pp. 218–21.

Laporte, Catherine. "Gary-Seberg: retrouvailles en douceur sur un plateau." *Elle*, 26 April 1971, pp. 233–4.

Quinson, René. "Dans *Kill* Romain Gary dresse son réquisitoire contre les trafiquants de drogue." *Combat*, 20 January 1972, p. 13.

_____. "Romain Gary veut régler ses comptes avec les trafiquants de drogue." *Combat*, 8358, 2 June 1971, p. 13.

Seberg, Jean. Private letter to Gary dated 22 January 1972, published in Myriam Anissimov, Romain Gary, le caméléon. Paris: Denoël, 2004, p. 475.

Tessier, Carmen. Interview with Seberg and Gary. *France-soir,* 21 January 1972, p. 12.

*Unifrance film*: *La Production cinématique française.* August 1971.

## Reviews

*ABC* (Madrid), 20 October 1972. L.L.S., p. 92.

*Amis du film et de la télévision*, 192/3, May/June 1972. J.B., p. 29.

*Analyse des films saison 1973* (Fiches du cinéma, 482), p. 294.

*L'Aurore*, 25 January 1971. Claude Garson, p. 10.

*Le Canard enchaîné*, 26 January 1972. M.D., p. 7.

*Cinéma*, 164, March 1972. Tristan Renaud, p. 152.

*Cineinforme*, 10:146–7, March 1972, p.52; 11:163, November 1972. A.F., p. 11.

*La Croix*, 31 January 1972. J. Ro.

*L'Express*, 1073, 31 January 1972. François Nourissier, pp. 59–60.

*Le Figaro*, 26 January 1972. Pierre Mazars, p. 18.

*France nouvelle*, 15 February 1972. Albert Cervoni.

*France-soir*, 26 January 1972. Robert Chazal, p. 9.

*Hollywood Reporter*, 22 February 1973. Alan R. Howard, p. 4.

*L'Humanité-dimanche*, 31 January 1972. S. Lachize.

*Intermezzo*, 27:5–7, June/July 1972, p. 12.

*Minute*, 513, 9 February 1972. Jan Mara.

*Le Monde*, 23 January 1972. Jean de Baroncelli, p. 14.

*Positif*, 136, March 1972. Albert Bolduc, p. 73.

*La Revue du cinéma / Image et son*, 258, March 1972. Raymond Lefèvre, pp. 133–4.

*Télérama*, 1151, 6 February 1972. Jean d'Yvoire.

*La Vanguardia española*, 2 June 1973. M.T., p. 55.

*Variety*, 15 December 1971. Gene Moskowitz, p. 22.

# *This Kind of Love*
# *(Questa specie d'amore)* (1972)

"She was transformed into the Giovanna I had imagined. When the film was in progress she went ahead spontaneously."—Alberto Bevilacqua

A Mario Cecchi Gori / Fairfilm S.p.A. Production; A Tinaus release

Original release: in Italian; releases with English dub

Also known as: *Ce genre d'amour* [France]; *Eine merkwürdige Liebe* [Germany]; *Esa clase de amor* [Spain]

Running Time: 98 minutes

Format: in Technochrome

CAST: [* denotes above the title billing] Ugo Tognazzi* (Federico Ferrari and his father Giuseppe); Jean Seberg* (Giovanna); Ewa Aulin (Isina); Fernando Rey (Giovanna's father); Angelo Infanti (Bernardo); Evi Maltagliati (Federico's mother as older woman); Marisa Belli (Irene); Pietro Brambilla (billiard playing youth); Margherita Horowitz (party guest); Anna Orso (Federico's mother as a young woman); Gianfranco Rolfi (Carabiniere guard); Andrea

Salvini (Federico as a boy); Bianca Castagnetta and Sara Simoni (Carmen and Yvonne, *Le Lucciole*); Ezio Marano (priest); Fernando Cerulli (civil lawyer); Giulio Donnini (Monsignore)

PRODUCTION CREDITS: *Director:* Alberto Bevilacqua; *Producer:* Mario Cecchi Gori; *Screenplay:* Alberto Bevilacqua, adapted from his novel; *Photography:* Roberto Gerardi; *Art Director:* Carlo Leva; *Editor:* Alberto Gallitti; *Music:* Ennio Morricone; *Music Conductor:* Bruno Nicolai; *Cameraman:* Roberto D'Ettore Piazzoli; *Director of Production:* Enzo Mazzucchi; *Assistant Cameraman:* Franco Bruni; *Sound:* Domenico Dubbini; *Boom:* Benito Alchimede; *Costume Designer:* Franco Carretti; *Costumes:* Carmen Pericolo; *Soundtrack:* Fono Rome; *Dubbing:* Cooperativa Doppiatori; *Studios:* Dino de Laurentiis Cinema; *Ugo Tognazzi's wardrobe:* Piatelli; *Makeup for Ugo Tognazzi:* Alberto De Rossi; *Cosmetic Lens:* Vittorio la Barbera; *Flowers:* Saracchi; *Music Editing:* General Music-Sialom; *Production Manager:* Luciano Luna; *Inspector:* Renato Fié; *Secretaries:* Alvaro Spada, Giandomenico Stellitano; *Administration:* Nando Vistarini; *Makeup:* Eligio Trani; *Hairstyles:* Adalgisa Favella; *Continuity:* Elvira D'Amico; *Assistant Director:* Riccardo Sesani; *Assistant Editor:* Roberto Sterbini

## Synopsis

Federico, the son of Giuseppe Ferrari, is married to Giovanna, the elder daughter of a wealthy and cynical businessman who is now his employer. Federico is haunted by childhood memories of persecution suffered by his parents for his father's antifascist principles. In contrast, Giovanna and her sister Isina have led a pampered and protected bourgeois life in the family villa outside Rome. Federico feels misplaced, and doubly humiliated by Giovanna's blatant affair with family acquaintance Bernardo. He tries to bridge the gulf which he has allowed to separate him from his father, but when Giuseppe joins a reception at the villa he becomes a figure of fun.

Giovanna's pregnancy seems briefly to draw the couple closer, yet a miscarriage plunges her into depression and withdrawal. Federico decides to return to his father's house in Parma. Here he reconnects with his roots, reliving past experiences, and when Giovanna joins them unexpectedly she too seems to relish the calm and simplicity of this place. After Giuseppe takes the lead in honoring local antifascist Picelli it is Federico who confronts the hooligans who have vandalized his garden in revenge.

Tensions between the couple remain, but the old man's funeral and a visit to Federico's mother in a mental hospital bring greater understanding and respect. Their final parting is amicable.

## Reviews

"[Tognazzi] walks off with these honors at the head of a strong cast in which Jean Seberg as a rich, spoiled wife and Fernando Rey as her aristocratic father give fine character portrayals.... Bevilacqua's second film is a serious but imperfect try to cut through contemporary social confusions and examine alternatives for the intellectual loner."—*Variety*

"... we don't know what greater triumph [Tognazzi] can expect ... fine Seberg ... In short, Bevilacqua has avoided any significant banana skins on the ever difficult road of a second film, and we can count him among the most interesting directors of the moment."—*La Stampa*

"A serious and demanding work, not entirely transparent but shaped with great sincerity ... [Tognazzi] gives new proof of his versatility as an actor ... [Seberg is] among the other actors worthy of applause in a film which deserves discussion."—*Corriere della sera*

"Some awkwardness, some slackness of pace, some trace of coldness are here and there avoidable: but overall the film, well scripted, rich in local coloring, is certainly noteworthy, not least for being interpreted with a rare humanity of tone by Tognazzi, here with more commitment than ever...."—*Il Resto del carlino*

"Beside Bevilacqua we must place Ugo Tognazzi, who in this film is not only an incomparable actor ... but a collaborator with the director.... Bevilacqua has put faith in him. Tognazzi has repaid it with interest. For this congenial partnership too, *Questa specie d'amore* is an important film and a testimony of our time."—*Giorni*

## Notes

Alberto Bevilacqua's first film *La Califfa*, screened at Cannes in 1971, was based on his highly successful novel of the same name from 1964. With *Questa specie d'amore* there seemed every prospect of repeating that success. This second novel had been awarded the Premio Campiello in 1966. It is in the form of monologue, largely addressed by the central character to his wife Giovanna, interspersed with loosely connected scenes from various periods of his life. As it stood it was certainly unsuitable for screen adaptation, but the central themes and certain key episodes provided the basis for a reworking in cinematic language. As Bevilacqua told Luigi Scorrano in 1982, you can't simply turn a book into a film, and that had never been his intention. Even so, this film retains a very meditative literary flavor, which is pointed up by the director's frequent use of voice over.

The changes Bevilacqua made to his story actually go well beyond those dictated by a different medium. Characters and situations are substantially altered, though the relationship between Federico and his father, now the central focus of the story, is essentially the same. This was, as the director explained, "my own story," and depicted a part of Italian history which had profound personal significance. The director's strong emotional attachment to the region and people of Parma is also much in evidence. Authenticity of location and atmosphere were fundamental. Thus the crucial scene of the banquet of St. John was shot over three successive nights with local people who were encouraged to behave naturally. The well-known mental hospital of Dr. Basaglia near Parma was the setting for another important scene. The ceremony honoring the watchmaker Picelli was a staged invention, though the events of 1922 referred to are historical. Bevilacqua's careful planning did not preclude spontaneous changes. The vandalizing of the garden was an almost last-minute addition, for example, inspired by a real incident of violent hooliganism which occurred during the shoot.

The choice of Tognazzi for the triple role was never in doubt, for his rapport with the director was already established and based on their common link to the Po region and its dialect. In Seberg Bevilacqua saw an "exceptional artist" whose background ideally matched her "outsider" role as he had conceived it. He revealed that she had been his first choice for the role played by Romy Schneider in *La Califfa*, but Seberg had not been free at the time. Intensive discussions with the director prior to the shoot enabled her to interpret her character exactly as he had imagined her and without further prompting. Journalist Donata Giachini was able to interview Bevilacqua and his leading players in September 1971 on location by the river Po, not far from Parma. Seberg spoke warmly of Tognazzi, of the director and of Parma, and referred to a film project with Omar Sharif in Bulgaria (which would come to nothing), but vowed to be home in Paris with her son for Christmas at all costs. Although personally unlike her character Giovanna, she saw resemblances to many women in her. She loved to work with writer/directors, she threw in, and this one was very strong in both fields. For his part, Tognazzi was equally appreciative of his partner: "Because Jean is a very serious actress and a very nice lady. Also, and this is most important, she doesn't pose, she doesn't adopt false attitudes...."

The film is episodic, like a series of vignettes, at times unashamedly nostalgic and intro-spective, a rich multi-layered Proustian rumination which is sometimes esoteric. The very loose narrative structure is composed of fragmentary scenes and conversations interspersed with monochrome flashbacks which can seem arbitrary or rather mechanistically sparked by association. An oblique presentation of character and story, something noticed by critic Gio-vanni Grazzini, is integral to the purposely hesitant and ambivalent mood. In addition, at times, a first person commentary provides contextual guidance. From this incomplete jigsaw we are invited to construct our understanding of the central character and the key relationships in his life. Were it not for the quality of the performances here, Bevilacqua's leisurely-paced film would surely struggle against its own wordiness. Tognazzi accomplishes a tour de force in playing the father, in youth and old age, and the son, and the director too deserves credit for making this gamble work on screen. Again, the benign anti-fascist, as accomplished as a public speaker as in chair making or horticulture, might well have appeared an over idealized figure. In fact Tognazzi gives us a well rounded and convincing portrait of a man in harmony with his own nature, one who accepts his fate with stoicism and even humor, but for whom infidelity to the principles which have shaped his life is unthinkable.

Five years of marriage to Giovanna and dependence on her father have established Fed-erico within the circle of high bourgeois Roman society, a world remote in every sense from that of his origins. He has accepted subservience to the father for the daughter's sake, not, he insists, for material gain. Nevertheless, in accepting a bargain he sees as cowardly he has for-feited self-respect and the respect of a wife who now openly betrays him. The couple bicker and exchange sarcastic comments, and the bond between them appears at breaking point. We find him at a crisis, when scarcely suppressed memories of a traumatic childhood are renewed by the arrival of his father in the capital. As Federico tentatively renews contact he begins to understand the man behind the remote and quasi-magical figure he had remembered.

**With Ugo Tognazzi in *This Kind of Love* (*Questa specie d'amore*) (Tinaus).**

Bevilacqua uses two key scenes to establish the contrast between the cold artificiality of Roman society and the warm, spontaneous life of his own rural background in Emilia-Romagna. When Ferrari visits the aristocratic villa in Rome the old "bolshevik" with his rustic ways and strong dialect is treated with patronage or disdain by all except Isina. The counterpart to this is Giovanna's presence at the cheese ceremony in Parma. Here it is she who is the fish out of water, but she is quickly made welcome in an atmosphere of boisterous conviviality and flowing Lambrusco. A genteel baroque setting, with a musical backdrop from Rossini, is opposed to a painting by Brueghel garnished with a chorus from Verdi.

Having returned to his roots, Federico finds acceptance and the peace of mind he has not known. Giovanna, when she visits him in this alien setting, sees him in a new light, and it almost seems that they can rebuild their relationship. The reality of Giuseppe Ferrari's life in his own community shows his son, in adulthood, the nurturing values his own life has lacked. There is a sense that this heroic model need no longer oppress him with a sense of unworthiness. Giovanna and her sister Isina are both pampered products of their background but differ sharply in temperament. Seberg interprets her role with sensitivity and fine judgment, showing a woman of shifting moods, a snob, highly strung and capricious, but also capable of warmth and self-examination. The loss of her child brings her closer to the husband she has never understood. After removal from her familiar protective environment and exposure to a different moral universe, Giovanna feels cured of earlier maladies: "Now I'm an adult," she tells Federico with only a hint of irony. It is not clear whether their parting will this time be permanent.

Eva Aulin as the more outgoing Isina makes an effective foil to the "nervous sensibility" of her sister. Their father is urbane but cynical, a patrician whose cordiality to Ferrari is patently insincere and a man of culture who can quote a Shakespeare sonnet simply to salve his own bad conscience. Sensing his son-in-law's moral disapproval, he cuttingly reminds him that he too is compromised. Rey has all the suave malice this part requires, but strong performances are also found in several smaller roles. Evi Maltagliati as Federico's elderly mother, whose mind has been blighted by the persecution of her husband, is touching and believable. Marisa Belli's Irene too could not be more perfectly pitched.

One of the film's strong assets is a score from one of Italy's masters of this medium, Ennio Morricone. The composer is able to set the mood of this low-keyed drama unerringly, a story in which superficial action often belies emotional narrative. The music evokes Federico's melancholy introspection powerfully with a rich orchestral texture, yet can balance the earnest with the playful. Thus Morricone deploys the idiom of Vivaldi, complete with mandolin and harpsichord, to depict the ambience of Roman society. The transition between scenes is sometimes jarringly abrupt, but this may be in part due to some careless re-editing. The lack of natural fluidity in the film's construction has to be seen as one of its more serious flaws in any case.

Giovanna's words connect the title to her relationship with her husband explicitly, yet Bevilacqua's film is clearly concerned with many different kinds of bond, both personal and abstract, which give meaning to his characters' lives. The director's personal faith in the importance of cultural roots and tradition are clearly proclaimed. In addition, he seems to assert no less strongly the healing power of the past, however hard it may be to confront its ghosts and lies. It is clear from his own comments that he saw Tognazzi's roles as representing two opposing life forces. He is apt to stretch his polarities and his didacticism too far, but his film has more than enough subtlety, intelligence and humanity to rise safely above the trite or merely sentimental. The writer/director extols the virtues exemplified by the old man and the region which has molded him, and the political message is clear, but he offers no facile solutions to the problems of Federico and Giovanna. The ending is deliberately inconclusive, suggesting only that what they have experienced here will help them to find their own future paths.

*Questa specie d'amore* was released in Rome in February/March 1972. It won the David di Donatello award for Best Film 1972 and was selected for the Locarno and Karlovy Vary film festivals. Despite a generally favorable response from critics, with particular praise for Tognazzi, the film appears to have had rather limited foreign distribution.

After Jean Seberg's death Bevilacqua recalled, "I met her when working on the story for a mediocre film called *Congo Vivo* in which she took the lead. I saw an ambivalence in her, a desire to live and a fear of life—she was the kind of person capable of facing up to her fears. She was nice, sensitive, courageous, I liked her a lot" (*Jeune cinéma*, 1980).

## References

Bernardini, Aldo. *Ugo Tognazzi*. Rome: Gremese, 1985, pp. 186–8.

Bevilacqua, Alberto. *Questa specie d'amore*. Milan: Rizzoli, 1966.

_____. "Vi racconto le mie attrici." *Corriere della sera illustrato* 2:51/52, 23 December 1978, pp. 36, 38.

*Bianco e nero*, 33, 1972, p. 18.

Borsellino, Nino, and Walter Pedulla. *Storia generale della letteratura italiana*. Motta, 1999, pp. 75–6.

Brunetta, Gian Piero. *Storia del cinema italiano*, 3d ed. Rome: Editori Riuniti, 2001, pp. 456–7.

Campari, Roberto. *Parma e il cinema*. Banca del Monte di Parma, 1986.

Cebollada, Pascual. *Biografia y peliculas de Fernando Rey*. Barcelona: C.I.L.E.H., 1992, p. 268.

De Bernardinis, Flavio. *Storia del cinema italiano*, vol. XII, 1970–1976. Marsilio: Edizioni di Bianco & Nero, 2008, pp. 356–7.

Desbruères, Michel. "Alberto Bevilacqua, romancier de l'échec" [interview]. *Arts*, 56, 19 October 1966, p. 35.

XXV Festival Internazionale del Film, Locarno, 3–13 August 1972. Catalogue, p. 34.

Giachini, Donata. "Tre Tognazzi per il nuovo film di Bevilacqua." *Bolero teletutto*, 25:1274, 26 September 1971, pp. 24–7.

Incerti, Corrado. "É facile diventare regista: intervista con Alberto Bevilacqua." *L'Europeo*, 28:16, 20 April 1972, pp. 80–5.

Micciché, Lino. *Cinema italiano degli anni '70*. Venice: Marsilio Editori, 1980, pp. 114–7.

Poppi, Roberto, and Mario Pecorari. *Dizionario del cinema italiano. vol. 4: I film 1970–79*. Rome: Gremese, 1996, ii, pp. 208–9.

*La Produzione italiana 1971–72*. Unitalia Film, 1972, pp. 180–1.

Scorrano, Luigi. *Alberto Bevilacqua*. Florence: La Nuova Italia, 1982.

Toscani, Claudio. *Invito alla lettura di Alberto Bevilacqua*. Milan: Mursia, 1974.

Tournès, Andrée. "Entretien avec Bevilacqua." *Jeune cinéma*, 129 Sept./Oct. 1980, pp. 11–2.

## Reviews

*La Casa*, 3 March 1972. Aldo Bernardini, pp. 138–9.

*Cineforum*, 110/111 Jan./Feb. 1972. Ermanno Comuzio, pp. 130–2.

*Cineinforme*, 10:149, April 1972, pp. 16–7.

*Corriere della sera*, 25 February 1972. G[iovanni] Gr[azzini], p. 15.

*Epoca*, 23:1117, 27 February 1972. Domenico Meccoli, pp. 108–9.

*Filmspiegel*, 19, 13 September 1972. Michael Hanisch, p. 7.

*Filmspiegel*, 26, 19 December 1973. p. 15.

*Giorni*, 15 March 1972. Davide Lajolo.

*Intermezzo*, 27:3, March 1972, p. 10.

*Il Resto del carlino*, 5 March 1972. Dario Zanelli.

*Rivista del cinematografo*, March/April 1972, pp. 167–9.

*Sipario*, 310, March 1972. Sergio Frosali, p. 62.
*La Stampa*, 3 March 1972. L[eo] P[estelli], p. 7.
*Variety*, 7 February 1973. Werb., p. 18.

# *The French Conspiracy (L'Attentat)* (1972)

"Jean brought a great deal of honesty to her role."—Yves Boisset

A Transinter Films, AMLF (Paris) / Sancrosiap, Terza Films (Rome) / Corona Film-produktion (Munich) co-production; A Two Worlds Films presentation; Released by Cine Globe, Inc.
Original release: in French; dubbed in English
Also known as: *Plot*; *The Assassination Attempt*; *Tödliche Falle / Das Attentat* [Germany]; *L'Attentato* [Italy]; *El Atentado* [Spain]
Running Time: 125 minutes
Format: in Eastmancolor

CAST: [* denotes above the title billing] Jean-Louis Trintignant* (François Darien); Michel Piccoli* (Kassar); Jean Seberg* (Édith Lemoine); Gian-Maria Volonte* (Sadiel); Michel Bouquet (Lempereur); Daniel Ivernel (Acconeti); Philippe Noiret (Garcin); François Périer (Superintendent Rouannet); Roy Scheider (Michael Howard); Jean Bouise (security official); Bruno Cremer (lawyer Michel Vigneau); Georges Staquet (Inspector Paul Fleury); Daniel Ivernel (Antoine Acconetti); Jacques François (Lestienne); Denis Manuel (Azam); Karin Schubert (Sabine); Pierre Santini (Meulun); Nigel Davenport (CIA man); and Karl Otto Alberty, Roland Blanche, Jean Bouchaud, Jean-François Calvé, Marc Mazza, Jacques Richard, Claudine Berg, Aude Loring, Henri Gilabert, Michel Beaune, Jean Launay, André Rouyer, Jean-Louis Tristan, Jean-Pierre Moreux

PRODUCTION CREDITS: *Director:* Yves Boisset; *Producer:* Yvon Guézel; *Screenplay:* Ben Barzman, Basilio Franchina; *Adaptation and dialogue:* Jorge Semprún; *Photography:* Ricardo Aronovich; *Assistant Director:* Claude Othnin-Girard; *Sound:* Jean-Claude Laureux; *Editor:* Albert Jurgenson; *Art Director:* Marc Desages; *Music:* Ennio Morricone; *Music Conductor:* Nicola Samale; *Music Publisher:* General Music, Rome, SAAR Music Publishers, Milan; *Mixer:* Jean Nény; *Cameraman:* Jacques Assuérus, *Photographer:* Jean Kerby; *General Production Manager:* René Fargéas; *Exterior Production Manager:* Henri Vergne; *Production Administrators:* Georges Martin-Cocher, Jacqueline Calvet; *Director of Production:* Jean-Pierre Spiri Mercanton; *Wardrobe:* Pierre Nourry; *Makeup:* Serge Groffe

## Synopsis

Shadowy figures in French and American security target exiled North African opposition leader Sadiel as a threat to national interests. They plot to coerce Darien, a radical reporter trusted by Sadiel, to act as go-between without revealing their true purpose, that once on French soil his friend can be delivered to the African regime's ruthless police chief Kassar. Darien's career and relationship with hospital administrator Édith have failed, and furthermore he has a police record. A commission from television producer Garcin and a flattering approach from American journalist Howard promise a complete change in his fortunes. He dismisses his doubts.

Darien visits Sadiel in Geneva and explains the TV project. Sadiel agrees to travel to Paris, where he can also announce plans to return to his own country. Arriving at Brasserie Lipp, where he is to meet Darien, Garcin and Howard, Sadiel is discreetly intercepted and escorted away by police.

**With Jean-Louis Trintignant in *The French Conspiracy* (*L'Attentat*) (Cine Globe).**

Darien becomes increasingly alarmed at Sadiel's disappearance, tracing him to the house of notorious racketeer Acconeti. When he raises the alarm and threatens to reveal the conspiracy, Darien is forced into hiding. Édith conceals him and appeals to policeman Rouannet for help. Darien's taped confession seems his only safeguard. He telephones Howard, offering him the tape and arranging a meeting. The call is tapped. Howard arrives in time to shoot Darien and escape just as the police arrive. Finding the tape handed to him has been switched, Rouannet can prove nothing. Officially, the disappearance remains a mystery. Darien is discredited and the case closed.

## Reviews

"Jean Seberg makes a somewhat surprising appearance, still sounding like the girl who betrays Belmondo in [*Breathless*].... The script is only adequate.... [The film's] main strength seems to derive from the integrity of individual performances from the highly professional actors who at present enrich the French cinema to such an extent."—*Films and Filming*

"... the only thing the film does is make one more appreciative of the skills of Costa-Gavras ... the film is so oddly staged that, in a moment of high drama, when Jean Seberg is telling her man that she loves him, she almost gets her nose caught in the closing of the door of a subway car."—*New York Times*

"It's excellent suspense cinema, reinforcing its effect by constant reference to actual facts still present in everyone's mind...."—*France-soir*

"The method of this picture could stand as a textbook demonstration of how not to make a political movie."—*New Yorker*

"You are happy to see a French film of this quality, gripping throughout ... you don't know whom to praise most among an extraordinary cast.... What a cast! But also, what a film!"—*Le Canard enchaîné*

"... much of it is cleverly staged ... and Boisset begins to indulge a nice line in Hitchcockery: the assassination of Sadiel's student friend in a crowded street (right out of the second version of *The Man Who Knew Too Much*), the *Psycho* shock of Trintignant's execution...."—*Monthly Film Bulletin*

"When you take on a subject like that, you have to be careful it doesn't rub off on the quality of your movie. The makers of *The French Conspiracy* weren't careful enough."—*Chicago Tribune*

## Notes

On October 29, 1965, outside the celebrated Brasserie Lipp in the Saint-Germain-des-Prés district of Paris, two policemen accosted and detained an exiled Moroccan opposition leader, Mehdi Ben Barka. The subsequent total disappearance of this prominent spokesman for third world radicalism was to trigger one of the scandals of the decade, just weeks in advance of the French Presidential elections. The investigation which ensued uncovered a mystery never fully elucidated, but what soon became apparent was that Ben Barka had been interrogated under torture and killed by agents of the Moroccan secret services, who subsequently disposed of his body.

The abduction itself was, however, only the culmination of a conspiracy, which lured the victim from Switzerland for the purpose of making a documentary film. This involved a number of French and foreign subjects in various ways. The judicial inquiry raised troubling questions and suspicions, for it revealed a murky world in which governments and their security services appeared to collude with violent criminals in order to deal with troublesome individuals. Soon a key figure in the plot began to talk. Georges Figon, the convicted criminal who was to have produced the documentary film, made a taped confession which was published in the weekly *L'Express*. He evaded the police until traced to an apartment building. As police closed in a shot was fired and Figon was found dead. The circumstances of this "suicide" were very odd.

There were assurances from no lesser authority than General de Gaulle, who was furious at being embarrassed in this way, that no high level officials were implicated in *l'affaire*. Nevertheless, journalists persisted in questioning the precise role of France's own security service, the SDECE, and speculated on the involvement of two other countries in the conspiracy. The head of the SDECE was hastily retired. Six individuals were charged, and seven others fled beyond the reach of French justice. In the spring of 1967 Antoine Lopez, Air France official and SDECE informant, and police captain Louis Souchon were jailed. Figon's lawyer, the deputy for Yonne, was disbarred for three years. In addition, the Moroccan Minister of the Interior and secret service chief Mohamed Oufkir, right hand man of the King Hassan II, received a life sentence in absentia. But even this was far from being the end of the mystery.

Even seven years after the Ben Barka affair it was audacious to make a film loosely based on the scandal, yet such a film would be guaranteed intense public interest and discussion. As Boisset told an interviewer from *Cinématographe*:

*L'Attentat* was a very difficult film to make. I had a very good understanding with the actors, and it's really thanks to them that it got made. A number of people were implicated, specifically, if not by name; obviously they didn't want the film to be made. The stars, in this particular case, made it financially viable and were a kind of protection from the threats to which we had been exposed.

The French authorities were in a difficult position. However undesirable it seemed that the painful episode should be revived in dramatized form, feeding suspicion of far-reaching skullduggery by agencies of the state, any direct intervention would simply lead people to assume that there was more to hide. Clearly, too, there were legal constraints of all kinds on the film's producers which needed to be carefully negotiated, quite apart from general political pressures. Any pretense that the film was simply a work of fiction was not sustainable; there were just too many correspondences. The director explained his approach in a special feature published by *Le Nouvel observateur*:

> *L'Attentat* isn't a reconstruction of the Ben Barka affair. It's a fictionalized adaptation, a "story" for the general public. Jorge Semprún and I wanted to go beyond the Ben Barka affair to look at the principle of assassination as a form of political action. We didn't want to make a police dossier....

This blend of fact and fiction permitted him in some cases to base a character on a fusion of two real people, but the director claimed that only the police superintendent Rouannet played by Périer was entirely invented. Boisset and Semprún had early on considered making a documentary about the abduction. This, they concluded, was impractical, but by making a "commercial" adaptation they could bring the underlying issues to the notice of the general public. Boisset believed that working "within the system" would involve compromise, but not the sacrifice of his central purpose. One compromise was evidently the late alteration of the screenplay in a way which seemed to shift responsibility from the French authorities to the Americans, a switch recalled with some irritation by Philippe Noiret.

In February 1972 the Paris police must have wondered whether they would be obliged to arrest four famous film stars. The director had been refused permission to film at the scene of the abduction, outside the Brasserie Lipp. In justification, it was said that traffic conditions prohibited such activity, whether day or night. Trintignant, Volonte and Piccoli were undaunted and prepared to risk working without a street filming permit, even if it meant committing a technical offense. Seberg was not in the scene in question but joined them to give moral support. When the crunch came, the authorities backed down, all too aware of the publicity which could follow any heavy-handed tactics. *L'Express* ran an article headed "Conspiracy against *L'Attentat*" in July 1972 in which various examples of obstructive action by official bodies were cited.

For one early scene advantage was taken of a real anti–Vietnam War demonstration. Trintignant and Seberg mingled incognito with the protesters, while scuffles with the police broke out around them, all captured unnoticed on a hand-held camera. Fortunately the two stars could be removed in good time and unscathed from the developing mêlée.

When the heavily publicized film was released in October 1972 it reopened wider debate about "political" films in general, but it was also strongly challenged as an account of the real events it clearly depicted. Some writers felt that it let the French government off the hook by implying that the CIA had been a prime mover in the plot (something contested by Semprún). Others compared the film unfavorably with Costa-Gavras' *Z*, also written by Semprún, but more skillfully. In reality, Boisset had probably attempted the impossible. He and his writers had set out to tell the story essentially as it had happened, with all the shocking circumstances. Yet they had also claimed the freedom of imaginative fiction in order to make a film which would have a message as well as being good entertainment. The Ben Barka story was too complex and still too obscure to allow much chance of success with this twin-track approach. Furthermore, once names were changed and characters modified the film was open to attack on grounds of dishonesty. Simply as cinema it was compromised, being neither one thing nor the other, and it seems to struggle under the weight of excessive detail. Pauline Kael's view that it provides a textbook example of how not to make a political film is over harsh, but its patchiness and many technical lapses are all too apparent.

Although the reviews were mixed to say the least, its subject matter and familiar cast made *L'Attentat* one of France's top grossing films of the year. Generally praised were Volonte's portrayal of Ben Barka, rising above the sometimes trite or sentimental script, and Trintignant as the flawed reluctant hero Darien. There was no doubting the abundant talent in the subsidiary roles. Seberg received third billing for the only significant female role, but the character of Édith is unsatisfactorily handled, and her function is largely passive. In purely commercial terms, though, this might be regarded as the last relative success of her career.

Considering its star line-up, public interest in the scandal and a strong publicity campaign, *L'Attentat* made disappointingly little impact. This brave attempt by a young director to turn the lessons of the scandal into mainstream cinema was probably doomed to fail from the outset, yet it is fascinating even in its many shortcomings. It falters, as in the inept chase scene, but often captures an atmosphere of real menace, underlined by the nerve-jangling score of Ennio Morricone. It is worth recalling that it was also Morricone who had supplied the music for Pontecorvo's powerful 1966 political drama *The Battle of Algiers*.

Many books and articles have appeared since Boisset's film was made, bringing many more details about the Ben Barka affair to light. In 2000 some key documents were declassified and a television documentary was made, and in the following year revelations by a former agent of the Moroccan counter-subversion agency Ahmed Boukhari were published, while Ben Barka's son pressed for a renewed investigation. The 2005 film of Serge Le Péron, *J'ai vu tuer Ben Barka*, is testimony to the continuing fascination of this notorious episode in French history. Le Péron, in contrast to Boisset, uses real names and explains the roles of writer Marguerite Duras and film director Georges Franju in the story. In all innocence, they had been used by Figon to lend prestige and credibility to the documentary project which was central to the trap. Le Péron uses the narrative device borrowed from *Sunset Boulevard* in focusing on the events leading up to Figon's own death, in itself material for any thriller.

## References

Baecque, Antoine de, and José Garçon. "Un polar comme au cinema: le rapt de l'anticolonialiste marocain Ben Barka ... fait l'objet d'un film de Serge Le Péron." *Libération*, 30 October 2005, pp. 4–6.

Boisset, Yves. "Politics for the people" [interview]. *Time Out*, 173, 15 June 1973, pp. 19–20.

_____. "Spectacle et politique" [interview]. *Cinématographe*, 13 May/June 1975, pp. 32–4.

Braucourt, Guy. "La censure (II)." *Écran*, 4 April 1972, pp. 22–3.

Deglin, Paul. *Ciné Revue*, 52:41, 12 October 1972, pp. 8–9.

Derogy, Jacques. "Le deuxième mort de Mehdi Ben Barka." *L'Express*, 1111, 23 October 1972, p. 103.

Ferniot, Jean, et al. "L'affaire." *L'Express,*" 762, pp. 10–27.

Figon, Georges. "J'ai vu tuer Ben Barka: le récit d'un témoin." *L'Express*, 760, 10–16 January 1966, pp. 30–36.

K. J.-F. "Conspiration contre L'Attentat." *L'Express*, 1074, 7 February 1972, p. 36.

Kachmar, Diane C. *Roy Scheider: a film biography*. Jefferson, NC: McFarland, 2002, pp. 40–1, 195.

Kael, Pauline. *Reeling*. Boston: Little, Brown, 1972, pp. 208–9, 214–5.

Maillet, Dominique. *Philippe Noiret*. Paris: Éditions Henri Veyrier, 1989, pp. 144–6.

Mairal, Jean-Claude. "*L'Attentat* et la presse." *Image et son,* 270, March 1973, pp. 38–44.

*Le Monde,* 15 August 1978. "Il y a treize ans: l'affaire Ben Barka," p. 11.

*New York Times,* 17 February 1972, p. 44.

Powrie, Phil. "French neo-noir to hyper-noir," pp. 55–60, *European Film Noir,* ed. Andrew Spicer. Manchester: Manchester University Press, 2007.

Quinson, René. "*L'Attentat*: une analyse de la violence en tant que moyen d'action politique" [interview with Boisset]. *Combat,* 22 April 1972, p. 13.

Semprún, Jorge. "*L'Attentat* et Ben Barka" [with reply by Jacques Derogy]. *L'Express,* 1113, 6–12 November 1972, pp. 116–7.

Smith, Alison. *French cinema in the 1970s: the echoes of May.* Manchester: Manchester University Press, 2005, pp. 35–73.

Smith, Stephen. "Comment Ben Barka a disparu deux fois." *Le Monde,* 1–2 July 2001, pp. 1, 10–11, 14.

Teisseire, Guy. "R.A.S après *L'Attentat*: l'opportunisme politique d'Yves Boisset" [interview with Boisset] *L'Aurore,* 10 October 1972, p. 15.

Todd, Olivier, et al. "Les services secrets et le pouvoir [interview with Boisset]." *Le Nouvel observateur,* 413, 9 October 1972, pp. 44–6, 51–3.

Vecchiali, Paul, et al. "À propos de *L'Attentat*." *Image et son/La Revue du cinéma,* 266, December 1972, pp. 29–38.

Violet, Bernard. *L'Affaire Ben Barka.* Paris: Fayard, 1991.

## Reviews

*ABC,* 16 May 1973. Hermes, pp. 80–1.

*Amis du film et de la télévision,* 199, December 1972. P.L., p. 25.

*Analyse des films saison 1973,* p. 83.

*L'Aurore,* 17 February 1972. Philippe Bernert, p. 17; 12 October 1972. Claude Garson, p. 10.

*Blanco y negro,* 83:3186, 26 May 1973. Donald, p. 74.

*Le Canard enchaîné,* 57:2711, 11 October 1972. Michel Duran, p. 7.

*Chicago Tribune,* 14 January 1974. Les Bridges, s.2 p. 13.

*Cineinforme,* 11:164, December 1972, p. 25.

*Cinéma,* 170, November 1972. Tristan Renaud, pp. 125–6.

*Cinema T.V. Today,* 30 June 1973, p. 28.

*Combat,* 11 October 1972. Henry Chapier, p. 13.

*Commonweal,* 99:13, 28 December 1973. Colin L. Westerbeck, Jr., pp. 343–4.

*The Daily Telegraph,* 8 June 1973. Patrick Gibbs, p. 15.

*Écran,* 9 November 1972. Marcel Martin, pp. 65–6.

*The Evening News,* 7 June 1973. Felix Barker, p. 2.

*The Evening Standard,* 7 June 1973. Alexander Walker, p. 29.

*L'Express,* 1109, 9 October 1972. Claude Mauriac, p. 106.

*Le Figaro,* 13 October 1972. Louis Chauvet, p. 28.

*Le Film français,* 13 October 1972. A.B., p. 14.

*Films and Filming,* 19:11, August 1973. Margaret Tarratt, pp. 49–50.

*The Financial Times,* 8 June 1973. Nigel Andrews, p. 3.

*France-soir,* 12 October 1972. Robert Chazal, p. 15.

*The Guardian,* 7 June 1973. Derek Malcolm, p. 12.

*L'Humanité,* 18 October 1972. François Maurin, p. 8.

*Intermezzo,* 1:2–3, November 1972, p. 11.

*Jeune cinéma,* 67 Dec.1973/Jan.1973. Ginette Gervais, pp. 37–8.

*The Los Angeles Times,* 25 December 1973. Kevin Thomas, iv, p. 30.

*Le Monde,* 10 October 1972. Philippe Herreman, p. 26.

*Monthly Film Bulletin,* 40:474, July 1973. Tom Milne, p. 143.

*The New York Times,* 15 November 1973. Vincent Canby, p. 58.

*The New Yorker,* 49:39, 19 November 1973. Pauline Kael, p. 236.

*Le Nouvel observateur,* 414, 16–22 October 1972. Claude Michel Cluny, p. 21.

*Positif,* 146, January 1973. Gérard Legrand, pp. 83–4.

*Pueblo,* 28 May 1973. José Luis Jover.

*Rivista del cinematografo,* 11 November 1972. Maria Fotia, pp. 552–3.

*The Times*, 8 June 1973. David Robinson, p. 11.
*Variety*, 18 October 1972. Gene Moskowitz, p. 24.
*Village Voice*, 18:47, 22 November 1973. Molly Haskell, p. 81.
*The Wall Street Journal*, 30 November 1973. Joy Gould Boyum, p. 8.

# *Camorra* (1972)

A Mondial TE.FI (Rome) / Europa Films (Paris) co-production; A film by Pasquale Squitieri
Also known as: *Gang War in Naples*; *Les Tueurs à gages* [France]; *Omertà—Reden heisst sterben* [Germany]
Original release: in Italian
Running Time: 111 minutes
Format: in Eastmancolor

CAST: [* denotes above the title billing] Raymond Pellegrin* (Mario Capece); Fabio Testi* (Tonino Russo); Jean Seberg* (Louise); Charles Vanel* (De Ritis); Germana Carnacina (Anna); Lilla Brignone (Giulia Russo, Tonino's mother); Enzo Cannavale (Luciano, nicknamed "The Lame One"); Ugo D'Alessio (Pietro Russo, Tonino's father); Paul Müller (Politician), Enzo Turco (Silverio); Salvatore Puntillo; with Anna Zinnemann, Marcello Filotico, Benito Artesi, Alberto Farnese, Francesco d'Adda Salvaterra, Renato Chiantoni, Giovanni Guerrieri, Mirella Mereu, Leopoldo Mastelloni, Enzo Vingelli, Nino Vingelli, Sergio Serafini, Orazio Stracuzzi, Guido Lollobrigida, Vincenzo Fallanga, Gennaro Beneduce

PRODUCTION CREDITS: *Director:* Pasquale Squitieri; *Producer:* Sergio Bonotti; *Screenplay:* Pasquale Squitieri; *Music:* Manuel De Sica; *Editor:* Daniele Alabiso; *Photography:* Giulio Albonico; *Production Manager:* Giancarlo Marchetti; *Set Designer:* Fabrizio Frisardi; *Production Designer:* Nicola Losito; *Costumes:* Rosalba Menichelli; *Assistant Director:* Gerardo d'Andrea; *Assistant Editors:* Rita Triunveri and Adelchi Marinangeli; *Continuity:* Adolfo Dragone; *Cameraman:* Sebastiano Celeste; *Makeup:* Raoul Ranieri; *Hairstylist:* Marisa La Ganga; *Sound:* Angelo Amatulli; *Sound Effects:* Renato Marinelli; *Production Inspection:* Vittorio Biferale, Francesco Manco; *Assistant Cameraman:* Maurizio La Monica; The songs *Reginella* by Lama Bovio and *Chiove* by Nardella Bovio are sung by Roberto Murolo

## Synopsis

A fight with a local gang leader lands young Neapolitan Tonino in prison. His future looks bleak on his return to his family and girlfriend Anna in their impoverished neighborhood, yet his pugnacious spirit is noticed by powerful Camorra boss Capece. Tonino is determined to help his parents and marry Anna, and soon he and old friend Luciano are employed in Capece's meat business. This proves only a trial job, and before long they are given increasingly violent tasks. Despite a harsh lesson in obedience Tonino wins the organization's approval. He becomes alienated from his parents and Anna, who want no part of his new wealth, and begins an affair with Capece's mistress Louise.

A successful assassination crowns Tonino's rise from the ranks with greater control of illegal gambling. Capece, however, learns of Louise's betrayal and sends his former protégé into a trap. Tonino survives and returns to find Louise murdered. Capece takes Tonino's brother as hostage and flees the anticipated revenge. Tonino avenges Louise and his friend Luciano as the police appear. Finally he heeds the appeal from his father and surrenders without further bloodshed.

## Reviews

"... extremely violent and distressingly realistic scenes seem like clichés, inadequate to depict the material and moral degradation of a criminal background."—*Analyse des films*

"The film abounds in dramatic incidents which give it an elementary vigor and strong visual hold."—*Corriere della sera*

"[Squitieri] fails everywhere and on all levels, but his most serious mistake is to let his actors down. Jean Seberg is the principal victim. Fabio Testi will still have to wait for the role he deserves."—*Saison cinématographique*

"The unfortunate actors, though experienced, are powerless to make credible a text fit for backward schoolkids, or pass off this regrettable enterprise as a tough documentary."—*Cinéma*

"... Testi is the main interest in this conventional crime thriller ... with more violence than surprises, where morality triumphs—which, currently, could be considered an original point."—*France-soir*

"Pasquale Squitieri, screenwriter and director of this film, depicts the world of the Camorra for us with great attention to detail, permitting the spectators to experience two hours of suspense and genuine interest."—*Cineinforme*

"Thus Jean Seberg finds the worst role of her career and the film in which she is worst filmed."—*Image et son*

## Notes

The film director Pasquale Squitieri studied law before becoming briefly involved in theatre, working as a journalist and eventually deciding to make a career in cinema. He worked as assistant to fellow Neapolitan Francesco Rosi, the noted director of such films as *Salvatore Giuliano* and *Le Mani sulla città*. Squitieri's first film *Io e Dio* received the critics' prize at Venice in 1970, and in the same year a collection of his short stories received a literary award. *Camorra* was Squitieri's fourth project as director/writer, and its subject matter was a natural enough choice for someone of his background, interested in the social ramifications of the organized crime endemic to his native city. As his own statements have made clear, his allegiance to his region and its people is a major influence in his filmmaking: "My films are very much bound up with Neapolitan tradition, society and history, and also very strongly linked to the specific cinematic tradition of cinema dealing with Naples and the South from the 1950s." *Camorra* in particular was "a film in the crime genre, but tied to a precise social background." This looks like a promising basis for an effective thriller which might combine a committed social message with the kind of documentary-style realism employed by Rosi and others. The popular young actor Fabio Testi, who had a role in De Sica's 1970 *Giardino dei Finzi Contini* among his credits, would take the leading role.

*Camorra* follows the familiar archetype of gangster stories, the gradual rise and sudden fall of a boy from a poor background through increasingly violent involvement in a criminal organization. This process transforms his character and progressively alienates him from his family and loved ones. Love interest tends to polarize between the innocent and the corrupted. Eventually he discovers that in acquiring power and wealth he has sacrificed the things he cared most about. Parables of vaulting ambition may be as ancient as any kind of story telling, but they only retain their hold on us to the extent that they involve interesting individuals rooted in a distinctive and believable setting. Squitieri's attempt to set his personal stamp on this formula puts its faith in a harsh realism founded on thorough knowledge of the setting and its criminal underworld. Presumably the actual killing of a pig in a slaughterhouse is the kind of detail intended to contribute to this grim atmosphere, and similarly the generally rough-hewn finish of his film is doubtless a stylistic choice to give greater conviction and impact. If so, the director's strategy fails, for he is rarely able to reach beyond the instantly recognizable stereotypes and stock situations. Elements of everyday realism are not fully blended into the criminal drama, and even the street scenes of Naples have an alien feel, like afterthoughts to add local color. Attempts to introduce a note of humor, as for example the casino scenes, provide some relief from the dominant mood, but these too seem artificial and misplaced.

At the start of the film, by defending an unknown fellow prisoner and thereby jeopardizing his own release, the hero at once displays physical courage and an unselfish sense of justice. Shortly after this he moralizes to Anna in florid terms: "Men are like ships. Some won't go out to make a living unless the sea is calm, the weather good, the boards sound and the nets mended. But then there are others who go out when it suits them ... They damage and destroy and are allowed to get away with it." Testi tries earnestly to give some depth to his character, but it is hard to reconcile the sympathetic traits we are shown with the brutality he is so soon to display. The sociological message is clear, yet apparently Squitieri has few psychological insights to offer beyond the clichés of his chosen genre. The screenplay is far too much plot- and action-driven, failing to recognize the need to make us believe in and care about these individuals. This is one reason why the compelling score by prolific film composer Manuel De Sica (son of Vittorio De Sica, producer of Squitieri's first film) builds tension to little ultimate effect. Gloomy lighting of interiors, suggesting the twilight world of the inhabitants, tends to add to the confusion, while abrupt transitions make for a fast-moving story but work against overall narrative flow. The director had the services of the experienced cameraman Giulio Albonico, who had worked with Seberg on *Ondata di calore*, but here the results are far less satisfactory. The camera meanders as pointlessly as a home video at times, and action sequences are confused and poorly composed. More controlled camerawork and better editing might have helped, but could not have compensated for the other inherent weaknesses.

The actors make what they can of this series of predictable incidents and situations. Jean Seberg has little to do other than embody the expensive gangster's moll haunting the gaming tables. Louise's character is never developed, and it is with some justification that Paul Vecchiali in *Image et son* pronounced this the worst role of her career. She smiles sardonically and is given a few lines of trite dialogue, but nothing prepares us for the crude melodrama of her subsequent fate. She tells Tonino that their relationship works because they do not love each other—"we couldn't possibly. But that only makes it easier. We dropped everybody we ever cared about long ago, so all we can do now is play out our little game." When Capece discovers she has betrayed him with Tonino she expresses her contempt for him as a lover and spits in his face, with consequences wisely left to the imagination. Heavy-handed moralizing and careless writing leave all of the cast with an uphill struggle. Seasoned actors Raymond Pellegrin and Charles Vanel, whose distinguished cinema career dated from 1912, are not to be faulted as the ruthless gang bosses, but these are instantly recognizable types. While De Ritis shows a genuinely paternal side, Capece is the suave, showy upstart devoid of redeeming features. Even more of a commonplace is the sexually predatory moneylender Don Ciccillo. Central to these roughly sketched characters, the physically imposing Testi carries off his dynamic man of action role as well as circumstances allow. As we would expect, due deference is paid to the familial virtues.

Tonino is respectful to his parents, sympathetically played by Brignone and D'Alessio, but our acquaintance with them is fleeting. Germana Carnacina as Anna provides a sensitive vignette, but not even this relationship is sufficiently explored to offset the harsh tone and general gloom. Tonino's disabled friend Luciano is assigned the role of clown, all too obvious a foil to the romanticized hero. It scarcely matters that his dying words are incoherent, for his fidelity and gratitude to his more charismatic friend were implicit in his subservient status from the outset.

The final sequences of the film particularly bear the marks of haste. Like Cagney's Rocky in *Angels with Dirty Faces*, Tonino is finally urged to act like a coward in the face of the law so that the young should not be tempted to emulate him. The difference is that where Curtiz's film cleverly leaves us suspended in uncertainty with its ambiguous ending, Squitieri's *Camorra* simply runs out of steam. It only deepens the effect of bathos when a rising aerial shot shrinks the whole overcooked human drama to insignificance against the barren slopes of the sleeping volcano.

If we hope to learn something of the distinctive culture of Naples and its poor, Squitieri largely disappoints, and he tells us almost nothing about the real Camorra specifically that we did not already know or might have invented for ourselves. Fewer violent incidents would have left more space for human interest without diminishing the force of his message, and would surely have resulted in a more involving story. As it is, the constant focus on brutality leaves us with the impression that this is a society so corrupt and oppressed as to be almost beyond hope.

According to Squitieri's recollections, Jean Seberg had agreed to take part in the film

because she had been in love with Testi, but the latter had subsequently dropped her. Squitieri viewed her as too emotionally susceptible and inclined to put total trust in others, a trust which was constantly betrayed. Following the scheduled location work in Naples in March, the interior sequences were to be completed in the studio at Rome. In May the Spanish pictorial *Semana* featured Seberg and Testi on a balcony in a break from the shoot in the capital. The "story" was that a love scene for the two of them had had to be postponed at her request. She had been unable to concentrate on this, it was claimed, because she was thinking about her husband Dennis. It may have been partly embarrassment. When Testi had proposed this role for her the previous year it must have seemed that she was also romantically available. Her recent marriage to Berry had changed the situation as far as the handsome Italian was concerned, and shortly afterwards Seberg and Berry were pictured arm-in-arm enjoying

Her only cameo film role was in *Camorra* (with Raymond Pellegrin) as a gangster's girlfriend (Mondial TE.FI/Europa Films).

a delayed honeymoon in the eternal city. In an interview published by *Fotogramas* in 1973 Seberg firmly denied the suggestion that she had clashed with Squitieri about one of the scenes in *Camorra* she had thought excessive. She did, however, admit that she had not cared for the character of Louise: "I prefer more human personalities," she explained, citing the example of her role in *L'Attentat*.

The film was released in Italy in August 1972, and received its Paris premiere the following month. It seems to have made little impression, and it certainly failed to revitalize Seberg's gradually ebbing career. Some eighteen months later Squitieri would explore the Camorra theme again in the film *I Guappi* (*Blood Brothers*). This period drama, again featuring Testi and Pellegrin, but this time supported by Franco Nero and Claudia Cardinale, is considerably more accomplished and more effectively conveys the same social message, voicing a concern for the plight of poor people caught between the opposing forces of law and order and violent organized crime.

## References

Albano, Vittorio. *La Mafia nel cinema siciliano. Collana di cultura cinematografica 11*. Manduria: Barbieri, 2003, pp. 133–6.

*Bianco e nero*, 35:3/4, 1974, p. 35.

Brunetta, Gian Piero. *Storia del cinema italiano vol. 4, 1960–93*, 3d ed. Rome: Editori Riuniti, 2001, pp. 457–8.

*Cinematografia*, 40:1, January/February 1973, pp. 83–4.

*Corriere della sera*, 28 March 1972, p. 13.

*Intermezzo*, 1:1, September 1972, p. 11.

*Nuevo fotogramas*, 28:1288, 22 June 1973, p. 14.

Poppi, Roberto, and Mario Pecorari. *Dizionario del cinema italiano. Vol. 4: I film 1970–79*. Gremese, 1996, i, p. 140.

*La Production italienne 1971–72*. Unitalia Film, 1972, pp. 24–5.

Squitieri, Pasquale. "Entretien avec Pasquale Squitieri." *Jeune cinéma*, 92 Jan./Feb. 1976, pp. 19–21.

———. "Il cinema italiano d'oggi, 1970–84," in *Raccontato dai suoi protagonist*, Franca Faldini, and Goffredo Fofi, eds. Milan: Mondadori, 1984, pp. 443–5.

## Reviews

*Amis du film et de la télévision*, 201, February 1973. J.B., p. 30.

*Analyse des films*, Saison 1973, p. 459.

*Cinéma*, 169, September/October 1972. J.G., p. 143.

*Cineinforme*, 11:162, November 1972, p. 27.

*Corriere della sera*, 26 August 1972. L.A., p. 12.

*Le Figaro*, 2–3 September 1972. Pierre Mazars, p. 24.

*France-soir*, 5 September 1972. Robert Chazal, p. 11.

*Image et son*, 265, November 1972. P. Vecchiali, p. 139.

*Il Lavoro*, 29 August 1972. R. Chiti.

*Le Nouvel observateur*, 408, 4 September 1972. Claude Michel Cluny, p. 14.

*Rivista del cinematografo*, 10 October 1972. Antonio Mazza, pp. 504–5.

*La Stampa*, 15 September 1972. S.R., p. 7.

# *The Corruption of Chris Miller (La Corrupción de Chris Miller)* (1973)

A Xavier Armet Production; A Comflik Associates presentation; A Target International release; Laboratory Fotofilm S.A.E. Barcelona; Distribution: Warner Bros.

Original release: in English
Also known as: *Behind the Shutters*; *Sisters of Corruption* [UK]; *Maske des Grauens* [Germany]; *L'Altra casa ai margini del bosco* [Italy]
Running Time: 105/115 minutes
Format: in Eastmancolor; in Panavision

CAST: [* denotes above the title billing] Jean Seberg* (Ruth Miller); Marisol* (Chris Miller); Barry Stokes* (Barney Webster); Perla Cristal (Perla); Rudy Gaebel (Luis); Gerard Tichy (Commissioner); Alicia Altabella (Adela); Vidal Molina (Ernesto); Maria Bardem (Maria); Juan Bardem (Pedro); Miguel Bardem (Tin); Goyo Lebrero (peasant); Gustavo Re (shopkeeper); Carl Rapp (TV reporter); Antonio Parra (postman)

PRODUCTION CREDITS: *Director:* Juan Antonio Bardem; *Producer:* Xavier Armet; *Screenplay:* Santiago Moncada; *Photography:* Juan Gelpí; *Editor:* Emilio Rodríguez; *Music:* Waldo de los Ríos; *Art Director:* Ramiro Gómez; *Sound:* Jorge Sangenís; *Sound Operator:* Taffy Haynes; *Sound Assistant:* Angel Rodríguez; *Production Manager:* Ángel Monis; *Assistant Director:* Jaime Bayarri; *Special Effects:* Antonio Bueno, Antonio Parra; *Assistant Art Director:* Rafael Perez Murcia; *Assistant Editor:* Celestino Marba, Miguel Grau; *Wardrobe Designer:* Tony Pueo; *Makeup:* Julián Ruiz, Antonio Florido; *Hairdresser:* Vincenta Palmero; *Production Unit Manager:* J. Maldonado; *Production Assistants:* Jaime Fuentes, Juan Gracia; *Continuity:* Mary Luz Manzano; *Camera Operator:* Ricardo G. De Navarrete; *Camera Assistant:* Julio M. Levva; *Still Photography:* Simon Lopez; *Property Master:* Ramon Miró; *Dialogue Coach:* Lewis Gordon; *Songs:* Gregorio García Segura

## Synopsis

Ruth Miller, having been deserted by her husband, lives with only her teenage stepdaughter Chris in their secluded country villa. Chris still suffers the effects of a traumatic rape at school, and relations are tense. A charming drifter named Barney cajoles the women to let him stay temporarily as handyman. Sensing the strained atmosphere, he plays each off against the other. During a storm anger erupts, and Ruth orders Barney to leave.

A detective investigating a series of brutal murders observes the young stranger, and soon Ruth and Chris too become suspicious. When Barney breaks in overnight, ransacking the house, his guilt looks certain. He makes love to Chris, but in a sudden panic she stabs him. Ruth comes to her aid, and Barney collapses under their frenzied assault.

The next day the arrest of the real murderer is proclaimed. Barney's possessions show that he had been sent by Chris's father to retrieve valuables. Horrified, the two women bury the body and reunite in a pact to conceal their own crime.

## Reviews

"... the film becomes a movie conforming to current demand for the world's screens. The good offices of Bardem, who was always (despite some ups and downs) one of our best directors, are enough to rescue the absurd storyline of the work.... Good photography and some perfect sets by Ramiro Gómez complete the picture." — *Cineinforme*

"... the plot is overladen with red herrings, loose ends and obscure motivations.... A pity; the performances are too good to be wasted in clouds of obscurity." — *Cinema TV Today*

"In this new example of his art, Bardem confirms his standing as a reliable director with solid technique and clear and well-developed instincts for filmmaking ... Seberg and Marisol, the principal female characters, are both very good." — *La Vanguardia española*

"Muddled little psychological thriller.... Bardem piles on the agony with a heavy hand, turning up climaxes in a fair flurry but saving his most risible touch for the very end ... The direction is generally as plain and unadorned as the melodramatic excesses and the inane psychological explanations...." — *Monthly Film Bulletin*

"The film is typical of those of the later period of Seberg's life abroad. Seberg ... gives an extremely sincere performance that is never particularly convincing. Once again, though, she gives dimension to a film of no great interest just because her presence is so unexpected. What ... is this quintessentially American beauty doing in the middle of so much quintessential European decadence?"—*New York Times*

"Beneath the knifings and seductions, the images of Seberg are nonetheless of a beautiful, sensitive actress flinching at human contact and assessing the world through a pained squint."—*Village Voice*

## Notes

Salvatore Moncada wrote his lurid screenplay, originally entitled *Doble Y*, for the producer Javier Armet. The project, at first under the title *La Verdad tenia un cierto color verde* but later renamed after its younger female protagonist, was placed in the experienced hands of director Juan Antonio Bardem. It was intended as a vehicle for establishing Spain's popular young singer-celebrity Marisol (Pepa Flores) as an adult screen actress. Bardem was a director of considerable standing in Spain, having built a reputation with such films as *Cómicos* (*Comedians*, 1954) and the first Georges de Beauregard productions, *Muerte de un ciclista* (*Death of a Cyclist*, 1955) and *Calle mayor* (*Main Street*, 1956). In this case his material left him little room for maneuver, but he made what he could of the confused motivation of the characters, adding some scenes of his own. Barry Stokes, who played the male lead, had made his career primarily in British television drama and low-budget films, but the name of Marisol alone would be sufficient draw for the domestic market. The casting of Seberg could be expected to add further quality and facilitate international distribution. The shoot took place during the summer of 1972, with exterior filming in the vicinity of Comillas, in the scenic Santander area of Northern Spain. Studio work was completed at the Isasi Studios in Barcelona in September, where Seberg and Marisol gave an interview for the popular magazine *Lecturas*. Seberg evidently appreciated a role which was so unlike the sweetly feminine ones she had generally been offered hitherto. The production was filmed with English dialogue, and two alternative versions were produced, only one of which contained the more risqué scenes and was intended specifically for the overseas market. For British distribution the title was altered to *Sisters of Corruption*, crisper and perhaps even less subtle, but better reflecting the parity of the pivotal female duo.

This overtly commercial, if not to say sensational film locates itself squarely within the horror genre, and its erotic overtones are of course consistent with this. This was not the first of Seberg's films to touch on the theme of lesbianism or bisexuality, for Rossen's *Lilith* and Gary's *Birds in Peru* had already done this. Here it could have been a more important strand in the narrative, yet it is not seriously developed as an aspect of the women's ambiguous relationship, and seems employed to add little more than a frisson to the storyline. One Spanish critic was later to comment that the film demonstrated the imbalance of censorship, in that a few inches of flesh were seen as more alarming than torrents of blood. *Village Voice's* Tom Allen found both sex and violence exaggerated here, and that "the sex, because more repressed, is constantly steamy, predatory and anxiety-ridden."

Like many horror features, *The Corruption of Chris Miller* draws heavily on the bank of credibility. Whether its credit is judged good depends, as usual, on the extent to which it succeeds in entertaining the audience through its skill in handling the essential elements of plot, characterization and visual effects, and in avoiding stale formula. The components, found in such classic thrillers as *The Spiral Staircase*, seem predictable enough: a large isolated house, vulnerable female characters, an unidentified killer on the loose, thunderstorms, darkness and an atmosphere of menace. Bardem exploits such devices and motifs with some imagination, and the opening sequence is particularly effective, culminating in a scene of shocking violence which serves as a warning of what we must later expect.

This first scene, which establishes the mood of danger and perhaps insanity, is followed by one which introduces the two women central to the story. The unseen father of Chris and husband to Ruth, who has abruptly abandoned them both, is the key to their relationship. The hostility and suspicion of Chris is linked to the traumatic assault she has suffered at school, jarringly indicated by flashbacks of a sweaty weightlifter in a gym. We soon see that Ruth's composed air of sympathy and concern masks a program of manipulation, although whether her intentions are purely sadistic is not immediately clear. The arrival of Barney provides the final element for the drama which is to be acted out, and the railway is cleverly used to link the two scenes and to imply that the stranger has brought the danger with him. Ruth's initial reaction to the good-looking young man as an unwelcome intrusion gives way to fleeting desire and a sense that she can make use of him, but we are kept guessing as to her true motivation.

The visit by Chris to the house of their horse-loving neighbor Luis seems to relax the tension, and the pleasant rural settings are well exploited by Juan Gelpí's photography. Here, as elsewhere, Waldo de los Ríos' film score echoes the mood and successfully manages the transition from a nervy and ominous tone to the expansively romantic.

Despite the phony psychology of the scenario, the dynamics of the ensuing triangular power game are interestingly handled in some scenes, and it is probably here where Seberg

**With Marisol in** *The Corruption of Chris Miller* (*La Corrupción de Chris Miller*) (**Warner Bros.**).

makes her best contribution. Stokes and Seberg play well against each other as each probes for the other's weak points and seeks the upper hand. She issues an implicit challenge: "Men are all the same, but now I know how to handle them." The scenes between Ruth and Chris can also rise above the level of the mechanistic plot. There is a suppressed sensuality in Ruth's brushing of the girl's hair which suggests more than the simple desire to "corrupt" as a means of revenge. Ruth does not reply when Chris suggests she must hate her father, but observes that "you have the same eyes, the same mouth." Of their relationship Chris tells the newcomer "We spy on each other. We don't know whether we love or hate each other." Barney believes his wish (perhaps to take Chris away from the malign influence of her stepmother) will be fulfilled if he can complete his house of cards. It collapses. "Don't be upset," Ruth tells him, adding ominously "Nobody gets what they really want." The dialogue abounds with such gnomic utterances, as when Chris responds to Barney's feigned concern that he has scared her: "We should always be scared. We never know when something will happen: and when it does everything changes so suddenly."

Realizing Barney has become a threat to her power over Chris, Ruth engineers a scene to provide the pretext for his expulsion from the house. This is among the least convincing scenes, but prepares the ground for Barney's subsequent break-in, after they have been convinced that he must be the serial killer sought by the police. With the three now enclosed in a sealed house the scene is set for a cathartic climax, which sees the two knife-wielding women pursuing Barney from room to room like avenging furies. Their work done, they are roused to reality by the news that the killer has been arrested, a twist which many cinemagoers will have anticipated but which hadn't entered the minds of our heroines. Whereas the bloodletting seems to have a curiously sedative effect on Chris's neurosis, it is the friendly Luis who has proved to be the one authentically loco, and as he is driven away glassy-eyed in the police car he seems baffled by the hostility of the villagers: "Why are they acting like that? I needed the money to look after my horses." The realization that they have killed an innocent man puts matters in a different light, and, implausibly enough, it is Ruth who now seems helpless and only Chris who knows what to do.

After the gratuitous violence, the exposure of the killing is treated almost like comic relief. The asphalt road surface starts to split open before our very eyes, in a quick succession of time-lapse shots. Workmen are sent to investigate the startling crop of peas on the highway, and soon a policeman is on his way to ask uncomfortable questions. This final nod to the principle of justice is, of course, itself a cliché. Only too aware of this, Bardem is perfunctory in his winding-up (one might constrast, for example, Clouzot in *Les Diaboliques*), but he does leave us with the effectively lingering image of the two conspirators, now united by their guilty secret and unsuspecting that they are about to be exposed.

*The Corruption of Chris Miller* was harshly treated by most critics after its commercially successful Madrid release in mid–May 1973. Two years passed before an English language version was available in Britain, and it was not offered to the American public until after Jean Seberg's death in 1979. While some reviewers picked out certain redeeming points, others saw the film as the nadir of the director's career, tantamount to professional suicide. Certainly, there seems all too little evidence of the insights and sensitivity which made *Death of a Cyclist* such an absorbing exercise in film noir, or made *Main Street* such a withering indictment of provincial male chauvinism. If here too, as some writers have sensed, there are subversive political messages, they are rather more carefully coded. The negative reaction in Spain and abroad was predictable for a product so blatantly exploitative and geared to current popular tastes. Many found, and some will still think the final gory extravaganza tastelessly excessive, although, it could be objected, that might have raised few eyebrows on the Elizabethan or Jacobean stage. By the standards of later "slasher" movies or even current mainstream cinema this violence looks fairly routine. The sensational elements tend to obscure the film's merits, modest as they may be, not least among which was Seberg's performance, a valiant attempt to make sense of an imperfectly defined character. Some may actually relish the ludicrously overcooked plot. For those who do not, a practiced filmmaker's eye has adorned this gothic tale with many details (the sinister Chaplin mask, a child's toy, a puppet theatre, the exuberant spirit of the horses) which offer their own compensations.

## References

Batlle Caminal, J. "Caballos de refresco." *El País*, 16 August 1986, p. 34.

Besas, Peter. *Behind the Spanish Lens: Spanish Cinema under Fascism and Democracy*. Denver: Arden Press, 1985.

Cerón Gómez, Juan Francisco. *El cine de Juan Antonio Bardem*. University of Murcia, 1998, pp. 224–7, 333.

*Cinestudio*, 120, May 1973, p. 54.

*Equipo Reseña: Cine para leer 1973*, Ángel Camiña, pp. 78–80.

García-Fernández, Emilio C. *Historia ilustrada del cinema español*. Madrid: Planeta, 1985, pp. 212–15.

Hardy, Phil. *The Aurum film encyclopedia: Horror*. London: Aurum Press, 1985, p. 248.

Jordan, Barry, and Rikki Morgan-Tamosunas. *Contemporary Spanish Cinema*. Manchester: Manchester University Press,1998, pp. 86–8.

Lázaro-Reboll, Antonio, and Andrew Willis (ed.) *Spanish Popular Cinema*. Manchester: Manchester University Press, 2004, pp. 12–13, 132.

Martínez Carril, M. "Después de 27 años, Bardem se revitaliza." *Cinemateca revista*, 18, July 1980, pp. 23–8.

Montaigne, Pierre. "Jean Seberg: mieux vaut un vieux décor qu'une aventure douteuse." *Le Figaro*, 30 October 1972, p. 24.

*Motion Picture Guide, 1927–83*, p. 489.

Sanchez, Lolita. "Jean Seberg y Marisol ... en 'La Verdad tenia un cierto color verde.'" *Lecturas*, 29 September 1972, 11:1067, pp. 31–7.

## Reviews

*ABC*, 20 May 1973. Hermes, pp. 81–2.

*Blanco y negro*, 83:3187, 2 June 1973. Donald, p. 67.

*Box Office*, 4853, 22 March 1976.

*Cineinforme*, 11:177, June 1973. A.F., pp. 12–3.

*Cinema TV Today*, 8 February 1975. Marjorie Bilbow, p. 13.

*Monthly Film Bulletin*, 42:494, March 1975. Richard Combs, p. 53.

*Mundo*, 2 June 1973. José María Caparrós Lera.

*The New York Times*, 30 November 1979. Vincent Canby, p. 10.

*Pueblo*, 29 May 1973. Tomás García de la Puerta, p. 44.

*Triunfo*, 557, 2 May 1973. Fernando Lara, pp. 56–7.

*La Vanguardia española*, 89:33268, 24 May 1973. A. Martinez Tomas, p. 34.

*Variety*, 8 August 1973. Besa., p. 14.

*Village Voice*, 3 December 1979. Tom Allen, p. 55.

# *Mousey (Cat and Mouse)* (1974)

"When I was offered [*Mousey*] I thought I should do it because it meant more exposure in the States."—Jean Seberg

An Associated London Films Ltd. production; A Universal Television release; A Robert Stigwood Group presentation

Original release: in English

Also known as: *Cat and Mouse* [UK]; *Pris au piège* [France]; *Il Gatto e il topo* [Italy]; *Andersons Rache* [Germany]; *La Tercera víctima / Un Respetable asesino* [Spain]

Running Time: 89 minutes

Format: in Technicolor

CAST: [* denotes above the title billing] Kirk Douglas* (George Anderson); Jean Seberg* (Laura Anderson); John Vernon (David Richardson); Sam Wanamaker (inspector); James Bradford (private detective); Bessie Love (Mrs.Richardson); Beth Porter (Sandra); Suzanne Lloyd (Nancy); Bob Sherman (barman); James Berwick (headmaster); Valerie Colgan (Miss Wainwright); Margo Alexis (Miss Carter); Robert Henderson (attorney); Louis Negin (couturier); Stuart Chandler (Simon Anderson); Tony Sibbald (workman); Don Fellows (foreman); Francis Napier (engineer); Roy Stephens (hotel receptionist); Elsa Pickthorne (concierge); Mavis Villiers (Martha); Elliott Sullivan (Harry); Jennifer Watts (party guest)

PRODUCTION CREDITS: *Director:* Daniel Petrie; *Producer:* Aida Young; *Screenplay:* John Peacock; *Director of Photography:* Jack Hildyard; *Executive Producer:* Beryl Vertue; *Editor:* John Trumper; *Art Director:* Roy Stannard; *Sound:* Kevin Sutton; *Production Supervisor:* Christopher Sutton; *Assistant Director:* David Tringham; *Costume Design:* Emma Porteous; *Makeup:* Wally Schneiderman; *Hairdresser:* Ronnie Cogan; *Continuity:* Zelda Barron; *Camera Operator:* Chic Waterson; *Sound Editor:* Mike LeMare; *Dubbing Mixer:* Ken Scrivener; *Music:* Ron Grainer; excerpt from Tchaikovsky Quartet no. 1 in D op.11

## Synopsis

Introverted Halifax schoolteacher George Anderson is nicknamed Mousey by his pupils. His depression becomes profound embitterment when his wife Laura divorces him, taking with her their son Simon. Laura denies him access to the boy on the grounds that Anderson is not the true father, and now plans to marry Montreal architect Richardson. Hastily resigning and selling his house, Anderson finds lodgings in Montreal in defiance of a court order. He names Simon as beneficiary in his will provided the boy keeps his surname. Laura rejects the idea. Richardson hires a private detective to watch Anderson when he continues to stalk them even after their wedding.

Fixated on revenge, Anderson anonymously informs the police he will kill someone as a "warning" that night, a threat which he gruesomely executes. After he tricks the detective shadowing him into informing the Richardsons he has returned to Halifax, this man becomes his second victim. Anderson reconnoiters the couple's isolated new home before gaining entrance to the house of Richardson's mother where Simon is staying. Telephoning Richardson from here is simply a ruse, so that Laura is left alone and the police diverted. Anderson plays out his cat and mouse game with his terrified victim when she realizes she is at his mercy. Ultimately it is "Mousey" rather than the vengeful killer who prevails.

## Reviews

"Although this does eventually work its way to a taut and suspenseful climax, it takes an unconscionable time a-getting there.... This is the sort of story that gives the impression of having been plotted backwards from its climax, with the reasons why of each incident having to be thought out in reverse order...."—*Cinema TV Today*

"A good 'suspense' film, where the director Daniel Petrie shows a perfect knowledge of the genre and its devices. But nothing more than that.... Nothing original, but a good consumer product in the wake of yesterday's thrillers."—*Amis du film*

"The correctness of Daniel Petrie's direction and the mature craft of Kirk Douglas fail to bring any substance to this autumnal thriller shot by an English production team between Halifax and Montreal. The psychological profile of the central character follows the already worn-out formula of the individual driven to murder by frustration."—*Rivista del cinematografo*

"A thriller with some pretensions to psychological depth ... the film does attempt to extend some sympathy to Anderson, with the result that the final sequence in which one is encouraged to identify with Laura as she is pursued around the house by her demented ex-husband, bears little relation to the rest of the movie."—*Monthly Film Bulletin*

"Miss Seberg has never looked so beautiful or seemed so poised, Vernon behaves bravely (though not too intelligently), but *Mousey* seems to have been doomed from the start."—*Los Angeles Times*

## Notes

Canadian Daniel Petrie had already had considerable directing experience when he took on this project. He had, for example, made the distinguished screen version of Lorraine Hansberry's powerful play *Raisin in the Sun* in 1961, and, despite his share of misfires, later in his career he was to direct such films as *Resurrection, Fort Apache, the Bronx* and *Rocket Gibraltar*.

"It's the most interesting part I have been offered for a year," Seberg told Sue Clarke in explaining her role. She admitted being a fan of Kirk Douglas and curious to see how he worked. "He is a very serious actor, with what I call a psychological approach.... When he makes suggestions about the script they usually become changes."

Petrie had been slightly apprehensive:

I was concerned about Kirk, because he had a reputation of eating directors alive for breakfast. But that didn't come to pass in this encounter. He was great to work with, and Kirk was searching to make the film better. He would say, "Do I have to say this? I think maybe if I didn't say *that*, but if I said something a little more incendiary...." And I'd say, "Oh, yeah! Well, why don't we do that." And I'd ask Jean, "Is that OK with you?" [and she'd say,] "Oh sure, that's fine." In other words, she was not *into* the character of this silly thing that we were doing. She was there to serve, and she did.

Outwardly this seemed an odd role for Douglas, but in fact playing against type in this way was just the kind of challenge he relished. "I'd call this a fun picture," he commented during production. "I know the guy I play bumps off a couple of people. But he's so *interesting*. He's weak, and weakness is more interesting than strength.... What every actor wants to do is work against the star system, and refuse to stay pigeon-holed. With *Cat and Mouse* I've done that."

The production was filmed on location in Montreal and at the Pinewood studios in England, beginning early in November 1973 and lasting some nine weeks. *Mousey* premiered on ABC-TV in the U.S. on March 9, 1974, as one of the network's *ABC Suspense Movie* series. It was then released for international distribution with the title *Cat and Mouse*, and it was under this title that the film was screened in London in June 1974, packaged together with the Jack Palance horror *Craze*. It attracted little critical attention and had limited circulation, apparently being shown in the U.S., Italy, Belgium and Spain but not in France or Germany, and this is reflected in the paucity of published reviews.

Perhaps more than anything it is the writing which pegs *Mousey* in the category of made-for-TV or "straight-to-video" type products. Production values are good and the cast headed by Douglas is more than adequate, while there is sound technical support. John Peacock's story shows little originality in its conception, although the construction is workmanlike enough. Everything hinges on the character of "Mousey" himself, and the persona of Kirk Douglas undeniably brings weight and substance to this volcanic role. The banality of the dialogue, however, is something that even Douglas cannot overcome.

The Jekyll and Hyde character Douglas embodies is an intense and brooding presence throughout, but is crudely delineated, and there is insufficient characterization to make this tortured individual very sympathetic or genuinely interesting. It is clear from the start that this is a portrait of a man unhinged by the loss of everything meaningful in his life. The meek and dutiful nonentity is suddenly transformed into a crazed and violent stalker, obsessed with the thought of avenging the wrongs he has suffered. This proposition is both corny, Freudian references included, and melodramatic, yet it is one which might just be made to work in the hands of a more inventive writer. Part of the problem is that Mousey's transformation not only stretches credibility, but it also suggests a latent sadism which alienates us. This is a psychological thriller which is too intent on thrilling to pay enough attention to either plausible psychology or satisfying storytelling. The thrills it contrives, however, often rely on worn-out stock situations, especially in the culminating scene.

There are moments of real menace, it is true, and the seedy downtown atmosphere is well conveyed and intermittently effective. The photography and editing are very competent, and the score by Ron Grainer sets the downbeat mood appropriately. Yet some

**With Kirk Douglas in *Mousey* (Universal Television).**

troublesome queries linger. Does squeamishness about vivisection betoken the lack or loss of George's manhood? Does he see the gruesome slaughter of a Good Samaritan part of his redemption, or just a rehearsal for this? He is confused about many things, so even this might make some sense in his head, but Sandra's flirtatious behavior, coupled with the unpleasant ensuing scene, is redolent of slasher movie cliché. Again, why should he write an apology in blood on the wall? We can't be sure quite what territory we are in here. Perhaps one should not ask too many questions of what Douglas termed a "fun picture," but this may not be the definition which springs most readily to mind as we follow Mousey's sanguinary adventures.

Although Seberg's interpretation of Laura is as sympathetic as she could very well make her, we simply don't learn enough about this character to make us identify with her and share in her fear. Marriage to even the pre-crackup Mousey might not have been a picnic, but the bare facts available to us indicate that this is a rather cold-hearted woman who, having married for calculated reasons, had abandoned the man who had served his purpose. Her affluent new husband appears equally self-centered in his protective role. Instead of seeking to ratchet up the tension, it might have been better to give us some reasons for caring about the fate of this couple. This is ninety minutes of passable entertainment which finishes much like its eponymous hero. Having run his erratic course, "Mousey" finally deflates, all passion spent, with scarcely more than a whimper.

### References

Clarke, Sue. "Jean Seberg: my life has been a roller-coaster." *Photoplay*, 25:3, June 1974, pp. 29, 59.
*The Hollywood Reporter*, 228:37, 1 November 1973. "Jean Seberg to star in 'Mousey' telefilm," p. 5.
*The Hollywood Reporter*, 228:42, 8 November 1973, p. 16.
Lacourbe, Roland. *Kirk Douglas, ou l'acteur émancipé*. Paris: Éditions PAC, 1980, pp. 220–2, 327–8.
Munn, Michael. *Kirk Douglas*. New York: St. Martin's Press, 1985, p. 133.
*Sight and Sound*, 4:3, March 1994, p. 62.

### Reviews

*Amis du film et de la télévision*, 222, November 1974, p. 22.
*Cineinforme*, 12:201, June 1974, p. 12.
*Cinema TV Today*, 25 May 1974, p. 14.
*The Los Angeles Times*, 9 March 1974. Kevin Thomas, s.2 p. 3.
*Monthly Film Bulletin*, 41:485, June 1974. John Raisbeck, pp. 122–3.
*Rivista del cinematografo*, February 1975. P. Pisarra.
*Sight and Sound*, 43:3 Summer 1974, p. 188.

# *Les Hautes Solitudes* (1974)

"It's almost like going back to silent film-making. And I think it's healthy.
I don't think it's a regression. It's part of rebirth and growing."—Jean Seberg

An Elite Films production; A Capital Films release
Original release: silent
Running Time: 80 minutes
Format: in Black and White

CAST: Jean Seberg; Tina Aumont; Laurent Terzieff; Nico
PRODUCTION CREDITS: *Director, Producer, Screenplay, Director of Photography, Editor:* Philippe Garrel

## Synopsis

This is an experimental film in black and white, without story or soundtrack, composed of some eighty sequences. Garrel's principal subject is Jean Seberg, revealed in silent tableaux apparently without any specific interrelation or meaningful sequence. Tina Aumont is the camera's secondary subject, similarly treated, and there are also brief appearances by Laurent Terzieff and Nico. The majority of the shots are static, sustained close-ups, lasting for anything between a few seconds and several minutes, and capturing a specific mood or simple action. The faces which fill the screen are often backlit and silhouetted or almost enveloped in darkness, in an interior which is ill-defined and glimpsed only incidentally. There is one very brief outdoor sequence to relieve this feeling of confinement and claustrophobia for a moment. One or two interiors suggest a café or similar public place. Otherwise the setting is domestic—a bedroom, bathroom or lounge, where a single natural or artificial (electric or candle) light source casts deep shadows. A grainy stock emphasizes the contrasts, throwing the contours of faces into dramatic relief and at times creating almost abstract forms on the screen.

Sometimes the actors speak, apparently to each other or to someone else in the room unseen, moving wholly or partially outside the frame. Occasionally they look directly into the camera, conscious of the camera operator and at times seeming to address him, but more often they seem deep in their own thoughts. In a few short takes the camera shows two figures together, or glimpses of movement of another person moving in the room, but these are exceptions. The image may be duplicated or divided by a mirror or reflective surface. The film concentrates on the individual, at the same time isolated in the frame of the lens and in an inner and exclusive world of private experience.

There are moments of interaction. The actors have unheard conversation, Aumont combs Seberg's hair and comforts her at her bedside, Terzieff and Aumont embrace. Despite this, as the title suggests, the predominant moods are of isolation and introspection. Nico lies almost motionless or speaks with deliberation, Terzieff is shown slumped forward in an attitude of despair, Aumont sprinkles her face and neck with water, extinguishes a candle or toys idly with a switchblade knife. It is Seberg who occupies the prime focus, both in number and duration of scenes and their dramatic overtones and range of emotion. We see her calm and reflective or anguished, smiling or weeping, at times responding directly to the camera, at others seemingly oblivious of it and lost in her own thoughts. Only Seberg interrogates the viewer/camera operator on equal terms as well as allowing herself to be observed, her mobile face reflecting amused complicity, tenderness, fear, defiance, resignation, uncertainty—a kaleidoscope of shifting moods. She poses in a straw hat decorated with flowers, laughing self-consciously. In another scene she confronts the camera challengingly, several times turning abruptly to face it. Hooded, she smiles at a private thought. For an instant we glimpse her as a frenzied figure with flailing arms. She crouches broken in a corner wiping tears from her face, gazes pensively through a window or tosses restlessly in bed as if waking from a nightmare which still torments. Simple acts, such as combing or pinning up her hair or shaking it loose, are captured. Leaning forward, she grasps a pendant cross which she presses for a moment to her lips. She enters the door of a café only to re-emerge moments later. More dramatically, she swallows a series of tablets, drinks from a glass, and then takes more until the figure of Aumont rushes forward to intervene.

## Reviews

"Entirely silent, *Les Hautes Solitudes* is in a sense a return to the sources of cinema, to the time when the image retained all its power, without music or dialogue to dissipate the attention of the viewer.... You have to let yourself be carried along by these images, which you can watch passively, almost hypnotically."—*Télérama*

"Garrel's silences are there to teach us to look, I'd venture to say hear what isn't said. Accustomed to industrial cinema's cacophony, we've forgotten these stirrings of the soul, quivers of an eyelash, cries withheld. Thus the image assumes its true lyrical dimension on the screen...."—*Le Quotidien de Paris*

"You need eminently readable faces, actors capable of expressing everything in silence; but neither should it be in the style of silent film, resorting to the stylized excesses of expressiveness.... Laurent Terzieff is magnificent; Jean Seberg, the central figure, is deeply moving."—*Le Nouvel observateur*

"It's Jean Seberg who plays the role. Transfigured. Hardly recognizable. A moving mask, lit up or clouded by indecipherable secrets. You could speak of a dramatic performance, did not the film totally escape the normal parameters of dramatic expression."—*Le Monde*

"Jean Seberg looks at us. Then it's the turn of Tina Aumont. Then Jean Seberg again.... The room is lit up again. The 'spectacle' is over. It would seem that it's the portrait of a woman enclosed in her solitude. But is it a film?"—*Analyse de films*

"A piece of cinematic bravura. In the beginning it's hard going. I was irritated by the slowness of the images, by the greyness ... yet, after the first fifteen minutes ... I was often fascinated by images which seemed to me sometimes to convey privileged moments of truth: anguish, doubt, confusion on the part of the heroine...."—*Image et son*

"Perhaps the film conceals the primal drama of the actor: of not knowing who he is. ...Reality has no hold on them. Have they still an identity? Garrel supplies no element of an answer.... This dramatic intensity of the actor is given back its power with exceptional talent by Philippe Garrel. Absolutely to be seen."—*Politique hebdo*

## Notes

Philippe Garrel is now firmly established as one of French cinema's most original creative artists, but at the time he made this film, his eleventh project, his work still remained widely unknown. Despite the poverty of his background he had been experimenting with film from his teens, although art had been another youthful passion. Among key early influences were his father, who was a marionettist and actor, *Alphaville* and other work by Godard, Andy Warhol and the painting of Georges de la Tour. His relationship with the Velvet Underground singer Nico over a decade from 1969 marked an important phase in his career, with collaboration on seven films. Ascetic and uncompromising, he has shown little interest in conventional realistic narrative or the drama of superficial cause and effect. He once defined cinema as "Freud plus Lumière." For Garrel, who has always assiduously recorded his dreams, the unconscious mind has been a wellspring of creativity, giving access to more important levels of reality.

Garrel vividly remembered meeting Seberg in 1974. "Jean was infinitely superior to the image the Hollywood people had given of her," he told Thomas Lescure. "It only needed a camera for her to metamorphose into an extraordinary actress. In her presence I felt the irresistible need to film, to film as a cameraman." On her side, Seberg was struck by the idealism of this young radical who cared nothing for conventional notions of success. Mainstream cinema had apparently forgotten her, and besides, helping young film makers was something she had always found hard to resist.

The lack of technical sophistication in Garrel's early work was dictated by economic constraints, but there was also a genuine desire to "return to the sources" of cinema and assert the expressive primacy of the image. Critics have often noted the links to early masters of silent film such as Murnau, but in *Solitudes* there was no external drama that the actors were required to project through lingering close-ups, as for example in *Nosferatu* or *Sunrise*. Seberg's skill in improvisation added to her extraordinarily photogenic quality (remarked upon by Coutard so many years earlier) was really all that Garrel needed in terms of subject.

Even with Seberg's help and using the most rudimentary technology, the impoverished Garrel had real difficulty securing the funds necessary for this film's completion. He decided to shoot it on black and white 35 millimeter stock, using an Éclair Caméflex, with no sound, lighting or technical help. "I was sure that just showing [Jean's] expressions would have enough value for the audience," he said. One reason for his choice of Seberg was her ability to improvise in the way he wanted. "I don't think if I'd used a French actress this film would have been a success," Garrel commented. "She was different from other actresses. Among the actresses who worked with me, Jean was the best." (This view accords strikingly with a remark by Nicolas Gessner: "That was one of her qualities—to be able to relate to European realities of movie making, and still keep her American technique of perfectionism.") Garrel was determined to dedicate an entire film to Seberg, filming simply as a cameraman reporter might create a documentary. He took his title from a reference by Nietzsche to the "seven solitudes" and "loftiness of soul" in the foreword to *The Anti-Christ*. Garrel's comments to interviewers on various occasions throw much light on his thinking: "I like seeing the rushes before they have been edited, sitting with my staff at midnight as we work on a film, so I wanted to make something similar for the audience." He had footage of Nico which had been shot for an earlier film, and which he now decided could be incorporated into this one.

Seberg had welcomed the challenge Garrel's concept presented. "You have to be aware of laziness in improvisation," she warned at the time. "You can have endless self-indulgent wasting of time. But in a sense that's necessary, because from it you can arrive at something concise. You can look at a film that has been shot with the players improvising ... these things can be condensed then, and made into a scene or sequence. Some of the directors will just photograph faces and bodies, and there is no sound, but you can tell that these images are speaking to the public."

The film was shot over a period of two and a half months at Seberg's apartment, a hotel at the quai Voltaire or local cafés. Garrel would use up what film he had scraped together, sometimes imperfect or date-expired stock, and then break off filming until he could acquire more. The shoot was a bizarre experience, as Seberg later recalled: just Garrel and herself, doing close-ups and still shots. Despite her own belief in the director's talent, she acknowledged the film's appeal might be limited: "Of course, it's not everyone's cup of tea. It's certainly not something the masses are going to rush to watch. But it might be part of the beginning of a way of re-inventing the cinema." Once the editing had been completed the director brought her a copy, and he records her approval of the finished product.

Like Bergman or Godard, Garrel paints with light and shadow to make compelling landscapes from the contours of his faces. It is these faces, whether in repose or expressing various degrees of emotion, which the camera records with patient objectivity. Garrel chose not to "tidy up" this raw material in editing by using devices such as fades and dissolves. His editing can split a single take, inserting different footage in the break. He appears far less concerned with the aesthetic composition of images than with their emotional power. Flouting conventional assumptions about audience reactions, he follows his instincts and the inherent demands of his material. Even the imperfections of his film stock seem to express a struggle to reach the unattainable. This randomness seems willful, yet in his final product he achieves a kind of organic logic which is spellbinding. The intensity of silence is such, at times, that the cigarette smoke which drifts across these flickering shapes might almost be some ectoplasmic manifestation. Garrel creates a dream-like séance of visual poetry, taking us beyond the looking glass and deep into a world of intimate private experience.

For Garrel the very act of filming was a kind of violence, and his rapport with his actors, whom he saw as essentially fragile beings, was crucial. One of Seberg's ideas in February was to have a suicide scene. Garrel would later describe a moment of panic when he stopped filming, fearing that the actress was playing this scene for real, and recall Seberg's consequent irritation at the interruption. Sensing her vulnerability, he superstitiously added a sequence of her with a crucifix as a form of protection. For the spectator, at any rate, the line at which improvised "psychodrama" ends and reality begins is disturbingly uncertain. There can be no doubt that Seberg taps deep into her private pain for some scenes, making the film an unflinchingly honest and poignantly revealing self-portrait, yet these were essentially spontaneous exercises in mime. As soon as the filming stopped, Garrel explained, the actress would again become serene.

Garrel's camera distils the sculptural beauty of these faces with almost uncanny skill. The expressionless mask which Seberg turned to the camera for Preminger is an enduring image of *Bonjour Tristesse*, and Godard's Patricia gazes at us with the same emotionally frozen stare for the final frame of *À bout de souffle*. For *Les Hautes Solitudes* Garrel seems to invite Seberg to do the very opposite, for we feel that here nothing is withheld. Seberg is not, however, giving us a documentary about a disintegrating life. This is performance of an extraordinary kind, considered, concentrated and disciplined, and probably to be counted among her finest.

*Les Hautes Solitudes* played in a cinema in the Marais area of Paris for a month from mid–December 1974, attracting some 9,000 viewings, and was featured at some festivals. By Garrel's standards this was a great success, for the return almost trebled the tiny production cost of 3.2 million old francs. Thereafter it appeared intermittently in art houses which catered specifically for experimental films such as this, and it continues to do so. At a public showing in Tokyo's Institute Franco-Japonais in 2002 the reels were shown in the wrong order without anyone spotting and challenging the error. "This is a very modern work," Garrel remarked. "Since I admire Godard as my master, modernity is important to me. This film impresses the audience with its non-constructed style. So even if a projectionist screens the reels in the wrong order, it works. If a film has a constructed narration, it can't be like this."

Four years after *Les Hautes Solitudes* Seberg allowed Garrel to shoot *Le Bleu des origines* in her apartment at the rue du Bac. This also was shot on 35mm, but this time with a hand cranked camera which had come into his possession. In addition to Nico, Zouzou and Garrel himself, Seberg also fleetingly appears. The memory of Seberg would continue to haunt Garrel after her death in 1979. She was memorialized in his short 1984 film *Rue Fontaine* in the character of Génie. This was an affectionate name Garrel gave to Seberg while she was alive, punning on the sound of her name and the French term for "spirit" or "genius." The scenario is in part derived from his first meeting with her and a dream that the director had following her death (see Garrel and Lescure, pp. 102–20). Six years later in his film *J'entends plus la guitare* Seberg is again recognizable in the character played by Adélaïde Blasquez. John Orr has also pointed out that Garrel's 1999 film *Le Vent de la nuit* unmistakably alludes to an incident in which Seberg had slashed her wrist in the presence of husband Dennis Berry and the director. Here she is represented in the role played by Catherine Deneuve.

## References

*Catalogue de la production cinématographique française*, 1974, p. 47.
Della Casa, Stefano, and Roberto Turigliatto, eds. *Philippe Garrel*. Turin: Lindau, 1994.
Deniel, Jacques, ed. *Philippe Garrel*. Paris: Studio 43, 1988.
Etchegaray, Françoise. *Philippe Garrel, artiste*. Filmer les Arts: Cinéma de notre temps, 1998 [documentary film].
*Le Film français*, 1580 Cannes Special 1975, p. 126.
Garrel, Philippe. "Philippe Garrel, Serge Daney: dialogue." *Cahiers du cinéma*, 443/444, May 1991, pp. 58–9.
_____, and Alain Philippou. "Entretien avec Philippe Garrel, à propos de *L'Enfant secret*." *Cahiers du cinéma*, 344, February 1983, pp. 23–7.
_____, and Corine McMullin. "Entretien avec Philippe Garrel." *Cinématographie*, 48 June 1979, p. 15.
_____, and Emmanuel Mairesse. "Dix ans après: Philippe Garrel." *Cahiers du cinéma*, 287, April 1978, pp. 60–3.
_____, and Thomas Lescure. *Une caméra à la place du cœur*. Aix en Provence: Admiranda / Institut de l'Image, 1992.
Jolivet, Nicole. "Jean Seberg tourne pour son mari." *France-soir*, 14 December 1974, p. 22.
Jones, Kent. "Sad and proud of it: the films of Philippe Garrel." *Film Comment*, 33:3, May/June 1997, pp. 24–5, 27–30.
Kronsfoth, Barbara, and Till Müller-Edenborn. "Gesichter im Kino." *Nachtblende*, 4:9 Autumn 1996, pp. 26–35.
Morice, Jacques. "Deux solitudes en silence: Garrel et Seberg. Un jour de février 1974." *Cahiers du cinéma*, numéro spécial January 1975, p. 112.
Orr, John. "Out of noir: Seberg-Preminger-Godard-Garrel." *Studies in French Cinema*, 7:1, 2007, pp. 43–55.
Ramasse, François. "L'avant-garde française: *Utopia, Le Bleu des Origines, La Nuit Claire*." *Positif*, 219, June 1979, pp. 62–5.
Rosenbaum, Jonathan. "Confessions of an opium eater: Philippe Garrel." *Sight and Sound* 16:8, August 2006, pp. 24–7.
Salvatore, RosaMaria. *Traiettorie dello sguardo: il cinema di Philippe Garrel*. Padua: Il Poligrafo, 2002, pp. 14–5, 46–7, etc.

## Reviews

*Analyse de films 1975. Saison 1974*, p. 339.
*Cinéma*, 194, January 1975. Gérard Frot-Coutaz, pp. 135–6.
*Écran*, 33 February 1975. Marcel Martin, p. 59.
*Le Figaro*, 20 December 1974. Claude Mauriac, p. 28.
*Image et son (Saison cinématographique 1975)*, 299, October 1975, Christian Bosséno, pp. 171–2.
*Le Monde*, 15 December 1974. Jean de Baroncelli, p. 28.
*Le Nouvel observateur*, 529, 30 December 1974. Jean-Louis Bory, p. 57.
*Politique hebdo*, 9 January 1975. H.D.
*Le Quotidien de Paris*, 19 December 1974. Henry Chapier.
*Rivista del cinematografo*, February 1975, p. 108.
*Télérama*, 1300, 11 December 1974. Jean-Luc Douin; 1519, 24 February 1979 [*Le Bleu des origines*]. Christine de Montvalon, p. 90.

# *Ballad for the Kid* (1974)

"[The film is] an invitation to a small dream."—Jean Seberg

A Kangourou Films presentation; A film by Jean Seberg
Original release: in English; French dubbed
Also known as: *Ballad for Billy the Kid*
Running Time: 19 minutes
Format: in Eastmancolor

CAST: [* denotes above the title billing] Jean-François Ferriol* (Kid); Jean Seberg* (Star); Jacques Robiolles (photographer); Macbeth (the horse)

PRODUCTION CREDITS: *Director and Producer:* Jean Seberg; *Screenplay:* Jean Seberg, Jean-François Ferriol, Denis Berry; *Photography:* Ramón F. Suárez Pirata; *Sound:* René Guiffrey, Philippe Sénéchal; *Assistant Directors:* Christian Lopez, Alain David; *Driver:* François Valero; *Makeup:* Mabel Muñoz; *Hair:* Camille Albane; *Editor:* Caroline Maire, Caroline Biggerstaff (Ferriol), Denise de Casabianca; *Mixing:* Dominique Jugie; *Special Effects:* André Cagnard; *Technical Advisor:* Charles Nemes; *Music:* Anita and Bob Brown; *Music Production:* Étienne Robiol

## Synopsis

We see a busy highway in an urban landscape dotted with pylons. In the foreground a cowboy on a white horse comes into view and ascends a sandy bank above the road. In a hollow between sand hills a woman sits in a deck chair, a table with a telephone beside her. She listlessly replaces the receiver. The rider approaches and greets her:

KID: Howdy Ma'm.
STAR: (removing sunglasses) You made it, Kid.
KID: (he dismounts and the horse gallops off) I don't never let a lady down, Ma'm. (He pours drinks for them both) Times been good for you Ma'm?
STAR: Times been bad Kid, real bad. Give me some more of that. How about you?
KID: Everything sucks.
STAR: You can say that again. (The telephone beside her rings) I'm not in for anybody.

The caller proves to be Star's agent. She subjects him to a stream of abuse which suddenly turns into sugary compliance. Star asks the Kid about their baby, and is perplexed by Billy's assurance that there isn't one. They can't have one, she concludes, because "No one believes in us any more ... we're has-beens." His gallantry makes her kittenish, but when he finds a newspaper photograph of her, she tosses it aside: "The press is a bore." A Civil War era photographer in a top hat suddenly appears on the scene. As a wanted man, the Kid feels threatened, but the sight of a camera causes Star to apply some hasty lipstick. They tussle, and she falls. Scorned by Billy, she lectures him haughtily: "Even on my fanny in the dust, I'm a star, Kid. That's something you'll never understand." Seeing her dissolve in childlike tears, her face streaked with mascara, the Kid comforts her, turning to shoot the photographer just as he takes their picture.

Star reproaches Kid for his homicidal habits and for spoiling everything: "you really ought to see my doctor." Billy can't decide what made him like this—perhaps it was an unhappy childhood, "or because I can't love anymore," or perhaps it's simply insanity. "Don't you love me just a little bit?" Star pleads. Then her thoughts suddenly return to the baby, as she puts her ear to the sand: "I can hear him, Kid. I can hear him so well."

Billy infuriates her by his denials: "You'll always be alone, Kid. You deserve such loneliness." "You shouldn't say those things," he protests. "You had a baby in a movie. We never had one." Star is unsympathetic towards his gloom: "Compared to me, you don't even know what loneliness is." Billy comforts her and suggests another shot of tequila. She becomes playful, reminding him of their pact: "Don't forget to tell me when you're ready.... You aren't going to change your mind, are you? You don't know how much it means to me that you've chosen me." The Kid tells her how she is to shoot him facing the sun. Uncertain how this will work "in real life" and objecting that shooting him in the back is "not very nice," Star nevertheless meekly promises to do her best. As he counts to three, she shoots. "Good, good," he murmurs, as he lurches forward and collapses face down in the sand: "You were always the only one." Star kneels over his body, now distraught: "Kid! Kid! It's—it's what you wanted, isn't it? Kid! Tell me, Kid, tell me." The camera slowly zooms out, showing their figures in a panorama of desert-like landscape

## Notes

Jean-François Ferriol, who had a fascination with both the Old West and cinema in general, approached Seberg with the idea for this film after a chance meeting. A twenty-two-year-old without acting experience, he felt himself to be a reincarnation of the legendary outlaw, and impressed the actress with his enthusiasm. The two collaborated with Dennis Berry in drafting a script and were offered production help by Seberg's *Bonjour Tristesse* co-star, Mylène Demongeot. Demongeot and her husband Marc Simenon were founders of the production company Kangourou Films which provided the backing for this project and also for the Berry/Seberg *Le Grand Délire* the following year. As if to justify herself, Seberg predicted that "it won't be much different from a home movie," joking that she wouldn't be "on stage come Oscar night." "I had a name as an actress and I used it to get this [film] working," Seberg later explained. "I would say to anyone who wants to direct—go out and do it."

*Ballad* was filmed in seven days at Villejuif, near Orly airport, on the outskirts of Paris. This provided an ideal location for the shoot, with a freakish contrast between dreary urban landscape and barren sand hills which neatly expressed the theme of two

*Ballad for the Kid*: the actress turns producer, writer and uncredited editor in this film short, 1974 (Kangourou Films).

opposed worlds. The budget of under $9,000 was advanced by Seberg and Ferriol so that they would keep personal control. In total, the cast and crew numbered just eleven people. The free publicity received, once the international news media heard of Seberg's debut behind the camera, must have been worth at least as much as the capital investment. Journalists wanted interviews, and there were mentions in *Newsweek* and a *New York Times* profile.

Seberg was happy to explain the venture. "Our film is a story of the meeting of two myths of our time: the nineteenth century bandit Billy the Kid and a star in the thirties in decline. Both have always fascinated the public." Her approach was highly pragmatic. "If people are willing to go along, films can be made very cheaply. As long as private arrangements can be made with the crew, there are no union problems."

"I'm like a child learning to walk. Every day I learn something more. So, yesterday I spoiled something, but luckily we're ahead of schedule. Help from Dennis has made a big difference. Sometimes we don't agree, which isn't to say we argue, but we don't have the same idea for shooting a scene. I like a clean and simple style and need his best efforts to help me achieve that." Seberg recalled her early experiences with Preminger, and felt it was important to create an atmosphere of calm in which actors could concentrate and not lose confidence. Apparently this was not at all Dennis Berry's style of working. "I could never have done it without Dennis being there to help," she told Susan d'Arcy, "but in a disagreement I have the final say. It's very pleasant when we see the rushes and he agrees that I was right." Ferriol's inexperience troubled Seberg less than her own as director: "He has an amazing presence, and I think he will go far."

Ferriol defined *Ballad* as "something between a Bob Dylan song and a science fiction story," whereas Seberg spoke of it rather as a surreal dream. The Kid and Star are conceived as the last survivors of the human race, perhaps counterparts to Adam and Eve, acting out their parodic destinies in a bizarre pact of love, mutual support and death. Seberg overtly mocks the concept of stardom and the persona of the prima donna, with associated tantrums, delusion and vanity ("That's not my best profile!"), and there are humorous digs at show business hypocrisy and psychoanalysis. Although Star and the Kid are unable to recognize themselves as stereotypes, mere puppets in a mass entertainment industry, they have residual characteristics of humanity, with all its erratic and contradictory features. They sense the gap between roles and reality, even if unable to locate it or themselves precisely ("You had a baby in a movie" ... "I've never done this before in real life"). It's clear from the character of Star that Seberg wants us to know that she does not take herself too seriously. There are, nevertheless, unmistakable hints of her own troubles; her lost child, declining career and spells of depression ("Compared to me you don't even know what loneliness is"). If it is indeed a "home movie" in this sense, it is an unusually interesting one, especially for a first attempt, and it is to be regretted that it was to remain a "one-off."

For Seberg, this short was at once an experiment without unrealistic expectations and a learning process. She hadn't "been burning to direct for years or anything like that," as she explained to one interviewer. "It scared me a lot." At the same time, the idea of helping Ferriol to realize his vision had clearly appealed to her, and besides, she had always enjoyed creative writing. Looking back on the experience, Seberg told Jacques Chancel she felt it had been a big mistake to try to act and direct at the same time. She lacked the necessary technical assurance, she felt, and got almost "schizophrenic" worrying about both sides of the camera simultaneously.

The film was shown at the 18th London Film Festival on the 19 and 20 November

1974, as an accompaniment to Franju's *L'Homme sans visage* (*The Man Without a Face*). It also featured at the Amsterdam Film Festival before its Paris screening, but it was subsequently forgotten, and very few since then have had the opportunity to see it.

### References

Axelson, Lars. "Skådespelare som regissörer." *Chaplin*, 133, 6:1974, pp. 218–24.
Best, Betty. "Billy the Kid is alive and well and living in a sandpit near Paris." *The Australian Women's Weekly*, 42:17, 25 September 1974, pp. 24–5.
*Catalogue de la production cinématographique française*, 1975.
D'Arcy, Suzanne. "Adieu tristesse." *Films Illustrated*, 3:36, August 1974, p. 493.
Fincher, Terry. "Jean Seberg a triomphé de l'adversité." *Le Soir illustré*, 2201, 29 August 1974, pp. 26–9.
G, K. "Jean Seberg, 15 años despues, de actriz a realizadora." *Nuevo fotogramas*, 1348, 16 August 1974, pp. 6–10.
Jolivet, Nicole. *France-soir*, 14 December 1974, p. 22.
Mills, Bart. "A show-biz saint grows up, or, whatever happened to Jean Seberg?" *The New York Times*, 16 June 1974, D pp. 17, 34.
Pantel, Monique. "Jean Seberg: 'Être femme et metteur en scène ne pose aucun problème.'" *France-soir*, 21 June 1974, p. 18.
Radio France: Radioscopie de Jacques Chancel. 29 January 1976 [cassette tape].
*Time*, 104:1, 1 July 1974, p. 38.

# *White Horses of Summer (Bianchi cavalli d'agosto)* (1975)

A Rusconi Film S.p.A. production
Distributor: Cinema International Corporation [USA: Allied Artists Pictures Corporation]
Original release: English version (partially dubbed)
Running Time: 95 minutes
Format: In Technicolor

CAST: [* denotes above the title billing] Jean Seberg* (Lea Kingsburg); Frederick Stafford* (Nicholas Kingsburg); Renato Cestiè* (Bunny Kingsburg); Alberto Terracina (Aldo Terrati); Antonino Faà di Bruno (hotel manager); Ciccio Ingrassia (fisherman); Filippo Fantini (Pasqualino); Alberto Farnese (Arturo, friend of Nicholas); Carlo Gaddi (surgeon); Vanna Brosio, Paolo Paolini (nurses), with Paola Rosi, Lorenzo Piani, Vittorio Fanfoni

PRODUCTION CREDITS: *Director:* Raimondo Del Balzo; *Exective Producer:* Rolando Pieri; *Screenplay:* Raimondo del Balzo; *Photography:* Roberto D'Ettorre Piazzoli; *Film Editor:* Angelo Curi; *Music:* Franco Micalizzi; *Artistic Advisor:* Mario Longardi; *Sets:* Claudio Cinini; *Wardrobe:* Franco Carretti; *Camera Operator:* Franco Bruni; *Production Inspector:* Nicola Venditti; *Assistant Cameraman:* Maurizio Maggi; *Assistant Director:* Vito Bruschini; *Assistant Film Editor:* Maria Pia Appetito; *Continuity:* Marisa Calia; *Décor Assistant:* Andrea Fantacci; *Wardrobe Assistant:* Rosanna Andreoni; *Sound Technician:* Gianfranco Pacella; *Boom-man:* Ivano Tedesco; *Makeup:* Otello Sisi; *Makeup Assistant:* Gino Tamagnini; *Hairstylist:* Giancarlo de Leonardis; *2nd Assistant Cameraman:* Alberto Pisani; *Wardrobe Mistress:* Lamberta Baldacci; *Head Grip:* Eugenio Raimondi; *Gaffer:* Maurizio Micalizzi; *Prop-man:* Giuseppe Torresi; *Production secretaries:* Pino Pennesi, Loredana Ulpiani; *Administration:* Vincenzo Lucarini, Remo Stampiggioni; *Mixing:* Alberto Tinebra; *Dubbing:* Massimo Turci; *2nd Assistant Editor:* Daniela Vasta; *Dialogue:* Nona Medici, Alberto Liberati; *General*

*Management:* Rolando Pieri, Valdemaro Cauli; *Assistants:* Enrico Lucherini, Marghareta Rossetti, Matteo Spinola, Pier Luigi Villani, Stefano Pirro; Costumes by G.P.11

## Synopsis

Wealthy Americans Lea and Nicholas Kingsburg bring their eleven-year-old son Bunny on holiday to the Italian coastal resort Pugnochiuso. Their precarious marriage has been strained by Nicholas's bouts of drinking and sudden disappearances. Nicholas is bored in a place devoid of cultural interest, while his son, with only his collie Clipper as playmate, is troubled by his restless parents' constant bickering. For the solitary boy, fantasies of Arab horsemen or pirates offer an escape from unhappy reality. A young journalist called Aldo helps Lea with her intoxicated husband after a night out. The next day, when she apologizes for the incident, Aldo makes love to her. She soon learns that Nicholas has left for Pompeii. Nicholas returns unexpectedly to find Aldo with his wife and attacks him.

Nicholas departs once more, expecting Lea to look for him. This time she refuses, reassuring Aldo that he is not to blame. Bunny and the bell boy Pasqualino are trapped in an abandoned house while playing, and the dog brings Aldo to their rescue. Nicholas's friend Arturo brings the couple together again, but Bunny rebels against their plan to leave for Venice. When the boy suffers a fall his life hangs in the balance. The crisis, having saved his parents' marriage, finally passes.

## Reviews

"Presumably the film originates from personal feelings and moods, studiously nourished by a painstaking and sincere love of cinema, even if it tends to slightly studied effects. The presence of Cestiè ... and a few narrative twists which objectively look weak or familiar nevertheless leave on the film the gloss of a sentimental product for uncritical audiences."—*Rivista del cinematografo*

"The story line, written by [Del Balzo], is banal, weak and linear in its narrative development, rather slow in the first part and even tedious in the second. Nevertheless, the film has many good points, above all its visual elegance and the care taken even in small details."—*Cineinforme*

"Of particular appeal for a sensitive audience, not necessarily exclusively female.... At his surest, Del Balzo knows how to banish the specter of the 'tearjerker,' and it is at such moments, well sustained by the young Cestiè, Seberg and Stafford ... that one has to look."—*La Stampa*

"... Executed with practiced skill and considerable artistic elegance, the film nevertheless suffers from the rather slow pace and excessive attention to introspective pauses, while the emotions succeed each other along all too familiar lines."—*Corriere della sera*

## Notes

After breaking into film as a screen writer, Del Balzo combined writing and directing in a sentimental vehicle for popular Italian child star Renato Cestiè, *L'Ultima neve di primavera* (*The Last Snow of Spring*). *Bianchi cavalli d'agosto* was clearly an attempt to repeat that commercial success, using the same star and a similar formula. It was a repeat in another sense too, reuniting Seberg and Stafford in another colorful travelogue eight years on from *Estouffade à la Caraïbe*. This soft-centered family drama was a far cry from that and from the other, predominantly macho roles with which Stafford had made his name in the 60s. Del Balzo had set his story in a fictitious hamlet in southern Italy, but the availability of the Vacation Center of Pugnochiuso for location filming provided a highly attractive setting for the film as well as publicity for the resort itself.

There's a slender but adequate story line here, with a sympathetic portrayal of the isolation of an only child whose squabbling parents seem oblivious to his needs and aware of little beyond the failure of their own relationship. Del Balzo does make some attempt to flesh out his characters, but some scenes involving the husband during his separate travels or between the wife and the journalist were dropped either before production or at the editing stage. An occasional hiatus in the narrative points to the latter. The evident wish to make this a wholesome family film may well have deterred the director from lingering on Lea's adultery or Nicholas's alcoholism. There was a half-hearted attempt to introduce a gothic element, hinting at something sinister in the local inhabitants and emphasizing the gloom of a semi-deserted hotel, but this is not effectively pursued.

The familiar character of the "bored rich kid" who has everything but what he really wants, the time and attention of his parents and the company of his peers, is made believable and engaging by Cestiè. Bunny's spontaneous attachment to a friendly stranger and the tensions this produces are equally plausible, and there is nothing essentially far-fetched in the marital problems of the Kingsburgs. It is Stafford who has the greatest challenge here, and he seems ill at ease as the egocentric and self-pitying Nicholas. It is implied that his immature behavior stems from the failed relationship with his own father, but nothing we see of him builds faith in the "happy ever after" resolution the director tries to engineer. The boy survives his mishap, yet his future happiness seems to depend on a doomed marriage. Jean Seberg is excellent as Lea, a poised though brittle woman who is aware she owes her luxurious lifestyle to her marriage, and whose feelings for her husband have not yet been entirely destroyed by his intemperance and caprices. Seberg's performance seems entirely consistent with this character as we understand her. Little seems expected from Alberto Terracina as the young journalist beyond intense looks. A more imaginative screenplay from director Del Balzo could have given the leading players more scope for developing their characters. As it is they sometimes seem to struggle, and there's a resulting flatness to many of the scenes.

On the positive side is the camera work of Roberto D'Ettorre Piazzoli, which is more than acceptable and effectively exploits the craggy coastline of Apulia, the Gargano peninsula with its marine caves and the outlying islands. The white horses of the title refer to the repeated dreamlike vision of white clad Arab horsemen galloping through the surf, an image expressing Bunny's longing for adventure and excitement, the features so lacking in his materially comfortable but emotionally deprived existence. If Del Balzo well understands the emotive pull of childhood, he does not forget the infallible cinematic appeal of animals either. He may surely be excused lack of originality in giving Bunny's dog Clipper his own heroic and impeccably executed "Lassie" moment in rescuing the endangered boys. Micalizzi's score adds color and underlines the changes of mood, but his primary theme soon becomes too obtrusive and insistent. Dialogue was clearly dubbed for the English and Italian language versions, and the synchronization and sound engineering are not always perfect. In sum, this is an unpretentious film with a plot which, though serviceable, isn't satisfactorily developed and suffers from too many loose ends. Many who are not allergic to calculated pathos will feel that its charm and visual appeal go some way to make up for its obvious weaknesses.

The film was shot at the end of 1974 partly in Pugnochiuso and partly in the De Paolis-INCIR Studios, Rome, while additional exterior filming took place in Rome and

**With Frederick Stafford (right) and Alberto Terracina in *The White Horses of Summer* (*Bianchi cavalli d'agosto*) (Rusconi Film).**

Pompeii. It was shown in Rome in March 1975, followed by screenings in other Italian cities in April and May. Distribution elsewhere included Spain, the U.S. and Japan, but was on a limited scale, and it cannot have been considered a commercial success even as a low-budget production.

Seberg's role in this film was evidently taxing for her, notably in the scene at the hospital when her son's life hangs in the balance. So often her dramatic roles seemed to echo or foreshadow painful elements of her own life, yet her conscientiously professional approach enabled her to give another well controlled and truthful performance, despite her fragile psychological state at the time. Like Shirley Temple, Cestiè survived the perils of child stardom, later working mainly for television. Stafford would make three further films, but his screen career was, like Seberg's, now clearly in decline. By unhappy coincidence, the Czech-born actor's death in an aircraft accident would precede that of Jean Seberg by only a few weeks.

## References

*Bianco e nero*, 36:9/12, 1975, p. 7.
*Cinematografia*, 42:2, March/April 1975, pp. 105–6.
De Bernardinis, Flavio. *Storia del cinema italiano*. Vol. XII, 1970–1976. Marsilio: Edizioni di Bianco & Nero, 2008, 71–73.
Poppi, Roberto, and Mario Pecorari. *Dizionario del cinema italiano. Vol.4: I film 1970–9*. Rome: Gremese, 1996. I, pp. 109–10.

## Reviews

*Cineinforme,* 13:226/7, July/August 1975, pp. 34–5.
*Corriere della sera,* 3 May 1975. R.P., p. 16.
*Rivista del cinematografo,* October 1975. P. Pisarra, pp. 443–4.
*La Stampa,* 23 April 1975. L[eo] P[estelli], p. 7.

# *The Great Frenzy (Le Grand Délire)* (1975)

> "I found [the film] quite hard work. Dennis was very hard on his
> mother and very demanding with us all."—Jean Seberg

A Paris Cannes Production / Kangourou Films (Paris) / Film Cine Produktion (Berlin)
  / Arden Distribuzione (Rome) production; A Lugo Films release
Original release: in French
Also known as: *Pierre et Marie s'en vont ensemble* [France]; *Die grosse Ekstase* [Germany];
  *Prossima apertura casa di piacere* [Italy]
Running Time: 95 minutes
Format: in Eastmancolor

CAST: [* denotes above the title billing] Jean Seberg* (Emily); Wolfgang Preiss* (Uncle
Artmann); Yves Beneyton* (John); Pierre Blaise* (Pierre); Stefania Casini* (Sonia); Isabelle
Huppert* (Marie); Silke Hummel*; Gladys Berry (Mother); Jacques Debary (Georges);
with Oscar Freitag, Henri Marteau, Jean Mermet, Alexandre Astruc, Georges Adet,
Antonella Lotito, Robert Rondo, Danièle Nègre, Solange Skyden, Evane Hanska, André
Badin, Raymonde Vatier, Yvonne Dany, Jean Disses, Gilbert Labat, Daniel Léger, Jean-
Michel Mole, Madeleine Bouchez, Larry Douglas, Jillali Ferhati, Aurora Maris

PRODUCTION CREDITS: *Director:* Dennis Berry; *Producers:* Mylène Demongeot,
Marc Simenon; *Screenplay:* Dennis Berry; *Director of Photography:* Pierre Lhomme; *Editors:*
Renée Lichtig, Franz-Josef Fiedler; *Director of Production:* Armand Tabuteau; *Sound:*
Bernard Ortion; *Music:* Patrick Lanjean; *Cameraman:* Gilbert Duhalde; *1st Assistant Cam-
eraman:* Michel Cenet; *Script Girl:* Elizabeth Rappeneau; *1st Assistant Director:* Isabel Pons;
*2nd Assistant Director:* Emmanuel Clot; *Props:* Éric Simon; *Makeup:* Maud Begon; *Still
Photography:* Yves Manciet; *Set Decorator:* Jean-Pierre Bazerolle; *Production Assistant:*
Michel Pasquet; *Props Assistant:* Marc Rivière; *Perchman:* Gilles Ortion; *Sound Effects:*
Louis Devaivre; *Sound Mixing:* Lucien Yvonnet; *Sound Editor:* Emmanuelle Castro; *Assis-
tant Editors:* Annick Menier, Martine Fleury; *Administrator:* Myriam Éliez; *Production
Secretary:* Monique Goujon; *Chief Grip:* François Valero; *Chief Electrician:* Jean-Claude le
Bras; *Music Publishers:* Nouvelles Éditions, Eddie Barclay; Dresses worn by Jean Seberg:
Reinhart Luthier; Coats worn by Jean Seberg: Jacques Laurent; *Jean Seberg's hairstyles:*
Yvanyve's

## Synopsis

Pierre wants to turn his garage home into a nightclub. His bourgeois friends John
and Sonia will be partners if they can borrow the necessary capital from their father
Georges, but he refuses angrily. The dysfunctional household is further challenged by the
visit of uncle Artmann with sophisticated American friend Emily. Georges suffers a heart
attack while molesting Marie, their maid, and even fellow doctor Artmann cannot resus-
citate him. The latter breaks a leg in the confusion.

Pierre seems instantly infatuated with the teasing, independent-minded Emily. She
mocks him and simultaneously laughs at Artmann's jealousy. After the funeral John is
eager to sell up and divide his father's money, but Pierre suggests the house could be a

specialized clinic for elderly men—in effect a *maison close*. The longsuffering Marie is persuaded to enlist as the establishment's star attraction, and more recruits are quickly found. The enterprise proves a resounding success, but now John breaks it to Pierre that he doesn't really fit in here. His erstwhile friends offer a share of the profits, while Emily's car is her farewell gift to her disappointed suitor. Pierre acknowledges that it's time for him to move on.

## Reviews

"The idea is interesting. It could have given us a film rich in political implications. Unfortunately, when you cultivate malice and apply it to everyone, rich and poor, you risk losing sight of any message. ...Where is the element of sincerity, where is the element of indulgence? The theme is ambitious, the result doubtful. Which doesn't mean uninteresting."—*Cinéma*

"Film starts well in revealing a shrewd flair for notating the personalities of its characters and then becomes too overcharged to keep up its anarchic, liberating drive. And it tries for more targets than are usually encountered in a first film. ... Berry shows possibilities but more cohesive scripting is called for."—*Variety*

"Dennis Berry's sincerity sometimes leaves us baffled. The characters are monsters or Alfred Jarry-like archetypes. Clichés from which the director has not always been able to rid himself ... are followed by outrageous touches, the cruelty of which is not without effectiveness...."—*Amis du film*

"Beyond our 'shocked' amusement, our pleasure doesn't prohibit thought. This fine bourgeois home turned into a brothel? Logical development: the tyranny of money leads to prostitution in general."—*Le Nouvel observateur*

"Constantly aggressive direction piles up incongruous details, caricatures. Too much, it's too much ... except Jean Seberg, whose character relies on ambiguity."—*Le Monde*

"... it's the least 'delirious' and most boring film of the season. John Berry's son has made a poor start. A surprising rediscovery of Pierre Blaise (*Lacombe Lucien*), who extracts himself from this mess with the assurance of an old hand."—*Écran*

"The only shot worth mentioning happens to be borrowed from the admirable *Maison Tellier* episode in Ophuls' *Le Plaisir* ... appalling, were it not for the presence of Jean Seberg, who traverses these unpleasant adventures with radiant detachment."—*Positif*

## Notes

Dennis Berry was eager to forge a career in filmmaking as his American expatriate father John had done, and minor acting roles had financed a quirky short he entitled *Jojo ne veut pas montrer ses pieds* (*Jojo doesn't like showing his feet*) in 1969. Another short film, *La Mort d'un chat*, followed. His marriage to Seberg brought important contacts and the joint venture *Ballad for the Kid*, together with better prospects of funding a full-length feature based on a screenplay of his own. Needless to say, Seberg was to be the centerpiece of this debut, as she had been for Moreuil and Gary. The provisional titles of *La Boîte à conserves* (*The Tin Can*) and *Pierre et Marie s'en vont ensemble* eventually gave way to *Le Grand Délire*. Seberg's *Bonjour Tristesse* co-star Mylène Demongeot and her husband, Marc Simenon, had formed their own production company called Kangourou Films. They were approached to finance *Le Grand Délire*, as Demongeot recalls:

> We decided Dennis Berry was a talent of immense promise, and we decided to produce his first [feature] film. [The filming] did not go very well because Dennis was an angry young man. We had a lot of problems putting the film together—money and everything.

On the first day of shooting he came onto the set. He shouted that he didn't want the producers on the set and we should go away. We did. Marc always regretted it. He said, "I should have stopped that movie immediately the first day," because [Dennis's] attitude was unbelievable. But Marc said, "I cannot do that to a young man who's doing his first movie," but he regretted that he didn't do it. We couldn't go to the set and to see the rushes—that was difficult. Jean wanted to do the movie because she hadn't worked in a while, but we should have said, "OK, drop it—we lose $100,000." The finished film cost about $2 million. The movie was not really bad. It could go on television very well.

On the obvious level this is a satire on middle class materialism, a slapstick comedy which spares none of the inhabitants of the prosperous suburban villa which provides its main setting. While the young people are rude and self-centered, the corresponding vices of the older generation are simply ridiculous or pathetic. Berry plays the whole thing for laughs, and delights in taking a swipe at any aspect of bourgeois convention, not least the accepted canons of taste or political correctness. Such outrageousness amuses more often than it shocks, though there is at times a strand of cruelty which surfaces, challenging the normal bounds of mockery. This indiscriminately provocative tone works against the kind of satirical coherence we instinctively look for in Berry's film. The heart attack of Georges at a critical moment might be funny, if unoriginal, because it is deserved and because he is a caricature and nothing more. On the other hand, the treatment of Marie by the other characters and by the writer/director exemplifies what makes the laughter often uneasy, if not hollow, leaving us to speculate on Berry's own standpoint and how far he sees ridicule as a satisfying end in itself.

In Dennis Berry's feature film debut *Le Grand Délire* co-starring Pierre Blaise (Lugo Films).

Pierre is soon characterized by Emily as a sympathetic clown, and indeed Berry evidently conceived him as another incarnation of the eternal Pierrot. Pierre Blaise interprets his role in this style, while endowing this plebeian outsider with some quirky individuality. He is a free spirit who enters and leaves this absurd puppet theatre having been touched by nothing other than the beauty of this other intruder, Emily. Certainly, here is no Candide-like innocent, introduced to shine a light on a corrupt and heartless world. Still less should we be misled by Berry's passing joke about the crucifixion, seeing him as any kind of would-be redeemer for the unredeemable. He is no better than the others, even if he can't match their appetite for portable property. If he finally rejects their values, it is because, having served their purpose, he himself has been rejected.

Jean Seberg's Emily is the vision which mesmerizes Pierre, an exotic creature whose mere fur-draped appearance is enough to conjure ghostly wolf howls from thin air. She might bring out the best or the worst in Pierre, as we see, but she has little patience with his romantic notions and knows on which side her bread is buttered. This part was clearly tailored for Seberg, and it is not surprising if at times we sense that she is playing herself. Somehow she succeeds in rising above the sordid antics in which she too is implicated, preserving a dignity of presence which makes the anarchistic Pierre's fascination with her credible. Berry was fortunate in his cast for a beginner, and not least in obtaining the young Isabelle Huppert as Marie. Hers is not a grateful role here, but she too shines as the outrageously exploited servant who, we are supposed to believe, happily embraces a life of highly personal services for the elderly. Even more roughly handled is Gladys Berry as the mother. The compensation for her ordeals is that even she is not excluded from front line service in the new enterprise: "I have a customer!" she crows ecstatically.

Berry shows an inventiveness in detail which generally keeps things moving and prevents us from dwelling on any particular piece of silliness in the plot, but there are lapses. The excursion to the swimming pool is a tedious irrelevance, unpleasant in tone, and the sequence of Pierre and Emily by the river is unaccountably prolonged, with an incongruously portentous, quasi-tragic musical setting. The principal theme of the musical score by Patrick Lanjean is a mournful tune which well expresses the dismal urban industrial landscape of the opening sequence. Berry must have tried hard to find locations as ugly and depressing as the ones he shows us here. We are convinced, at any rate, that the family villa is a haven of undeserved privilege, and if it becomes more overtly a temple of Mammon this may be only a logical development. Being cast out of this particular temple is, unquestionably, a blessing in disguise for Pierre. He accepts expulsion philosophically, together with Emily's verdict, which he makes her repeat over and over, that she is "not a woman for him." The last we hear from him, as he makes a Chaplinesque exit down the highway, is that he's fed up with women. The viewer might be excused for concluding, on the evidence, that this is the best clue to what this film is essentially about. The ideas behind Berry's film may bring to mind associated themes in the films of Buñuel. Once this comparison is made it can only highlight the contrast between the lack of subtlety and deficiencies of technique here and the mastery of the Spanish director.

The shoot of *Le Grand Délire* began in Paris in mid–December 1974. The production was completed within the two months scheduled, despite the far from harmonious atmosphere on the set, and the Paris premiere followed in April 1975. It had a generally cool reception, although some critics saw potential in the young director. Berry was later to marry and work with another icon of the New Wave, Anna Karina, and has pursued a successful directing career, primarily in television. Pierre Blaise, newly discovered by Louis

Malle for the lead in *Lacombe Lucien* (1974), was killed in a road accident only months after completion of Berry's film.

## References

*Le Film français*, 1559, 20 December 1974, p. 23, 1584, 13 June 1975, p. 31.
Fougères, Roland. *Ciné revue*, 55:12, 20 March 1975, pp. 4–7.
Jolivet, Nicole. "Jean Seberg tourne pour son mari." *France-soir*, 14 December 1974, p. 22.
*Le Technicien du film*, 21:222, 15 January 1975, pp. 12–3.
Unifrance film. *La Production cinématographique française* 116/1975.

## Reviews

*Amis du film et de la télévision*, 244, September 1976. J.B., p. 26.
*Cineinforme*, 13:223, May 1975, p. 19.
*Cinéma*, 199, June 1975. Raymond Lefèvre, pp. 136–7.
*Écran*, 37 June/July 1975. Marcel Martin, p. 67.
*L'Express*, 1242, 28 April–4 May 1975. G.J., pp. 10, 13.
*France-soir*, 22 and 29 April 1975. Robert Chazal, pp. 18, 13.
*Image et son* (*Saison cinématographique* 1975), 299, October 1975, Jacqueline Lajeunesse, pp. 164–5.
*Le Monde*, 4 May 1975. J.S., p. 17.
*Le Nouvel observateur*, 546, 28 April 1975. Jean-Louis Bory, p. 85.
*Positif*, 171–2, July/August 1975. Olivier Eyquem, p. 105.
*Téléciné*, 200, June 1975. Stéphane Sorel, p. 23.
*Variety*, 23 April 1975. Gene Moskowitz, pp. 24–5.

# *The Wild Duck (Die Wildente)* (1976)

"Today I would rather not work at all than be involved
with something I don't believe in."—Jean Seberg

A Solaris Film production in collaboration with Sascha Film/Wien (Vienna) and West-deutscher Rundfunk (Cologne); A West German-Austrian production; A New Yorker Films release (USA)
Original release: in German; released with English subtitles
Also known as: *Le Canard sauvage* [France]
Running Time: 100 minutes
Format: in Color

CAST: Peter Kern (Hjalmar Ekdal); Jean Seberg (Gina Ekdal); Bruno Ganz (Gregers Werle); Anne Bennent (Hedwig Ekdal); Martin Flörchinger (Captain Ekdal, father of Hjalmar); Heinz Moog (Consul Werle, father of Gregers); Sonja Sutter (Mrs. Sörby); Heinz Bennent (Relling); Robert Werner (Molvik); Guido Wieland (Petersen); Anton Duschek (Graberg); Uwe Falkenbach, Erich Aberle, Bruno Thost

PRODUCTION CREDITS: *Director:* Hans W. Geissendörfer; *Producer:* Bernd Eichinger; *Screenplay:* Hans W. Geissendörfer, based on the play by Henrik Ibsen; *Photography:* Robby Müller; *Assistant Director:* Astrid Graue; *Music:* Niels Janette Walen; *Sound:* James Mack; *Synchronization:* Norbert Herzner; *Mixing:* Christian Dalchow; *Lighting:* Hans Kirchmair; *Art Direction:* Ulrich Schröder; *Wardrobe:* Edith Almoslino-Assmann, Lambert Hofer; *Editor:* Jutta Brandtstätter; *Assistant Editor:* Helga Beyer; *Production Manager:* Hans Weth; *Assistant Cameraman:* Martin Schäfer; *Still Photography:* Martin Schäfer, Ruth Walz; *Production Supervisor:* Gunther Witte; *Script Supervisor:* Barbara von Weitershausen; *Makeup:* Hannelore Uhrmacher, Adolf Uhrmacher, Lilli Zangerle; *Property Master:* Harry Nap; *Props:* Max Martinek, Alfred Nurschinger; *Production assistant:* Annie Oleon; *Associate Producer:* Peter Genée

## *Synopsis*

Hjalmar and Gina Ekdal, their eleven-year-old daughter Hedwig and Hjalmar's father live frugally on Hjalmar's photographic business. Once an officer and renowned hunter, the old man was imprisoned for theft during his partnership with Consul Werle. This disgrace weighs heavily on Hjalmar, who dreams of an invention which will restore their fortunes. In their attic, among tame rabbits and the duck given to Hedwig by Werle, father and son hunt imaginary game together.

Consul Werle's idealistic only child Gregers blames him for his mother's death. After a long absence as manager of Werle's timber works he returns home and visits his admired childhood friend Hjalmar. Gregers' suspicions are aroused on learning that his friend is married to Werle's former servant and that the couple's business was backed by his father. Werle has announced his engagement to his housekeeper, Mrs. Sörby, and wants reconciliation with his son, but Gregers denounces his dishonesty.

Now lodging with the Ekdals, Gregers is determined to strip away the illusions which diminish his friend. Despite the revelation that Hedwig will soon become blind, Gregers tells Hjalmar that Werle is her real father. The Consul's will and Gina's silence appear to confirm this. Hjalmar is shattered, and rejects the child. Hedwig is convinced by Gregers that she can only regain Hjalmar's love through sacrificing the wild duck she has nursed. A shot rings out in the attic, and both men are appalled at the spectacle of the dying girl.

## *Reviews*

"... splendid film ... By concentrating on his people and resisting all trite devices used by film makers to 'open up' a play on the screen, Geissendoerfer has succeeded in making *The Wild Duck* a genuine movie and not just a filmed play."—*Los Angeles Times*

"... the camera remains extremely reticent, always subordinated to characters' movements and never an independent commentator. This shows Geissendörfer's faith in his actors, who never for a moment abuse the freedom he allows them."—*Süddeutsche Zeitung*

"What a shattering experience it is to see Ibsen's *The Wild Duck* for the first time in the masterful German film version ... [Gina] played with cool authority by Jean Seberg...."—*San Francisco Chronicle*

"Jean Seberg as Gina ... is eye-pleasing in the role of the former housekeeper.... Robby Mueller's camera, with color tones and subtle touches throughout, as well as set design and costumes ... are worth the price of admission."—*Variety*

"Geissendörfer has just made one of the best film transcriptions of this play.... The film is astutely acted, especially by Kern...."—*New Yorker*

"Pruning of the text has taken place but this version is essentially faithful.... The director makes a few minor errors of judgment, including the uneasy stylization of the scene in the loft, and his admiration for Jean Seberg results in the film's single miscasting.... The other players are admirable...."—*Films and Filming*

"Seberg, who has become an actress of depth and sensitivity, is fine as Gina. Kern is excellent.... But it is Bennent, as the daughter, who is a real find.... Geissendorfer has beautifully fused the literary and emotional qualities of *The Wild Duck* to come up with a beautiful film...."—*Hollywood Reporter*

"Jean Seberg takes the role of Gina ... and gives a very fine performance.... The combination of the strengths which the actors and the technical elements contribute, added to the work of camera crew and wardrobe departments, make the film into a drama of extraordinary quality."—*Cineinforme*

"Geissendorfer opens up the play but not in such a way that he lets the life out of it....

With the exception of Miss Seberg, who is too chicly beautiful to be believable as the waddling, once-ripe housemaid she's supposed to be, the casting is nearly perfect."—*New York Times*

## Notes

*The Wild Duck* was shot in seven weeks during the early summer of 1976 in the Austrian capital. It was Jean Seberg's last completed film, and thus it happened that she ended her career as she began it, with a classic play. The circumstances of her debut and this modest art film's release, however, could scarcely have been more contrasting, for this time publicity and press attention were minimal. Seberg was happy to talk about her role and the reasons why it appealed to her:

I have always liked Ibsen and had read him when I was a child. I consider *The Wild Duck* to be one of his most interesting and profound plays. Hans Geissendörfer came to me in Paris and told me about his plan to film *The Wild Duck*. He spoke about his work with such passion and commitment that I was immediately won over for this project. I hadn't even seen the earlier movies of Geissendörfer before I accepted the role. I don't need to, I'm not much concerned about what a director had done previously: I decide to participate if I have a good feeling and a good impression of the director, and if the things he has told me about his movie have convinced me. I have been making movies for twenty years now, and yet only worked three or four times with people who loved their work and took it seriously. Today I would rather not work at all than be involved with something I don't believe in.

The role of Gina, which I play in *The Wild Duck*, represents a challenge, a new watershed for me as an actress; now I have entered on a new path: it's no longer enough for me to be Jean Seberg and look pretty and put on some silly cinematic airs. Gina is like a keystone in the architecture of a cathedral: she holds the whole family together. She doesn't say much, she stands rather in the background, but she's the basis of the family. She is no fascinating woman, she isn't beautiful, she works hard, but she stands with both feet firmly on the ground. While I'm acting I carry sand-filled weights under my feet, so that I have a really physical sense and consciousness of the nature of this woman. Gina has a painful past behind her, one she wants to forget. She has married Hjalmar and tried to build a home, a modest but secure refuge for her small family. When Gregers turns up she probably senses danger, but I believe she hopes right to the end that everything will be all right, and that

In the screen version of Ibsen's *The Wild Duck* (*Die Wildente*) with Anne Bennent (New Yorker Films).

Gregers will leave her family in peace again. For her, for her kind of intelligence and upbringing, it is inconceivable that this man can tell Hjalmar and the child the cruel truth. But neither is she the woman to speak out, to express herself, in order to defend herself. She has learnt to be silent, and she endures what befalls her.

To one journalist curious about her current career and plans, she explained succinctly that Hollywood was "dead" where she was concerned, adding that she now felt "much too European" for that.

As has often been noted (and not least by the author of *Saint Joan*), *The Wild Duck* seems to mark a deliberate thematic shift in Ibsen's work. In this play, significantly defined as a tragicomedy, the focus is less on society and its hypocrisy than on the plight of the individual attempting to find significance in his own fate. Thus Hjalmar clings tenaciously to the illusions which alone can make life bearable, while the intruder Gregers becomes equally set on his mission to purge the household of the "lies" which diminish the friend he so much admires. Old Ekdal, broken and disgraced, survives in the realm of fantasy and nostalgia which the attic represents, and which offers his sole alternative to alcoholism. It is primarily the womenfolk who provide the tenuous link with reality here, maintaining a precarious balance between acquiescence and practicality. Gina, assisted by Hedwig, keeps the family afloat economically as well as in a broader sense, freeing her husband to indulge in grandiose or sentimental flights of fancy. Ibsen is merciless in exposing the flaws of his characters, but it is often the words of the healer Relling which seem to reflect the author's viewpoint, contemptuously rejecting the self-serving "idealism" of Gregers which can only bring destruction. In contrast to Gregers, Relling accurately diagnoses the maladies of those around him, and perhaps also his own. The pessimistic note of the play's conclusion is underlined by the suggestion, explicit in Hjalmar's case and implicit in that of Gregers, that neither of these men will ever achieve self-knowledge.

Geissendörfer began his career in the 60s with documentary and experimental projects. This led to television commissions, and he soon became associated with the movement termed the New German Cinema, although less avant-garde than some of its exponents. Equally ready to use his skills in the service of popular drama or classic adaptations, he has gained particular respect both as a technician and visual narrator. Though he was found by one critic to be too slavishly faithful to Ibsen's play, Birgitta Steene has convincingly demonstrated the unfairness of this accusation, highlighting the film's divergences from the text and stage directions and analyzing their significance. It is arguable that in reducing Hedwig's age from fourteen to eleven the director has made his story more plausible, giving more scope for the imaginative world of childhood into which the male Ekdals also enter, at times to an absurd extent. Geissendörfer referred to the distance and artificiality resulting from the theatrical casting of an adult in the role of a child. He wanted to sweep away such barriers. On screen, as he put it, "Anne Bennent *is* Hedwig." Again, departing from Ibsen, the director brings his audience right inside the mysterious sanctum of the attic, accepting the risks this brings in dramatic terms.

The claustrophobic atmosphere more easily conveyed by a stage production is not dispelled by the brief outdoor scenes, but Geissendörfer shows a fine understanding of the cinematic techniques which can compensate for loss of theatrical impact. The contribution of distinguished cinematographer Robby Müller is important here, taking us into the private world of the child in a way simply not possible on stage. In the final sequence the camera dwells on Hedwig as she slowly and silently makes her way from room to room, takes the gun and enters the attic to gather up the wild duck. The contrast between this and the inter-cut shots of the garrulously self-regarding Hjalmar is potent. The theme of literal and figurative blindness which runs through the play is picked up on screen, but not over-insistently. Necessary cuts in dialogue inevitably affect balance and our view of the characters, but the essence of what Ibsen wrote remains here, even if the interpretation is open to challenge. The lighting, on which the playwright placed emphasis for the creation of mood, is used effectively for some fine camerawork by Müller. The subdued tones and slightly grainy quality have a somber richness which seems well attuned to the unfolding tragedy, and there are many images, composed as perfectly as paintings, which linger in the mind's eye.

What is most striking about Nils Janette Walen's music is the sparing way it is used, rendering the dramatic effect all the greater. Hjalmar's "conjuring" for Hedwig, Old Ekdal's account of the duck legend, the ironic hunting horns in the attic, Hedwig's birthday march played on the music box and the girl's last embrace of the duck are passing moments in the drama, but it is music which signifies their importance. Similarly, there is an unobtrusive but ominous interlude which precedes the fatal walk taken by Gregers and Hjalmar, a dividing point which is to precipitate disaster.

The film's casting seems almost impeccable, given Geissendörfer's view of the characters. Even those who would question the change in Hedwig's age must admit that Anne Bennent is impressive and touching in this role. Seberg was a more surprising choice for the part of the semi-educated, self-effacing but quietly capable Gina. It seems a pity that more time could not have been given to this character, and that the exchanges with Mrs Sörby in Act 4 were cut, but Seberg was right in seeing her role as a key one. Hjalmar takes his wife's subservience for granted, but there is surely no need to emphasize Gina's gaucheness or low social status. The reticence of Seberg's Gina is eloquent, and her graceful background presence as a woman accustomed to serve others and suffer in silence accords perfectly with the narrative. The director's gamble in assigning the actress a role so different from any of her previous ones seems amply vindicated, and leaves us to speculate just where Seberg's "new path" might have led her.

The film was premiered on September 10, 1976, in Munich and on November 26 in Vienna. It was selected for the 1976 London Film Festival and for the World Film Festival of Canada in August 1977. Praised in both Germany and Austria, it received the feature film award of the Bundesministerium in Bonn. In 1981 Geissendörfer was the only West German film director to have more than one film screened at a German film season in the Soviet Union (*Die Wildente* and *Die gläserne Zelle*). Despite this favorable reception, *The Wild Duck* suffered from the same lack of good distribution in the U.S. as had handicapped most of Seberg's post–1970 work. The film remains largely unknown, but its rare screenings have met with warm appreciation from audiences and critics, and indeed some have thought it decidedly finer than Safran's better known 1984 filmed version of the play, starring Jeremy Irons and Liv Ullmann.

*The Wild Duck* followed Geissendörfer's adaptation of the nineteenth century classic *Der Sternsteinhof* by the Austrian writer Ludwig Anzengruber, released in 1975. He was to direct a sumptuous international production of Thomas Mann's 1924 masterpiece *The Magic Mountain* some six years later. Both of these illustrate the same meticulous care for visual detail combined with unsentimental determination to reveal the underlying humanity of his characters, with all their flaws, that we see in his treatment of Ibsen's play.

## References

"10 Filme von Hans W. Geissendörfer." 29, Internationale FilmFestspiele Berlin, 1979.

*Besonders Wertvoll. Langfilme 1975/1976.* Verwaltung der Filmbewertungsstelle Wiesbaden, 1976, pp. 198–200.

*Bild + Funk,* 39, 24–30 September 1977, pp. 12, 48.

*Film-Echo/Filmwoche,* 30:19, 2 April 1976, p. 19; 30:35, 25 June 1976, p. 24.

*Filmkunst,* 82/83, May 1979, p. 11.

Fischer, Robert, and Joe Hembus. *Der neue deutsche Film 1960–80.* Munich: Goldmann Verlag, 1981, p. 262.

Ibsen, Henrik. *Vildanden* [The Wild Duck]. Copenhagen: Gyldendal, 1884.

Kino-Information, 3:24, 16 December 1976, p. 15.

Kirschner, Klaus, and Christian Stelzer. *Die Filme von Hans Wilhelm Geissendörfer: Gespräche, Materialien, Daten.* Erlangen: Videogruppe Erlangen, 1979, pp. 95–102.

*Motion Picture Guide, 1927–83,* p. 3853.

Pflaum, H.G. "Erfahrungen beim Verfilmen von Ibsen, Anzengruber und anderen." *Film-Korrespondenz,* 5 October 1976, pp. 3–5.

Rentschler, Eric. "Hans W. Geissendörfer, a precise craftsman." *New German filmmakers from Oberhausen through the 1970s,* Klaus Phillips ed. New York: Ungar, 1984, pp. 124–142.

Steene, Birgitta. "Film as theater: Geissendörfer's *The Wild Duck* (1976)." *Modern European Filmmakers and the Art of Adaptation,* Andrew Horton and Joan Magretta, eds. New York: Ungar, 1981 pp. 295–312.

*Stern Magazin,* 30:40, 22 September 1977, p. 286.

*Die Wildente: ein Film von Hans W. Geissendörfer nach dem gleichnamigen Theaterstück von Henrik Ibsen.* Munich: Filmverlag der Autoren, [1976?].


## Reviews

*Box Office,* 4941, 25 April 1977.

*Cineinforme,* 14:257, October 1976, p. 26.

*Film-Echo/Filmwoche,* 22 September 1976. Dr. Helmut Müller, p. 8.

*Films and Filming,* 326, November 1981. Mansel Stimpson, p. 43.

*The Hollywood Reporter,* 13 April 1977. Charles Ryweck, p. 2.

*Kirche und Film,* November 1976. Peter W. Jansen.

*Los Angeles Times,* 9 May 1979. Kevin Thomas (s.4 p. 26.

*Medium,* October 1976. Wilfred Günther, p. 34.

*The New York Times,* 29 April 1977. Vincent Canby, p. 12.

*New Yorker,* 53:12, 9 May 1977. Penelope Gilliatt, p. 124.

*Nürnberger Nachrichten,* 6 January 1977. F.J. Bröder.

*San Francisco Chronicle,* 21 March 1979. Judy Stone, p. 52.

*The Saturday Review,* 11 June 1977. Judith Crist, pp. 44–5.

*Soho Weekly News,* 28 April 1977. Bob Baker.

*Süddeutsche Zeitung,* 21 September 1976. H.G. Pflaum, p. 24.

*Variety,* 8 September 1976. Ron Holloway, p. 20.

# Postscript
## *The Story, Legend and Legacy*

"Whatever happens to me, either through myself or my associations, will be my own responsibility, no one else's."—Jean Seberg, May 1957

A real-life Cinderella story was and is manna from heaven for the copy writers. The further twists to the original "Jean Seberg story," successes and setbacks both professional and personal, merely refreshed the legend. When the press itself became part of the story, however, this added a further, unexpected dimension. The shocking circumstances of Seberg's death and the scandalous revelations of a government-funded conspiracy against her seemed incompatible with the screen personality the public knew and admired. How could all this happen, and how could it end so painfully? It is clear from the tributes which appeared in print at the time that many who had never met the actress had a feeling of personal loss. They wanted to explain why that was, and needed to make sense of this event. The dramatic story had become more than ever public property. The conflict between Seberg's champions and her detractors, often divided along political lines, would of course rage on, and, needless to add, with scant consideration for the sensitivities of her family.

Within the year following her death several authors were researching the Seberg story. Among these were the Washington *Star* drama critic David Richards and stage writer Christopher Adler. Richards' book was published in July 1981 by Random House under the unfortunate title *Played Out*, and large extracts featured in the *Chicago Tribune*. The French translation which appeared the following year was similarly excerpted in *Paris Match* to satisfy wider interest. In September 1981 there was a documentary video installation by Margia Kramer at the MoMA in New York (*Jean Seberg, the FBI, the Media*), with linked film screenings. In November 1981 Mike Wallace chose Seberg for the first in a series of half-hour television profiles for CBS-TV.

Christopher Adler, like other writers since, felt the need to interpret the facts in his own way. His idea for a musical drama based on Seberg's life led to Peter Hall's production *Jean Seberg*, which opened at London's National Theatre in November 1983. The National Film Theatre ran a "tribute" season of five of Seberg's films in association with this. Hall's production, scripted by Julian Barry and scored by Marvin Hamlisch, was a major flop, and plans for a Broadway run were abandoned. Hamlisch was deeply disappointed, later observing, "Maybe you have to be an American and have lived through McCarthyism to understand the emotional impact of the Jean Seberg story." Many others felt the same way.

Although several ambitious "biopic" projects came to nothing, Seberg's life was an obvious subject for documentary film. In 1995 Fosco and Donatello Dubini released *Jean Seberg, American Actress*, a laudably sober compilation of interviews, while in the same year Mark Rappaport's fancifully titled *From the Journals of Jean Seberg* took a very different

**211**

**Jean Seberg, 1958 (courtesy Manoah Bowman, Independent Visions).**

approach. Rappaport is occasionally insightful, but he is also tendentious, digressive, and seriously misleading, typifying the subjective spin so many have imposed on Seberg's story. By chance, New York's Film Forum ran an eleven-film retrospective in March 1996 which coincided with the screening of Rappaport's film. Other Seberg film seasons have been held in New York, Chicago and elsewhere.

Carlos Fuentes, with his 1994 novel *Diana*, is only the most distinguished of the writers who have chosen to interpret or explain Seberg by posthumously reinventing her. This inclination, however dubious and ultimately reductive it can prove, persists in France, where interest in Seberg and Gary has never faded and continues to manifest itself in books, articles and television documentaries. Imaginative works inspired by Seberg's life continue to appear. An experimental film by Joseph Lally, *The Murder of Jean Seberg* starring Daphne Guinness (2010), is just one interesting example. Fortunately, in recent years there have also been new publications well grounded in fact to counterbalance fantasy and invention. Even now fresh information still emerges.

Gradually, after all the distortion, a more balanced view of the actress has become possible. Two new biographies appeared in 2008, and the documentary *Movie Star: The Secret Lives of Jean Seberg* (Fourth Wall Films, written and produced by Garry McGee and Kelly and Tammy Rundle) was released in 2012. Continuing interest is reflected by the "Saint Jean" and other websites and a host of different internet links. In Marshalltown, Seberg's birthplace, a film festival was mounted at the Martha Ellen Tye Playhouse in 1992. The newly-restored Orpheum Theater Center, which hosted the U.S. premiere of *Saint Joan*, now has a permanent display of Seberg memorabilia. The Orpheum's first *Jean Seberg International Film Festival* held in November 2011 will, it is hoped, become an annual fixture.

Seberg's life story makes an absorbing and involving narrative, yet we should probably be wary of those who, for whatever reason, try to cast her as victim in their private three-act tragedy. Those who knew her almost always recall her vitality, playful sense of humor, quick intelligence and generosity of spirit. Indeed, all these qualities show themselves at different times in both filmed interview and performance. Her sufferings, real enough in her last years, are too often allowed to dominate our view of her. Portrayals of her life as tormented and joyless and of her film career as a catalogue of disasters are falsifications which bear no serious scrutiny. Tempting as it may be to seize on a life story as an exemplum or cautionary tale, to do so is to is to disregard normal human complexity. Alongside the bold self-assurance which impressed Preminger there were vulnerability and self-doubt too. Midwestern resilience helped her to cope with the psychological battering of her mentor and the "cruelty" of some early reviewers, though both left a lasting mark. Setbacks in her private life were balanced by periods of success, happiness and fulfillment. The "roller coaster" life of a film actress, with all its risks, was after all the life she had knowingly chosen and did not regret. Her political commitments and the price she paid for them were an aspect, but only one aspect, of the person she was.

The fascination with the Seberg story was no five-minute wonder. As with Monroe, somehow the disparate elements, political and personal, would unite to take a lasting hold on the popular imagination. Although she may not have been considered a "big" star in the Hollywood sense, the highs and lows of her career seem like a classic Hollywood fable. Journalists never quite lost sight of the image of the martyred Joan, cynically used by powerful men for their own ends, even if the conflation paradoxically downplays Seberg's courage and her personal ambition. Her marriage to Romain Gary, twenty-four years her senior, seemed for some an echo of the Preminger role or a new variation on the Pygmalion theme. Here was ample material for myth-making. Furthermore, this cinematic saint would not lack personal iconography. With the success of *Breathless* in 1960 Seberg would leave a mark on feminine hairstyle and fashion for generations of women and create an enduring point of reference. Somehow the youthful vendor of the *New York Herald Tribune* became, through the alchemy of Godard and Coutard, an image as evocatively Parisian as the Eiffel Tower itself.

Some screen personalities seem to have or acquire a mystique which has little to do with dramatic performance alone. With *Breathless,* Jean Seberg became at least a junior member of this exclusive circle. The mediocrity of some of her subsequent films never quite dispelled this aura. Nicolas Gessner defines her quality in simple terms as "Not better or worse, but different. She was unique." It was surely this distinctiveness, this striking yet elusive essence that Périnal's camera first captured for the screen, that fascinated filmmakers such as Godard and Garrel. Other directors sought to recreate that magic, though not all knew how. Opinions remain divided as to Seberg's standing as an actor, but those dismissive of her talent often reveal that they know only a tiny fraction of her work. The response must be: "See all of the films, the good, the bad, the quirky and the forgotten, and judge for yourself." The quest to do just that is challenging but rewarding. If this survey offers any resolute pilgrim a serviceable road map, its compilers will feel amply rewarded.

# Bibliography

## General

Alexandre, Jean-Lou. *Jean Seberg, ou la tentation de l'échec.* Biarritz: Séguier, 2007.

_____. "Une actrice sur la Vague: Jean Seberg." *CinéAction* 104. Corlet-Télérama, 2002.

Alpert, Hollis. *The dreams and the dreamers.* New York: Macmillan, 1962.

Anissimov, Myriam. *Romain Gary, le caméléon.* Paris: Denoël, 2004.

Assouline, Pierre, et al. *Lectures de Romain Gary.* Paris: Gallimard, 2010.

Austin, Guy. *Stars in modern French film.* London: Aurum, 2003.

Bona, Dominique. *Romain Gary.* Paris: Mercure de France, 1987.

Boston, Anne. *Lesley Blanch: Inner landscapes, wilder shores.* London: John Murray, 2010.

Coutard, Raoul. *L'Impériale de Van Su: comment je suis entré dans le cinéma en dégustant une soupe chinoise.* Paris: Ramsay, 2007.

Durant, Philippe. *Belmondo.* Paris: Laffont, 1998.

Frischauer, Willi. *Behind the scenes of Otto Preminger.* London: M. Joseph, 1973.

Fujiwara, Chris. *The world and its double: the life and work of Otto Preminger.* New York: Faber and Faber, 2008.

Gary, Alexandre Diego. "Je suis fier de mes parents [interview with Michèle Fitoussi]." *Elle* 3068, 18 October 2004.

_____. *S. ou l'espérance de vie.* Paris: Gallimard, 2009.

Gary, Romain. *Chien blanc.* Paris: Gallimard, 1970.

Geneuil, Guy-Pierre, and Jean-Michel Dumas. *Jean Seberg, ma star assassinée.* Paris: Édition 1, 1995.

Grob, Norbert, Rolf Aurich, and Wolfgang Jacobsen. *Otto Preminger.* Berlin: Jovis, 1999.

Guibert, Simon. *La mort de Jean Seberg: récit fragmenté.* Paris: E-dite, 2005.

Guichard, Maurice. *Jean Seberg, portrait français.* Clamecy: Jacob-Duvernet, 2008.

Hangouët, Jean-François. *Romain Gary: à la traversée des frontières.* Paris: Gallimard, 2007.

Hangouët, Jean-François, and Paul Audi. *Romain Gary.* Paris: Editions de l'Herne, 2005.

Hirsch, Foster. *Otto Preminger: the man who would be king.* New York: Knopf, 2007.

Kramer, Margia. *Essential documents: the F.B.I. file on Jean Seberg. Parts I and II* [privately published 1979–80].

_____. *Jean Seberg/the FBI/the media.* [handbook for a documentary video installation at The Museum of Modern Art, New York; privately published 1981].

Larson, Jean Russell, and Garry McGee. *Neutralized: the FBI vs. Jean Seberg, a story of the '60s civil rights movement.* Albany, Ga: BearManor Media, 2008.

Legouis, Philippe, and François Moreuil. *Un voyage en italiques.* Brussels: Artésis, 2007.

McGee, Garry. *Jean Seberg: Breathless.* Albany, Ga: BearManor Media, 2008.

Moreuil, François. *Flash back.* Chaintreaux: France-Empire Monde, 2010.

Orr, John. "Out of noir: Seberg-Preminger-Godard-Garrel." *Studies in French Cinema* 7:1, 2007.
Pratley, Gerald. *The cinema of Otto Preminger.* London and New York: Zwemmer/Barnes, 1971.
Richards, David. *Played out: the Jean Seberg story.* New York: Random House, 1981.
Schoolfield, Ralph. *Romain Gary: the man who sold his shadow.* Philadelphia: University of Pennsylvania Press, 2002.
Seberg, Jean. "Lilith and I." *Cahiers du cinéma in English* 7, January 1967.
_____. "Reflections on acting." *Oxford Opinion* 4:5, 31 October 1959.
Willoughby, Bob. *Hollywood, A Journey Through the Stars.* New York: Assouline, 2001.

## Selected Interviews

*ABC Film Review,* 9:2 February 1959. Elizabeth Hardie.
*Art Films,* 1:4 April–May 1964. Stanley Paley.
*Ciné revue,* 44:21, 21 May 1964. R. Mann. "Jean Seberg et l'amour," pp. 18–9.
*Ciné revue,* 49:35, 28 August 1969. Roderick Mann.
*Ciné revue,* 51:31, 5 August 1971. Jacques Baroche. "Jean Seberg: 'je suis un "dingue" du cinéma!'" pp. 34–5.
*Ciné revue,* 54:32, 8 August 1974. Roderick Mann.
*Cinémonde,* 1342, 26 April 1960.
*Cinémonde,* 1470, 9 October 1962. Gilles Durieux. "À Paris Jean Seberg fait l'apprentissage du bonheur," pp. 20–1.
*Combat,* 16 July 1966. Pierre Kyria. "Jean Seberg ... à batons rompus," p. 8.
*Continental Film Review,* 22:11 September 1975. "Jean Seberg and the French scene," pp. 16–7.
*Cosmopolitan,* 166:3 March 1969. Joan Barthel. "Jean Seberg loses her innocence," pp. 110–13.
*Daily Mail,* 24 October 1958. Robert Muller. "The dinner dilemma of St. Jean," p.6.
*Elle,* 1271, 27 April 1970. Catherine Laporte. "Jean Seberg et le prix de l'indépendance," pp. 92–4.
*Elle,* 24 January 1972. Catherine Laporte. "Jean Seberg: 'J'ai choisi l'aventure de la Vie,'" pp. 4–7.
*Evening News,* 25 April 1968. William Hall. "Baptism of fire...," p. 10.
*Films and Filming,* 20:9 June 1974. Gordon Gow. "Re-birth," pp. 12–9.
*Films Illustrated,* August 1974. Susan d'Arcy. "Adieu tristesse," pp. 490–3.
*Fotogramas,* 28:1288, 22 June 1973. Ariana Ripa. "Jean Seberg, corrupciónes aparte," pp. 14–15.
*Grand Hotel,* 27:1346, 20 April 1972. N.A. "Ha sposato il terzo uomo ma vuole ancora bene al secondo," pp. 8–9.
*Guardian,* 27 June 1974. Bart Mills. "Miss Submissive's getaway," p. 13.
*International Herald Tribune,* 8 February 1979. Jane M. Friedman. "Actress says FBI plotted to smear her," p. 4.
*Interviews.* New York: Macmillan, 1970, pp. 124–30.
*Le Journal du dimanche,* 1711, 16 September 1979. "Deux semaines avant son suicide, Jean Seberg confiait."
*Jours de France,* 637, 28 January 1967. Léon Zitrone.
*Look,* 26:14 July 3, 1962. Joseph Roddy. "The restyling of Jean Seberg," pp. 45–8.
*Los Angeles Times,* 7 February 1958. Philip K. Scheuer. "And Bonjour, Jean Seberg," Section II, p.7.

*Los Angeles Times*, 8 December 1968. Joyce Haber. "Jean Seberg, her life and good Times," calendar p. 13.

*Le Monde*, 21 June 1972. Nicole Jolivet. "Jean Seberg: 'Deux hommes-grenouilles me protégeaient...,'" p. 22.

*Movie News*, 5:4 April 1969. Derek Hunter. "Success is bitter-sweet for Jean Seberg," pp. 12–3.

*The National Observer*, 5:6, 7 February 1966. Joseph N. Bell. "At 27, There's a new bounce in Jean Seberg."

*New York Herald Tribune*, 22 August 1957. Joe Hyams. "Jean Seberg finds films are work," p. 17.

*New York Herald Tribune*, 5 February 1958. Joe Hyams. "Can't quit when you're behind, Jean Seberg says," p.15.

*New York Times*, 21 March 1965. Peter Bart. "Paris to Hollywood with no stop at Marshalltown," s.2 p.11.

*New York Times*, 11 August 1968. Rex Reed. Reprinted:*Conversations in the raw*. New York: World, 1969, pp. 166–73.

*New York Times*, 16 June 1974. Bart Mills. "A show-biz saint grows up...," Arts pp. 17, 34.

*Observer Magazine*, 10 March 1974. Des Wilson. "A star is reborn," pp. 24–32.

*Paris Match*, 657, 11 November 1961. Bernard Giquel. "Je voudrais avoir une vie ennuyeuse," pp. 126–9.

*Perspectives (Le Soleil, Québec)*, 7:26, 26 June 1965. Stephen Franklin. "Polie par Paris, Jean Seberg fait sa rentrée à Hollywood," pp. 6, 8–9.

*Photoplay*, 25:3 March 1974. Sue Clarke. "My life has been a roller-coaster," pp. 29, 59.

*Radio France*. Radioscopie de Jacques Chancel. 29 January 1976.

*Saturday Evening Post*, 236:23, 15 June 1963. Pete Hamill. "Jean Seberg," pp. 20, 23.

*Semana*, 32: 1623, 27 March 1971. Manuel Roman.

*Seventeen*, 16:5 May 1957. Edwin Miller. "New-penny bright," pp. 122–3, 184.

*Seventeen*, 22 March 1963. Edwin Miller. "Jean Seberg revisited," Reprinted: *Seventeen*

*Show*, 3:8 August 1963. Donald W. LaBadie. "Everybody's Galatea," pp. 76–7, 98.

*Star Weekly Magazine (Toronto Star)*, 11 May 1957. Marjorie Earl. "Teenage St. Joan," pp. 31–2.

*Stop*, 28, 1 August 1976. "JS: No me conformo con ser actriz," pp. 4–7.

*Sunday News (NY)*, 20 October 1968. Ernest Leogrande. "Real hippies—like 1853," pp. 29–30.

*Télé 7 jours*, 306, 29 January 1966. Geneviève Coste. "Jean Seberg: Jeanne d'Arc a fait de moi une petite Française," pp. 30–31.

*Télérama*, 887, 15 January 1967. Claude-Marie Trémois.

# Index

Numbers in *bold italics* indicate pages with photographs.